SOUND ADVICE
The Musician's Guide to the Recording Studio

SOUND ADVICE
The Musician's Guide to the Recording Studio

Wayne Wadhams

Illustrations by Robin Coxe-Yeldham

Schirmer Books
An Imprint of Simon & Schuster Macmillan
NEW YORK

Prentice Hall International
LONDON · MEXICO CITY · NEW DELHI · SINGAPORE · SYDNEY · TORONTO

To Ning and Dad,
Aunt Jo,
and Uncle Sal,
with love forever

Interview with Billy Joel and Jim Boyer by David Schwartz, copyright © 1984, *Mix* magazine. Reprinted with the permission of the Publisher.

Interview with Al Schmitt and Val Garay copyright © 1983, *Recording Engineer/Producer*. Reprinted with the permission of Intertec Publishing Corporation.

Interview with Daniel Lazerus by Ralph Jones copyright © 1985, *Recording Engineer/Producer*. Reprinted with the permission of Intertec Publishing Corporation.

Interview with Bruce Swedien by Alan di Perna, copyright © 1984, *Mix* magazine. Reprinted with the permission of the Publisher.

Interview with Roger Nichols by David Schwartz, copyright © 1987, *Mix* magazine. Reprinted with the permission of the Publisher.

Interview with Alan Parsons copyright © 1986, Richard Elen. Reprinted with the courtesy of the author.

Interview with Bruce Swedien, copyright © 1983, *Recording Engineer/Producer*. Reprinted with the permission of Intertec Publishing Corporation.

Interview with Phil Ramone, copyright © 1980, *Mix* magazine. Reprinted with the permission of the Publisher.

Interview with George Massenburg, copyright © 1984, *Recording Engineer/Producer*. Reprinted with the permission of Intertec Publishing Corp.

Interview with George Massenburg copyright © 1988, *Recording Engineer/Producer*. Reprinted with the permission of Intertec Publishing Corp.

Interview with Daniel Lazerus, copyright © 1985, *Recording Engineer/Producer*. Reprinted with the permission of Intertec Publishing Corp.

Interview with Humberto Gatica, copyright © 1981, *Recording Engineer/Producer*. Reprinted with the permission of Intertec Publishing Corp.

Interview with Quincy Jones and Bruce Swedien by Jimmy Stewart, copyright © 1982, *Recording Engineer/ Producer*. Reprinted with the permission of Intertec Publishing Corp.

Schirmer Books
An Imprint of Simon & Schuster Macmillan
1633 Broadway, New York, NY 10019-6785

Library of Congress Catalog Card Number:

Printed in the United States of America

printing number
       7 8 9 10

Library of Congress Cataloging in Publication Data

CONTENTS

PART **IV**

ILLUSTRATIONS

PREFACE

FEAR is the enemy of creativity and success. This maxim is true whether applied to record industry business affairs or to the studio recording process itself. While it's healthy to take risks, it is equally healthy to worry about failure, and all musicians who undertake a recording project face many unknowns. Some focus their fears on the enormous financial risk of spending thousands of dollars on studio time, tape, and whatnot. But at a deeper level, every musician's darkest fear is that the finished tape will not be acceptable and pleasurable to its intended audience. What could be worse than playing your newest musical creation for a friend and sensing an indifferent attitude in return?

To avoid this fate, musicians have developed an instinctive drive to lavish as much studio time and money as possible on each composition in the hope that a master quality tape will reveal the underlying quality of the music itself. And certainly, a well-recorded tape is preferable to a home demo, performance and all other factors being equal. However, keeping the musical factors equal is the tougher challenge—using the studio to improve what's already there without losing the essence of the experience the musician hopes to give his or her listeners.

Certainly, no mere book nor any linear course of study can guarantee a musician the ability to move his or her audience or achieve success. However, recording technology has reached a state of such sophistication that, to an inexperienced live performer, the studio may seem like a forbidding monster peopled by chips and concepts beyond the understanding of mere mortals. Furthermore, Madison Avenue and equipment manufacturers have hoodwinked many into believing that records simply cannot be made without the lastest and most expensive equipment. Faced with the dual dragons of unfamiliar technology and lifelong indebtedness for studio costs, what singer can simply belt out a song without at the same time crossing his or her fingers?

I learned about recording before there were college courses, before there were textbooks, and long before anyone dared to recognize engineering and production both as crafts and art forms. Back in the 1960s, the only way to learn about recording was to be in the studio—as an artist, roadie, or whatever—and keep your eyes and ears wide open. As a recording artist fortunate enough to have a label paying the studio bills, I watched every knob the engineers turned, noted how much they turned them, and the changes wrought in each sound. Equally important, I observed how these audio adjustments affected my emotions and those of listeners. In this way, I amassed a library of observations and techniques by which one can connect the craft of recording with its underlying goal of portraying emotions.

Simply stated, I hope this book may help eliminate the fears that musicians harbor about the recording experience. Unlike texts written for aspiring engineers, this book will not deal with the minutiae of circuit design. Recording musicians simply do not need to understand the innards of every device in the control room. They do, however, need to know what the major studio and control room components are, how they function (in simple, nonmathematical terms), how they can be interconnected, and the ways in which each can manipulate or alter sounds to achieve different emotional effects. They should also learn that listeners expect very different things from live and recorded music and that a good engineer can fill in the missing visual and physical experience of the live gig with the right studio tricks.

Beyond this, musicians should know how every instrument makes its sounds and how these sounds behave in the relatively small rooms in which they are most often recorded. Why, you might ask, should an acoustic bassist know how drums are recorded? First, because there are many similarities in the way drums and bass produce their sounds. Knowing these can give both players fresh ideas about how to use the studio in every session. Second and more important, the bassist and drummer are musical collaborators working toward a single goal: making a strong and unified musical statement on tape. Understanding their respective musical and audio roles can wipe away insecurity and obviate the all-too-common studio vanity of perfecting one instrument's sound at the expense of the blend of all.

I further hope the knowledge this book imparts will relieve studio tensions and facilitate truly creative use of the studio for each purpose and budget, without cluttering the mind with engineering trivia that diverts attention from winning the musical war. All of my discussions are based on the simple fact that every studio operation has both a sonic result and an emotional impact. By working backward from their desired musical goals through the range of options by which these can be realized, musicians should quickly develop a "nose" for the kind of studio equipment and techniques that can take their sound in the right emotional direction.

Some readers will find certain concepts discussed or recording techniques suggested of little interest. Nor, for that matter, will every reader agree with the kind of sound I think is appropriate for this or that purpose. After all, recording is a highly subjective topic, and tempers run high when an engineer or producer fails to achieve the sound the artist imagined. However, the larger a musician's base of studio understanding, the more confidence he or she will bring to every session. This alone will facilitate good communication with engineers and producers, save studio time and money, and instill a faith in the studio's ability to enhance the music.

To my knowledge, this is the first book designed for musicians that attempts to demystify the entire field of audio engineering. If my own fascination with certain technical matters goes a bit too far for your curiosity, use my excess to learn how engineers and producers think and what goals motivate them. Whatever your judgment, I am deeply honored to have this opportunity to help musicians launch and nurture their recording careers. As a former professional musician, I have tried to speak directly to your real studio needs and concerns. If this book can achieve even a few of these lofty goals, my effort will prove more than worthwhile.

WAYNE WADHAMS

ACKNOWLEDGMENTS

So many people have contributed to the *Musician's Guide to the Record Industry* and the *Musician's Guide to the Recording Studio*, I hardly know where to begin. Perhaps I should begin at the very beginning. I wish to extend my deepest gratitude to Kevin Gavin, who in 1964 plucked my first rock group out of the backroom of the Paradise Bar & Grill in Springdale, Connecticut, and booked us into A&R Studios, where a certain Mr. Phil Ramone engineered our first releases for United Artists. The love of making records that was born then still burns bright. For that act of faith, that vote of confidence, and for enduring the chaos of managing us throughout three years and as many labels, I dedicate this book to you, Kevin.

Twenty-two years later, enter the late Robert Share, then provost of Berklee College of Music. With the building of Berklee's new Music Production and Engineering Department nearly completed, Bob suggested I contact *Downbeat* magazine's Jack Maher and Charles Doherty, who had expressed interest in a series of articles explaining basic recording techniques to musicians, with special attention to session planning and budgeting, as well as "shopping" or marketing of finished demo and master tapes. Reader response to the resulting series of "Pro Session" columns showed the need for a complete expose of technical *and* business aspects of the record industry. Many printer ribbons later, a combined guide to the studio and the record industry emerged.

The impetus to enlarge the scope of the project and issue separate guides to the record industry and recording studio came from reviewers of the composite text, members of MEIEA (Music and Entertainment Industry Educators Association), my own students at Berklee, as well as several recording artists and clients who, immersed in their careers, expressed a desperate need for a comprehensive overview of their own industry. Unfortunately, many recording artists, by virtue of a scarcity of independent courses and the speed with which their careers may have bloomed, simply do not understand the minutiae of music publishing, broadcast royalties, artist royalties, or other subjects that have a profound effect on their income.

Together, the two guides have drawn direct input from hundreds of professionals specializing in areas from record retailing to entertainment law, digital circuit design to dance-floor feedback. Among those who supplied facts and figures, procedures, precautions, and panaceas or otherwise shaped the final product are: Les Arnold, Mark Parsons, and Jeff Ehrlich of LaSalle Audio, Boston; Ned Berndt and Linda

Stone, Q Records, Miami; Dr. George Butler (A&R), Steve Berkowitz (product mgmt.), Mitchell Tenzer (business affairs), Jack Rovner (v.p. merchandising) and Mickey Eichner (sr. v.p.), all of CBS Records; Scott Cooper, financial consultant, Boston; Jonathan Davis, remix engineer and producer, New York; Kevin Dixon and Tom Ketterer, Capitol Recording Studios, Los Angeles; Marty Feely, associate publisher, *Billboard* magazine; Mark Fischer, esq., Boston; Bill Gitt, Berklee College; Ira Moss, MMG Records, New York; Jeffrey Largent, Lexicon, Inc.; Eric Kuehnapfel, Video Post Supervisor, Target Video Productions, Boston; David Mash (chairman), Thomas Rhea (asst. chair) and Jamshied Sharifi, Music Synthesis Department, Berklee College; Anthony Plessas, composer and producer, Athens, Greece; Marshall Rushford, EMI-Manhattan Records; David Schwartz, Publisher, *MIX* magazine; David Sonenberg, esq., New York; Michael Szakmeister, APPV engineer, Editel Productions, Boston; Cosmo Wyatt, New England Disc Jockey Association, Boston.

The following people gave lavishly of their time to conduct the Great Sounds survey for the studio guide and compile its results; to research and gather materials for both guides, here, in New York, and California; to prepare charts and other materials, proofread manuscripts, and hammer both books into shape: Peter Christensen, Dave Dickerson, Ken Furutani, Fred Katz, Minoru Kaneko, Paul Kopchak, David McEachern, Paco Ojeda, Jim Pistorio, Mark Rettenmeyer, Ingrid Pashulak, Paul Ruest, Shane Swisher, Talley Sherwood, Lisa Togno, James Viviano, and Steve Ward.

To Suzanne Hollander, Salli Lastra, Stacey Stanley, Andrew Roshberg, Catherine Carlesimo, Tony Berkeley, Amy Hoffberg, Whitney White, Charles Taylor, and Kevin Dunning, my thanks for long hours and meticulous assistance during the final edit and preparation of indices for both guides.

I owe a special debt to the incredible people who made the CD package that is available for the studio guide a reality: coproducer and engineers for the project Robin Coxe-Yeldham and John Servies, assistants Charles Abbott, Brian Bilick, Christine Carere, Michael Dobkowski, Kevin Dunning, Tim Metzinger, Brad Safford, Elaine Spellman, Jesse Tolbert, Karla Tolbert, and—for the design and layout of the booklet—Paco Ojeda and Curt Johnson. A mammoth undertaking lovingly completed. Full credits appear in the CD booklet itself.

For permission to reprint materials originally issued by the distinguished organizations and trade magazines that guide this industry, my deepest thanks to:

Victor Fuentealba, president; Patrick Varriale, Richard Gabriel and Steve Young, AFM: New York, Los Angeles, and Boston
Mortimer Becker, Carolyn Friday, and Ira Sills, AFTRA
Michael Citrin, executive director, AMRA
Paul Adler, director of membership, ASCAP
Marty Feeley, *Billboard*
Gary Roth, senior attorney, BMI
A&R Administration Department, CBS Records
Registrar of Copyrights and the Library of Congress, Washington, D.C.
Edward Murphy, Harry Fox Agency and NMPA
David Schwartz and Penny Riker Jacobs, *Mix* magazine
Mel Lambert, Sarah Coleman, and Cynthia Sedler, recording engineer/producer
Recording Industry Association of America

Laurie Hughes, esq., Legal Department, SESAC
Keith Spenser-Allen, publisher/editor, *Studio Sound* magazine

Authorship credits for each reprint accompany the text.

For bearing with me through two years of continual expansion, reshaping, updates, and revisions of both guides and the CD package, I wish to thank Maribeth
Payne, editor in chief of Schirmer Books, Mssrs. Fred Weiler and Robert Axelrod,
editors in charge of this project, and production supervisor Sylvia Kanwischer. A personal Grammy to all at Schirmer for their patience and perseverance.

Finally, I send my love and sincere thanks to my dear friends Larry and Alma
Berk, founders of Berklee College of Music; to Bruce MacDonald, director of development; Don Puluse, division chair of music technology, Dave Moulton, chairman of
music production and engineering, and to the administration of the College. They
encouraged this book to take shape, allowed field-testing of various materials in class-
room and studio courses, and generously granted over two-hundred hours of digital
recording and editing time, without which the studio guide CDs would not exist.

INTRODUCTION

To my knowledge, this is the first book of its kind. There are many fine textbooks for aspiring engineers, each examining with mathematical rigor the design and deployment of various types of studio equipment. These volumes—by Eargle, Woram, Pohlmann, et al.—are invaluable to those whose job it is to know every wire and junction in the control room. But what about the musician who wants to understand the basic functional aspects of a studio, specifically those that affect how an instrument sounds and is recorded there? Where does the drummer find a thorough treatment of drum recording or the guitarist of guitar recording? Until now, this crucial information was simply unavailable.

Studio and computer hardware is designed and most easily used by people with technical, not purely musical, backgrounds. Moreover, the terminology of studio equipment, from decibels and microvolts to control channels and dither, may seem totally forbidding to a studio novice. For these reasons, musicians feel cut off from any real engineering know-how. From lack of knowledge, when making demos they place mics exactly as they must on stage and add only a touch of reverb, assuming that the mix will sound the same in the living room as in a control room. The all-too-frequent result is wasted time and money: one track or the whole tape needs to be remade later. Worse yet, sometimes a brilliant performance must be scrapped for poor recording quality.

On the other hand, overspecialization in engineering per se can take its toll in reverse. With no understanding of the musical and emotional goals to be achieved in each song, even the finest engineer is virtually useless. What an awful stalemate: many musicians have insurmountable difficulty communicating with the engineers recording their music, while some engineers believe that great sound alone will let the music and its meaning shine through.

This book should facilitate productive communication between musicians and engineers, and it will help musicians make professional-quality recordings whenever the expert help of a seasoned engineer is unavailable or unaffordable. It is a collection of facts and advice, with equal emphasis on what you need to know and how this can be bent to serve your musical purposes on every session. I view the guide as a studio cookbook. Thus, like a good cook, you should be able to make a good meal in any kitchen with at least the bare essentials on hand.

HOW THIS BOOK IS ORGANIZED

This book is divided into four parts. Part one examines the basic gear used in professional recording, with just enough attention to the design and operation of each type to discover why it was invented and to consider how varying its basic parameters can broaden its potential uses. We will also investigate how all the components of the studio are interconnected and discover that proper installation and maintenance are as important to the product as the quality of the equipment itself. Along the way we will look at the behavior of sound, how it travels, behaves, and misbehaves in various rooms and spaces. Sound, after all, is the raw material from which the finished tape is made.

Part two turns the mirror back on the reader and reveals the perceptual problems so many musicians encounter when playing and hearing their music in the studio, rather than live in the rehearsal hall or on stage. To do this, we will examine how studio and control room acoustics differ from real-life environments and how playing in the studio can drain excitement or energy from good performers; we will poke holes in some common misconceptions that often lead studio clients to spend much more time and money on their tapes than is necessary for the purpose at hand.

Part three, by far the longest, contains the recipes in our cookbook, namely, chapters devoted to each instrument or orchestral section that is commonly recorded in a studio. In each, we will look at how the instrument produces its sound and how that interacts with the studio, and explore a range of microphones, signal processors, and techniques that can be applied to the original sound to capture its best parts and relocate or package it best for various types of music. Because instruments of related construction share underlying characteristics of sound generation—for example, acoustic instruments with wooden bodies, from the kick drum to violin or acoustic guitar—I strongly advise that all readers, even vocalists, read the entirety of Part three.

Part four is a brief look at how to plan and execute finished tapes from a production standpoint. Here we will consider the emotional intent and market of the finished mix, define how various musical elements can be used to establish and reach these goals, and see how the studio can better aim each of these at the emotional target. There are an infinite number of methods for producing fine demo and master tapes. No one mode of thought is right for every purpose. Yet, just seeing how a logical approach can be applied to something as ill-defined as *production* may help you find the approach best suited to your own musical style and your intended audience, not to mention your budget!

SOME REAL-WORLD EXTRAS

Sprinkled through the text are some fifteen interviews with or articles by producers and engineers whom you will recognize, identified by a microphone where each interview begins. Each is located at a point in the text where its subject matter complements or contrasts with my own approach or suggestions. Why include suggestions that contradict my own? Few cooks prepare recipes exactly as the book states:

one may like more spice, another less. The important thing is to understand what the original recipe yields, then vary it to taste according to who is coming to dinner!

You will also find charts and lists of microphones and other equipment that is currently popular in studios. Some of these brands and models will fade from studio racks in the future, but the underlying functions they serve will remain. Thus, the text concentrates not on how to operate this or that specific device but on what the device does to sounds and on the common parameters that are embodied in all devices of its type. The principles of good recording revealed herein will serve you for many years to come.

Because this guide is aimed primarily at musicians, I have tried to avoid some of the rigors of most textbooks. First, without any sacrifice of the precise terminology crucial to a clear understanding of technical topics, the tone is conversational, not formal. Real examples, tips, and asides are interjected liberally, both to lend real dimensions to the technical data and to keep the whole book user-friendly. There is also much built-in repetition and review of basic concepts as they apply first to one instrument, then another. I hope this helps solidify your understanding and encourages you to experiment, both in home recordings and in the studio.

It would be impossible to include a glossary of every technical term used in a volume of this scope. I assume that readers know what tape and tape recorders are, along with a host of other common-knowledge items and concepts. Those terms that are briefly defined within the text are printed in italics at that location. By directing the reader to these locations, the italics listings in the index thus serve as an embedded glossary. For complete definitions of the full range of production, recording, and music business terms, readers may turn to my earlier *Dictionary of Music Production and Engineering Terminology*.

THE COMPACT DISC SET AND RECORD INDUSTRY GUIDE

Another resource intended to supplement this guide is a set of two CDs containing some 160 digitally recorded examples of specific studio techniques, many of which are explained in the current text. Disc 1 embraces the entire recording process, demonstrating various miking and signal processing techniques for drums, bass, piano, voice solo lead instruments and sections. Disc 2 contains two complete mixdown sessions, working track by track from raw 24-track tapes up to a finished mix, showing the effects of equalization, compression, noise gating, reverb, and other effects as they are applied to each track, leading to a finished mix.

A hefty booklet accompanies the package, with complete recording data for each example: every mic used and how it was positioned and adjusted; every processing device and how its parameters were set—equalizer bandwidths, compression ratios, delay times, the works. This data should help you figure out how familiar records were engineered and allow you to use similar techniques in your own sessions.

For musicians who need to learn about business aspects of launching their recording careers, I have also written a companion book, *Sound Advice: The Musician's Guide to the Record Industry*. Together these two guides constitute a career cookbook that demystifies the technical and business aspects of making records as one's principal profession.

Even if you consumed every book available on recording and the record industry, remember there is no substitute for expert help, whether in the studio or in business affairs. Engineers have the most complete knowledge of the equipment and capabilities of their studios. Do not cancel a session because the studio you have booked has no AKG 414s or because the engineer prefers brands or models of equipment other than those suggested here. Engineers spend thousands of hours in their own studios: you may spend a few dozen hours at most. The good nose you develop via this guide will help you tell professionals what you need and keep them focused on the real problems, rather than on niceties or noncrucial details. It will not, however, replace the experience gained through years of professional engineering.

Finally, nothing should take your attention away from writing and performing, the two activities at the heart of every musical career. Remember that great studio sounds, a magic mix, and even a spectacular contract are no substitute for good music and a good performance. The public buys only that which moves the emotions. Nobody ever had a hit record because of the kick drum equalization or the flanging on the tambourine. You can and should take pride and pleasure from good craftsmanship in every facet of your work. But remember: to the public, the bottom line is feel, emotion, heart, meaning, and humanity. Without these qualities, the finest recording is merely a collection of lifeless sounds.

SOUND ADVICE
The Musician's Guide to
the Recording Studio

Part I

INTRODUCTION TO THE RECORDING STUDIO

1

A BRIEF HISTORY OF THE MULTITRACK RECORDING STUDIO

As I write this, the original 1961 version of Ben E. King's recording of "Stand By Me" is number one in the Billboard Hot 100. It is the theme of a hit movie, but this alone will never sell records. What will is a strong message: heart! Your favorite record of the 1950s or 1960s is both a landmark and a personal challenge. Listen to some of these "oldies" and hear how much was achieved without high-tech equipment. To make recordings that transcend the technology used to create them—recordings that the next generation of musicians will admire as you admire those of the past—is the real challenge.

There have been four separate stages in the development of music recordings studios, roughly aligned with each decade since the 1950s. Until the late 1940s, music was recorded in two ways, both mono. Many recording sessions were done direct to disc, with one or more lacquer masters cut right in the studio. If the music was for a film soundtrack, it was recorded directly onto a 35mm optical soundtrack negative. Running at 18 inches per second, and with about 55 dB signal to noise ratio (abbreviated S/N, a parameter we'll define later), this method gave better overall sound quality than any disc of the time.

Tape recording, developed by the Germans during the Second World War, was used both in radio broadcasts and for the deciphering of intercepted code messages. The poor sound quality obtained on that early equipment, due largely to inferior tape, soon improved with the introduction of commercial recorders and new tapes by Telefunken in Europe and Ampex in the United States. These machines were mono, full track (one 1/4″ wide track), running at 15 ips for music-quality performance. Lower speeds were usually reserved for voice recording. It was discovered early that

3

you could overdub by playing back a previously recorded tape through a mixer, blending that with live mics, and sending the composite signal to a second recorder. In the history of record production, this simple step rivaled the invention of the wheel.

Obviously, the pretaped music lost a bit of sound quality and gained a bit of noise. Nevertheless, this technique did allow artists to add layers of new music. Such mono-to-mono copy-overdubbing was the standard in pop music production up until 1962. Until that time, pop and rock records were made to sound good on AM radio—in highly compressed mono. Not much attention was paid to true stereo in pop and rock until 1967, when the Beatles brought out *Sgt. Pepper's Lonely Hearts Club Band.* While stereo was entering its second decade for classical and jazz recording, these genres were played primarily on FM. Rock was usually confined to AM until the early 1970s.

Throughout the 1950s, record companies owned most of the better recording studios, renting unbooked hours to outside users for radio and TV commercial productions. There were very few independent studios of any real quality. For rock, the large, well-designed acoustic space did not matter as much as the engineer's ear for getting excitement into the mix.

Of the staff engineers at major labels, certainly Billy Porter of RCA stands out. His work on Elvis Presley's earliest hits is a marvel, both for its fine technical quality and many innovative techniques. In the jazz field, Rudy van Gelder engineered the Blue Note and Prestige sessions of John Coltrane, Miles Davis, and other artists. The crisp and clean cymbal and horn sounds on these tapes challenge even the compact discs on which they are now being rereleased.

In 1955, hit guitarist Les Paul commissioned Ampex Corporation to build a custom recorder, with eight parallel tracks to be inscribed on special 1″-wide tape. He and his wife, Mary Ford, had done many tape-to-tape records, layering six or more guitar and vocal parts, but they were displeased with the buildup of noise and distortion, not to mention the limited control inherent in the mixing process. The first Ampex 8-track was delivered the next year, and Les and Mary proceeded to make a string of Top 10 hits on it. He developed almost all the techniques and tricks that later became standard in multitrack sessions—headphone or cue mixing, sel-sync overdubbing, bouncing tracks, prelaying effects and delays, and special varispeed operations.

The late 1950s brought an acceptance of the 2-track recorder in rock sessions, but mostly as a convenience in producing mono records. Basic tracks could be laid down on one track, some instrumental overdubs (perhaps even horns or strings) on the second track (recorded while these musicians heard a headphone playback of track 1 via the record head, later called *sel-sync*), then both tracks mixed onto the first track of a second machine along with another live overdub. The vocals might then be added on the remaining track of machine 2 and a mono mix made on to a full-track recorder.

This process saves at least one tape generation on the basic tracks, gives better control over the level of each overdub, and does allow a remix of at least the vocals and completed tracks. The resulting 2-track tape makes pretty artificial stereo, as evidenced by hits as late as the Beatles' "Nowhere Man," in which all voices and the guitar solo are on one channel and everything else is on the other. As George Martin has pointed out, however, most records produced this way were not meant for stereo issue. The two tracks merely allowed better control over elements in the final mono mix. Record companies, in the wake of public demand for stereo, simply released anything they could find, no matter how artificial it sounded, and regardless of how much the artists objected.

Ampex introduced a stock model of its 1/2" 3-track machine in 1960. It offered sel-sync on all tracks and gained its first acceptance with producers of jingles, mainly because a narrator could be added on the third track, rather than on a subsequent pass on 1/4" requiring another generation loss of the music. The 3-track did enable some of the first quasi-natural stereo pop records, however, since the lead vocals could now be mixed into the center, with the music on left and right channels. On the other hand, some rock engineers really had no idea of how to use the medium. There is even one story of a top engineer who used the third track only for acoustic or electric bass.

My own favorite early multitrack memory is an afternoon in 1964 at A&R studios, then on 47th Street next door to the original Manny's Music Shop. Another engineer burst into the control room where my group was working and declared, "It's here." Our own engineer (now a major producer) took us out to witness the unpacking of A&R's first 4-track Ampex. The entire staff was speechless, circling it as though a space-craft had landed. Then our engineer, with genuine puzzlement, said, "What are we going to do with *four* tracks?" Twenty years later I read an interview in which he discussed the awful artistic limitations of working with 24 tracks!

That afternoon we were recording 2-track at what was perhaps the top independent studio in New York, a literally state-of-the-art setup. The cost was $30 per hour, including engineer, a very high price even in New York. The paperwork indicates that in four afternoon sessions over the next week, we recorded three sides for United Artists. It took a total of 17 hours and cost about $600, with tape. In the mid-1960s $6,000 was a huge studio budget for a rock album. Just four years later, when 8-track became the pro format for rock, and when independent studios began springing up in every loft or converted office space, rentals rose to an unheard-of $60 per hour.

This pushed 1969 album studio budgets up to around $10,000 with mixdowns—an amount that might only be approved for established artists—which still did not include AFM or AFTRA musicians' and singers' payments. A decade later, the average studio bill jumped to well over $30,000, with a few privileged artists spending up-wards of $500,000 per album just in studio costs. Yet in the same period of time- '69 to '79, retail album prices went from $6.98 to $8.98 list price, an increase of under 30%.

Until around 1968, it was fairly standard practice to do two completely separate mixes of singles and albums—one for radio play in mono, the other for home play-back in stereo. This caused sales and promotional problems when the mono and stereo mixes of a particular tune had a different sound or feel. Since the mix can make or break a record, labels wanted only the "hit" mix—mono—to be played on the air. Meanwhile, FM rock stations, then developing their first legs, insisted on play-ing stereo whenever available. As a stopgap some stations installed primitive delays and reverbs to simulate stereo. Others actually bootlegged stereo tapes of hits out the back door of certain studios—unauthorized midnight mixes made by underpaid engineers.

CBS came up with a novel solution: *Compatible Mixing.* This was really nothing more complex than mixing to stereo tape while monitoring the process with both channels mixed to a mono signal. The finished mixes maintained their characteristic sound or punch whether played in mono or stereo. Often, simultaneous full-track and stereo machines ran to give a first-generation mono and stereo product. The process was discontinued in the early 1970s, when the major labels stopped pressing mono albums and singles.

By 1970, 16-track was gaining acceptance for rock production in the United States, though even the Beatles continued to use 8-track through most of *Abbey Road* and *Let It Be* in that same year. The Ampex MM-1000 16-track package cost almost $35,000 and required a much more elaborate console than was previously available. Split designs became the standard, the main bank of faders used for mic/line inputs feeding the recorder, the monitor section off to the right used to provide cue mixes and other submixes for reverb chambers, and so on. Although Ampex and Scully announced 24-track models to come, there was little rush to buy them because of the noise build-up inherent with so many separate recorded signals.

The real demand for 24 tracks came from clients—artists and producers who wanted the control and versatility, even at the expense of more noise and cost. The Dolby A system provided just enough noise reduction to bring 16 tracks of tape noise back down to the noise level of a good 2-track machine, but the first systems were expensive—almost $2,000 a track! Not many studios could afford it, and not many artists wanted to pay the extra in rentals. By 1970 top studios were charging more than $100 per hour.

Aside from refinements made in existing devices—quieter and more precise parametric equalizers, smoother compressors and better plate reverbs—few new tricks except mechanical flanging were added to the engineer's bag. First made popular on a single named "Itchycoo Park" by the Small Faces, *flanging* was accomplished by playing two copies of a finished tape back on two machines and mixing their outputs. One copy was started a fraction of a second before the other, and drag was manually applied to the playback machine's feed reel, slowing its speed just enough to bring the two copies into, and then past, exact alignment. The dramatic swishing underwater effect of the resulting comb filter began appearing on every record and really established the commercial demand for a whole range of effects that are now available in various digital units.

As more artists in pursuit of a signing found independent funding to make demos and even master tapes, privately owned studios sprang up everwhere during the late 1960s.

By 1972, when Caribou Ranch and other so-called alternative-environment studios were established, many successful artists began working on master tapes during United States and foreign tours, on vacations, or wherever they happened to be. Recording vans could be brought to the Grand Canyon or Great Pyramid if necessary. The Band's first two albums were recorded in the basement of their pink ranch house. Meanwhile, major independent studios offered all the equipment and conveniences of the labels' own flagship rooms, including great engineers. To accommodate the traveling plans of major acts, some of the best engineers went freelance for the first time, billing their services as consultants to the budgets of whichever album was in progress.

Other engineers—such as Phil Ramone, Bill Szymczyk, and Geoff Emerick—moved on to production, allowing the house engineers wherever they were working to concentrate on what they knew best: their own equipment. Some artists used their own money to produce albums completely on the road, then asked for a reimbursement, or recoupment advance. Still other artists, flush with profits from hits and wary of the creative accounting practices of their labels, retained ownership of their master tapes, merely leasing them to the majors. Just as the film industry had converted from studio to independent production in the late 1950s, so the record industry left the nest ten to fifteen years later.

The 1970s brought new formats and devices—both for studios and musicians. The Kepex and other noise gates were invented and used to great effect in albums such as Jeff Beck's *Blow By Blow*. After Roy Halee had used multiple reverbs to create the cavernous effects on various Simon & Garfunkel hits, such as "The Boxer," EMT finally brought out a true stereo plate reverb around 1970. The first delay lines came out in 1973, including the Cooper Time Cube, with around twenty milliseconds of Acoustic Delay (created via flexible tubing through which the input sound was sent from a small speaker to a microphone at the other end, with a preamp to bring the signal back up to line level).

Expanders, Aural Exciters, and the first generation of digital toys such as Eventide's first digital delays appeared on the scene by 1975. Next came EMT's now-famous Model 250 reverb, which (retailing at a mere $28,000) looked like a small red android and was later compared to R2D2. This was the first unit to allow programming of various digital spaces, and also developed enough heat (with hundreds of internal memory chips) to fry an egg on top! The biggest development of all—console automation—began with the API/Allison system in 1975. This system stored automation data on one or two tracks of the 2″ tape. In 1978 Neve introduced its NECAM system, using floppy discs to store the data and identical SMPTE time code on the 2″ tape and floppy to synchronize the whole operation. The other hot new device was BTX's system for interlocking sound and video playback. As you might guess, the BTX was developed for use in film scoring and jingle work, where perfect sync is mandatory. The idea of using the system to interlock two multitrack tape machines came later, and with it the birth of 46-track, 69-track, and the other baroque formats used today. To my knowledge, the ultimate is still Arif Mardin's 1984 production of the Italian group Scritti Politti, for which five 24-track machines were locked up during the mix.

Digital recording as a medium for pop and rock really did not happen until the mid-1980s, when compact discs made it possible to get all the added and expensive quality out to the public. However, 3M Corporation did bring out a 32-track digital machine—the legendary DDS—in 1977. With the 4-track mixdown machine and all the interconnects, the package ran a mere $180,000 (about $450,000 today, taking a decade of inflation into account). Only a few rock albums—notably Steely Dan's *Gaucho* and Ry Cooder's *Bop Til You Drop*—were recorded on this system because of the extreme cost and complications involved. Studio owners were still reeling with the almost-yearly cost of converting their operations from 4- to 8- to 16- to 24-track, adding $30,000 worth of Dolbys, and buying new consoles one moment and trading them in the next.

Digital, with all its obvious sonic advantages, was financially just out of the question, and as a result, 3M sold only a few dozen of its systems in a five-year period, discontinuing the line in 1982. Sadly, many engineers believe the DDS sounded better than any digital multitrack available today. Meanwhile, classical and jazz recording took to 2-track video-based digital systems like a duck to water. No overdubs—no punching in—limited editing, but what sound quality! The first Sony Analog-to-Digital converter cost under $2,000 and could store its output on almost any VCR, although 3/4″ gave the least dropout and error problems, and the tape cost about $25 an hour—less than 1/4″ analog tape recorded at 15 ips.

If studio owners were dizzy with new equipment in 1980, they certainly had no idea what was in store by 1988. The most important new types have been the computer-monitored mixing consoles such as the Solid State Logic, digital reverbs, and dedicated effects systems (ranging from inexpensive models by Korg and Ibanez up to the Lexicon 224 XL, 480, and later models), synthesizers with *MIDI* (Musical Instrument Digital Interface), drum machines and sequences, digital multieffects devices (such as the Yamaha SPX-90 with dozens of internal programs), and finally the Apple Macintosh computer, used by musicians to write and arrange music and by studio engineers to control the simultaneous operation of sequencers, samplers, consoles, and tape machines. One of the primary reasons the major studios formed SPARS (the Society of Professional Audio Recording Studios) in 1977 was to restore a reasonable pace to the rapid conversion from one professional recording standard to the next. The continuing costs of obsolescence, downtime for the installation of new equipment, and retraining of house engineers all add up to a bill that most studios can't pay. Only a few lucky ones have the name to attract round-the-clock bookings or capture the prize sessions: lockout or block bookings for stars working on top-shelf major-label budgets and Hollywood film-scoring projects.

Today many musicians are feeling the same pinch. Every new generation of synthesizer that comes out obsoletes the last—first Moogs and Arps, then Sequential Circuits, Korg, Roland, and Yamaha with FM tone generation. While the new toys are fun, few musicians have enough current work and/or income to merit the investment.

Wonderful as all these machines are, they have again made it very difficult to maintain professional status without raising studio rentals sky high. In fact, rates at the hottest studios for rock and pop production, whether it be the synth-equipped Unique in New York or the spacious and beautiful rooms at Fantasy Sound in San Francisco, can approach $400 per hour if you are using 48-track digital with a host of SMPTE interlock video, synth, and computer-driven equipment. Everything but the studio itself may be added to your bill à la carte at its own hourly rate.

On the other end of the spectrum, many 24-track studios in Boston, Atlanta, and Detroit, and even lesser-known rooms in New York and Los Angeles, can be rented at under $50 an hour, often as low as $35 with block bookings. While this is great for recording artists and labels, in a way it is just not fair. The recording studio is the instrument without which hit records cannot be made, yet studio ownership is among the worst financial bets in the industry.

2

SOUND SOURCES AND MICROPHONES

T HE purpose of chapters 2–8 in part one is to familiarize you with the basic types of equipment found in professional recording studios. We will discuss the most common design parameters of each equipment genre, the inherent limitations and problems with each genre of equipment, and the underlying considerations that guide many professional engineers and producers in the selection and use of the equipment at their fingertips.

INTRODUCTION

In short, these chapters may help you become a good cook in the kitchen known as the *control room*. As with any field of knowledge—musicianship, for instance—the first things you need are facts. When you apply these and develop a technical toolkit, you are on the way to audio craftsmanship. Beyond this level, when you instinctively know how to achieve desired sounds and can concentrate on deciding what sounds are needed, craftsmanship may finally yield to artistry.

Each step takes a lot of time and experience, but with luck you will develop the chops and the nose for recording techniques that are right for your music and that reinforce the emotions you want to bring to your audience. If some of this information proves to be a review, I guarantee you will find more than a few new concepts to chew on, so please do not brush by, even if you have had a lot of studio experience—even if you are a working engineer.

No two recording studios are alike. The simple demo studio may have only 4 or 8 tracks and very limited sound-processing gear, while a mastering studio can afford 48 tracks or more and has over $1 million in equipment. Yet the basic goal of every studio is the same: to help you express your emotions via music and to capture that expression on tape or another storage medium. Certain genres of music are very equipment-intensive, while others demand little more than two mics and a stereo recorder.

Sometimes, too much equipment can actually stifle creativity. Toys are tempting to use. An engineer with a rack of expensive new digital processors will doubtless think of ways to use them in your session, even if they are not necessary or appropriate in your music. Playing with toys takes time away from playing music. Then, too, the cost of the toys is built into the hourly rate you pay for a studio. If you are paying for things you don't need, these toys are robbing you of additional studio time to play your music. The solution is to follow the precepts of philosopher E. F. Schumacher: *Use technology appropriate to the job at hand.* If the job calls for the highest of tech, fine—use it and pay for it. If not, go to the simplest and least expensive studio that meets the needs of each project. Remember, you could still produce *Sgt. Pepper* with two 4-track machines!

To put some order into our discussion, let us discuss studios in the same sequence as signals flow—from sound sources and studio acoustics to microphones, consoles, tape machines, outboard signal-processing equipment, automation, control room acoustics, and duplication services. Some topics may be irrelevant to your current project. However, my underlying goal is to help you develop good common sense for future projects, as well as a healthy sales resistance to the lure of equipment fancier and costlier than you really need. Important technical terms will be printed in italics when they are first defined.

STUDIO INSTRUMENTS

The Studio Piano.   What instruments a studio must have depends on the type of music you play. It also depends on how easily you can find and rent important instruments from other sources and how easily they can be moved into the studio you select. For the moment, presume that you are recording music that requires a good piano. We define *good* by the use for which the tape is being made. If you are doing a demo to get live gigs, a great piano is not necessary. In fact, club owners who have lesser pianos may respond better to a tape that gives them an idea of how you will sound on location. All the studio piano needs in this case is a decent action and even response. If you have any doubts about a specific piano, ask the studio for a sample of how it sounds on tape.

On the other hand, if you are producing a master tape, the studio's piano may determine where you record. There is no way to make a fair piano sound great. Moreover, if the action is wrong, you will have two strikes against you during every take. The third strike will be your own attitude playing an inferior instrument. However, *beware the great name tag.* There are plenty of Steinways, Baldwins, and other classic pianos that do not live up to their reputation. Every manufacturer has good and bad years. Moreover, piano maintenance is a delicate and expensive proposition. Better to play a lesser name in better condition than a Bösendorfer in poor repair.

Request some time to play the studio's piano, lid up, and without any baffling in which it may be housed. If there are any problems in its action or voicing, demand they be fixed before your sessions begin. You should especially check for the evenness of volume over the keyboard; absence of pinging or wooden clunking when keys are struck (indicating that felt silencers and other parts need replacement); uniform damping of notes when they are released; proper and quiet operation of the pedals; quiet mechanical operation throughout; and absence of buzzing, slight crackling sounds, or metallic resonances. These may signal misadjustment of hammers, loose parts in the action, or even cracks in the soundboard.

Next, have someone else play while you put your head inside the lid for a careful listen. Anything that sounds amiss will be twice as bad on tape. Furthermore, do not agree to help pay for repairs. It is the studio's piano—they will reap the resale value, not you. If they want your business, the repair bill is just a part of their expenses. If you are booking more than a few hours of time, the studio should provide a complete tuning immediately prior to your initial session and daily tweaking if you are doing basics for a full album.

Concerning the instrument's sound, the brighter the better for rock and related genres. In general, piano hammers get harder with time and use, causing a brighter sound. However, when they become petrified, a metallic ringing sound sets in. A piano that is fine except for this problem can be toned down by having the hammers pin-pricked by a trained technician. In any case, I have never recorded a piano that did not require a brighter equalization, even for jazz and classical music, so an overly mellow instrument will be useless for a recording session.

Studio Drums.   Many studios have a house drum kit used mainly for jingles and other commercial projects. While the engineer doubtless knows the kit intimately and can quickly set up to record it, the kit may not have the right basic sound for your tapes, especially for master tapes. If the kit has the type and size drums you are used to, ask to hear how it sounds on tape with music similar to yours. If the sound is fine, spare yourself the agony of lugging your own kit around and the risks of its taking longer to set up and yielding inferior sound because the engineer is unfamiliar with it.

In any case, before agreeing to use a house kit, check the tightness of the shells (there should be no cracks or rattling sounds, and all mufflers should work properly); the condition of the hardware (there should be no stripped screws or cracked clamps); the type and condition of the heads (if you want different heads, be prepared to replace bad ones yourself, unless those on the kit are just plain worn out); and the proper operation of stands and accessories (from kick and hi-hat pedals to the shims and adjustments on cymbal stands, and tom-tom mounts). Ask for some studio time to adjust the entire kit to your height and layout preferences, and give it a brief run. Ask the studio to repair any obvious shortcomings, and plan on bringing your own accessories, from pedals to cymbal pads, and at least two drum keys. Also, take special note of the snare sound. If it has a clear pitched resonance even after tuning (i.e., it sounds primarily at one note usually between G below middle-C and middle-C itself), do not use it. Drums with this problem require extraordinary equalization, which cures one ailment but may create others.

Studio Keyboards.   These days most studios have several synthesizers on hand. If the brands and models they own are usable, so much the better. But do not assume that they will work like, or as well as, your own. Manufacturers often build more than one revision of the same instrument, with different patches or presets, with or without

MIDI. In particular, if your session does require MIDI interconnection of two or more instruments, or if you need to interlock the operation of instruments by internal clocks or other sync pulses, do not assume this hook-up will work. Ask the engineer to demonstrate that the synths do in fact function properly in these applications, and get a money-back assurance that they will do so in combination with the instruments you are bringing in.

In general, the newer the synchronizing system, the more bugs you will encounter among different manufacturers featuring it. Right now this is often the case with higher-order *PPQN* (96 pulses-per-quarter-note and up), *FSK* (frequency shift key) clocking and tape-sync systems, and MIDI synchronization. A failure at either end— sending or receiving—means no session.

If you plan on interfacing two or more instruments via computer, get a further assurance that the specific computer and software you intend to use will be compatible with studio equipment. That way, if there is a problem, you can at least avoid paying for studio time wasted. And whatever you do, make sure the studio has duplicate sets of all MIDI and sync cables you will need. Finally, if you plan on overdubbing or mixing elsewhere and will require the use of the same interfaces in these operations, check with all the studios involved to make sure their systems are compatible with your own equipment and with each other's. Otherwise, you may forfeit a studio deposit without getting anything down on tape.

MICROPHONES AND DIRECT BOXES

Microphones are the most important equipment in any studio. Do not assume that because your studio of choice has a great console or outboard gear that it has good microphones in top shape. No amount of equalization or processing can make up for a poor signal from the mic. Thus, I reccommend that you inform the engineer of all the sounds you intend to record, find out what mics he might use, and make sure that there are more than enough of the right types and matched pairs to accommodate the most complex sessions in your project.

There are dozens of types of mics, each suited to a particular range of recording applications. So that you will be familiar with their major characteristics, let's first discuss the three broad categories of internal design and function. Every microphone consists of a *capsule*, (the enclosed component that converts sound into an electrical signal), a *housing* or case with some active or passive electronic components (*active circuits* require battery or other outside powering, *passive circuits* do not), and internal wiring and a cable to carry the signal to the console. The capsule contains a thin membrane, or *diaphragm*, that vibrates in reponse to impinging sound waves. How these vibrations are changed, or *transduced*, into an electrical signal is what distinguishes the three basic types of mics. Cross-sections of each basic capsule design appear below.

The *dynamic* mic works like a loudspeaker in reverse. A tiny coil of wire is attached to the rear of the diaphragm. When the diaphragm vibrates, this coil moves within the field of a small permanent (or electro-) magnet, which in turn induces a minuscule flow of electric current in the windings of the coil. Electrons flow in one direction as the diaphragm and coil move forward from the rest position, then switch direction as the diaphragm and coil return through rest position during the second half of each sound wave. The resulting *alternating current,* whose *frequency* varies directly and continuously with that of the incoming sound waves, is sent via the mic cable to an amplifying circuit in the console.

There are three important factors determining the absolute quality of a dynamic microphone. First is the weight of the diaphragm and coil: the heavier this apparatus, the louder a sound has to be in order to vibrate it. A heavy apparatus is less responsive to high frequencies (high-pitched sounds composed of short, rapidly vibrating sound waves), and thus has a limited *frequency response.* Finally, weight will determine how quickly the diaphragm can respond to a sound that begins instantaneously, a parameter called *transient response.*

Also important are the number of windings and strength of the magnetic field and the elasticity of the diaphragm's mounting. These together determine the mike's *sensitivity,* or the signal strength it generates in response to a sound of known volume level.

Finally, the coil-wire *gauge* or thickness and the number of internal windings together determine a mic's electrical *impedance* flow, or effective *resistance to current.* This parameter is important for two reasons. First, the lower the impedance, the longer the mic's cable can be without a loss of high frequencies in the signal. Second, low-impedance mics and their cables are less susceptible to outside fields that induce hums, buzzes, and other *RF* (Radio Frequency) interference. All professional studio mics are *low impedance* (600 ohms or less).

The *output* of almost all mics is very small and easily degraded (with loss of level or high frequency response and the introduction of noise) if connected to a *high-impedance* amp or console input. In order to provide for efficient energy transfer, most consoles have *bridging input circuits,* which can accept any mic whose impedance is lower than or equal to the input's nominal impedance. A standard 600 ohm bridging input will work well with some studio mics (mainly ribbon types) whose impedance is as low as 50 ohms. (The symbol for ohms is the Greek letter omega, written Ω.)

Because the diaphragm responds only to changes in air pressure immediately in front of it, the simplest dynamic capsule, called a *pressure type,* responds equally to sounds from any direction and is thus *omnidirectional.* We will see how this pickup pattern can be alterred later.

In a *ribbon* microphone, the diaphragm is usually a thin, pleated ribbon made of or coated with a conductive metal and suspended between and two poles of a magnet. As the ribbon vibrates in response to sounds, a current is induced, which in turn passes to the console's mic input. Without special housings, ribbon mics naturally respond only to sounds coming from in front or behind the flat side of the ribbon. Most ribbon mics are thus *bidirectional.*

Since the ribbon itself replaces the diaphragm and coil of the dynamic, you can easily guess what parameters control the quality of its output signal. Most current ribbon mics have very lightweight ribbons, providing excellent frequency and transient response, though sometimes at the expense of output level. While the ribbons in older mics were quite fragile, suited only for gentle in-studio handling, newer

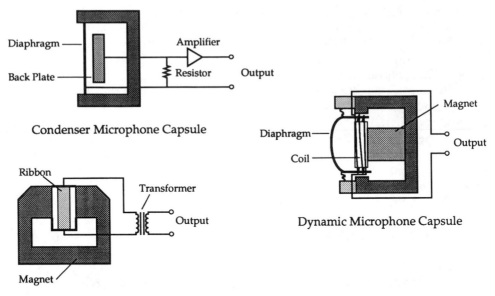

Condenser Microphone Capsule

Ribbon Microphone Capsule

Dynamic Microphone Capsule

Figure 2.1. Cross sections of dynamic, ribbon, and condenser microphone capsules. The axes of the dynamic and condenser capsules are to the left; that of the ribbon mic extends off the page toward and away from the reader.

models, like most of the Beyer line, have tougher ribbons and more protective internal mountings. Yet even some of the latest are susceptible to damage from the high sound-pressure levels encountered in tight-miking of drums or guitar amps.

Condenser or *capacitor* microphones operate on a totally different principle. Instead of a magnet, the capsule contains a membrane in close parallel proximity to a metal plate, each of which is charged oppositely by an outside source of constant *DC* or *direct current* voltage (either a battery or highly filtered power supply). An electrical field is thus established between membrane and plate. Any movement of the diaphragm in response to sound waves changes the strength of this field. This, in turn, induces an extremely small (well under one microvolt, or one millionth of a volt) change in the supply voltage—so small and susceptible to outside interference that a *preamplifier* circuit must be installed inside the mic or within a few feet via cable. Here, the sound-induced changes in supply voltage are sensed, amplified, and sent on to the console.

If the capsule is sealed like the simple dynamic mic shown above, the diaphragm be responsive to sounds from all directions. A vented or open capsule may only hear sounds coming directly from in front, making its response *unidirectional.* In any case, the quality of a condenser microphone depends on several new factors. Its diaphragm must be lightweight to have good high frequency response. However, unlike the dynamic, whose rigid diaphragm is web-mounted to the capsule and thus moves linearly in and out, the condenser's diaphragm can act like a drum head, vibrating in one or more modes at once. The first mode corresponds to uniform motion of the entire diaphragm in and out, the second (as when a drum is struck off-center) causes the

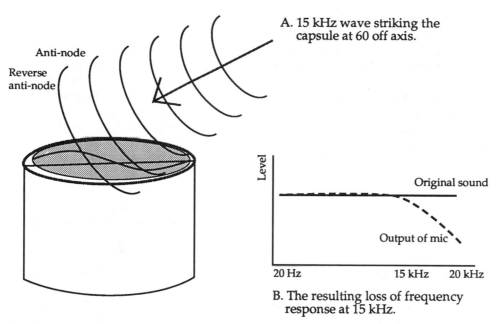

Anti-node

Reverse
anti-node

A. 15 kHz wave striking the
capsule at 60 off axis.

Level

Original sound

Output of mic

20 Hz   15 kHz   20 kHz

B. The resulting loss of frequency
response at 15 kHz.

Figure 2.2. A. Second-mode vibration of a mic diaphragm in response to an off-axis, high frequency sound wave. B. The original signal and the mic's output, showing the resultant loss of high-frequency response in this situation.

diaphragm to behave as two separate heads, one moving in as the other moves out. (For further details, see chapter 12.)

Upper-mode vibrations can cause distortion in the mic's output. However, with a diaphragm less than an inch in diameter, only the highest-frequency sound waves approaching at a severe angle can cause such an asymmetrical stimulus. A 20 kHz wave (20,000 cycles per second, one full wavelength of which is about 1/2″ in length) approaching at a 45 degree angle pushes one side of the diaphragm in and the other out. Since the size and weight of the condenser mic's diaphragm have nothing to do with its output, the diaphragm can be made extremely light and therefore quite responsive to high frequencies and transients. However, this same feature can produce a harsh, spitty top end in situations where *off-axis* ambient high frequencies are present at high levels. (*On-axis* sounds approach the capsule perpendicular to the diaphragm.)

Power for condenser mics can be supplied by internally mounted batteries or by a nearby power supply that converts 110 volts AC (Alternating Current, itself a high-powered audio signal which has a frequency of 60 Hz in the United States or 50 Hz in Europe) to the DC voltage required to charge the capsule and run the preamp. Many current consoles have a feature called *phantom powering,* a circuit that delivers 48 volts DC to all the mic inputs in such a way that DC flows through the signal conductors without affecting the delicate sound signal itself. Another family of mics, the *electret* condensers, have capsules that are permanently charged at the factory. However, even these need a second DC supply—usually batteries—for their preamps.

Flexibility and Convenience Factors.   One factor that determines a mic's suitability for any specific use is its maximum *SPL (sound pressure level),* or the level of the loudest sound that it can hear without producing a seriously distorted signal. This is determined by how far the diaphragm can move from its rest position without reaching the end of its ability to flex smoothly and in accurate proportion to the pressure of the sound wave at hand. The human threshold of pain occurs between 120 and 140 decibels (abbreviated dB) SPL, depending on whose standard dB scale is used. Regardless of the scale, this threshold differs at various frequencies—lower than the quoted SPL at frequencies to which the ear is most sensitive (2–4 kilohertz or kHz) and higher for extreme bass and treble. Similarly, the published Max SPL of mics reflects an average for any combination of frequencies in the mic's frequency response range.

You will (I hope) never hear a live performance louder than about 125 dB, and most microphones work well up to at least that level. So why worry about max SPL? Because the actual sound level two inches about the head of a snare drum, or right in front of the speakers of a guitar amplifier, can approach 160 dB, a level that can in fact shatter the diaphragm of some older condenser mics. Life was simply quieter then.

Furthermore, some microphones, when overdriven, produce more pleasant-sounding distortion than others. Dynamic mics, whose diaphragms are rigid and cannot vibrate in different modes, produce smooth overload distortion in comparison to the average condenser. Thus, it is important to inform your engineer of the volume at which your drummer and amplified musicians like to play. Then, too, even on-axis sounds above a condenser mic's max SPL can cause modal distortion as the diaphragm is wrenched out of shape. For groups consisting of acoustic instruments (except drums), max SPL will have no influence on mic selection.

Another important factor is *directionality.* The housing in which the capsule is mounted can be designed to reinforce or completely change the inherent directional characteristics of the capsule itself. In addition to vents in the capsule, the housing may contain *side* or *rear ports,* openings through which sound waves approaching from various directions (on or off axis) can enter the housing and reach the diaphragm. There are two ways in which these ports can be designed to cancel or phase out sounds approaching from off-axis.

First, if the path by which an off-axis high-frequency sound enters a port and reaches the front of the diaphragm can be made one-half a wavelength longer than its frontal entry path, the frontal and port components of the sound will cancel at the diaphragm, at least partially. Second, if the path length by which a wave entering a side port and reaching the *rear* of the diaphragm can be made equal to the length by which the same sound reaches the front of the diaphragm directly, then the two *wavefronts* will cancel at the diaphragm, regardless of the sound's frequency or wavelength. The result is no overall pressure change at the diaphragm, no diaphragm movement, and no signal in the output. The mic can employ both of these principles to achieve its overall response pattern.

Mics whose response tapers off with off-axis sounds, with minimum response toward the rear, are called *cardioid,* since the angular graph of output with respect to a sound source moving around the mic (called a *polar pattern*) is roughly the

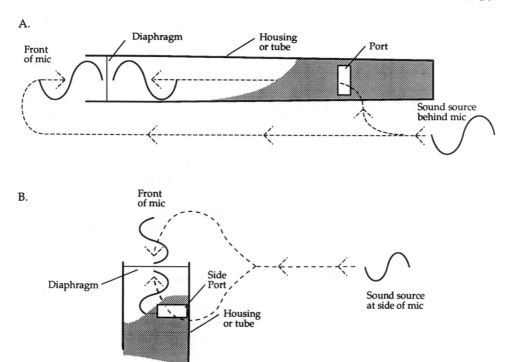

Figure 2.3. Acoustic cancellation of off-axis sound, two ways. A. Creating different path lengths so that sound reaches the front of the diaphragm 1/2 wavelength after it reaches the rear. B. Reaching front and back sides of the diaphragm at equal pressure, thereby not moving the diaphragm.

shape of a heart. While such *side* and *rear rejection* helps the mic eliminate leakage from other nearby sound sources, the ports can also cause a proportional increase in the amount of low-frequency output from frontal sources. Since lows have wavelengths longer than the body of the mic itself, they can enter ports and reinforce the waves striking the front of the diaphragm directly. The resulting boost in bass response for nearby sound sources is called the *proximity effect*. While this can be used to good effect on stage, it may cause havoc in the studio.

Esoteric housing designs, with concentric tubes and elaborate systems of ports, can lead to even more directional mics with *supercardioid* and *hypercardioid* polar patterns. While these patterns provide higher overall rejection of side and rear sounds, the result may be a very uneven frequency response to side and rear sound waves. The strange sound of the resulting leakage (called *off-axis coloration*) is sometimes manifested as a nasal "telephone effect" or spitty high-frequency *sibilance* and can therefore call more attention to itself than a higher level of leakage (as from a less directional mic) with fairly smooth or so-called flat off-axis response. For stage use of hand-held mics, remember that the performer's hand may cover up some or all of the ports, undoing the rejection for which it was purchased.

In the mid-1970s, Crown International first marketed a new type of mic called the *PZM (Pressure-Zone Mic).* Now fairly common in studios, PZMs are basically dynamics, but the capsule is mounted at the surface of a thick metal plate about 5 inches on a side. The plate acts like a miniature wall, shielding the capsule from sounds on its far side, especially reflections of sounds originating on the live side. The resulting pattern is thus hemispherical. When taped to a wall or any solid surface, live side toward the desired sound source, PZMs are alleged to produce a signal free of many of the problems of room acoustics. If a PZM mic is mounted inside a piano lid, for example, sound reflections off that lid are effectively eliminated from its output.

Multipattern microphones, which have several possible polar patterns, are achieved in two ways. In a dynamic or ribbon mic, a switch can be used to cover or reveal certain ports, thereby altering how much sound reaches the diaphragm from various directions or in varying phase relationships. Or there might be more than one ribbon, each aimed in a different direction. The mic's output can be derived from one or the other or be a blend from both. In a condenser, the electrical outputs of two separate diaphragms, mounted on either side of the plate and powered by the same source, can be combined in varying proportions to give a wide range of polar patterns. Of course, each pattern has its own on- and off-axis response with inherent colorations. The five most common polar patterns for studio mics are shown below.

The concentric circles represent output levels spaced five decibels apart: the farther the graph is from the center at any angle, the higher the mic's output in response to sounds from that direction. With respect to an on-axis sound that generates full output (confusingly designated 0 dB) on the cardioid pattern, a 5 kHz sound coming from the rear produces an output 20 dB lower. Ergo the 5 kHz polar pattern for this mic crosses the -20 dB circle 180 degrees off-axis. However, remember that the on-axis output of each mic is not necessarily equal. We set this group at "0 dB" for easy comparison of different patterns.

Internal controls can facilitate or limit the use of certain mics for particular applications. Among the most common controls provided is the *attenuation pad,* a simple electronic circuit that allows the output of the microphone to be reduced when it is used with extremely loud sound sources. In most cases, the pad has no effect on how the diaphragm moves; it will not reduce the incoming sound level to an SPL within the mic's undistorted range but merely reduces the voltage of the output signal to prevent overloading of the console or amp input that follows.

In condenser mics, the pad may reduce the signal level from the capsule to the mic's internal preamp, preventing overload there rather than at the console. In either case, pads do not affect the frequency or transient response of the mic or its polar pattern. Most pads are designed to reduce the output by 10 or 20 dB, reducing the output voltage by about 70% and 90%, respectively. Many mics also have internal low-frequency roll-off or attenuation switches and circuits, affecting frequencies below one or more fixed turnover frequencies—perhaps 75 Hz, 150 Hz, or even higher. This can be used to defeat the proximity effect if you are tight-miking an instrument or vocalist. Handier yet is the continuously variable low roll-off circuit, the extremes of which are usually marked Music (no roll-off) and Voice or Speech (taking out frequencies below 500 Hz or so).

In chapter 12 you will find a chart of most popular studio microphones, listing

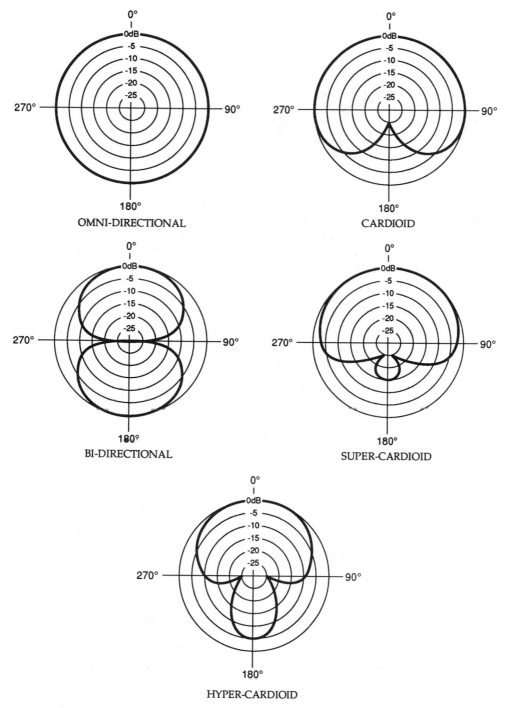

Figure 2.4. Common microphone polar patterns. Polar pattern is the thick line. Mic axes are at 0 degrees.

fairly complete technical data for each and a sampling of the instruments on which they are commonly used. Overall, a studio's supply of mics and their condition are a dead giveaway about its commitment to getting good sound on tape. Microphones are easily damaged in studio use. One good drop onto a hard floor from four feet, or one good smash by a drum stick, can destroy the capsule as well as the housing. If a studio lists its mic inventory in sales literature or ads, ask to inspect the mics (casually) before booking. The physical condition of mics is a good indicator of how well they will perform . Once banged up, a mic should be factory tested. If it needs repair, the studio will more than likely also want to pay to restore its looks. An engineer who says that this crushed tube just came back from factory repair may—or may not—be telling the truth.

There are no rules about what mics every studio should have. Certainly you should find a selection of dynamic, ribbon, and condenser models. It's also a good indicator if there at least a few Neumann, AKG, Sony, or equally costly multipattern condenser types. You should also check to make sure that there are enough matched pairs to record the instruments and sources you want in true stereo—which for a jazz group might be piano, drum overheads, percussions, vocal backups, and a horn section— totaling a minimum of five pairs. Beyond this, it is important to have more than the number of mics you will need for your biggest setup so that you can try a second or third choice on some instruments if the first choice doesn't sound good or turns out not to be working properly. For specific mic/instrument suggestions, refer to the individual chapters on each instrument in part three.

STEREO MIKING TECHNIQUES

There are many musical sources that benefit from stereo miking. Some of these, like the grand piano, have one large sound-producing mechanism; others, such as vibrophones or rack toms, are actually a set or collection of separate instruments each of which produces only one note. Most of the two-mic stereo recording solutions can be grouped into two broad categories; coincident and noncoincident miking. *Coincident* mics are placed so that their two diaphragms are as close as possible without the mics touching. Sound waves that reach both mics equally will therefore produce audio signals that are in phase with each other. This is particularly important with bass and midrange frequencies that carry the weight and power of many instruments.

Where then is the stereo? This depends on the choice of specific mics and the direction in which each member of the coincident pair is aimed. The simplest and most popular coincident configuration is called *XY miking*. Here the diaphragms (usually of two identical cardioid mics) are placed one over another, the axis of one mic aimed between 30 and 50 degrees to the left of the center line of the sound source, the other mic's axis aimed the same angle toward the right. Each mic picks up midrange and highs arriving along its own axis, but both mics pick up lows equally, regardless of where these lows come from.

The stereo image produced by XY mics is very realistic. Someone hearing an XY recording could visually pinpoint the left to right position of each source or player in front of the original mics. However, because the mics hear little beyond their com-

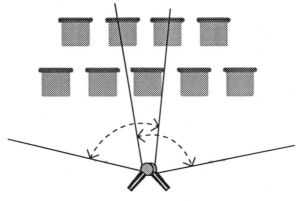

XY (coincident) configuration. Two cardioid mics, one aimed to the left, the other to the right of the center of the sound source.

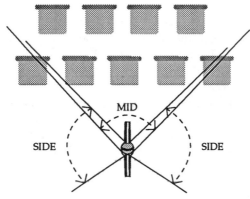

M-S (coincident) configuration. A cardioid "mid" mic is aimed directly at the sound source. A bidirectional "side" mic is oriented with its axes perpendicular to that of the cardioid, picking up left and right ambient sounds. The signals from both mics are combined by an electronic matrix to give the final left and right stereo signals.

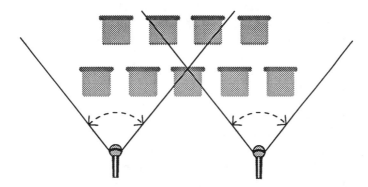

With a spaced pair, it is easy to get too close or too wide, and lose the sound source in the center.

Figure 2.5. Coincident and noncoincident miking schemes for a nine-person brass section showing the on-axis angles of mid- and high-frequency receptivity for each mic.

bined 120 degree frontal view, XY pairs give little sense of the size of the room itself or its inherent sound. Imaging is optimized at the expense of sonic drama.

MS (Middle-Side) miking is a coincident scheme that captures the room or hall and surrounds the listener. Here a cardioid mic is aimed along the center line of the sound source, while a bidirectional mic is mounted directly above or below, with its axis perpendicular to the center line of the source. To obtain left and right signals from the two mics a circuit called an *MS matrix* simultaneously performs two functions. First the matrix adds the two signals, reinforcing whatever is common to both signals, namely audio information from the left of center. At the same time, the matrix switches the original phase of the bidirectional mic signal and adds this to the cardioid mic signal again. Because sounds from right of center push the bidirectional mic diaphragm to the left, the second addition reinforces signals arriving at both mics from the right. The two resulting signals, now useable as left and right stereo channels, represent everything happening in an arc of about 270 degrees around the original mics.

In general, MS miking is best reserved for very large sources such as big bands and orchestral sections, where the MS pair can be 10 to 15' from the source, and where the room or hall itself has fine acoustics. Do not use MS pairs where the pair must be located within about 6' of the source, or in very small or dead studios, or—worst of all—in isolation booths.

The simplest and most frequently used noncoincident scheme is called the *spaced pair*. Here two identical mics (usually omnidirectional or mildly cardioid) are mounted in front of and aimed at the sound source, with the mics between 2 and 10' apart laterally. This gives a broad, spacious stereo, but lacks the left/right imaging accuracy of coincident techniques. The greater the distance between the pair, the more dramatic the sonic results. However, beyond a certain point the left and right signals will have little in common, which produces a so-called hole in the middle. Even those sound sources right on center will lack a clear center image.

Because each spaced pair mic is located a different distance from any sound source to the left or right of the pair's center line or axis, the combined mic signals from off-center sources have phasing problems at all frequencies. Low frequencies will seem less solid or tight than with any coincident pair. For this reason, spaced pairs are not recommended as the only or primary mics for ensembles where the bottom end must be solid, unless the sources of the lows can be separately close-miked to restore the desired weight and focus.

If the spaced mics are spaced closer than about 2', the phasing problems will become more obvious in the midrange and confuse the stereo imaging even further. For a sound source located 45 degrees to the right of the center line of a spaced pair mounted only 2' apart, the distance from source to the left mic is about 12" more than the distance from source to the right mic. A sound of 550 Hz, one full wavelength of which spans about 2' or 24" in air, will be essentially phased out when the spaced mic signals are blended to mono. The 550 Hz wavefront striking the left mic is always one-half wavelength later than that striking the right mic. Similar cancellation will occur at frequencies where one foot equals 1.5, 2.5, 3.5 wavelengths, namely around 1.4 kHz, 2.3 kHz, 3.2 kHz and so on.

For sources producing highs over a wide horizontal angle, the spaced pair works beautifully. Spaced pairs also produce pleasing stereo in less than perfect rooms, and even in isolation booths, making them popular for drum overheads, especially since the kick, snare and toms—all sources of lows—are often miked separately. If the source produces highs unevenly from left to right, the choice of different individual mics for the spaced pair can restore some measure of balance. For a big band seated with all the trumpets to the right of the spaced pair's center line, a broad cardioid or omni for the left mic will draw the trumpets closer to the center, even if a tighter cardioid pattern is used on the right mic. Thus, any two mics with a similar overall sound can be used in a spaced pair, as long as they produce the desired stereo effect.

If you plan on recording one or more electric instruments without amps or mics, check the studio's supply of *Direct Boxes,* or *DIs (direct input);* do not plan on using your own on-stage preamps or impedance-matching devices. The noise and distortion specs of most of the inexpensive units for stage use are simply not up to studio snuff. Make sure the studio has more than enough good DIs to accomodate your worst-case scenario. Despite the nominal specs on studio DIs some of them produce unpredictable results—unexplained grounding problems or RF hums— when used on certain synthesizers, guitars, or instrument pickups. Chasing such problems can eat up a lot of time and money. Having extra DIs around will also eliminate the need to overdub a part that, for musical reasons, should be laid down with basic tracks.

Remember as well that a drum machine requires one DI per output or up to eight in order to record each drum or cymbal output on a separate tape track. Inform your engineer ahead of time what drum synth you have and how many outputs you'll be using during the session.

3

CONSOLES FOR RECORDING AND MIXING

CONSOLES are a hot topic, thanks to the amount of publicity that manufacturers like Neve and Solid State Logic receive in the trade magazines. Overall, I advise you to forget the hype and concentrate on the task at hand. If you will be mixing forty or more tracks and have to return night after night to get the same sounds on song after song for an album, the SSL can be a real time saver. At the risk of alienating friends at SSL, however, if you are laying basic tracks or overdubbing, you just do not need many of such a board's features. These stages of a demo or master project can be carried out with equal speed and precision on a wide variety of console brands and models.

MAJOR COMPONENTS

With that in mind, let us look at the major components of all boards in the order in which the signal flows. The first circuit an entering signal encounters in each *module* (a vertical column of controls and internal circuits allocated to one signal) of the console is a microphone and/or *line preamplifier,* usually incorporating an input gain or volume control called the *trim* and one or more internal pads. The three important parameters of this input stage are low-circuit noise, low-circuit distortion, and sufficient headroom to handle the entire dynamic range of your instruments or vocals. The input stage boosts a mic signal level between 40 and 70 dB, from *mic level* (in the 50–100 microvolt range) up to *line level* (about one volt).

Headroom is a measure of a circuit's ability to accept signals higher than its

24

nominal input level, then accurately process and output them and generate an output signal proportionately higher than its nominal full output level (in the mic/line preamp, about one volt). For example, a bass guitar can have transients well over 0.1 volt. Each factor of two in voltage corresponds to a change of 6 dB in signal level. Compared with a mic whose output is 100 microvolts, or 0.000100 volt, the bass's output is 1,000 times greater. Since 1,000 is about 2 raised to the tenth power, and each doubling of voltage implies a 6 dB increase of signal level, the bass level is 10 × 6 dB or about 60 dB higher than that from the microphone. In order for a console mic input to accept input signals over such a wide voltage range, the trim control usually preceeds the mic preamp or input stage itself.

Moreover, when the trim is set so that the average level of a bass note produces full level in the console, the input preamp must be able to handle bursts of energy during particularly loud sections of the song. Instruments such as drums, piano, and voice produce transients 20 dB or more above their average level. To pass this without distorting, the input stage thus needs 20 dB headroom. In the example above, 20 dB above 1 volt implies that the preamp must be able to produce a clean output of 10 volts. Most professional consoles provide at least 20 dB headroom. The weak link in the recording chain turns out to be the tape itself, which generally has no more than 12 to 15 dB headroom, depending on frequency.

To take the guesswork out of headroom, many pro tape decks have LED overload indicators installed inside the VU meters for each track. Even when the VU meter cannot move fast enough to show the actual level of a transient, these LEDs indicate signal peaks at or above the top of the headroom buffer zone. Of course, all headroom figures depend on what you call normal full *operating level* or 100 percent modulation level. The same circuit can have 12 dB headroom if you call 1 volt its operating level, or only 6 dB if its nominal full level is rated at 2 volts. Either way, once distortion occurs, it cannot be removed. Thus, it is important that everything else in the chain have more headroom than the storage medium itself—in this case, the tape.

VU VERSUS PEAK-READING METERS

The *Volume Unit (VU) metering* system was developed in the 1920s, long before tape recording was even conceivable. In essence, VU meters display the average ongoing program level, and so give a good indication of whether a radio transmitter, record groove, signal processor, or tape is being used to a reasonable degree of efficiency. However, the VU meter gives little indication of the exact signal level at any moment of the program. A meter's *ballistics* describe how the meter moves or responds in reaction to various types of signals. By the time a VU meter responds to an incoming transient at full level, the needle might move only halfway to a full level indication, so VU meters are considered to have rather slow ballistics.

A peak-reading meter, on the other hand, has fast ballistics, which means that its indicator (whether a needle or series of LEDs) shows the highest instantaneous peak levels occuring in the program signal. Because transient signals like voice or drums cause a peak meter to gyrate wildly, peak-reading meters are straining to the eye. For this reason, and because the circuitry inside a peak meter is more expensive

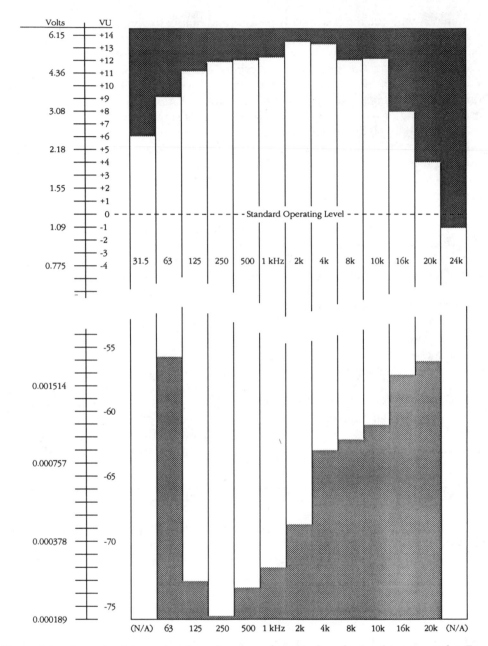

Figure 3.1. A graph of the entire dynamic range of a typical professional tape recorder. For steady tones, standard operating level is shown at the dashed line and is defined as 0 on the VU meter. From this point the headroom in each frequency range ends where the dark gray begins above, e.g., +12 dB VU at 1 kHz. The noise floor of the machine occurs where the light gray begins below. At 1 kHz, this machine's noise level is thus −72 dB VU. The actual input signal voltages that produce the corresponding VU levels in most professional recorders are shown in the left column.

to build, VU meters are still standard on most tape recorders and in many consoles. In other consoles, where the meter indicators are LEDs, or liquid crystal displays (not mechanical needles), the engineer can choose to read a specific signal or the master outputs by either VU or peak ballistics.

While there is no exact mathematical relationship between VU and peak readings that holds for any type of program signal, in general, when a VU meter reads full level (called 100 percent *modulation*), the same signal would cause a peak meter to indicate a level of +12 dB. It is confusing that 100 percent modulation is designated as "O dBVU" until one understands that with respect to this level, a reduction of 6 dB in signal level occurs when the voltage of the signal is reduced to half its initial value. Thus, on a VU meter, 50 percent modulation occurs at −6 dBVU, 25 percent modulation at −12 dBVU, and no level at all is designated as −∞ in VU terms. Modulation is thus a direct measure of the incoming voltage, while the decibel readings relate to the human ear's tendency to judge relative volumes by a non-linear scale. (In fact the scale is logarithmic, but we need not go into the details here.)

Because meters respond differently to signals containing various frequencies and types of transients, it is handy to have peak meters available in the studio. Using peak meters, one can match the highest peaks of a drum signal to the limit of the headroom on the tape being used, and so take advantage of all of the tape's magnetic capacity without causing tape saturation. However, for most applications, VU metering is adequate, and an experienced engineer will know what peak levels are present in each type of sound, over and above the VU reading indicated. Remember too that full level is different for different types of tape, so recorder meters (and the actual electronics) need to be calibrated to properly indicate normal level, headroom characteristics, and absolute saturation level for the type of tape a particular studio uses. If you bring your own tape to a studio and notice the engineer riding levels lower or higher than nominal full-level on his system, it is most likely because he knows that your tape has a lower or higher normal *operating level* than the brand or type his studio stocks in-house. Remember that consoles and most processing equipment have far greater headroom than tape, so even when console meters look disastrously high, the signal being delivered to tape can be clean and undistorted.

CONSOLE STRUCTURE OR ARCHITECTURE

Most studios have what are called *in-line consoles,* in which all the circuitry and controls associated with an individual mic/line input or recorded track appear in a vertical column or module mounted on a single faceplate. These modules are lined up next to each other across the width of the entire board. Above the modules is a *meter bridge* (usually with one meter per module or track, and to the left and right, a *patch bay* with jacks connected to various inputs and outputs of circuits within the console and to all the outboard equipment in the control room. Sometimes called a *jack field,* it is generally mounted above or adjacent to the so-called producer's desk. Most of today's in-line consoles consist entirely of two to four types of modules.

I/O Modules (Input/Output).   *I/O modules* are lined up next to each other and numbered from left to right, generally form the bulk of the entire console. The mic/line preamp and trim controls discussed earlier are located here. A direct output stage or preamp is usually included, allowing the engineer to patch any module direct into any track of a tape deck. However, the O of I/O does not represent this direct output.

For convenience, a group of buttons in each input module allows the engineer to select any of a number of output channels to which the signals in one or all modules can be sent. Usually there is one output channel for each track of the multitrack, but not necessarily one for each input module. Despite the ubiquitous I/O name tag, however, the actual input and output circuits are electronically separate and sometimes even designated separately as I and O modules. Each output module has its own level meter, normally mounted vertically beyond the end of the I/O module. Together, all these meters form the so-called *meter bridge.*

The so-called *size* or *configuration* of a console is designated by the respective number of Is and Os. A 32 × 24 board, for instance, has 32 input modules, and the signal from each of these can be sent to any of 24 separate output paths, or *buses.* In this case, there are 32 Is but only 24 Os. A few manufacturers add a third number to their size (usually the middle number) to indicate the number of channels available for monitoring functions.

The Master Module.   The *master module* contains the the stereo master and submaster volume faders, along with all the controls for studio and control-room monitoring, such as speaker selection and playback volume. The master controls for reverb and studio headphone *(cue)* mixes may also be located on the master module or may be located separately on a *cue master* and/or *reverb master module.* In rare cases, there may be a separate *monitor module,* taking speaker control for studio and control room over from the master module.

The Automation Master Module.   If present, the *automation master module* will have controls related to the automated mixdown system, and these days it may also provide circuits to interface with outboard SMPTE (Society of Motion Picture and Television Engineers)- and/or MIDI-controlled equipment.

Each I/O module receives signals from three sources: a mic input in the studio or isolation booths, a line level input that is accessible through the *patch bay* (one or more rows of input and output jacks), and a direct feed from one track from a multitrack or other tape recorder. In most boards, the tape track signal is not a separate input but connected to the line level input by depressing the Tape button. Thus, the module actually has two inputs, one at mic level, the other at line level. The tape source is there to spare the engineer the effort of patching in tape playback so frequently.

When any signal source is permanently wired into a circuit or module (i.e., it does not need to be patched in every time it is used), it is *normaled* to that input. Some sources or signals, like those from mics, are not only normaled to each module but actually *hard wired.* A hard-wired connection cannot be accessed at the patch bay or rerouted to another destination without manually reconnecting or resoldering it inside the console. Only line level signals flow through the patch bay. Mic level signals are just too fragile and subject to interference, and are thus hard wired to the mic inputs.

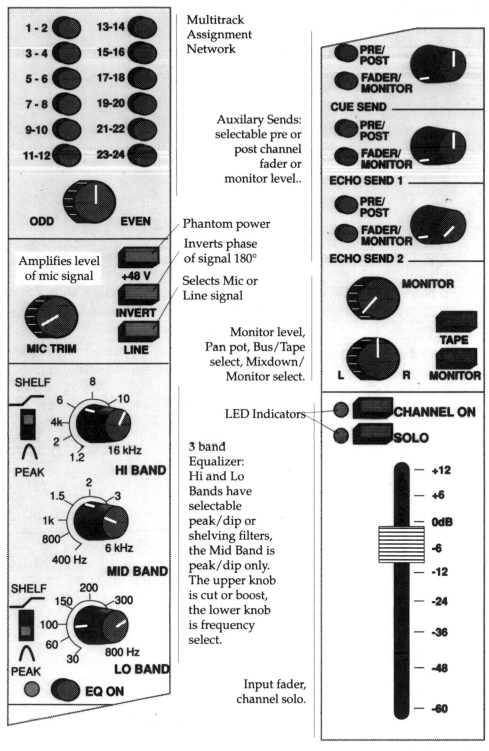

Figure 3.2. A typical I/O (Input/Output) module, upper half on left, lower half on right

Each of hundreds of normal connections within the console is routed through a particular pair of *jacks* (electrical receptacles or sockets) in the patch bay, one jack for the output signal of each circuit, another jack for the input of the circuit to which it normally flows. To derive a copy of one of these signals without interrupting a normal, the engineer *patches* (inserts one end of a patch cord) into the output jack of the pair. The other end of the patch cord can then be inserted into the input jack for another device or circuit. However, by inserting a patch cord in the input jack of a normal pair, the engineer can break the normal and send some other signal to that input. Clearly, each circuit can have only one input at a time. In any case, each circuit input or output accessible via the patch bay is called a *patch point*.

The studio recording process requires that all engineers have access to, and control of, at least three separate copies of the input signal being handled by each module. First and most important, engineers must control the volume and quality of each input to be sent to a tape track for recording. Next, they need separate control of the volume at which each of these inputs is heard in the control room. Third, they must be able to separately control the level of each input that goes to the musicians' headphones while recording or overdubbing. To allow the engineer to send different amounts of each input signals to several destinations, and to blend all the signals going to each destination to suit its particular requirements, is the essential function of the console while recording.

Once a mic signal is raised to line level, or the proper line level signal selected in any module, the console allows the engineer to use copies of this signal for each desired purpose, separately adjusting the volume of each copy and introducing individual signal processing (with in-board circuits or outboard devices accessible via the patch bay), to some or all of the copies as best suits each individual need. The volume of a particular mic as heard in the control room has no effect on the level of that mic heard in the headphones, and neither of these levels affects that being recorded on the assigned tape track.

Each signal-copy from an individual module can be mixed together with the corresponding copies of signals from other modules via individual mixing circuits called *summing amps*. Each such resulting blend travels to its destination through an electrical path or bus. Thus, the headphone copies from all modules are summed and sent to the headphone or cue bus. Two summing amps and two busses are necessary if the console allows stereo cue mixes. The monitor buses carry the sum of left and right stereo monitor summing amps, ultimately to the control room power amplifiers and speakers. Still other copies of each input signal can be mixed together via auxiliary summing amps and buses and sent to outboard processors such as reverb units and delays.

Most I/O modules have three sections, each with its separate volume (and other) controls, each capable of carrying a separate signal. The *input* or *program section* is operated by the main faders—those nearest the engineer. During recording the signals from each of these faders is normally sent to tape. The meter over each module may display the signal level immediately after the trim or after the main fader, depending on brand and model of the console. The engineer can also send the combined signals from the program faders to the stereo master buses, in which case the entire blend will appear on the main stereo output meters and be controlled by the stereo master fader.

Most often the engineer doesn't want to hear the relative balance of these signals exactly as they are going to individual tape tracks. In this event, he or she can use the *monitor section* of the I/O modules for listening, adjusting the level of each signal via its own separate monitor *pot* (short for *potentiometer,* or volume control). A *pan-pot* allows individual signals to be placed anywhere in the left/right stereo image. Normally monitor and master imaging are selected by the lone pan pot. The monitor signals are summed in stereo, their level set by a stereo monitor master pot, after which they take a pair of buses to the monitor amp and speakers.

The third section of each module is its *output section,* by which the engineer selects where to send the signal. This is discussed later.

Another block of pots on each input module allows the engineer to make completely separate mixes of all the signals for other purposes. Many brands of modules provide two stereo *reverb-send* pots and associated pan-pots and up to eight additional *effect-send* pots, some in stereo pairs with their own pan-pots. The latter can be used to send one or more sources or tape tracks to devices such as digital delays, flangers, and so on. The first stereo reverb send pots on all I/O modules lead to a pair of buses, where all the signals to be reverbed are summed in preparation for input to the reverb device. Other buses collect summed signals from similarly numbered effect-send pots on all the modules.

Most consoles allow the engineer to send the signal to reverb or effects either straight from the input stage, called a *prefader* signal (sent before its volume is affected by the main fader), or after the main fader, called *postfader.* In the former case, no matter how the engineer rides the fader, that signal will go to the reverb-send pot at full level; in the latter, the level sent to the reverb send pot will vary in proportion to the changing program fader level. Choice among these options is made via a *pre/post* switch adjacent to each send pot.

On some consoles, no specific sends are normaled to reverb or headphone amps. Instead, buttons on the master, reverb, or cue module allow the engineer to select any desired *aux send* (auxiliary send) for these purposes. The *reverb returns* (outputs from the reverb devices) usually appear on the master module, adding their signals to that passing through the stereo master fader. In any case, the summed aux sends, reverb sends, and returns are generally accessible via patch points.

It is often necessary to vary the signal levels from two or more faders with a single finger if, for example, the level of all drum mics must be lowered simultaneously. To this end, some consoles have *group assignment* buttons, wheels, or selectors adjacent to or above the main fader. By choosing one of among perhaps eight *submaster* groups, the signal in that module and others assigned to the same submaster will all be controlled by a single designated stereo fader in the master module. The fader at each module in the group will still control the individual amount of its own signal in the submaster blend, but the level of the entire group can be varied by the submaster. (We will see a variation of this feature in the discussion of console automation in chapter 4.)

A few consoles have *fader-flip* buttons, which allow the engineer to swap func-

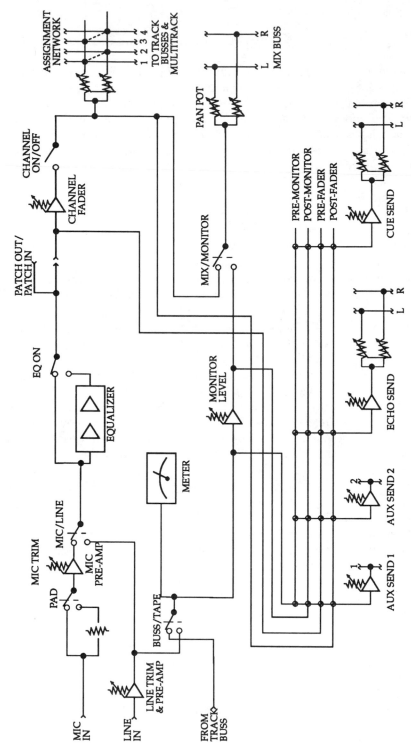

Figure 3.3A. Flow chart for a typical in-line console I/O module

32

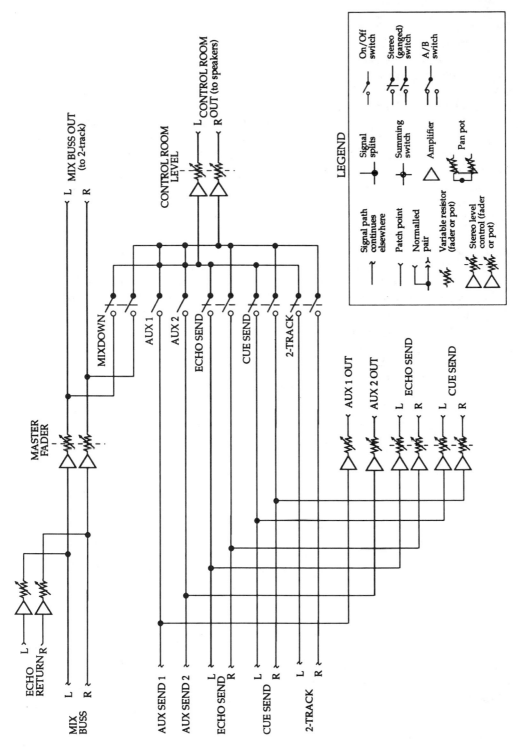

Figure 3.3B. Flow chart for a typical in-line console master section

33

tions between the main or program faders and monitor pots. The scheme can get very complex on more sophisticated boards. Beyond these options, each input module has an in-line equalizer, which in some consoles is switchable, affecting either the program or monitor signal. A few high-end consoles also provide in-line compressors and noise gates for each module, but now we're talking SSL, NEVE, and the like.

The output section of each I/O contains its *track* or *bus assignment matrix,* a rectangular field of buttons by which the program signal from the module is sent to one or more output buses. Each module can be sent to a separate bus, or they might all be sent to a single bus. Similarly, each numbered bus could be patched to any destination but is generally normaled to the sequential inputs of an 8-, 16-, or 24-track recorder, bus 1 to track 1, and so forth.

A pan-pot is usually provided in the output matrix of each module, allowing its signal to be distributed to two sequentially numbered buses that can serve as left and right stereo destinations for the collected program signals from a number of modules. By this method, six mikes used on woodwinds, for example, can be directly mixed to stereo and recorded on a single pair of tracks. The engineer would merely assign all six mics to buses 5 and 6, using the pan-pot at the matrix to place each wind in the desired left-to-right stereo position.

During overdubbing and mixing, various input and output or I/O modules can be used to reproduce already-recorded tracks from tape; to bring live mics or D.I. inputs in from the studio and assign these new sounds to unused or clean tape tracks; to bring "live" drum machine or synth sources into the mix, synched with the multitrack tape by MIDI and/or SMPTE signals (these can be treated exactly as if they were already on the multitrack tape, effectively increasing the number of tracks available for your session); or to control reverb and effects that are then sent to players' headphones, the control room speakers, or direct to tape in combination with new material and/or tracks recorded earlier.

Here again, modules can be assigned to groups for control by a submaster. When this is done, any assignment of those signals to reverb and effects buses remains in full force.

Split-console design is an alternative to the standard in-line architecture. Here, one bank of input modules with faders, equalizers, and so on feeds the multitrack machine during recording and accepts the various track outputs during mixdown. A completely separate bank of monitor faders and mini modules is positioned off to the right. These feed the monitor buses, cue (and sometimes reverb) sends, and so on. For recording basics and overdubbing the split design is visually easier and quicker to use, since the engineer deals with the signal to tape on one side, and the signal-to-ears on the other. Overall, both types of architecture achieve all the same functions: only the layout is different. However, a 40-input split board can be nearly fifteen feet wide including patch bay and producer's desk. You would need roller skates to operate anything larger. For space reasons alone, most studios opt for in-line consoles.

Figure 3.4A.   Photo of a section of Sony MXP-3000 console showing I/O modules, echo send/ return module, and master module. Photo courtesy of Sony Corporation.

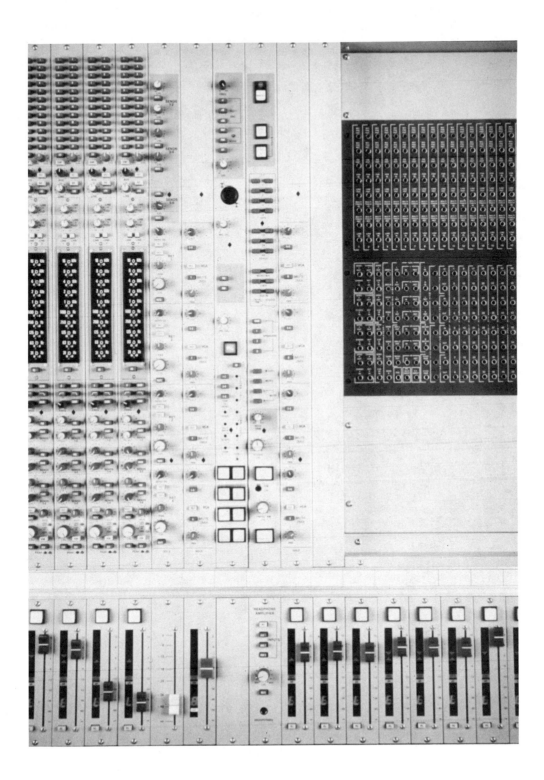

IMPORTANT FACTORS FOR YOUR SESSION

The basic job of the board is to provide flexibility and control of all inputs—and to do so quickly, quietly, and without adding distortion. Although the noise specs for most boards are more than adequate for analog recording, overdubbing, and mixing, a big variable in actual performance is the quality of the installation. Even an SSL can be noisy if there are grounding problems in the control room, if the mic lines themselves are improperly shielded or pick up ambient fields, or if the engineer does not use the various stages of amplification (from mic input and trim to master fader) to maximize signal and minimize noise. Sloppy signal control can also introduce severe distortion.

First, determine whether the console has enough input and output (or I/O) modules and track-assignment buses to handle your project. Just because a studio has a 24-track deck doesn't mean it can record all 24 tracks at once. If the board is 24 × 12, you may be able to record only 12 tracks at a time. (Even if the others can be patched direct from the other modules, you may not be able to monitor them all through phones.) While this may be passable for a rock demo, it probably is inadequate for a careful big-band master tape. Beyond that, determine whether there are enough reverb and effects sends to allow separate generation and control of each additional sound you need and enough returns (spare input modules that are not needed for direct track playback) to bring the effects all back into the console during mixdown.

Some studios have a smaller 8-, 12-, or 16 × 2 mixer off to one side, into which returns and reverbs are patched. The outputs of this mixer then appear on two faders or pots leading to the master fader, perhaps at the normal in-board reverb returns. One way or another, if you need 24 tracks and 10 total returns, there must be 34 places for signals to be entered ahead of the stereo master fader.

Next I would ask the engineer to turn up one I/O module (with mic input selected) to full gain with no mic plugged in, turn the master fader up full, and then turn the control room monitors carefully up full. There should be a considerable hiss but virtually no audible hums, buzzes, or recognizable radio interference. If there is, the system has something amiss. If the engineer says that such problems are "way below your music level" when the speakers are turned down to listening level, it is still risky because such problems can be compounded and amplified when mics or DIs are plugged in. Furthermore, they often indicate unauthorized high-frequency signals (often well above the audible range) scurrying around in the board. These can later interfere with highs from musical sources like cymbals, generating substantial audible by-products including intermodulation distortion, feedback (called *oscillation*), leakage among various modules or tape tracks (called *crosstalk*), or all three.

If the board is relatively inexpensive or an unknown brand, ask the engineer to play back a stereo master mix through a pair of I/O modules, and try out the in-line equalizers. This is the only circuit in the board that should affect the quality of your

---

Figure 3.4B. Photo of section of Sound Workshop Series 34 console showing I/O module, echo send/return module, and master module. Photo courtesy of Sound Workshop.

sounds. If the equalizer has scratchy pots, causes distortion when you crank one or more bands, or adds a harsh or metallic quality to the mix it can do the same thing to your instruments or recorded tracks.

Different boards, despite manufacturer protests, do have different sounds, and much of this difference is in their respective eqs. Among the high-end boards, Neve, Harrison, and Amek are rumored to have a smooth, musical sound—an indefinable and unmeasurable "warmth" that many producers believe adds to the performance and the finished tape. Others, like SSL, Trident, and Studer, are thought to be accurate almost to the point of sounding clinical, giving a cooler, crisper, uncolored sound. Still others, like Sony and Sound Workshop, have fairly neutral sonic reputations. All distinctions aside, great records and many hits have been made on every make of board, so don't get overly fussy until you can afford this luxury.

In terms of helping musicians while laying basic tracks and overdubs, the most important section of the console is its headphone or cue mix and send circuitry. It is crucial that musicians not only hear each other well in phones but have a good idea of the audio ambience in which the final mix may be dressed. Thus, the cue system should be stereo and capable of delivering reverb and a couple of effects to the musicians' headsets. Positioning of various instruments in left-to-right stereo will help players focus on those sounds on which they rely for the right feel when playing live.

A second cue mix can be particularly handy for the drummer and/or bassist, who may want to concentrate more on the rhythmic sources in the arrangement than on its melodic or chordal elements or who may simply need more headphone level. Here, a mono cue mix won't hurt much. Many boards have both stereo and mono cue systems. To make sure you get what you will need, try on the studio phones for comfort and sound. No amount of expensive in-board electronics will make up for $10 phones or good sets with blown-out drivers in one or both ears.

Beyond these few factors, you may or may not need console automation. If your tracks are carefully recorded, with consistent and high level, and without a lot of talk and audio garbage between the good lines of music and vocal, automation can waste as much time as it is intended to save. If you want to remove or mute short instrumental lines and fills, popping various tracks on and off a lot during the mixdown, automation will be helpful for its ability to remember and perform these mutes. However, a fully automated mixdown can require two dedicated tracks on your multitrack tape. Mutes can usually be written on a single track.

In my opinion, most mixes can be accomplished just as well manually. Even if the two-track master has to be spliced together from several sections mixed separately, or from pieces of several complete passes, it can have a life and spontaneity that repeated automation passes can drain away in the search for audio perfection. Do not let automation affect your studio choice unless your mix will take six hands working the console simultaneously.

4

MULTITRACK AND OTHER TAPE RECORDERS, NOISE REDUCTION, AND STUDIO ACOUSTICS

Tape recorders and noise reduction work together as one device from the moment signals leave the console until they return from tape. There are a couple of basic problems in multitrack recording that you can't avoid, so we might as well expose them right now, before examining the niceties of specific systems.

TAPE RECORDERS AND NOISE REDUCTION

First, 2″ 24-track is too noisy a medium for recording masters at 15 *ips* (inches per second) tape speed, unless you use some form of noise reduction. The same is true for 1″ 16-track, 1/2″ 8-track, and other *narrow-guage* or semipro multitrack formats. It is impossible to squeeze a high enough *signal-to-noise (S/N) ratio* out of these formats without Dolby, dbx, or the like. (*Signal-to-noise ratio* is the decibel difference between the highest signal a system can pass without distorting, and the system's inherent noise level when no signal is present.) Thus, your only alternative is going to 30 ips for all recording at double the tape cost and with a maximum length of 15 minutes on any single cut—the playing time of a 10.5″ (2,500′) roll of standard 1.5-mil-thick tape (one mil = 1/1,000 of an inch).

In many circumstances 30 ips actually gives better overall sound than noise reduction. If you have to *bounce tracks* (rerecord sounds from one tape track to another, perhaps adding new sounds to those already recorded, as in double- or triple-tracking vocals),a Dolby or dbx has to encode and then decode the material during every new bounce or generation. By the time you have bounced a track three times and play back the final version, the original sound has been through eight coding and decoding operations. Even the small distortion inherent in a professional noise reduction system (and every circuit adds some distortion to a signal) will certainly be noticeable, if not objectionable, by that time.

Furthermore, most noise-reduction systems are *companders*. They compress (reduce) the dynamic range of part or all of the signal during recording, proportionally increasing low-level signals toward 100% modulation or nominal "full" tape level. During playback the recorded signal is expanded (increasing its dynamic range again) in exactly the opposite fashion. This restores each sound to its original input level. Tape noise or hiss is subjected to the same playback expansion, and its level is thereby reduced during soft musical passages. All companders are *level-dependent* with respect to their input signals in that the amount of compression or expansion applied depends on the instantaneous signal level going to or coming from the tape.

Since the level at which multitrack decks record and play is not entirely uniform from studio to studio, you can run into serious problems if you record with noise reduction at one studio, then overdub, bounce, or mix down in another studio. There are in fact two industry standard record/playback levels in use at different U.S. studios. Since these standards are about 3 dB apart, serious playback errors can occur in tapes recorded here and mixed there.

Such errors can impart a fluttery, breathless quality to recorded music, the result of the expander not exactly undoing the compression that was applied during record. The problem can be avoided only if the recording engineer lays test tones at the head of each multitrack tape, allowing the mix engineer to adjust playback level of each track to match. Of the systems in use at most studios, the Dolby A is most sensitive to improperly matched record and play levels. This system generates its own warbling reference tone, a sample of which should be recorded on all tracks at the beginning of each new reel of tape for later playback level alignment.

The Dolby SR (Spectral Recording) and the dbx systems are theoretically impervious to such problems, although I have heard traces of mistracking in the latter when record and playback levels are way off.

The original Dolby A (invented in 1968 and still in use at many studios) eliminates about 10 dB of noise by dividing the frequency spectrum into four bands and companding each of them separately. The Dolby SR system affords over 30 dB noise reduction by an even more complex process. dbx units equalize and compand signals in a single broad band, also achieving about 30 dB reduction. In double-blind tests many engineers have preferred the SR to digital multitrack, both for low noise and overall sound quality. As of this date, however, few low-budget and midline studios have SR equipment.

Noise reduction cannot eliminate noise emanating from the source: your instru-

Audio control panel: Master and individual track monitoring selection and record ready status. The LEDs light to reflect the chosen mode.

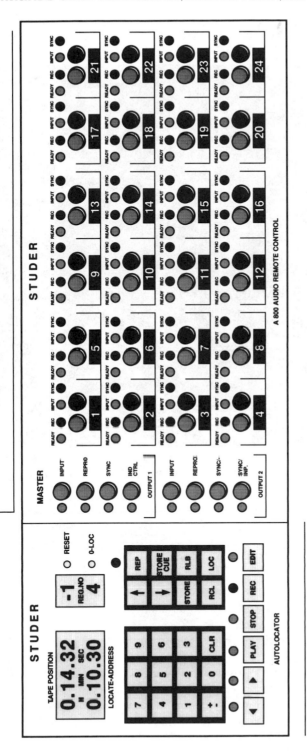

Transport and Auto Locator control panel:
REP allows the operator to set up a repeating play / rewind loop, STORE CUE takes the current tape position and stores it to a memory number, RLB is Rollback which locates a tape position a number of seconds in advance of the number displayed, for cueing purposes. There are 20 location memories, 0 through 9 and -0 through -9 accessed using STORE and RCL (recall). LOC locates the tape to the time displayed in the address window. The up and down arrows move numbers back and forth between the tape position and locator-address windows.

Figure 4.1A. Multitrack remote controls. Studer A800 24-track remote and auto-locator

Current tape position and locate address displays, RST key to reset the display to 00.00, LOC to locate the locate address, and varispeed controls.

Keypad, store, recall, and repeat keys.

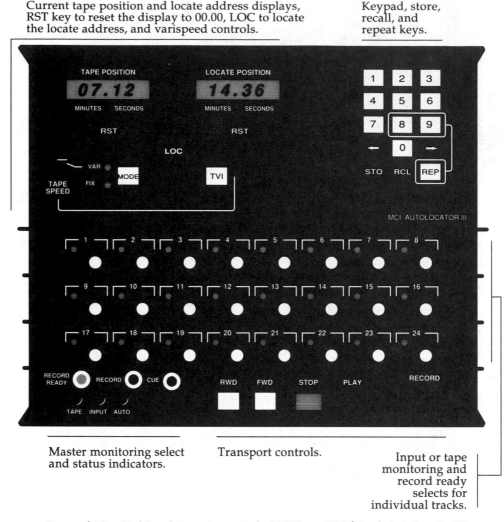

Master monitoring select and status indicators.

Transport controls.

Input or tape monitoring and record ready selects for individual tracks.

Figure 4.1B. **Multitrack remote controls: MCI/Sony JH-24-track AutoLocator III**

ments, amplifiers, on-stage or studio processing devices, or the recording console. It only reduces the amount of noise inherent on tape and any noise added in the playback electronics of the recorder itself.

Regarding analog multitrack recorders, within any price range there are more differences in features and conveniences than in the sound quality each machine puts on tape. Certainly the Rolls-Royce of machines is the Studer 820-SR, but its price tag of nearly $80,000 is between twice and thrice the cost of several workhorse brands like MCI (now renamed SPPC for Sony Professional Products Corporation) and Otari. Again, the printed specs of all models look very impressive, so it is pointless to discuss minor variations in S/N (signal to noise), frequency response, and distortion. Hits and

Record ready/Safe select switches for each track. LEDs indicate status: blinking shows the track is armed, on shows the track is recording.

Monitoring status selection and display. Master buttons at left allow override of the individual select switches at the bottom.

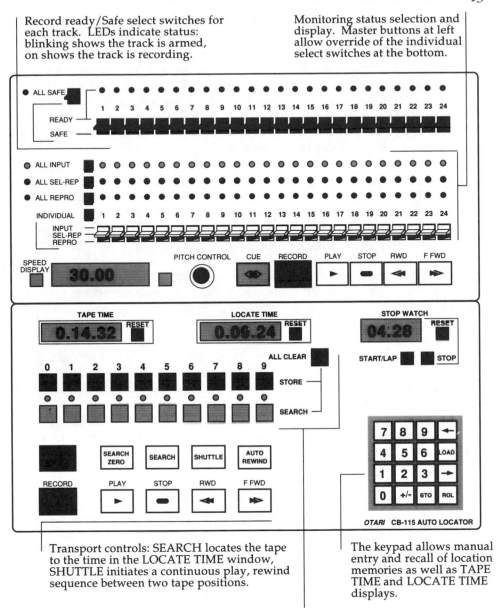

Transport controls: SEARCH locates the tape to the time in the LOCATE TIME window, SHUTTLE initiates a continuous play, rewind sequence between two tape positions.

The keypad allows manual entry and recall of location memories as well as TAPE TIME and LOCATE TIME displays.

Tape position memories. The upper button stores the current tape position, the lower button initiates a search for that position. The LEDs indicate which memories are in use.

Figure 4.1C.   Multitrack remote controls: Otari MTR-90 24-track remote and auto locator

Grammy winners have been made on all brands and models, which indicates that the machine is less important than the musicians and engineers using it. However, I must note a few user features that may affect your studio choice.

All recent multitracks should allow you to punch in and out on any track without adding clicks and pops. Ask the engineer if the deck has problems with punching noise. In addition, older or improperly maintained machines may respond rather slowly to punching instructions, which makes it difficult to accurately insert short phrases or single notes on an individual track. If you think this will be necessary on your session, tell the engineer before booking.

Second, there are two ways of monitoring sounds during recording: sending the mic signals directly to the monitor section of the board, and sending these signals directly to the multitrack and monitoring the outputs of the respective tape machine channels. Of these, the latter is much better, because it tells you exactly what the machine is hearing. If a signal level is too hot for the machine, you will hear distortion: if the Dolby is mistracking on the way to or from the machine, you will hear it. You would not hear these problems if monitoring straight from the console faders. Most multitrack machines automatically send their input signals to the respective outputs for any channels put into record mode, which makes through-the-machine monitoring a simple matter of selecting tape for the line input of the console monitor pots.

Current multitracks help save studio time through faster winding and more accurate location of selected tape positions via *auto-locator* and equivalent systems and SMPTE interlock. A machine that enables the engineer to note and memorize tape positions corresponding to different musical events in a take, then recall these points quickly, can save hours of overdubbing time during an album project. In addition, when you are recording inserts or correcting short mistakes, the ability of the machine to loop or cycle back to a desired tape position can help you get the right feel, pitch, or other quality in fewer takes, while the important musical info to remember from the last try is still fresh in your mind.

Let me remind you, however, that multitrack is not the right medium for every tape. For gig demos, I seriously recommend that you consider going to a top local studio and recording direct to 2-track. Certainly, for small jazz or classical groups where players can execute all the parts at once, direct-to-2 is the solution. It can also be quite productive and enlightening for a hard rock group. First, it puts the musical pressure back on the artist, forcing you to rehearse thoroughly and decide what elements are most important to the effect of your tape. And since 2-track rates are lower at top studios, for the same money you might spend at an inexpensive multitrack facility, you will be able to work at a great studio and learn from a top engineer, both of which will prepare you for the time when a master tape is at hand and nothing but the best will do.

TWO-TRACK RECORDERS AND DIGITAL MIXDOWN

Let me be quite frank. Half-inch 2-track recorders running at 30 ips, as well as DAT and 1/2″ and 3/4″ video-based PCM digital 2-track formats, do give you astounding quality on your mixes. It is also flattering to know you are working in the same formats

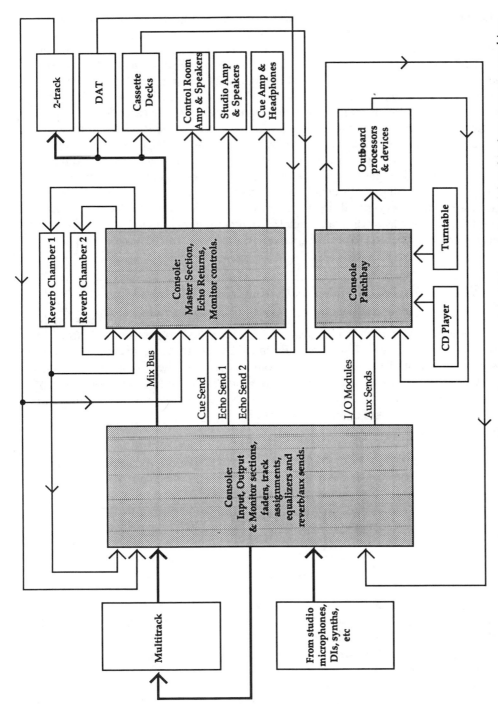

Figure 4.2.   Typical signal flow in a control room. The gray boxes are sections of the console, and the white boxes are tape machines and various outboard gear. The heavier line shows the basic path from incoming signal to mixdown.

as the hitmakers you respect. But do you really need the quality? Only if your tape is headed straight for digital release. If not, think twice about spending the extra money. First of all, you will have no use for the 1/2″ or digital master outside the studio. Moreover, 15 and 30 ips quarter inch are still the standard at many LP mastering studios, and cassette duplicators invariably request 7.5 ips or 15 ips 1/4″ master tapes.

My recommendation is to mix to 15 ips 1/4″ for *all* demos. Noise reduction is superfluous, since 1/4″ is so much quieter than cassette in any case. For masters of records for local release, mix to 30 ips 1/4″ if you insist. If you think there might be a compact disc release, make a simultaneous DAT or 3/4″ U-MATIC. After making the PCM digital master of all your mixes, put it on the shelf until it is worth spending the money to edit and sequence the CD. Although 1/2″ VHS and BETA digital sounds great on playback, all 1/2″ systems have substantial dropouts and errors. Thus, 1/2″ videocassette masters do not always transfer to a good 3/4″ premaster for CD pressing. Some CD mastering labs will not accept 1/2″ digital masters but DAT is now accepted everywhere. (See chapter 5 for an explanation of how digital systems work.)

STUDIO AND CONTROL ROOM ACOUSTICS

While there are some elements of room acoustics on which most listeners agree, there are as many opinions of what makes for good studio and control room acoustics as there are clients. Thus, despite who designed the acoustics in a particular studio, it is your judgment of the sound of the room that counts. The bottom line is this: if the studio does not make your instruments sound good and provide the comforts you need, and if you do not like the way some of your favorite records sound when played in the control room, go to another studio. No apology is necessary; your taste is the law.

There are several distinct schools of studio and control room design. Until the late 1970s the ideal studio was a "dead" space, one large enough and oddly shaped to prevent room resonances from affecting the musical sounds produced in it, and with enough sound-absorbent materials in the walls and ceilings to kill any reverberation that might reach the mics. In theory, such a space will ensure that the mics hear only the direct sound from the instruments and voices, without any coloration. Moreover, such a space affords the best possible separation between individual mics and, hence, the best control of sounds in the control room. Reverb, from plate, spring, or chamber, can be added during the mix. The inherent reverb time of the studio itself was kept to under 1/4 second for all midrange and high frequencies.

While this approach works well on paper, and does give the mix engineer lots of flexibility with application of ambiences, dead rooms make real instruments sound terrible! Any musician knows that. Ordinary rooms, be they basements or clubs, give music a helping hand. Their reverb and echoes gloss over small errors in pitch and timing and meld separate instruments and vocals into a unified performance. In addition, because the walls return some of the sound that strikes them, musicians do not have to push so hard to put out comfortable volumes. To get an idea of what the industry considers live and dead, and what reverb times complements different kinds of music well, refer to the charts below. Remember too that a room can generate

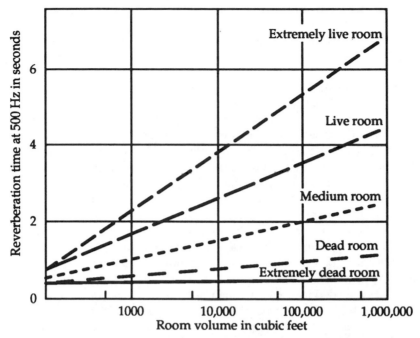

Figure 4.3A.   Graph of reverb time (T-60) versus volume for so-called live, medium, and dead rooms or halls. A room whose volume is 1,000 cubic feet might be 10′ × 12′, with an 8′ ceiling height. A room of 100,000 cubic feet might be 60′ × 80′, with a 21′ ceiling height, i.e., a 400-seat auditorium.

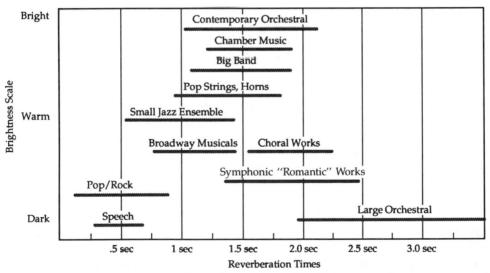

Figure 4.3B.   Good reverb times for studios or rooms in which to record various genres of music. The reverb in "bright" rooms is most noticeable between 1 and 2 kHz, giving a metallic quality. A "warm" room has most reverb in the 500 Hz range, smoothly blending the sounds of instruments like cellos and violas, woodwinds and lower brass. A "dark" room has most reverb at or below 300 Hz, giving more weight to low notes and allowing higher pitched sounds like vocals to retain clarity and intelligibility.

47

more reverb at some frequencies, less at others. Thus the timbre of reverb can be quite different even in two rooms whose overall reverb time and "liveness" are identical.

In the late 1970s the trend started to reverse. Studio designers began using so-called *live-end/dead-end acoustics* for both rooms. Half the studio is built live, with uncovered parquet floors and hard wall and ceiling surfaces. Movable baffles can be set up to darken or deaden this end, but for horns and strings or an open drum set, bright reflections give a snap that is impossible to add via artificial reverbs or even real chambers. The other end of the studio is left dead to facilitate separation or for instruments whose final effect or ambience in the mix is yet to be decided.

In the control room, the dead end encompasses the front half, surrounding the window and monitor speakers. The lack of reflections here gives the engineer exact information about stereo *imaging* (the L/R positioning of various sounds in the mix), the level of artificial reverb and effects, and the highest possible detail in the sound of each instrument or voice. The live end, wrapping behind the engineer and client, simulates the way the music will sound in a real room but not so much as to interfere with the clarity needed for precise equalization and effects adjustment.

Live end/dead end construction generally gives better acoustic results in low-budget studios than in their corresponding control rooms because many such control rooms are small enough that the equipment itself (such as consoles, recorders, and racks) destroys much of the acoustical effect being sought. The presence of a large glass surface in the dead end can undo the imaging that the surrounding absorptive material aims to provide. Then again, the tendency to put bulky, soft furniture to the rear of the console—in the live end—removes some of the warmth that the hard surfaces create.

The fact that this scheme has become a standard would be no problem if these rooms were designed by professional acousticians or by Chips Davis himself, who originated the idea and owns the LEDE trademark. However, in the hands of an amateur, LEDE can lead to an acoustic disaster. If a studio advertises a LEDE control room, find out who designed it. If you are doing a master tape and have any doubts about the room's sound, I would not hesitate to call the designer, both to make sure he really did design it and to ask for tips that might give you a better handle on how to record or mix there. If anyone knows the room's acoustic triumphs and tragedies, certainly its designer will.

Concerning the control room, this research and analysis is irrelevant if you really do not like the sound you hear. My recommendation is to bring in two well-recorded albums by artists in your musical field and ask the engineer to play you one of the studio's best tapes of the same genre. Play these at medium level, not full tilt, and listen carefully to the sound of the major instruments in each. If you do not like what you hear, you will have problems recording at this studio. Even if the engineer knows the room well enough to get good sound to tape, your own instinct during every playback will be to change the sounds, and dissatisfaction with the control room sounds will show up as uneasiness in your performances.

More recently, realizing that it is easier to tone down a bright room with baffles than to brighten up a dead one, studios are being built with lots of exposed wood on all surfaces, giving open reverb times of up to 1.5 seconds. Such rooms are great for a big, ambient rock or heavy metal drum sound. Because the room gives so much of the music back, performers love playing in these rooms. However, they offer relatively little separation among mics. And if the basic sound of the room is not complementary to the specific sound quality required in your project, it's difficult to neutralize the room's contribution. Before you get too excited about what fun it is to play in a live studio, think of whether its particular type of life suits the mood, feel, or drama of the music you'll be recording there.

Most studios have several moveable baffles that can be used to partially or totally enclose one instrument, player, or amplifier. These usually consist of four to six inches of sound-absorbent insulation mounted inside a wooden frame ranging from

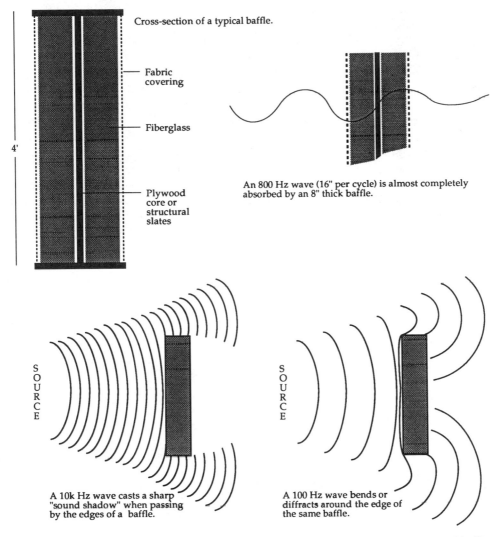

Cross-section of a typical baffle.

Fabric covering

Fiberglass

Plywood core or structural slates

4'

An 800 Hz wave (16" per cycle) is almost completely absorbed by an 8" thick baffle.

SOURCE

A 10k Hz wave casts a sharp "sound shadow" when passing by the edges of a baffle.

SOURCE

A 100 Hz wave bends or diffracts around the edge of the same baffle.

Figure 4.4.   Sound absorption by baffles and diffraction of sound around the edges of baffles

$3' \times 4'$ in size up to wall sections perhaps $6' \times 8'$ high. Strictly speaking, however, a baffle is anything used to achieve isolation, even a piece of heavy felt cloth attached to one side of a drum mic to reduce leakage from a nearby cymbal.

Baffles are the best tool for adjusting studio reverb in the mid and high frequencies. However, there is no way to prevent low frequencies from reverberating except through proper room design and in-the-wall absorbers. Here are two examples, (1) Since sound travels at about $1,100'$ per second, the wavelength of a 1.5 kHz tone is about 9 inches ($1,100$ ft./sec. $= 1,500$ Hz $\times .73'$). A baffle half this thick can contain a half wavelength at this frequency, effectively absorbing the entire sound. In contrast, the wavelength of a 100 Hz tone is about $5.5'$, much greater than the thickest baffle. No single movable absorber can contain half the wave, so it passes through pretty much unscathed. (2) Lows bend or diffract around corners, while highs do not. Where a baffle placed in front of half a tweeter's sound field will produce a so-called shadow, substitute a woofer and its wavefronts will fold right around the baffle and continue unimpeded.

If a studio has a long reverb time in the lows, low frequencies from your drummer's kit (unless the drummer is in a well-isolated booth), the grand piano, or an amplified bass will leak into every mic in the room and make the resulting tracks somewhat muddy and unmanageable in the mix. To test low-end reverb in the studio, have the engineer send a sequence of short low-frequency tones (or play a recorded kick drum) to the studio monitors at high volume. You will be able to hear and time the reverb pretty accurately. Walk around as you do this to see if it varies from one side or location to another. If it collects in certain spots, no acoustic instruments should be placed there, since their soundboards will act like resonators for the ambient lows. If you are playing any type of music where a drummer has to be in the open studio, a low-end reverb time of one second or more is a real problem.

5

REVERBERATION AND DIGITAL RECORDING

THE studio and control room acoustics, mic collection, console, and tape recorders act as a single system. The choice of board and the way it is wired into both rooms are decisions made before most studios are built. Most often, the installation crew spends the vast majority of its time making sure that the mics, console, and recorders function smoothly together, without ground loops and other systemic problems. Indeed, console and recorder manufacturers are quite careful to make sure their products are compatible. Imagine the drag of having to take back a costly and bulky piece of gear that doesn't interface well with others. Once this system is up and debugged, the installer's job is largely done.

However, processing equipment becomes obsolete faster than fashion trends. Since many outboard devices cost well under $1,000, studio owners buy and junk them at will. Little attention is paid to how well any specific unit will interface with the studio's guts—the console and recorders. Thus, the different clocking frequencies of various digital devices can cause audible beating, or interference with each other. Similarly, non-standard input and output levels of certain compressors and equalizers may lead to excessive noise or distortion when they are patched into a board set for standard professional levels. Much incompatibility derives from the growing in-studio use of signal processors designed for interchangeable stage and studio use. These units may be ideal for neither function, and while minor problems will be drowned out in live performance, not so on master tapes.

Beware when studio shopping that what the studio has in the racks is only half the story. The other half—how it works with the console/recorder system—is something you may not find out until it's too late.

51

ARTIFICIAL REVERBERATION SYSTEMS

There are basically three types of artificial reverb systems used in professional studios today: mechanical, digital, and real acoustic chambers. Under mechanical I include both plate and spring systems, diagrammed below. The principle behind these is quite simple. A *transducer* (any device that converts one form of energy into another, here basically a speaker) attached to the springs or *plate* (a large piece of sheet metal) introduces sound waves derived from the reverb mix sent by the console. The plate or springs shake as those waves bounce around internally. Another transducer, located at or near the opposite end, senses the vibrations and converts the reverb to an electrical signal that is sent to the console's reverb return.

Most good mechanical reverbs allow the engineer to adjust the effective reverb time from perhaps 0.5 second to 6 seconds. As the time is reduced from max, one or more dampers are brought into contact with the springs or plate, which of course stops them from vibrating as they would if undamped.

Needless to say, the quality of mechanical units depends on their materials and design. Top of the line is EMT's Model 240 gold foil unit. Because the foil plate in this case is so thin, it responds beautifully to high frequencies, like the diaphragm of a condenser mic. The heavier the spring or plate, the more high frequencies must be boosted before entering and upon leaving the unit. The more boost the more noise. Thus, for obvious reasons, the foil unit is quietest of all. At about $10,000, the Model 240 is by far the most expensive mechanical reverb around.

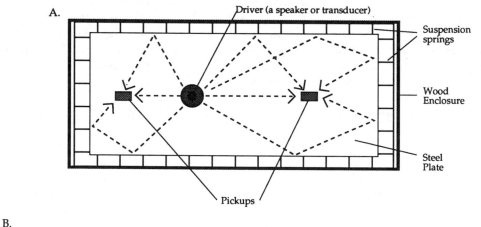

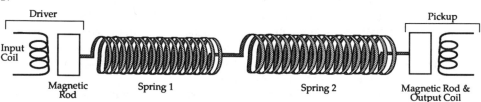

Figure 5.1.   A. Cross section of a plate reverb system. B. Cross section of a spring reverb system

In spring reverbs, AKG units are generally ranked among the finest. However, because sound can travel back and forth only in one dimension on each spring, springs tend to produce a discreet series of apparent reflections when used on very transient signals like drums. Damping can help, but for the smoothest continuous decay, plates beat springs by a mile. Again, among traditional large plates (up to 4 × 8 feet), EMTs are top-ranked. Echoplate and other brands also yield fine results.

Bear in mind that plates and springs can have two output transducers, each picking up waves from separate points in the system. These two outputs simulate stereo reverb, as in real rooms or halls. However, just as most live instruments are essentially single-point, mono sources whose reverb spreads throughout a room or hall, most spring and plate systems combine the stereo inputs from the reverb send into one mono channel. Thus, a mono-in/stereo-out reverb cannot return the reverb of any single sound to just the left or right channel of the mix. Two complete reverb systems are usually required for full stereo reverb, each fed by one channel of the reverb send. If your music requires discreet left and right reverb return, ask the engineer if the studio's plate or springs will provide this.

The *acoustic chamber* is even easier to understand. A small, highly reverberant space (for example, a tile bathroom or basement storage room) is equipped with a speaker system and two mics. The speaker plays whatever the engineer feeds to one of the reverb sends. This sound simply reverberates in the live room, enters the nearby mics, and treks back upstairs to the console, where the mic signals become reverb returns. Though it takes time, the chamber's inherent sound can be varied by moving its speaker and mics, altering its wall surfaces, or by equalization of the signals sent to the speaker and coming back via the mics. Though chambers have only one reverb program, they provide the only true reverb of all artificial systems. Even the finest digital units cannot mimic a chamber's three-dimensional feel or duplicate the physical impact a live chamber can add to snare drum and other power sounds.

Digital Reverb systems have much more flexibility than springs, plates, and chambers, but many of them have problems with transient signals like drums. The root of this problem is inherent in the medium. If you strike a drum in a live room, there will be a series of discrete *early reflections* from the first bounce off the ceiling, floor, and walls. These reflected waves will in turn bound off other surfaces, and so on. Each reflection occurs at a definite time interval from the original drum beat, and the collected reflections slowly diminish in volume. In a real room or any reverb system, the nominal *reverb time,* called *T-60,* is the number of seconds from any loud transient to the moment its reverb level is 60 dB below the original sound's level.

A digital reverb has a program in it for each type of room or hall and uses a series of digital delays to simulate the measured time intervals, volumes, and frequency contents of the entire series of reflections that happen in the real room. When the drum beat is input, the delays store it and release copies at the prescribed times and volumes, and with the corresponding frequency contents. This scheme sounds fine, but something is missing.

Notice that in a real room the sound of the drum beat strikes each wall over its entire length, not just at the center. The reflection from the center arrives back at the drum soonest, and the other reflections do not come back directly at all but bounce off other walls. Each possible combination of bounces has a corresponding path

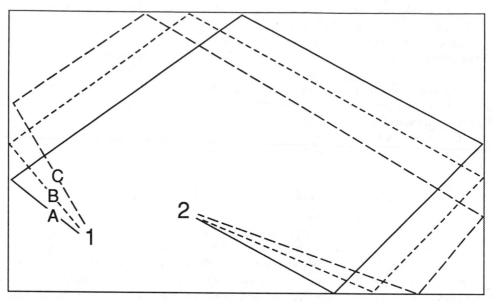

Figure 5.2.   Three adjacent paths by which a sound emanating from point one might reach point two after four reflections. Path A is the longest; path C the shortest. There are an infinite number of other path lengths available via walls, floor, and ceiling, giving rise to a continuous series of reflection times. Together, these create real acoustic reverb.

length and takes a corresponding time to reach the drummer again. The total number of paths and times at which these waves return is thus infinite. Real room reverb is thus not completely definable by any limited series of timed reflections. Every room calculates and outputs an infinite number of reflections, while the digital room, operating only within the dimensions of its computer-defined mathematical matrix, creates a limited number of reflections.

So much for the limitations—now for the advantages of digital systems. What the unit does with the sound to achieve each program is defined by a series of equations. By altering the equations we can instruct the unit to imitate any type of reverberation—from rooms and halls of any size and construction to plate and/or spring reverbs by any specific manufacturer. We can even define nonexistent spaces in which the reverb gets louder after the initial note, fades out and then in again, warbles, or changes pitch.

The graph of reverb volume with respect to the time from the original sound is called the *reverb envelope,* and that is what each program generates. The reverb volume at any moment is the summation of sound reaching the listener via all possible paths at that instant. For a real room, this can easily be measured and graphed. For any fictitious space, we simply invent the envelope and program the digital reverb with equations that will result in that envelope for any sound that is input.

At this writing the top of the digital reverb line are Lexicon's 224 XL and 480, for which Lexicon periodically supplies new software programs and updates. The 224 control panel allows the operator to select from several variations of each basic pro-

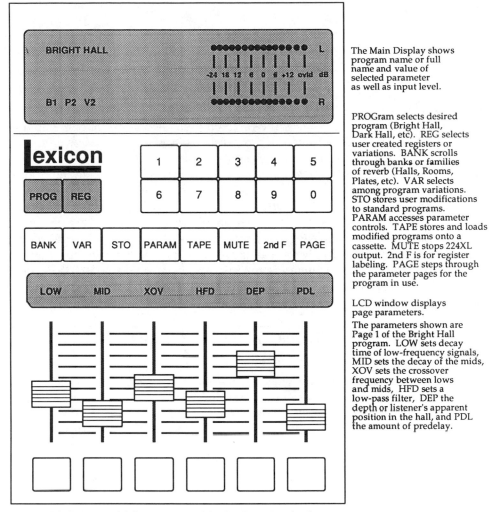

The Main Display shows program name or full name and value of selected parameter as well as input level.

PROGram selects desired program (Bright Hall, Dark Hall, etc). REG selects user created registers or variations. BANK scrolls through banks or families of reverb (Halls, Rooms, Plates, etc). VAR selects among program variations. STO stores user modifications to standard programs. PARAM accesses parameter controls. TAPE stores and loads modified programs onto a cassette. MUTE stops 224XL output. 2nd F is for register labeling. PAGE steps through the parameter pages for the program in use.

LCD window displays page parameters.

The parameters shown are Page 1 of the Bright Hall program. LOW sets decay time of low-frequency signals, MID sets the decay of the mids, XOV sets the crossover frequency between lows and mids, HFD sets a low-pass filter, DEP the depth or listener's apparent position in the hall, and PDL the amount of predelay.

The buttons and faders activate and display the settings for the parameter named above each.

Figure 5.3A.   The Lexicon 224 XL remote control, displaying the reverb parameters that can be varied on four "pages" of a typical factory-supplied program, called "bright hall."

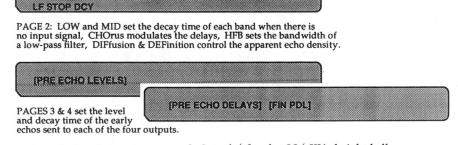

PAGE 2: LOW and MID set the decay time of each band when there is no input signal, CHOrus modulates the delays, HFB sets the bandwidth of a low-pass filter, DIFfusion & DEFinition control the apparent echo density.

PAGES 3 & 4 set the level and decay time of the early echos sent to each of the four outputs.

Figure 5.3B.   Parameter pages 2, 3, and 4 for the 224 XL's bright hall program

gram for standard sources, such as halls, rooms, chambers, plates. Once a program is selected, there are between eight and twenty-five variables that can be altered by the engineer. These include the overall reverb time, and within this the separate reverb times of high and low frequencies, what frequency divides the high/low bandwidths, *predelay* (the time between an input sound and the onset of its reverb), and the density of reflections per unit of time (controlled by parameters called depth, chorus, diffusion, definition, et al.). The program even allows control of the number and strength of very early reflections that simulate the way sound bounces around on stage, before it reaches the audience (called *preechoes*).

The price of good digital reverb is coming down in proportion to the price of computer memory chips. There are a number of acceptable stage versions (mono) for under $400. On the other hand, the complete 224 XL package costs over $12,000. It is beyond the scope of this book to review individual studio units. However, when a studio proudly boasts of having this or that digital reverb, ask to hear it demonstrated on the toughest family of sounds—drums, percussions, or any transient source. If you hear discrete, fluttering reflections rather than a smooth decay, make sure the studio also has a good-old plate or live chamber.

DIGITAL RECORDING AND ITS OFFSHOOTS

Conventional analog circuits deal with audio signals as a continuous graph of their voltage with respect to time. Thus, an *analog recorder* imprints on tape an uninterrupted and continuously changing magnetic field that corresponds to the changing voltage of its input signal. When the instantaneous voltage is positive, the record head creates a north field proportional to the voltage's strength; when the voltage is negative, it creates a south. Similarly, an amplifier generates a sustained, powerful output (measured in watts that double for each increase of 3dB in the input signal's voltage), then shapes its waveform to exactly match the waveform of the tiny audio signal that arrives at its input. The amplitude of its output is virtually a photographic enlargement of the input. At any instant in either of these devices, the important fact about the signal is the numerical value of the voltage itself.

Digital Recording Theory Without Much Math. Digital recording and signal processing are derived from one simple question: What if, instead of making continuous copies or enlargements of the input, we repeatedly measure or *sample* the instantaneous voltage of the input signal and write each numerical value down in sequence? Is it later possible to reconstruct a continuous wave from these numbers and hear the original audio signal? The answer is obviously yes. If logic tells you that the ear does not work this way—one instant at a time—you are right. But the process works anyway if we take samples at such close time intervals that the ear cannot hear the discontinuity. In the same way, if you make the points on a dotted line close enough, the eye will perceive them as a continuous line. This is why we see television images, half-tone photos, and color lithography as a single picture rather than a field of closely spaced dots.

The most difficult obstacle to implementing this principle is finding circuits that can take samples and later reconstruct them fast enough to fool the ear. First of all,

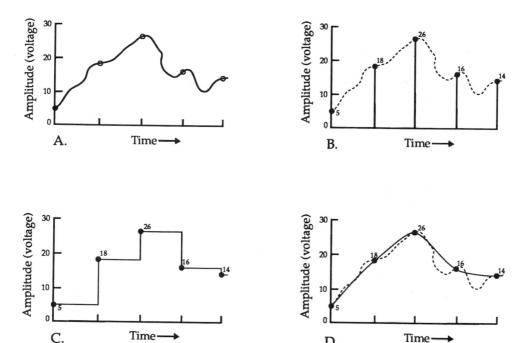

Figure 5.4. An analog sound wave (A) is sampled for digital recording (B), stored as binary digital information (C), then reconstructed for playback (D). Note that with only five samples taken during this small portion of the wave, much detail of the original (the dotted line in D) is lost in the final output signal (solid line in D).

our samples have to be timed closely enough to pick up the plus-to-minus voltage sweeps of the highest frequency we can hear, about 20,000 Hz. This requires that we catch plus-to-minus changes that happen in one-40,000th of a second (the time period of one-half wavelength at 20 kHz). It turns out that 40,000 samples per second is also more than enough to fool the ear into perceiving a reconstructed series of samples as a continuous sound waves. As many of you know, the sampling rate selected for encoding and reproduction of compact discs is 44.1 kHz, or 44,056 samples per second, to be exact. Professional recorders by various manufacturers use 44.1 kHz, 48 kHz, 50 kHz, and even 100 kHz. Higher sampling rates do give a closer approximation of the original analog waveform, though the companies whose equipment uses the lower rates claim that there is no audible difference to the listener.

Next we have to make sure each sample represents the numerical value of the signal voltage to a reasonable precision. In studio equipment, signal voltages vary from about −1 to +1 volt (without headroom). The question boils down to what precision each sample needs in order to produce an output that will fool the ear again.

For this answer we need to look not at the voltage itself but at what the voltage represents to the ear, namely an instantaneous sound level, measured in decibels. The smallest difference in level that the average ear can detect is about 1 dB. For each sample taken, the digital system can write down a corresponding voltage of limited accuracy. In essence the system rounds off to the closest available approximation for that voltage. In order to ensure the system will have well under 1 dB error at any instant from its input to its output, we need to have enough available approximations or steps (called *quantizing increments*) so that the maximum possible error corresponds to less than 1 dB. That way, if an error occurs, it will be too small to notice.

But where do errors come from? Suppose our digital system could only generate numbers accurate to the nearest 0.1 volt for each sample taken. What happens when the sampled waveform is exactly at 0.25 volts, right between the steps at 0.2 and 0.3 volt? No matter which way the system is programmed to round off, there will be a half-step or 0.05 volt error in this sample. At it turns out, to keep the total error (record and playback) under 1 dB, we have to hold the error level in each operation to under half a dB. This implies a step accuracy of 1/4 dB in the initial sampling stage, which also turns out to be sufficient for even the most discriminating ear.

What total range of input volumes must we be able to approximate? The best professional analog recorders, with noise reduction, are able to reproduce sounds over about a 85 dB range. Why bother with a new system unless it tops that? As it turns out, what we really need depends more on how well analog consumer products work than on their professional counterparts. Until recently, the best S/N ratio in a home system was about 60 dB for a fine turntable. From here, 100 dB would be heaven! In any case, to record sounds varying over a 100 dB range, with each sample accurate to 1/4 dB, we need to assign every voltage sample to one of 400 steps. At the instant when the input signal is completely silent (0.0 volt), step 1 will be noted and recorded; when the signal is 100 dB higher (1 volt in our example), the system writes step 400.

Computers are the only devices capable of taking samples fast enough and writing down the step number that corresponds to each one. But since computers deal only in binary code, expressing all numbers with respect to base 2 instead of decimals, we need to convert all our samples into binary. How many binary digits (called *bits*) does it take to represent the decimal number 400? Just as each of the three places in 400 stands for one power of 10, each place in a binary number stands for one power of 2.

$$400 = 2 \times 2 \times 100, \text{ or } 2 \times 2 \times 2 \times 2 \times 2 \times 2 \times 2 \times 2 \times 1.57$$

This equals a little under 2 raised to the 9th power (written 2^9). Thus we need a binary number of at least 9 digits. This makes sense because $2^9 = 512$, which is more than enough whole numbers to specify any of our 400 steps.

Now we have a complete picture of how to make a digital recording system meet our specifications. It must take more than 40,000 samples per second for each audio channel to be recorded and generate for each sample a binary number of at least nine digits representing the instantaneous voltage of the audio signal. If the medium on which these numbers are written assured complete accuracy of the recording and playback of this data, it would be just that simple. But the only medium available at the beginning of digital was good old recording tape, and the only inexpensive machine capable of handling this volume of data is still the VCR.

Like audiotape, videotape has *dropout*—moments on tape where the oxide is uneven, or where dust interferes with head contact—so there are a lot of instants at

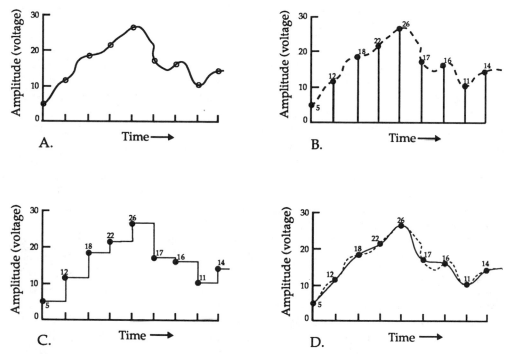

Figure 5.5. If more samples are taken during the same portion of the original wave, the final output signal is more faithful to the original.

which the audio samples might not be accurately written on or read from the tape itself. Suppose the machine tries to make sense of a sample with dropout: 1 0 1 * * * * 0 1. It will not know what voltage to make of it, so this sample should be ignored. How does it know to ignore it? We can add one more digit at the end of each sample that says whether the number of 1s in each sample is odd or even—a O if it is even, a 1 if it is odd. That way, when the machine counts the number of 1s and finds that it does not match the last digit, or if the final digit is missing due to a dropout, the machine just repeats the last sample that worked (called *last valid data*).

This is the simplest of what are called *error detection and concealment* schemes; the case in point is called *parity checking*. It turns out that there is enough dropout on tape to require that we come up with several other methods of double-, triple-, and quadruple-checking the data before it is reproduced as sound. For each such scheme, we have to add more digits to our samples.

We can also add digits to each sample to accomplish a number of other functions. If we want to encode the time at which each sample was taken (with respect to some starting point), we can write it in extra digits. If we are recording stereo, one extra digit will indicate whether each sample corresponds to the left or right audio channel, and so on. Luckily, most current computers are based on chips that speak to each other in words that are 16 bits long, which is more than enough to satisfy all our demands.

DIGITAL EFFECTS DEVICES AND TOYS

So far we have assumed that our goal is to construct the samples in the same order and at the same spacing as they appeared in the original input signal, thereby reproducing it exactly. However, we could play with the samples in all kinds of ways, and that is exactly what happens inside delays, flangers, harmonizers, and a host of other audio Cuisinarts that have hit the market in recent years.

The range of digital circuits on the market for various studio applications is staggering. Except with the very simplest—the delays themselves—the only user rule is *what sounds good is good.* Since all of these devices produce sounds not heard in nature, use them without blinking if they suit your music; including any distortion or technical flaw that complements the input sound or its emotional intent. What fuzz tones and Wah-wah pedals did for rock guitarists in the 1960s and 1970s, the digital processor can now do for any musician.

The underlying principle for many of these devices is quite simple. Instead of having the delayed signal return the same interval after each input signal, what happens if we devise a way of changing the delay time while the device is operating? If we shorten the delay time, the electronic "wall" off which the sound reflects is moving toward the listener like a train. Just as a train's whistle has a higher pitch when it is moving toward you than when at rest, the delayed sound will increase in pitch while the delay time is decreasing. Conversely, when the delay time is increasing, the wall moves away like the train gone by, and the musical pitch goes down. (The underlying acoustical phenomenon is called the *Doppler effect.*) By repeating the variation in delay times cyclically, we introduce an apparent vibrato to the input signal, as the pitch of the output wavers around its nominal frequency.

By controlling the variation of delay time and the envelope of the delayed sound that follows each input signal, we can come up with endless effects. As in digital reverbs, the delay-time variations are internally defined by equations. Some units even supply graphs of the envelope and time variations. Since the controls of most delays are labeled numerically, it is handy to know a bit of math when you want a certain effect, but the bottom line is discerning when this effect sounds good.

The *harmonizer* or *pitch transposer* continuously and repeatedly cycles through a fixed range of delay times but always in one direction—increasing or decreasing. When it reaches the end of each cycle, it jumps back to the other end of its range and seamlessly connects each cycle with the next. The result is that its wall seems to move continuously toward the listener (when the delay time decreases continuously) or away from the listener (when the delay time increases) at a selectable constant speed. An input signal thus comes out at a musical pitch above or below the original, respectively, exactly like the approaching or receding train whistle.

By setting the direction and speed of the wall, the operator can make the musical pitch of the processed signal harmonize with the original; hence the device's name. Adding a touch of an octave above a male voice can lighten it, while adding the octave below a trumpet line will create the ghostly illusion of added trombones. The word *harmonizer,* used loosely for any such device, is actually a trademark of the Eventide Corporation.

Flangers allow the engineer to specify the period in which the delay will cycle

A. A 100 Hz wave,

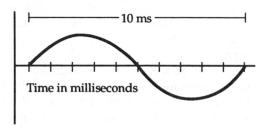

with 1 ms of delay added for each ms of elapsed time,

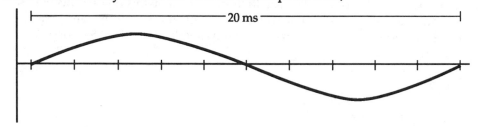

the same waveform now spans 20 ms of time, and is output as 50 Hz (cycles per second).

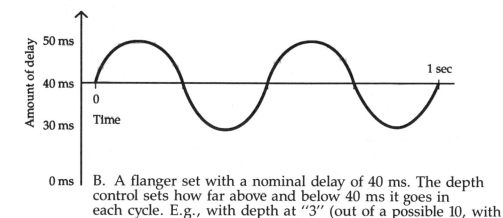

B. A flanger set with a nominal delay of 40 ms. The depth control sets how far above and below 40 ms it goes in each cycle. E.g., with depth at "3" (out of a possible 10, with no specific units implied), the delay varies from 30-50 ms.

Figure 5.6.   Graphs of delay time versus time. A. Harmonizer set for an octave pitch drop. B. Flanger with rate set at 2 cycles per second

up and down once through a specified range (called *rate*), the amount of change in the delay time within each cycle (called *depth*), or degree of pitch bending. This is analogous to the speed of an approaching and receding wall and depends on whether each cycle will be made smoothly (via a sine wave) or in jumps (via a square wave or some other discontinuous function). Most units also permit the operator to send a selectable percentage of the output signal back to the input (called *feedback* or *regeneration*) and sometimes to create delay *subroutines* within each cycle, superimposing smaller delay cycles over the main one. The resulting effects vary from simple vibrato, which can be used to texturize constant tones like dull synth patches, to hilarious warblings of prehistoric or extraterrestrial origin.

At the other end of the effects spectrum are processors like Yamaha's SPX 90 family, which offer over 70 preset programs—from simple reverbs, delays, and flanging to special effects that Disney never dreamed of. These are instantly accessible by pushbuttons, and the operator can switch among them quickly with no clicks, pops, or other audio problems. Moreover, changes between one patch and another can be cued by external MIDI or SMPTE data. In three years' time this unit has become standard studio and stage equipment with all kinds of musical groups and spawned a whole generation of magic boxes manufactured by Roland (the DEP-5), Korg, Yamaha, and so on.

6

OUTBOARD SIGNAL-PROCESSING DEVICES—ANALOG AND DIGITAL

MOST outboard processors allow the engineer to change one of two parameters in the sound source: its dynamic range or its frequency content. Changing a sound's dynamic range is one way of altering its envelope, and this is what compressors, limiters, and noise gates do. The simplest of these devices work only in proportion to the level of the sound signal at any instant. However, we can also make them operate in response to other criteria, such as the presence or absence of certain frequency ranges in the signal, the presence or absence of a completely separate sound signal, or cues from an outside clock. Any user-supplied information or parameter that tells the device when and how much to work is called a *key,* and it is sent into the device's *keying input.*

In the first case, the key might be derived from the output of an equalizer fed by the same source signal. Without that equalizer, the compressor responds to the absolute voltage or level of the input signal, regardless of its frequency content. However, if we reduce low frequencies going through the equalizer and into the keying input, the compressor will, in effect, not hear as many lows in the program material and will only compress when highs are present. If we then boost the highs in this equalizer by 10 dB, the compressor will respond as if the highs in the original signal were boosted by 10 dB: it will compress high frequencies 10 dB lower in level than those that would previously have been affected.

The keying input of any processing device thus tells the device what to see or react to and how much of it is there, which can have little relation to the signal that is then processed. If it responds to cues from an outside clock, we might send the output of an electronic metronome into the keying input. Regardless of what is happening in the program signal, every time the metronome ticks, the compressor compresses. With all this in mind, let us look at what various dynamic range devices actually do.

COMPRESSORS

As the name suggests, a *compressor* reduces the dynamic range of an incoming signal. This means that the range of amplitudes in the output waveform is less than in the input waveform. The absolute level of that output depends on how much the signal is amplified by the unit before *and* after compression occurs. Since compression is a basic recording tool, and because the action of good compressors is hard to detect, we'll spend extra time investigating them in detail. These illustrations demonstrate two of the basic reasons for using compression. In speech, the human voice is often entirely silent between words. Words that begin with a consonant, like *tease,* have a steep opening transient—the *t*—followed by an extended vowel sound during which the volume changes gradually. Notice, however that the final *s* sound in *tease* is low in volume. If there were some music playing behind the voice and a drummer chanced to tap his hi-hat just as the *s* occurred, the highs from the hi-hat could easily obscure the *s* and the listener would probably hear *tea.* Quite a difference!

We could try to increase the volume of the entire word until the final *s* could be heard, but the transient might overload and become distorted. By adjusting the input level to the compressor so that only the beginning of the word triggers compression, we can reduce only the level of the transient t, after which the level will return to normal, ensuring that the final *s* shines through. Similarly, the harder a drummer strikes a snare, the steeper the transient. In many recorders the snare is the loudest sound, and the cutting stylus that carves the record groove can only make each groove so wide, after which it overloads. Without compression, if the drummer hits certain beats much louder than the rest, the mastering engineer has two choices: let the loud ones overload, or turn down the entire volume on the disc until nothing distorts. The "hotter" or louder a disc is cut, the better it sounds to most listeners, so the answer is simple: the engineer compresses the entire tape to control the snare transients and increase overall level on the disc.

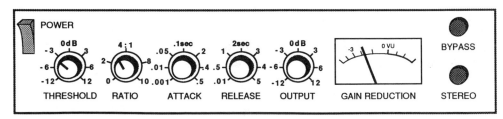

Figure 6.1. **A typical compressor control panel**

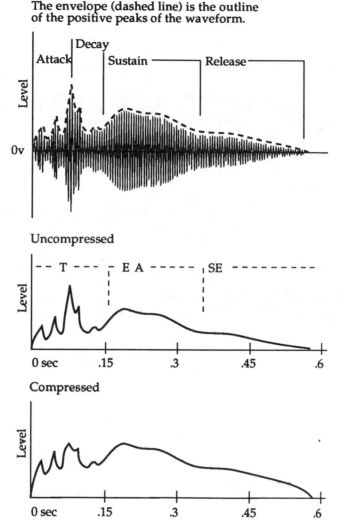

Figure 6.2. Sound envelopes of the word "tease," uncompressed and compressed as described. The attack is reduced in level; the sustain and release are boosted. With the peaks proportionately lowered, the level of the compressed "tease" has been boosted to match its previous, uncompressed peak level. Thus, overall level of compressed sounds can be recorded much higher on tape, or blended higher in a mix.

The other function illustrated here is to even out the level of an entire performance so that details, like the *s* in *please* or the trailing off of guitar notes, do not get lost. Every sound envelope is made of four sections: an *attack* (in percussive instruments called the *transient,* in which the signal rises from zero up to its first peak), *decay* (in which the initial peak level comes down to the continuous level), *sustain* (the continuous level of an extended note or word such as *ahhhh . . . ,* and *release*

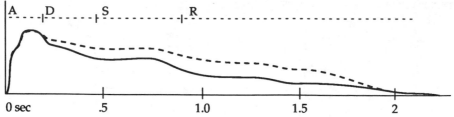

A piano note compressed to give more apparent sustain using a slow attack time (.2 sec) to retain its percussive character. Note that the release begins when the player lifts his finger from the key. The soundboard continues to resonate for another 1.5 seconds.

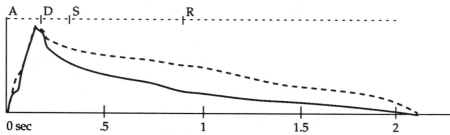

Two consecutive clarinet notes compressed using a quick attack and a quick release. The louder first note is reduced in level. The softer second note is essentially unchanged.

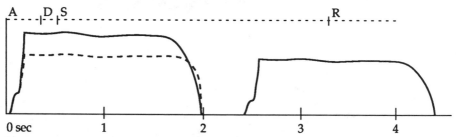

An acoustic guitar note compressed to increase the note's sustain. Note that the attack is unchanged, and again the body resonates long after the note is released.

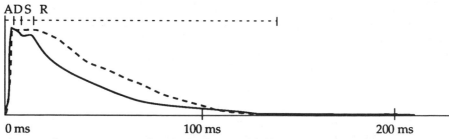

A snare drum compressed to make it sound fuller or more sustained, using a fast attack and a fairly quick release.

Figure 6.3. Sound envelopes of various musical instruments before compression (solid lines) and after compression (dashed lines). As in figure 6.2, the levels of compressed piano, acoustic guitar, and snare drum envelopes above have been raised so that the compressed peaks are as high as the previously uncompressed peaks.

66

(what happens as a guitar string is damped or when a clarinetist stops blowing and the note ends). The entire group is known as ADSR.

As you can see, the snare drum has the same four parts, ADSR, but the length of the entire envelope is very short—so short that the ear can easily think the sound is all transient. Because of the extreme level differences in the transients or attacks of various sounds, the speeds with which these transients decay to the sustained level of the sound, and the nature and importance of hearing the release of many sounds, we need to be able to control our compressor in some detailed ways.

First of all, we need to be able to select the signal level above which the unit will reduce the volume, called its *threshold*. Next, we need to control how much the unit reduces the signal's gain above this threshold. *Gain* is the ratio of the signal level at the output of an audio device to the signal level of its input, and can be expressed as a simple ratio or in decibels. Beneath the threshold, a compressor's output will increase *linearly*, meaning that each dB increase in input level will result in the same 1 dB increase in output level. If output level equals input, the resulting gain is 1. (In case you are wondering, negative gain does exist, but not in standard compressors. A gain of -5, for example, means that for every 1 dB increase at the input, the output goes down by 5 dB.)

If, for instance, we never want to allow a signal to increase above threshold, the compressor becomes a *limiter,* since it potentially has to apply an infinite amount of *gain reduction* to lower extremely loud input signals to threshold level. As you can imagine, however, a limiter can completely remove the dynamics a musician puts into his performance. Most of the time its is better to reduce dynamics proportionately, compressing the output level of an input signal above threshold by a designated factor or ratio.

For example, if a signal enters at $+9$ dB above threshold and we want that peak reduced to $+3$ dB, we can apply a compression ratio of 3:1. Such a ratio would reduce an input signal at $+3$ dB to $+1$ and a steep transient of $+15$ to a respectable $+5$, as long as the *attack time,* the time it takes the unit to apply its full gain reduction, is short enough to catch the transient before it sneaks through. Although a limiter's compression ratio is by definition infinite, most engineers regard as limiting any compression ratio over about 10:1. To accommodate different instruments, most studio compressors allow the user to vary the attack time from 1 millisecond (ms) or less to 20 ms or more, continuously or in steps.

The final parameter of compressor operation is *release time*. Once an input signal is again below the threshold, the compressor stops working, but not instantly. Instead, its overall gain glides back to its value prior to compression. If an instrument plays a soft note right after a loud one that had activated the compressor, the release time must be short, perhaps 0.1 second, so the soft note will be restored to its full level. On the other hand, if the release on each note is very long, or if there is unwanted noise between notes, compressor release time should be much longer. This will minimize our awareness of valve, key, or damper noises associated with each released note. Most studio compressors permit continuous adjustment of release time from 0.1 second to 5 seconds or more.

Moreover, instruments release according to different, envelope curves. Acoustic instruments generally have accelerating releases. When the string is muted or wind

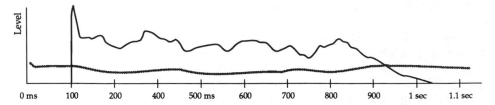

The envelope of a Stratocaster guitar chord (solid upper line) and the guitar amplifier's continuous noise level (lower grey line).

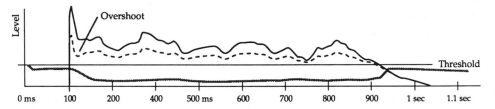

After 2:1 compression, the same chord (dotted line) and amp noise. Note in particular that the amp noise before and after the chord is proportionately higher than before compression. Pumping and breathing refer to the audible rise and fall of such noise. (In a vocal signal, the singer's breathing and mouth noises would be increased.) This problem usually results from too fast an attack and release time.

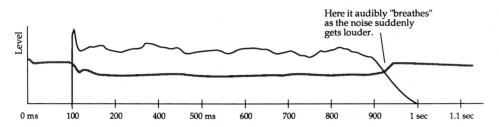

Raising the level of the compressed guitar back to it's pre-compression average, the pumping and breathing are exaggerated even more. The amp noise is also much louder between notes than before compression.

Figure 6.4.   Pumping and breathing problems resulting from incorrect compression

stopped, the vibration tapers off slowly at first, then drops rapidly, as shown in figure 6.5. Unmuted guitar notes, on the other hand, have decelerating releases. The string loses lots of energy quickly, then continues to ring ever softer for up to 10 seconds. When compressing an instrument, it would be ideal to find a compressor whose *release curve* sounds best with the instrument's. In reality, each studio compressor has a characteristic release curve—accelerating, linear, or decelerating. Although this specification is rarely printed in sales or operating manuals, it is an intergral part of the unit's sound and an important factor in choosing the right compressor for each instrument during recording and mixing sessions.

Compressors also have *attack curves* that are an equally important component of their sound. Although the attack applied to a steep transient like a drum can be

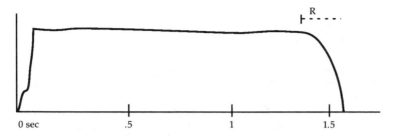

Clarinet note, showing an accelerating release curve.

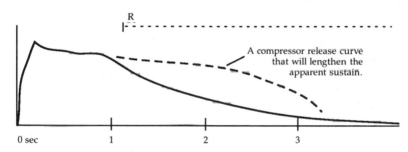

Harpsichord, showing a decelerating release.

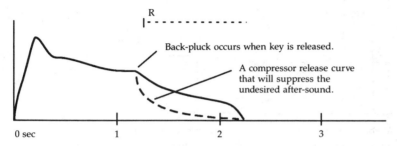

An electric bass note shows a decelerating curve.

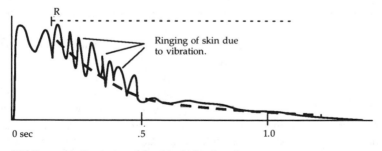

Mid Tom - note the ringing of the skin during the release.
Average level, shown as a dashed line, is a decelerating curve.

Figure 6.5.   Release curves of four instruments

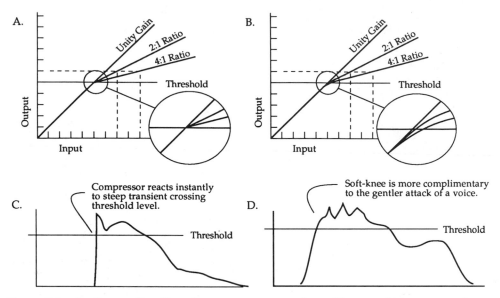

Figure 6.6. **A.** shows a "hard-knee" compressor curve that will respond instantaneously to the steep incoming transient of a kick drum, whose envelope is shown in C. For contrast, see the "soft-knee" compressor curve (**B**) that will more smoothly compress a sound such as a voice singing the word "reach" in D.

accelerating, linear, or decelerating (just like release), the two curves encountered most commonly are slightly more complex. They are called *hard knee* and *soft knee,* named the way their graphs look on paper. Again, a part of the reason a particular unit works well on bass or kick drum has to do with how its own attack curve matches or complements that of the instrument.

Beyond these "personality traits," most compressors have downright design flaws. Like people, compressors can overreact to a sudden stimulus. This *overshooot,* perhaps upon receiving our +15 dB sample transient, might cause the unit to reduce gain by more than the 10 dB desired in the example above, which in turn will obscure the decay and part of the sustain of the sound. As any mechanical flaw can sometimes make an artistic contribution, you may find particular cases where overshoot sounds great.

If a narrator is to be compressed and heard solo, for example with no music or other sound mixed behind his or her voice, a short release time will allow every breath between words to come through loud and clear. If the narrator pauses without a breath, the compressor's release will momentarily bring up room tone and any system noise. This phenomenon, called *breathing,* is very annoying to the listener. Thus, for a solo narrator, a longer release is probably better. However, any music in the background while he or she speaks will mask the compressor's and narrator's own breathing and may further necessitate higher level on the ending of each word. Here a shorter release time might work better.

Pumping is another phenomenon associated with some compressors. If, for example, one instrument in a mix is louder than the others, its volume will be the factor that causes the compressor to function. When that instrument stops playing, even for a moment, the apparent level of the other instruments will increase dramatically. Thus, every time the dominant instrument starts and stops, it will squash and release the level of the others, audibly pumping the others down and up in level.

DE-ESSERS

The *control circuit* of a compressor, expander, or noise gate (reacting in response to the keying signal) tells the unit at what time and at what capacity to operate. Known electronically as a *side chain,* the control circuit performed the keying in the examples above. While the side chain responds to the signal level or anything we send to the keying input, the device's output—the sound we will finally hear—travels through a completely separate path, as illustrated in figure 6.7.

Boosting highs going to the keying input, as we did earlier, is actually called *de-essing.* Several manufacturers make de-essers, all of which are basically compressors with a high-frequency boost introduced to the key input or control circuitry. In essence this boost lowers the threshold for highs only, so the unit begins compressing highs when their level in the input signal is below the nominal user-selected threshold level. This technique is particularly helpful in recording close-miked vocalists who produce loud *sibilants* (*s* sounds) that might otherwise overload tape and cause distortion. Dense highs can cause tape overload at much lower levels than low frequencies, turning innocent-looking meter readings into a recorded disaster.

To control these, a de-esser shelf boosts the highs above 5 kHz going to the control circuit, sometimes by up to 15 dB. In this case a sibilant whose actual level is −15 dB seems to the unit to be at 0 dB, or nominal threshold. If the de-esser has a 5 : 1 ratio, a vocal sibilant input at −5 dB is now 10 dB above our −15 dB plateau. The unit compresses those 10 dB by 5 : 1, producing an output 8 dB above this plateau. The resulting instantaneous output is thus at −13 dB.

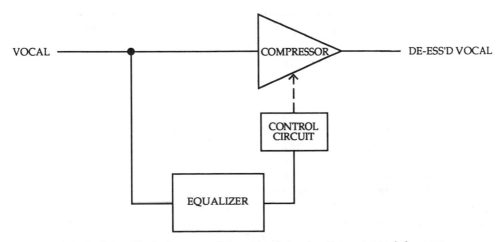

Figure 6.7.   Block diagram of the side chain circuit in a typical de-esser

Because vocal sibilants are very brief—as little as 20 milliseconds in duration—the de-esser has very fast attack and release and may have a variable ratio. Prudent de-essing maintains intelligibility on all lyrics (or narration) and permits vocal levels to be ridden much hotter in the mix before overload occurs. However, be aware that compressing or limiting without de-essing actually boosts the proportion of highs in a signal and causes distortion. Since the incoming signal level of vowels is higher than that of sibilants, the compressor reduces the gain on vowels, letting the sibilants pass at full level. To restore apparent *unity gain* (where output level of a device equals input level), the engineer boosts the output signal, with an increased proportion of high frequencies.

EXPANDERS AND NOISE GATES

Expanders and noise gates do just the opposite of compressors and limiters: they increase the dynamic range of incoming signals. Recording engineers need this capability when the original performance has few dynamics and needs more energy. When the engineers who recorded the original performance applied too much compression, or when they need to get rid of the system or tape noise between words, notes, or chords. These days, with noise a prime concern in high-quality pressings and CDs, most expansion is done for the latter reason.

The parameters we need to control in an expander are much the same as those we identified in compressors. Most expanders are designed so that the operator can select a threshold below which the unit will reduce the level of an incoming signal. Again, we need to select the attack time to fit the nature of any transients in the signal. Then we need to specify the expansion ratio that the unit will apply to sounds below threshold.

With a 0 dB threshold and a 1:5 ratio (the larger number is always on the right for expansion), an incoming signal at −1 dB would exit at −5 dB; one at −3 dB would leave at −15 dB and so on. However, we might also want the unit not to reduce any signal beyond a certain bottom-line level, for fear of losing it entirely. That level is called the *range* or *floor* by various makers. Finally, we need to specify how long the unit will take to stop expanding once the signal returns above threshold, called its *release time* or sometimes its *fade*. In some cases, we may want the gate to stay open for a user-preset time after each signal above threshold. To this end, some manufacturers include a hold control, with a time range selectable between 0.1 and 20 seconds. When the designated hold time has elapsed, the specified fade time takes effect, reclosing the gate.

Common musical uses of expansion are to add percussive quality (and more energy) to rhythm tracks like funk guitar parts, clavinets, or chordal synth backups. Or we might want to add dynamics to the notes of a synth solo played on an instrument without touch sensitivity. Noise gates and expanders can also be controlled through a keying input. We can instruct the unit to operate only in response to certain frequency ranges or to function in time with other musical or outside events. For instance, if we key the noise gate on a rhythm guitar with the snare drum track, every time the drummer hits the snare the gate will open and the guitar will be heard for a period defined by the hold and fade. Whenever the snare track is below threshold,

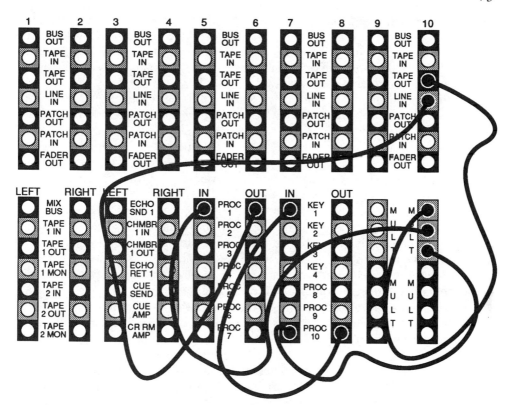

Figure 6.8. A typical console patchbay using TTL-type patchcords, showing the patch routing for the de-essing circuit in Figure 6.7: TAPE OUT of module 9 (lead vocal) goes to a MULTiple patch point, splitting the signal to be patched out to a compressor (PROCessor 1) and a parametric equalizer (PROCessor 10). The output of the equalizer is then patched to the KEY IN of the compressor, the output of the compressor returned to LINE IN of module 9.

(as, for example, between each snare hit), the guitar level is reduced to the designated floor.

The noise gate is designed primarily to help eliminate any type of noise between desired signals such as amp noise, breathing between words, tape noise, and noise from effects boxes. The threshold of the unit must be set low enough so that every desirable sound comes through. When the input signal falls below threshold, it will

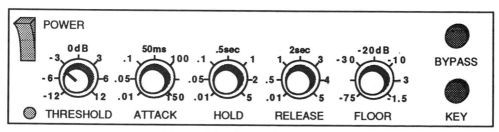

Figure 6.9. A generic noise gate

be reduced by a selected ratio or directly to a selected floor level. Gates can thus shorten the sustain and release sections of sounds like a kick drum envelope. The ungated drum may continue vibrating for nearly a second, although all we want is the initial transient and a short puff of lows thereafter. The solution is to adjust the threshold, floor, and fade to eliminate what follows.

Aside from getting rid of unwanted sounds, noise gates are useful for special effects such as gated reverb. For example, you might want to hear the snare reverb continue for a certain duration after a snare hit, then stop dead. First, you will need a separate reverb unit just for the snare. Then patch the noise gate in on the reverb return, set the threshold and hold time as desired, and you have it. Or you might use the hold and fade controls together to hear the reverb sustain for a certain time, then fade out gently over a second preset time interval.

Like compressors, expanders have a few inherent problems. They can overshoot, reducing the level more than the engineer or producer desires and sometimes opening on transients that do not quite reach threshold. Also, even the fastest circuit may not be able to open in time to allow the attack of a snare to be heard. Since the gate essentially switches off at each transient, it can give an audible click. This may not be noticeable in a snare sound, but it would definitely be audible on a kick drum. The lower the floor level between notes, the further the unit has to open, and thus the louder the click. It is therefore important to adjust the floor, hold, and fade to get as close to the desired sound as possible without generating unwanted gate clicks in the process.

You should also beware that different manufacturers use different terms for noise gate variables. What Ashly calls the floor, Kepex calls range; one brand's hold is another's sustain. Someday manufacturers may realize that such conflicting terminology can cause users to misuse their equipment and mistakenly accuse it of poor performance or design.

7

EQUALIZERS AND SPECIAL EFFECTS PROCESSORS

THERE are hundreds of different types of equalizers, and musicians, engineers, and producers are more outspoken about their favorite types, brands, and models than about any other signal-processing equipment. This is appropriate, because more than any other device, an equalizer changes the basic sound of any signal—the internal balance of various frequencies by which one instrument or voice is recognized and distinguished from others.

EQUALIZERS

Internally, every equalizer divides the incoming signal into two parts: those frequency ranges whose level will not be altered and those whose level will. Much of the characteristic sound of various equalizers derives from the way each unit affects frequencies where these two ranges meet. The simple fact is that every circuit that selectively alters the volume of frequencies within a signal also causes some *phase shift* or delay in those frequencies it does alter. Electronically, it takes a small increment of time to make the change, and thus the frequencies altered will be delayed, perhaps by only a few millionths of a second.

No listener would be able to hear this tiny delay, but the fact that one range is delayed and another is not can cause a perceptible change in the timbre of the resulting sound. Strictly speaking, such phase shifting is a type of distortion, but again—as with fuzz tones and flangers—some people make the effect a part of their music, while others will go to any length to avoid it.

75

The three quantities that we need to control in an equalizer are:

1. what *center frequencies* will be boosted or dipped
2. the width of the range of frequencies *(bandwidth)* that will be boosted or dipped
3. how many decibels of boost or dip we will apply.

It would be nice to have full control of each of these variables, but that is electronically more complex and more expensive than living with certain preset values for the center frequency or bandwidth.

The fully *parametric* equalizer does allow individual control of all three and may have up to six sets of controls to allow the engineer to separately equalize six different bands within the input signal. The bandwidth for each band or range of equalization is usually expressed in musical octaves and is often designated by the letter Q. If, for example, the unit is set to boost at 500 Hz with a bandwidth of 0.2 octave, it will produce a rise or dip in frequency response starting 0.1 octave below 500 Hz, with the highest rise at 500 Hz itself, and will continue to boost frequencies up to 0.1 octave above that center frequency.

One octave below 500 Hz is 250 Hz, and one octave above is 1,000 Hz, so that in this example the unit boosts the range between about 475 and 550 Hz. If we leave the bandwidth at 0.2 and raise the center frequency to 10,000 Hz (10 kHz), the boosted range will extend from about 9,500 to 11,000 Hz, or 0.1 octave below and above 10 kHz.

Parametric equalizers are great for finding and dipping specific resonances or problem frequencies in a signal (a technique called *destructive equalization*). They can also locate the frequency at which the pluck of a bass note happens, perhaps to diminish the instrument's attack. In both these functions, the equalizer is vicariously used to affect the dynamic range of the signal by removing overaccentuated frequencies. In most of these situations, it is better to equalize before applying compression or noise gating. You may actually find that the equalization makes compression unnecessary. On the other hand, *constructive equalization,* used to rebalance the usable musical frequencies present in the signal, is normally applied after compression.

A type of very narrow-band equalizer designed mainly for destructive uses is called the *notch filter.* It is widely used to eliminate 60 Hz amplifier hums and buzzes; to get rid of camera noise in film-making; or to reduce the level of any unwanted narrow-band noise in the program signal, room, or location—rumble from air-conditioners or heating systems, the 14,750 Hz tone emitted by television sets, or even the clocking, sync, or carrier frequencies of some less expensive drum machines and synthesizers.

A *filter* is normally defined as an equalizer that can only dip certain frequency ranges. It is *passive* if there is no internal amplifying circuit to boost the output level back up to unity gain and *active* if such an amplifying stage is included. Most passive filters do not require a source of AC or DC power.

Many consoles have *semi-parametric* or so-called *"sweep" equalizers* and related hybrids. Some semi-parametrics allow continuous control of each center frequency but not of the corresponding bandwidth. Others have full parametric controls for one or two midrange bands, with preset frequencies for low- and high-frequency equalization. Before going further, we need to define *peak* and *shelf equalization.*

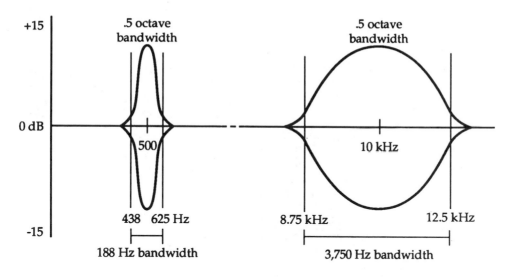

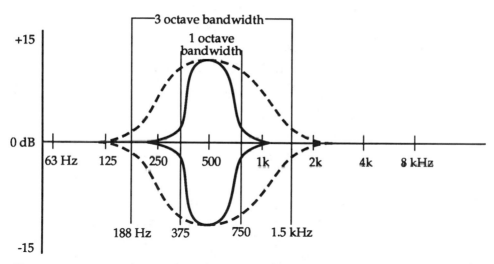

Figure 7.1. Boost and cut curves of a parametric equalizer, showing various bandwidths around a center frequency of 500 Hz and 10 kHz. Horizontal frequency scales in graphs can be misleading. If the scale is linear, with each length representing the same number of hertz, an 0.5 octave boost will look skinny in the bass and broader in the treble ranges, as in the upper drawing. The lower drawing uses a logarithmic frequency scale, where each *octave* is allocated the same distance on the horizontal axis. Here, 0.5 octave boost will be the same width at any center frequency.

As you can see, in figure 7.2 peaking equalization creates a smooth rise or dip around the center frequency. In contrast, suppose we want to boost or dip all frequencies above or below a certain point. We need to designate the frequency at which the equalizer achieves the desired boost (called the *turnover frequency*) and the height or depth (in dB) of the shelf to which it raises or lowers frequencies beyond this point. Conventional tone controls in stereo amplifiers are shelf equalizers, although

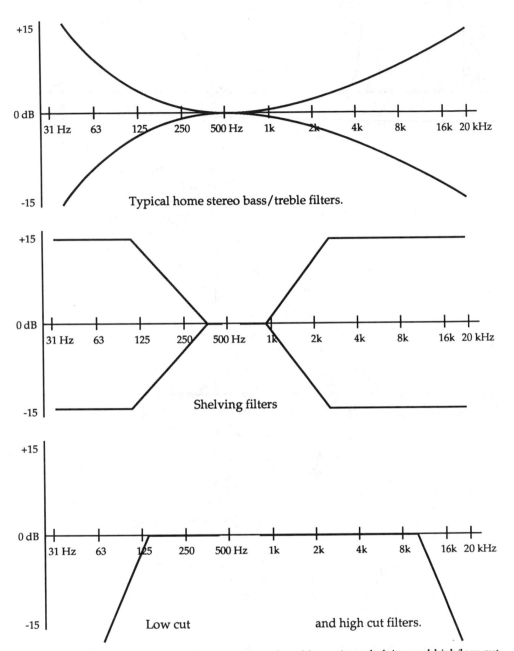

Figure 7.2. The frequency response curves produced by various shelving and high/low cut filters

in many cases the shelf is not flat: frequencies further from the turnover are boosted more than those adjacent to it.

The simplest type of in-board equalizers are two-, three-, or four-band types with fixed bandwidth settings and several selectable center frequencies for each band. These are often adequate for shaping the sound of instruments, but they are of little use in destructive applications. It might be better to run a problem signal through an outboard notch filter or parametric first, then through a noise gate and/or compressor, and finally through the in-board equalizer to finalize the desired sound. We will discuss this further in part three.

Graphic equalizers offer a picture of what the unit is doing to the frequency response of the input signal (ergo the name *graphic*). Each vertical slide-control affects the band around one center frequency. A single channel may offer from 5 to 30 or more bands, each separately and simultaneously adjustable. Most studio graphics have 10, 12, or 15 bands, and thus offer more flexibility for general sound shaping than a 3- or 4-band parametric. But since you cannot vary the center frequency or the

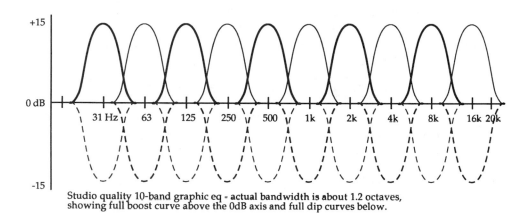

Studio quality 10-band graphic eq - actual bandwidth is about 1.2 octaves, showing full boost curve above the 0dB axis and full dip curves below.

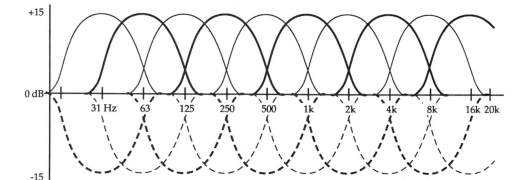

Home stereo quality 10-band graphic eq - actual average bandwidth is about 2.2 octaves.

Figure 7.3.   The boost and cut curves of a studio-quality 10-band graphic equalizer (approximately $500) and a home stereo 10-band (approximately $100). The studio unit permits much more precise boost or dip at each center frequency.

bandwidth of each band, graphics cannot be used to pinpoint resonances and other unwanted frequencies.

Let me dispel one bit of misinformation. The third-octave graphic, with 27 or more bands per channel, is *not* the preferred outboard equalizer for session work. There are two simple reasons for this. First, because there is so much circuitry associated with this many bands, it takes a very expensive unit to match the noise and distortion specs of simpler equalizers. These units were originally designed for equalization of control-room monitors, a function for which they are usually adjusted once and mounted in the back room with the monitor amplifiers. Second, the very number of controls on 27-banders makes use during a session inconveniently slow. There are just too many options, and it is easy to get carried away hunting for the "lost equalization" instead of pushing ahead with the mix.

Table 7.1 lists specific brands and models of outboard signal processors that are most often found at good demo and mastering studios. Audio quality, flexibility, durability, client "impressiveness," price, and many other factors influence the buying decisions of studio owners. No single equalizer or compressor can claim to be the finest in all of these decision-making categories. Yet the fact that the devices in table 7.1 are standards indicates that each has a combination of high marks from owners and clients alike. It also means that you are familiar with how they sound on many records.

AURAL EXCITERS AND SAMPLING DEVICES

There are a number of mystery special effects devices on the market. In many cases their manufacturers seal the entire circuit in plastic so that electronics wizards cannot copy the design. Others, not quite so protective, simply use proprietary, custom-designed chips and other components, effectively masking how the device works. Of these, the most widely used is the Aphex *Aural Exciter*. A signal fed into the exciter comes out brighter in the high frequencies, with a touch of apparent compression (very fast attack and release) in the highs. In addition, the unit seems to add a touch of one or two harmonics to signals, but again only to the very high frequencies in the input. The resulting output has an indefinable sizzle, a quality that separates it from unexcited sounds in a mix.

The Aphex first came into prominence in the mid-1970s, when it was used to enhance vocal tracks. After exciting, a vocal will draw the listener's ear, even if it is fairly low in the mix. Then someone discovered the Aphex for guitar and sax solos, and for a while it was not uncommon to find engineers running complete mixes through a pair of exciters. Like all effects, however, less is more—too much excitement is worse than none at all.

There are several types of *sampling and triggering devices* available to output sampled sounds on external command. All of these have the same basic features. The first circuit is a digital *sampler,* which is essentially an area of *RAM* (random access computer memory) in which an audio input signal called a *sample* can be stored as digital data. One might load a kick drum sample (from a live mic, before or after signal processing) into the device by hitting the start button and having the drummer

Table 7.1. Signal Processors Commonly Found in Current Studios

Reverbs	Equalizers
Lexicon PCM 60	Urei 535 Graphic
PMC 70	Ashly Parametric
200	Valley Int'l. Maxi-Q
224 Series	Orban Parametric
Yamaha Rev 1	Klark-Trecknic Graphic
Rev 7	
SPX 90 Series	Noise Gates
Eventide SP 2016	Ashly SC 33
Alesis Microverb, MIDIverb and Quadraverb	Kepex II
EMT Plates	Drawmer DS 201
Echo Plates I, II, III	
	Compressor/Limiters
Delays	DBX 165 and 160
Lexicon PCM 41	160X
PCM 42	900 Series
Prime Time II	Urei 1176 LN
Roland SDE 1000, 2000	LA-2 and LA-4
3000, etc.	Valley Int'l. 610
	Gain Brain
Flanger	Dyna-Mite
Loft 450	Ashly SC 50
	Orban De-Esser
Special	
Eventide H949 Harmonizer	
MXR Pitch Transposer	
Aphex Aural Exciter	
Yamaha SPX-90 Series Multi-Processors	
Roland DEP-5 Multi-Processor	

sound one good kick. More expensive units have larger RAMs, enabling longer mono samples and even stereo samples to be stored.

Next is a group of circuits that allow the stored sample to be edited. You may want to trim the beginning of the sample to eliminate the time after the start button was hit and before the attack of the kick, or trim the end after the drum's release is finished. Furthermore, if the sampled sound is too long or contains unwanted moments internally, you can slice out a portion of the trimmed sample. More expensive sampler/triggers allow the user to chop out time increments by the millisecond or even one digital sample at a time, where each sample represents less than 1/40,000 or 0.000025 second. (Be careful not to confuse the meanings of the word *sample* in these two contexts.)

Some units even display an image of the entire sample's waveform, showing both its envelope and the exact points where the audio wave crosses zero from positive to negative voltage. For most internal editing, the user splices two portions of the wave together at instants where the voltages are zero, or at moments where the voltage of each portion is rising or falling similarly. Most sampler/triggers allow the user to preview each edit before permanently discarding the head, tail, and internal trims.

The final circuit is the *trigger,* which plays back the finished sample on command. This can be cued manually, or (as in the control circuit of a noise gate) by the occurrence of an audio event in another incoming signal, for example successive hits of a poor-sounding kick drum as heard by its mic or recorded on tape. The most popular current sampling and triggering device is made by TC Electronics, with AMS brand units a close second. Both of these feature enough editing features for easy manipulation of drums and other commonly replaced sounds, and both have triggers that can output the stored sample less than 2 ms after each trigger command. While 2 ms may seem virtually instantaneous, this much delay can be enough to subtly alter the feel of a drum part being replaced. Keep your ears open for such problems, and avoid improving individual sounds or tracks on a tape at the expense of the entire song's feel or groove.

CONSOLE AUTOMATION, SMPTE SYNCHRONIZATION, AND THE BASICS OF MIDI

AUTOMATION is used only during the final mixdown, the last stage of a recording project. Because it takes a substantial amount of time to set up and deal with the automation system during each mix, using the system can add to rather than save time on the project as a whole. Thus, automation is one of those items with which many studios impress clients but which relatively few clients have the time, patience, money (and often, the need) to use in their projects.

THE ADVANTAGES OF AUTOMATION

There are several types of automation systems, but all work on the same underlying principle. When a console fader is used to vary the signal level allowed to pass through, no record is made of its position or setting at various points during a mix. However, it is possible to introduce a device that keeps such records. Instead of allowing the fader to directly control the signal flow, we use the fader only to generate a voltage that varies in proportion to its setting, and then use that voltage to control the signal flow. By keeping a record of the fader's changing output voltage that is in sync with the ongoing recorded performance, we can later use that information to replay the changes in signal level originally imparted by the engineer. In effect, we have adopted the principle of the player piano to capture and replay the engineer's fader movements.

This process requires several new devices installed in the console. First, we need faders that generate the required *control voltages*. Next we need a circuit, called the *voltage-controlled amplifier* (or VCA), that can vary the level of an output signal in response to changing control voltages supplied by the fader. We also require some way of continuously observing and writing down the setting for each fader on the console. Finally we need a place to write all this information down. The latter is simple: we can just write it all down on an empty track of the multitrack tape. Or we can put timimg information or codes on one track of the tape, line them up with identical codes written on a floppy disk, and write the fader information corresponding to each point in time on that disk.

More difficult to arrange are the circuits that actually read the position of each fader as the engineer does a mix, then use the replayed copy of this data (from the 2″ tape or the coded floppy disk) to generate the same voltages during the automated playback and thus control signal levels as though the engineer were doing it manually. The solution turns out to be a computer-based circuit that sweeps across the entire console many times a second, noting the position of each fader during each sweep, and writes the fader information onto the designated automation track or floppy disk.

In theory, if we use volume controls and switches throughout the console that generate control voltages corresponding to their position, we could automate the entire console. The SSL Total Recall system goes about halfway, noting the position of pan-pots and equalizer adjustments. It does not, however, reset all these components by itself. Beyond controlling the main faders like other systems, Total Recall displays all its other notes on a television screen, allowing the engineer to see what was done on previous takes and improve the mix from there. At the moment, only the Harrison Series 10 console is fully automated.

Because of the ease with which computer data can be handled, it is possible to separate data during a playback and alter just that which came from specific faders. We can update what we did with one or more faders, while retaining the information about other channels whose levels are acceptable as last manipulated. The updated information is then substituted back into the datastream and written onto a second track of the tape, or as a new program on the floppy disk, without erasing what was done on the last try. In this way, the mix can be improved on succeeding passes until the final data represents all the fader changes on all channels of the console, including reverb and effects returns.

Most console automation systems have three basic operating modes:

1. *Write mode:* The computer circuits scan the board and write down (on tape, or floppy, or even in RAM) the position of each fader many times per second.
2. *Read mode:* Data are read back from tape or floppy and used to reproduce the engineer's fader movements in real time.

3. *Update mode:* Data are read from tape or floppy, and the engineer changes what he or she did with one or more faders. This new data replaces the corresponding parts of the old, and the updated datastream is again written on tape or floppy.

In addition to fader level information, it is quite useful to have the system mute and unmute various channels during the mix. This is ordinarily done to eliminate tape noise from tracks when there is no signal present; to eliminate unwanted recorded noises such as coughs, breaths, feet shuffling, and the like; and to edit out unwanted musical material such as chords, notes, or fills in an effort to give proper shape, build, and decoration to the arrangement or mix. Muting data is usually written in a separate pass, before the engineer begins playing with fader levels, so that the unwanted sounds will not affect creative judgments.

Operating in the read mode, most automation systems reproduce what the engineer did without actually moving the faders as the playback progresses. Only the Neve NECAM and the GML systems achieve true "player-pianohood" via small motors that move each fader during playback exactly as the engineer did during the write or last update pass for each console channel. While it can be helpful to see and hear what you did last, this feature has drawbacks. Since the motors are still coupled to the faders (and all nonautomated console functions) during write mode, each fader is a bit heavy or sluggish to adjust. Also, when the automation system first locks onto data during a playback pass, the faders may move unpredictably for a few seconds, so keep your fingers clear of the faders as they kick into action. Like any system with so many added movable parts, NECAM and GML downtime is generally high.

The ARMS system (in Figure 8.1) is employed on MCI (now called Sony or SPPC), Harrison, and Sound Workshop consoles, among others. Note that each fader has only two mode buttons and associated led (light-emitting diode) indicator lights. These clearly cannot accomplish all the things we might like the system to do. The ARMS buttons on the master module work like typewriter shift keys, changing the function of the individual ARMS buttons on each module, thereby expanding the number of jobs each button can do.

To do a rough mix without muting any channels, the engineer merely presses the Master Write button, placing the entire system in Write mode, and does the mix, sending the data to an empty tape track. But to do one pass for mutes, before making any level changes, the engineer configures the shift keys on the master module so that the lower button at each fader becomes a Mute button, inscribing mutes on the automation track or floppy. On a subsequent pass made to adjust levels, the system will also note and remember a fader's level even during sections where a mute was specified earlier. The resulting track of automation data thus contains mute and level information.

To hear this take, the engineer pushes Master Read and listens, noting what needs alteration in the next pass. When ready for another pass, the engineer selects the desired mode or status on the channels to be altered. The rest of the system remains in read mode. The composite data (old from those channels in read, new

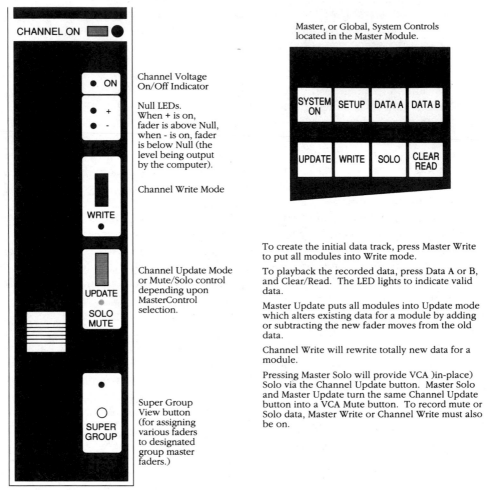

Master, or Global, System Controls located in the Master Module.

Channel Voltage On/Off Indicator

Null LEDs. When + is on, fader is above Null, when - is on, fader is below Null (the level being output by the computer).

Channel Write Mode

Channel Update Mode or Mute/Solo control depending upon MasterControl selection.

Super Group View button (for assigning various faders to designated group master faders.)

To create the initial data track, press Master Write to put all modules into Write mode.

To playback the recorded data, press Data A or B, and Clear/Read. The LED lights to indicate valid data.

Master Update puts all modules into Update mode which alters existing data for a module by adding or subtracting the new fader moves from the old data.

Channel Write will rewrite totally new data for a module.

Pressing Master Solo will provide VCA)in-place) Solo via the Channel Update button. Master Solo and Master Update turn the same Channel Update button into a VCA Mute button. To record mute or Solo data, Master Write or Channel Write must also be on.

Figure 8.1.   Close-ups of the ARMS Console Automation System, as installed in a Sound Workshop Series 34

from those being altered) is recorded on a second track of the 2″ tape. In subsequent passes the engineer refines the mix, bouncing the automation data back and forth between two tracks, or to different locations on the floppy disk. Because the system can simultaneously mute/unmute and change the levels of each channel, the final automated mix may contain more instructions than a whole team of engineers would be able to execute in real time.

It is beyond the scope of this book to give a complete course in how to operate automation systems. There are many other possibilities even with the ARMS system. My intention is for you to understand the advantages and disadvantages of these systems. Once you have decided to use automation, your engineer will take the pilot's seat.

THE DISADVANTAGES OF AUTOMATION

The first and major disadvantage of automation systems is that they are confusing even to engineers who use them daily. In many systems, several buttons and LEDs must be checked just to identify the system status, which means you can waste a lot of time doing passes, before you realize that the updates were not written properly or cannot be properly read back from tape or floppy. Make sure that the engineer doing your mix is thoroughly familiar with the system and uses it regularly. If you have any doubts, talk with another client on whose project the system was used. Did it save or waste time? Did the client get a better mix with the automation than without it? You would be surprised how often the answer to both questions is no.

Second, in order to make full use of automation on 24-track 2″, you must reserve at least two tracks for the automation data itself. Sonically, this data is a shrill, warbling tone. If recorded at too high a level on tape, the data may be audible as crosstalk in adjacent musical tracks. Conversely, the data will not properly control automated playbacks if recorded too low. It is sometimes necessary to reserve tracks adjacent to automation data for a low-level sound in the mix, for example, a rhythm guitar or other instrument that can be gated to eliminate crosstalk between notes or chords. On the other hand, a percussive instrument recorded next to an automation track may bleed into the data and cause errors. In the worst case, it may be necessary to leave the nearest track blank. If 24 tracks are barely enough for you, you will want to avoid reducing the available tracks to 20 or 21.

If you decide to put SMPTE (Society of Motion Picture and Television Engineers) time code on one track of the 2″ and use a synchronized floppy disk for the actual data, you still have the same problem. SMPTE codes are even shriller and more subject to crosstalk and *print-through* (transfer of sound from one layer of magnetic tape to adjacent layers) than automation data. Even though some brands of automation can operate well on SMPTE signals recorded at −10 dB or below, you may still have to throw away one track between that containing SMPTE code and any track with music, reducing you to a total of 22 usable tracks. However, an on-tape SMPTE track gives you the added advantage of being able to synchronize the multitrack with any other SMPTE-driven deck, audio or video.

Third, there is always the chance that the system will not play back exactly what the engineer wrote. Most automation manufacturers guarantee that the levels you hear in read mode will be different from those you wrote by no more than 1/4 dB. If the system is working properly, that is close enough. If not, you may not recognize the problem. In a complex mix, you probably will not notice that one or more levels have slipped up or down by a couple of decibels. It may be necessary to check out the system before doing a critical mix.

Record some tones on blank 2″ tape at full level (O dBVU), and write a trial pass with the automation, adjusting the playback levels to a verifiable series of meter readings, say −10, then −3, then −6, then +3, and so on. See how closely the system reproduces these levels in read mode, and see if it maintains accuracy over two or three consecutive playback passes. If there is any doubt that the system will work right, do not use it! Do the mix manually until you have a complete take or pieces that can be assembled to give you what you want.

SMPTE INTERLOCK SYSTEMS

Until a few years ago, all the sound for television programs was edited and mixed exactly as was sound for motion pictures. The original recordings of dialogue, narration, sound effects, and music were *transferred* onto sprocketed *magnetic film*—(clear motion picture leader coated with magnetic oxide) generally 35mm in width—and edited into separate rolls of dialogue, music, and effects (between 5 and 50 total rolls). During the mix each roll was played in mechanical synchronization with the edited picture. Even today, with the advent of broadcast-quality portable video cameras, many top-rated television shows are shot and edited on motion picture and magnetic film.

However, the bulkiness of the mag film method, plus the need for high-quality stereo music in films and TV, finally necessitated a way of synchronizing multitrack audio with motion picture projection and video playback. In the 1950s the Society of Motion Picture and Television Engineers (SMPTE) standardized a numerical code system by which any *frame* (a single image lasting 1/30 second) in a complete show can be uniquely indicated. Each SMPTE *address* contains four 2-digit numbers separated by colons. From left to right, each pair indicates the number of hours, minutes, seconds, and frames from a designated starting point of 00:00:00:00 to the frame in question. The picture frame with SMPTE code number 01:29:13:08 is exactly 1 hour, 29 minutes, 13 seconds, and 8 frames after the starting point.

Let us assume that an edited videotape is *striped* with a continuous SMPTE code; that is, a code is written on one of the tape's analog tracks for the entire length of the program. Each video frame will then have a sequentially numbered code address recorded right on the videotape. It is certainly possible to stripe one track of a multitrack audiotape with the same SMPTE code. Now, if we design a device that reads the SMPTE code from the video, tells the audio tape recorder each video code address as it passes, and controls the playback speed of the multitrack machine so that its own SMPTE code is kept in perfect numerical alignment with that from video, we have a SMPTE synchronizer.

Notice that the SMPTE code from one of the two decks—in this case the video deck—controls the motor speed of the other. The first deck is therefore the *master,* the latter its *slave.* In theory, the code from the master can control any number of slaves, as long as each of their motor speeds can be independently varied to keep the code on that machine in perfect alignment with code from the master. Moreover, there is no reason that both machines cannot be audio recorders. As long as each roll of tape has the same series of SMPTE codes on it, a slave really has no idea of what kind of machine the master is.

Taking the concept even further, it does not matter if the code on the master and slaves contains the same SMPTE numbers. As long as each machine can read an uninterrupted stream of codes, the slaves can be made to advance exactly one frame for each frame the master advances. In this context, the codes are analogous to the sprocket holes in film that, although unnumbered, keep any number of sound and picture rolls in sync. However, the minute there is a dropout in the SMPTE code of master or slave, that machine will revert to its nominal tape speed and lose sync for the duration of the dropout. Furthermore, while trying to restore proper sync, the speed of the machine may vary wildly, along with the pitch of any musical material recorded on it.

In current broadcast videotape production, the original live or location sound can be recorded directly to the analog soundtracks of the videodeck (a Sony 1″ C format, 3/4″ U-Matic or even 1/2″ Beta-cam or VHS), or simultaneously to a separate audio recorder, with the same SMPTE code recorded on audio and video decks. As the picture is edited, the matching segments of sync sound can be easily copied in SMPTE sync to tracks of a multitrack tape that has been prestriped with a continuous SMPTE code at least as long as the entire program.

Using the videotape as the master and slaving the multitrack(s), any sound that must precisely sync with events on screen can be *laid over* to the multitrack while the picture is viewed. On 2″ tape, once in sync, always in sync. Finally, the entire multitrack tape is *mixed to picture,* the mixdown recorder also inscribing a SMPTE code identical to that on the video master or multitrack. If this mix is made on a separate sync audio tape, we can later perform a *layback* onto the edited video master for dubbing and distribution.

You probably will not use SMPTE interlock in making demos, but you may need to record or mix to picture if you plan a music video. Although I cannot explain the minutiae of videotape production here, let me just caution you that SMPTE code and interlocking procedures are not something that can be reliably used by a novice. If you do make a music video that requires precise timing of sound and image, put a professional in charge of the interlocking devices. The time, energy, and money needed to make even the simplest video is not trivial, and there are many things that can go wrong with interlocking audio and video machines in the field. If you do not have clean and continuous SMPTE codes on all your original tapes—audio and video—the project may prove uneditable at worst, or very time-consuming as well as expensive to postproduce.

MIDI IN THE CONTROL ROOM

No one could have imagined that the Musical Instrument Digital Interface (MIDI) system developed by Roland in 1983 could become an industry standard so quickly. Nevertheless, MIDI code generators and slaving circuits are now being built into most professional synthesizers, drum machines, some recording consoles, and even grand pianos. The original intent of MIDI was to allow a player to use one keyboard to control the sound-generating circuits within any number of synthesizers. In its simplest form, every time a key is depressed or stroked on one synth, data is generated and sent via MIDI cables to the sound-generating circuits of another instrument. The second instrument, believing the data came from its own keyboard, generates the same notes played on the first. Here MIDI codes serve as a remote control, the local synth telling a remote instrument when to generate what notes, and using what sound or patch. MIDI merely specifies the nature and timing of various events.

However, the data capacity of each MIDI command or *word* is sufficient for many additional instructions. For instance, the player can change patches on the second synth from the keyboard of the first, or apply the full range of dynamics in his keyboard performance to all remote MIDI instruments via *touch sensitivity* commands included in the MIDI codes. By writing all the MIDI instructions on a floppy disk in alignment with a SMPTE stripe or other continuous timing data, all MIDI'd instruments will automatically and repeatably play in perfect alignment with sounds on a similarly striped multitrack tape. The multitrack reads its time code into a computer, which knows (from the floppy) the code addresses at which each MIDI command is to be executed, on which synth, with which patch, and with what performance parameters or details.

These days, it is not unusual to find an Apple MacIntosh computer acting as the interface between multitrack tape and a host of drum machines and synths, the instruments MIDI'd together via computer, and the computer SMPTE'd to the tape. This effectively adds tracks to the tape, since each MIDI'd performance will be identical from take to take. The drum machine and other instruments can play directly into the mixing console, while vocals and live instruments play back from tape. All will stay in perfect sync, so the only limitation is the number of input modules in the mixing console itself. In this way, MIDI has enabled 4− and 8−track studios to turn out master-quality tapes that actually include 24 or more separate channels of musical material.

As cautioned earlier, make sure your own synths and MIDI-based devices are compatible with necessary components owned by the studio you have booked. Manufacturers often change circuits and systems, and many users make their own modifications that can inhibit the proper interaction of factory-supplied hard- and software. Furthermore, make sure the engineer for your project is completely familiar with the normal and abnormal operation of all these systems. A blank stare when "System Error" is displayed may quickly translate into "Session Abort"! There really is no arguing with or fudging your way around computers.

Again, the details of MIDI as a composer's and artist's tool are beyond the scope of this book. However, there is now a growing list of studio processing equipment that can be operated remotely by MIDI commands. Digital signal processors with a host of different effects are perfect candidates for such outside control. The times at which the device is to switch from one kind of processing to another can be entered on a floppy disc with other MIDI data. During a mix, the switching can be done automatically and perfectly, allowing the engineer and producer to concentrate on creative decisions.

Even if your music is entirely acoustic, the MIDI system with computer interface may help you achieve more repeatable and quicker results. However, do not rely on MIDI as a crutch. If your music is synth-based, and most of your programming can be done before setting foot in the studio, you already know MIDI's capabilities. If you are not familiar with MIDI and feel that your type of music requires the freedom of live performance with its inherent tempo variations, do not let an engineer convince you to refashion your production to take advantage of this new technology.

In an interview with Jeff Burger, published in *Recording Engineer/Producer,* engineer/producer George Massenburg shares his feelings about the impact of this new technology on recordings.

I hate the way records are made today. All these machines are supposed to be our salvation, but they don't make better music. They just make more confusion. Most of the MIDI studios are not turning out wonderful music that touches people; it's just crap. Now, I use it all, but I like to think that we can still make records that have a sense of themselves, a sense of time, and a sense of place—records that are artistically executed and entertaining. We're entertainers, not magicians!

I think we're going to see exactly the same thing we've seen for 300 years: a single "sense" of a piece of music. You put on a Rolling Stones record and you don't hear a DX7 or a drummer, you hear a record with a sense of itself. Huey Lewis said, "The song tells us what to do next." Overdubbing is just a tool. However, rather than coming full circle away from machines, I think the people who know how to operate the machines are going to demand more performance out of them.

People would like to think that in ten years somebody will come along with the magic processor that will run just one edit list and just wrap everything up into one neat package—an 80 × 64 console, all reverbs and effects, machine control and Winchesters attached everywhere. That is not going to happen. I think recording equipment will still be modular, and people will have their favorite pieces of equipment. As long as engineers act like hairdressers they're going to carry their favorite tools around with them. Those black boxes will eventually develop into software tools, but it will take a hell of a computer to run them.

What about the big, integrated studio of the future, you just feed information into it, and get music out of it? That might be a good 50-year plan, but by the time processors become that powerful, there will be countervailing forces. A funny thing happens in the balance between art and technology. When there is a tremendous leap ahead in technology, people react by increasing the human factor in their art. In other words, I do not predict a simplification of the recording process.

Go into the studio knowing just how your music will make its way to tape. The insecurity of trying to adapt to a new medium while you are recording master tapes will creep into your performances. If you are not comfortable and confident of how the tape will turn out, it will probably not turn out well.

Part II

MIND OVER METERS: PREPARING FOR THE COLLABORATION WITH ENGINEER AND MACHINE

9

SESSION PLANNING AND ENGINEER COMMUNICATION

ALL too often I have seen groups stroll into a recording session, even to record a master tape, without having met their engineer or planned anything about the session in advance. In doing this, they are counting on magic happening when the tape rolls. Any magician will tell you that planning and practice are the building blocks of a good act: the same is true of recording a demo or master tape. There are just too many things that can go wrong.

Let us presume that you have selected a particular studio based on its tracking capabilities, room, and console—all the basic equipment and pricing considerations. After booking the session, there are several decisions you should make before the sessions. We will consider:

- The purpose of the master tape
- How many songs to record
- Session scheduling
- Intended instrumentation and Vocals
- The most crucial sounds
- The best order in which to record the song's basic tracks
- Recordings selected for studio reference

Write down your answers to the above, meet with your chosen or assigned engineer, and—together—plan how you will achieve each goal. Bring in one record each of the two artists you identified in the last item above, the best available previous recording you have made, and introduce the engineer to the whole project—its tech-

95

nical, musical, and emotional aspects. Remembering that the studio and engineer will be temporarily joining your group, we will consider the following:

- Arranging players in the studio
- Acoustic isolation of instruments or players
- Arrival and equipment setup
- Effects boxes and accessories
- Planning for problems
- Budget planning with the studio engineer

THE PURPOSE OF THE MASTER TAPE

If you are making a tape to get gigs, examine the gig market in your town. Who books the clubs where you want to play? Call them and ask how much they rely on tapes in making booking decisions. How much material do they need on tape to make a decision? Whose tapes have impressed them? Was there anything in common among these favorites—the kind of material, arrangements, vocals, the overall recording sounds? With an unlimited booking budget, what acts would best please their audience?

Asking too many questions can leave a bad impression, but try to get as much information as you can, and discuss it all with your group. Everyone wants to please audiences and be accepted. Laying these booking and audience ideals out on the table should not cause everyone to change style and wardrobe. However, if you want your audience to know and like you, you must know and like the people who make up that audience.

If your group and music are the direct opposite to the market you discovered, you are either in the wrong city, trying to get booked in the wrong clubs, or both. If your group persona fits in with the market, each of you will have a conceptual bridge that ensures your finished tape has at least some elements to which that market responds. You have to attract ears before they will really pay attention to what you want to say.

If your upcoming tape is primarily aimed at attracting a recording contract, the questions you must answer are totally different. You may in fact find the answers to a lot of these in the bins at a good record store. What labels have signed acts anything like your own in the last two years? Which of those acts were first timers? Were the first-timers well-established live performers before their first album was released? Who was/is the A&R person at each of these labels?

Next, call the labels to ask if they are accepting demos now. If so, an A&R assistant (but probably not the secretary) can tell you how much material the tape should contain, if the label prefers to buy completed master tapes or to work with their artists on sponsored masters, how much the label relies on reviews of live performances, and if there are radio stations, critics, or anyone else whose opinion you should obtain and include with your tape.

Next look at the airplay market: are any of the first-timers getting radio play in your area? If so, call the stations or DJs who play them most and ask what cuts they like best, what other similar groups they like and play on the air, if you may send them your tape, how much material you should put on it, and whether you can put them on your mailing list for future gigs.

Few record labels sign artists without getting several corroborating opinions. An A&R person always has some guidelines to go by: a few critics or club bookers who share his or her musical tastes. If you find the right third parties to recommend you, that can reduce by months the label conversion time. As a seller in a buyer's market you must use every technique available to find out to whom to send tapes, what makes these people respond to an unsolicited package, and what other information will help them make up their minds.

When you are on the brink of recording a master tape—something to release commercially, representing the best you can do—all of this investigating should be behind you. Instead of asking how to sell your package, the question now is how to package what you want to sell. Major aspects of musical content are already decided. It now remains to use the recording studio to dress the music with a sound and ambience that identify its future market for the listener. Master tapes, from the artist's point of view, break down into two categories: (1) those you are self-producing with your own or independent funding and (2) tapes commissioned and paid for by a label. The comments that follow apply to your own productions, to be completed before a label comes on board. In this case, your two overriding concerns will probably be quality and cost. To clarify the planning process, for the moment we will think in reverse: we will pretend that you are doing an album with an unlimited budget and need worry only about making a great and salable recording.

Record labels prefer to buy masters mixed and ready for release, because it minimizes guesswork regarding the product's quality and allows the A&R people to play the tape around and get solid opinions before authorizing a buyout payment or recoupment advance to its backer(s). However, nine times out of ten, even when ready to buy the label will want to pay for a remix of the intended single and one or two other potential follow-up releases. In some cases, they will have a specific idea of the target market for the finished album and feel that the present mixes are too harsh, too soft or whatever. Or the label may just want one final shot at improving the product. A second mix does not cost much, and then the label will have two versions to choose from.

In light of this, I advise that you spend most of your own independent budget perfecting the performances on tape. Then just rough-mix the whole album, with one final on the tune you think will be singled out. Often a remixed single no longer fits with other cuts already mixed. Thus more remixes follow to unify the whole album. To fine-mix the whole project once to the label's taste and discard a cheap rough mix is an efficient and cost-effective strategy. In addition, because master tapes do wear out and lose sound quality after hundreds of hours of overdubs and mixes, it is best to spare your tapes until someone else is paying for the final mix.

From the creative standpoint, there is an even better reason to do roughs rather than a final. Artists often begin a project with a firm notion of the emotions they want to capture, and then get wrapped up in technical details during the production. Certainly every detail of the recording is important, but once all your performances are on the multitrack, the tough question returns: Did you get the emotions you had in mind from the start? A "ruff" mix is the chance to find out without spending a fortune.

In one or two hours, can you identify the instruments, phrases, fills, and other materials that constitute these emotions? Like an outline of a well-written paper, a good rough mix shows the potential of the multitrack and acts as a guide when you have the budget to spend 4 to 8 hours in a final mix. Plenty of major hits have in fact been the rough mixes that felt right, rather than final mixes that had technical perfection but no life. The public buys feel, impact, and emotion, not technique.

The most important thing you can tell an engineer before recording anything is the emotional result you want from each song. The knowledge that a song is meant to be happy, angry or tragic will guide the engineer's every move—from picking mics to making the right cue mix (the most important thing to help you play well); from equalizer decisions during track-laying to predelay settings on the reverb chosen for the roughs. The engineer is the window through which your emotions get on tape. He or she is a creative partner—to keep any artistic secrets from your engineer is asking for failure. For starters assume that he or she knows nothing about what you want. The more explicit your verbal picture, the easier it is for the engineer to repaint it in sounds.

In today's market, unless you are working in multitrack digital, you have to think hard about how your finished product will sound when played digitally on compact disc. Because the final tape will only be as quiet and clean as its noisiest or dirtiest tracks, the engineer has to know about any audio pitfalls ahead of time. Warn him or her if you must use your guitarist's onstage effects boxes, a noisy amplifier, or synthesizer.

The other consideration in final mixing is speed and efficiency. An album that takes three weeks to mix will be expensive and may lack continuity. It is very difficult to get uniform drum sounds and overall blend every night for weeks on end. Artistically, it is much better to mix quickly: anything you can do in laying tracks to effect that is well worth the time spent planning. Continuity of tracks is of primary importance. Make sure the same instruments and vocals are recorded on the same numerical tracks for each tune in which they appear. For any sounds, such as lead vocals or drums, that should be consistent throughout the entire project, spend your time once to get the right sound before laying tracks. Then make sure that instrument goes down with the same sound in every tune. Take copious notes when reviewing takes; note problems that must be cured in the final mix to avoid disasters like "Oh no, we forgot to mute the sneeze on track 6!"

HOW MANY SONGS TO RECORD

In making gig tapes or label demos, the fewer songs you record the better. It is wise to leave listeners wanting more, and it behooves you to pick the few songs that work best as entertainment events. Live audience reactions to your songs will tell you most of what to record. If you have a hunch that one song that does not come off well live will succeed on tape, record that too. Of course you want to tape the tunes that allow players to show off their strongest solos or chops, favorite patches, or equipment, but if these tunes are not crowd pleasers, record something else. Never ignore an audience's ability to pick winners.

Next, remember that if booking agents are busy, so are the club owners for whom they will play your tape in an effort to get you gigs. Shorten song arrangements wherever possible—if not in the recording, then in editing. Short versions of four different songs packed into a twelve-minute tape are better than six-minute stage versions of only two. Avoid medleys, simply because it's difficult for listeners to locate the song or section they like best when playing the tape again.

Each A&R person at a major label receives dozens of unsolicited tapes weekly in addition to solicited ones. Since your tape is optional listening, it must make its point quickly and decisively—no three-minute introduction on the first song, no teaser before the single. Every song has to work from start to finish. In my opinion, a demo tape for any artist, type of music, or any purpose should be under 20 minutes long, preferably between 12 and 15 minutes. The agent or A&R person can always ask for more.

SESSION SCHEDULING

How many sessions to schedule and when depend on two factors. The first is group and studio availability. The second hinges on when your group plays best. If the players are really best in early evenings, that should be your first choice, at least for basic tracks. Develop a list of total studio hours needed for basics and for each type of overdub, and pick optimal times. I prefer to pay more for the right time slot at the right studio than to pay a cheaper rate at another studio. Switch studios rather than take a time slot when the players are not comfortable, alert, and up! No amount of overdubbing will correct problems with the basics.

I also strongly suggest that you try to book each phase of the project in a short stretch. Recording all the basics for an album in a few nights will keep them cohesive, like a continuous live performance, even if you wait weeks before adding vocals and overdubs.

How many hours is the group good for in each session? Most musicians play better in two 4-hour sessions than on 8-hour stretch. Thus it may be wise to book a *lockout* for two or three days (i.e., make a deal to have the studio for your use only, around the clock). This will enable you to leave all the mics and board set up through the basics sessions, saving a lot of setup time and player frustration. Even if it is more expensive than four or six graveyard shifts (late evening sessions), a lockout takes pressure off you. The group might knock off three tracks on a night when players' energy stays high or break if it's not happening. Next day the setup's still there, ready to pick up where you left off. The pressure is only on once—on the last day of the lockout.

As for how much time to book, I generally add at least 30 percent to the amount of time each basic, overdub, or vocal "should" take. If you project three hours per basic, allow yourself four in the studio. You'll know early if you're ahead of pace and may be able to cancel the last session without financial penalty. Conversely, if you run over after booking just enough time, the studio may not be able to extend your lockout or give you more sequential evenings. Think always in terms of reducing the musical pressure, even if a little extra money is involved. Your total budget will dictate how far you can bend on these matters.

Don't try to record in bits and pieces of players' spare time—for example, after work or between other gigs. Any studio tape is an investment and a challenge. You can't possibly do a great tape when you're exhausted from a day gig or on the fly between commitments. If taping is a special event, set aside a special time when everyone can relax in preparation and be clear of daily problems. This may mean one or more people taking some time off work—at least afternoons before each basic session. It is worth the trouble, however, because even if you do not hear player tensions in the finished tape, an objective listener will.

INTENDED INSTRUMENTATION

Write a list of all the instruments, overdubs, vocal parts, and sweetening to go onto each song you will record. You might even use ledger forms to construct a track sheet and priority list for each tune, laying the same instrument into identical line numbers for each tune. This will help see which songs have most instruments in common and reduce the number of necessary mic and board setups. This will help the engineer maintain consistent treatment of instruments and vocals, even if each song is set up from scratch.

Whereas certain parts of your musical plan will be mandatory, other overdubs and sweetening tracks are often optional. Use this information to prioritize overdubs. Separate the "musts" from the "maybes." This will help you monitor your remaining studio time and budget as sessions progress. If, for instance, you are using more time than planned, you can make sure all the musts are finished before any maybes. If you are unsure whether certain fills should be played on a synth or guitar, plan ahead which instrument to try first—and try it while that instrument is set up to do musts on another tune. Again, the less time spent on studio and board setups, the more time for playing. *Spend studio time making music, not decisions.*

CHOOSING THE MOST CRUCIAL SOUNDS

When your instrumentation sheets are complete, write in anything crucial about the sound, feel, or effects you want on individual tracks of each song. If the snare drum should be fatter on one song, note it. If the sax must be extra crisp on another or if a delay or flanger will be needed on the rhythm guitar, write it in. This is time-saving info for the engineer, who can then pick mics, prepatch outboard signal processing while you set up and rehearse, and change control room setups between tunes. In addition, it flags specific sound goals that are often forgotten in pursuit of a better solo or a new twist in the arrangement. If you are recording a full album on label backing, I suggest you use the Production Grid form shown and explained at the end of this chapter. Such rigorous planning in this situation may save thousands of dollars, but will not be necessary for a quick demo tape.

RECORDING ORDER

Use proposed track and planning sheets to decide the order in which to record your basics. In planning a film shoot, it makes financial sense to complete all the shots that take place in one location, regardless of where these scenes occur in the script, before moving to the next site. The same with recording: group all the tunes that use the same instruments and/or sounds in the basics, and record each group in continuous or adjacent sessions.

Also, be sure you take the length of your sessions into consideration when planning the recording order. During a time slot when you normally rehearse or perform, energy should be best following the warmup, so put an important or difficult tune first on the list. However, if your studio time starts in the morning or at 2 A.M., it will take a while for everyone to settle in to the right groove. In that case, begin each session with an easier tune or something good for warming up. It often works out well just to jam on songs you do not intend to record, until the entire group finds the same wavelength, then roll the tape.

As for overdubbing order, I recommend that you put lead instruments and vocals on as soon as possible after doing basics. Do not wait until sweetening and percussions are recorded, because the basics and leads are the song. In a first listening, the feel and featured emotions may be the only things that stick with a booking agent or A&R person. These must be winners before overdubs or solos are worth doing. It is also wise to take a few days' break after putting on the leads. Take home a very rough mix and make sure you are happy with basics and leads, or take notes on what needs recutting. Then go back to work with the major hurdle behind you.

SELECTING RECORDINGS FOR STUDIO REFERENCE

You know perfectly well whose records sound best to you at home. Take a couple of these into the studio before you book studio time, and use them to check out the control room's "listenability." If these records sound good there, bring them back during the sessions for your own and the engineer's reference. If they sound quite different (and you book sessions anyway), adjust your ears to how these records sound in the control room. If your own tapes match the records' control-room sound, the tapes will sound like the records in your living room too.

Although the control room is a new environment to you, remember that it is a living room to your engineer. Above all else, trust the engineer's ears because he or she wants to give you the best sound possible. Engineers usually assume that sound is your first priority too. If you have not worked a lot in studios, let me suggest that you make sound your second or third priority and physical comfort and ease of movement your first priority. The more at home you feel in an otherwise cold and clinical environment, the more natural and confident your product will be. Approach the studio as if it were an unfamiliar stage. The more comfortable your setup, the better you can hear your own performance, and the better that performance will be. Billy Joel discussed the process of relating to his engineer, Jim Boyer, in an interview with *Mix* magazine publisher, David Schwartz:

To me, the engineer is like one of the guys in the band, and he's got to bring his own particular personality and creativity to his instrument [the studio]. I talk to him like I talk to the musicians. Jim and I have a language that we've developed, a kind of short-hand that helps get things done. If I can get something without going through a lot of rigamarole, that just helps everything.

He's with me through the entire process, and he's there after I'm gone, when they're mastering. To me, he's the key figure—even more than the band, because the band goes away and they don't hear what's going on with the overdubs, what kind of sound effects, or the mixing and sequencing. They're not involved with 65 or 70 per-cent of what's going on.

The producer is the X-factor: the wild card. Phil [Ramone] will come up with some-thing out of left field that neither Jim as a technician, nor I as a musician, might have perceived. It's some kind of spiritual thing. . . . The good producers that I know, like Phil and Quincy Jones, are song-oriented. The producer's role has changed as musicians have become more and more technically aware, and as engineers have gotten more creative.

Jim Boyer shared the studio techniques he applies on Billy Joel's albums in the same interview.

[The drummer] is elevated enough to be able to see everybody in the room. He's the focal point, after Billy.

I use Beyer M88s and M69s for toms, Sennheiser 435s for overheads. I like small-transducer mics because they sound a little clearer; they're a little more trans-parent for cymbals. I like [Neumann] KM84s on the top of the snare and a [Sennheiser] 421 or [Shure] SM57 on the bottom, and [AKG] D 12s for the bass drum. That's the contemporary miking. I don't really like to use condensers on toms. I never have, be-cause of the leakage.

[On guitars,] we use Neumann U-87s, or AKG 451s or 452s—condenser mics—because they just sound better than dynamics for this application.

Mostly [we take bass] direct. Doug [Stegmeyer] uses a Yamaha bass amp. I've miked his speaker with an [EV] RE-20, and I've used an AKG D 12. But there's a new mic by Fostex [M77RP] which looks like an old Shure. It's long and it's got ribs on it. It's an incredible bass amp mic, one of the best I've ever heard.

ARRANGING THE PLAYERS IN THE STUDIO

If you like the floor plan you use in rehearsal, ask the engineer to duplicate it for the basic sessions. Visual contact is important for exchanging cues, but it goes far beyond that. Do not forget that every group expresses itself physically as well as musically—to the audience and among its members. Musicians get energy and feel from each other's movements, postures, and facial expressions, and these add a lot to the performance. Make sure each of you gets the cues you always get in rehearsal.

If the engineer persuades you that leakage among the drum, piano, and other acoustic instrument mics will be a problem, impress him or her with the urgency of a tight grouping, suggest more directional mics, and make some minor audio sacrifices. A less-than-perfect sax or piano sound may be restored in a mix; an uneasy feel in the tracks cannot. If it makes anyone nervous to have people staring from the control room, put up a baffle between the group and the window. In other words, use the studio and its furniture to create an environment where you are focused on the music and on each other. You should not be diverted by anything until each take is done. The only etiquette that counts is that which results in a great tape.

It's important, I've found, to keep the musicians close to each other in the studio [reveals engineer Al Schmitt]. It sounds better, because the musicians can hear better and adjust to the room. Some engineers tend to separate the players to get more separation on the tracks. It may be psychological, but musicians play louder when they are further away from each other. By moving them closer together, they play a little softer, and you get a tighter, punchier sound.

The conga player [on *ToTo IV*] was almost in Jeff's [the drummer's] lap. They were right next to each other, and there were no flats [baffles] in between. Jeff was up on a riser about a foot and a half high. When they were fooling around without headphones, they could hear each other really well during the run-down. When they put the headphones on, they played the same. That subtlety shows up in the music. The music 'breathes' better; the dynamics are better.

[For producer Val Garay,] preproduction starts with the setup. I let the band choose whatever makes them comfortable. Their rehearsal arrangement doesn't necessarily have to reproduce their normal stage or recording studio locations. As a rule of thumb, the drummer usually sets up in the middle of the room, because everybody is listening to him. Then the bass player puts his amp near the drummer, so they can play easily together. From there it's pretty much up to the band members. A semicircle seems to work. . . . As far as levels go, the band pretty much figures that out for themselves too, because there's an instant relationship among the members of a professional band. To hear each other in the room, there has to be a balance. . . . Once you get that balance, you can stick one mic in there, open it up, and you're ready to make a work tape.

I like to make recordings of each arrangement as we go along. I use just one little cassette machine with one little microphone. You'd be amazed at how much you can get on one of those recordings. It's very close to the actual recording in the studio. The cassette tells you whether an arrangement works or not. The great test is how the song wears, and for that you have to keep listening to it over and over. The old adage is, "If it has legs, it will walk." . . . If everything about the song is comfortable, it will keep going. If not, it starts to grate.

When we go into the studio, I like to cut everything live—everything at once. I mike everything close for isolation and also put very loud instruments, like distortion guitar parts, in separate rooms. To make the separate tracks blend back together, I run feeds to two PA speakers in the rehearsal studio [adjacent to the main studio]. I have two Neumann U-76s that I can move anywhere in the room, or right next to the cabinets, for any desired effect. I just open the mics up and add them to the original sound at the board.

I guess you could say I'm a purist, but don't confuse that with traditionalism; a traditionalist I'm not. I would prefer to play with the guitar player's amp and get the

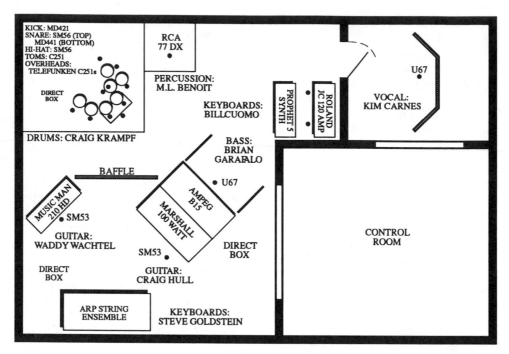

Figure 9.1.   Room and mic layout for "Bette Davis Eyes," by Kim Carnes; engineer/producer: Val Garay; Studio: Record One

sound at his station, rather than attempt to manufacture what's needed in the control room. All I try to do is capture what he's got. In essence, the secret is that the studio and all the equipment must remain transparent in the overall process of recording.

To achieve an open sound on his recording for the Bill Evans Trio *You Must Believe in Spring* album, Al Schmitt placed all the players close together.

We tried to get that "trio" sound. We didn't worry about the bass or the drums leaking into the piano or piano into the drum mics and so on. We actually tried to achieve that [leakage]. Once we locked in the sounds, we recorded one tune and brought the group into the control room. After they knew what it sounded like, it was simple. I could have sat back, put my feet up on the console, and just taped it. They produced their own dynamics. The album took four days.
   Somebody like Bill [Evans] is amazing. The grand piano sounded so great when we started to record, but there were just a few notes a little louder than the others. After playing for a while, he learned which notes rang out and would play those softer. All of a sudden the piano sounded even and balanced. . . . Instead of trying to equalize a little more bottom from the piano, he'd play the bottom a little harder to even it out. Those are things that most musicians don't think about doing. But when you're working with these kind of pros, it makes the job a lot easier.

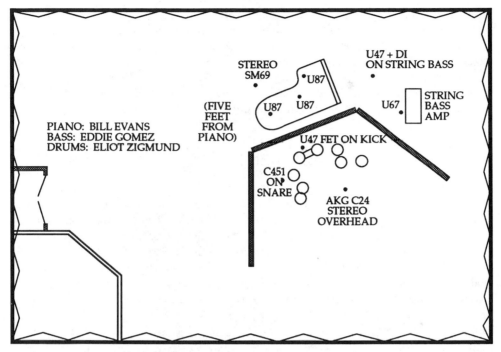

Figure 9.2. Room and mic layout for Bill Evans Trio sessions at Capitol Studios, Hollywood; Engineer: Al Schmitt

You'll get some phasing, but that's natural. The leakage is what makes the record sound good. Instead of having this big, open piano sound, and a tight, little drum sound, it sounded like a *trio*.

Eddie Gomez has such a great bass sound. We had it wired with a pickup and took that direct, as well as through his amp, with a mic in front of his instrument. I used a Neumann 47 tube on the bass itself, aimed toward the middle of the f-hole, and about one foot in front of it (primarily for arco passages); a direct box for the pickup signal; and a Neumann U-67 about a foot away from the front of the amp. It was a small amp with not very much bass [output], so we got a lot of top-end from there.

ACOUSTIC ISOLATION

Isolation booths and baffles are meant to deal with one basic problem: *leakage* (e.g., the unwanted sound of drums that is audible through a mic set up specifically for acoustic guitar). Leakage is worst when a group contains two or more acoustic instruments playing at different volume levels. We will investigate the acoustics of iso booths in chapter 14. For now, think of how the physical limitations of booths can affect the length of your sessions and the feel of recorded takes. First, it is difficult and time-consuming to set up and adjust mics around a drum set in a booth. If you have a choice of boothing drums or the acoustic guitar, go with the latter. Even if you encounter a little leakage with drums in the main room, the group will feel the impact of live drums—a good physical stimulus for exciting performances.

Do not isolate a player who is the physical center of attention. If the pianist leads the group, insist on good eye contact between him or her and everyone else. Engineering factors are always secondary to musical goals. Before you or the engineer spends a lot of time on isolation, think again of the purpose of the tape. If it is primarily to get gigs, a bit of leakage among instruments is not important.

ARRIVAL AND EQUIPMENT SETUP

There are two human curves at work in most sessions. One charts the accuracy or precision of taped performances. This is usually an ascending curve: the more takes you do, the more accurate they become (until the players collapse from exhaustion). The other is a descending curve of excitement, enthusiasm, and feel. With groups used to playing a song once on stage, the members generally muster up their best studio energies for the first few takes. After that they get more correct but less vital. This means that everything you do before tape rolls should help save your energies for that first take. When you plan the sessions, ask the engineer to help with optimal preparation for the all-important early takes. Everyone should have enough time to recover from the physical exertion of bringing in equipment before the session really begins. Ask if you can leave your equipment off in the studio or a storage area a couple of hours before your session. If you book sequential sessions, ask to store your big items overnight. If you are worried about theft, call your insurance company ahead and make sure you are covered. If not, buy an *equipment floater* to cover the few days when your things are in the studio. It is inexpensive, especially if the studio is alarmed. In any case, do not count on the studio having third-party coverage.

No one likes to lug equipment up back stairs, set it up in a hurry, then wait for hours while other players get sounds. Find out how much time the engineer thinks it will take to set up each instrument and in what order it should be done. If it will take two hours to get a decent drum sound and half an hour to mike and isolate the piano, why should the rest of the group sit around in the control room or lobby? Tell the drummer to arrive first, the pianist two hours later, and everyone else after that. Boredom in the setup will convert to low energy on the tape. Prepare those who set up first to take a break or get food while the last instruments are miked and their sounds adjusted. Once the session begins, everyone will be locked in the same two rooms for quite a while. A breather before it starts will keep energy up, frustration down.

EFFECTS BOXES AND ACCESSORIES

Studio signal processors are generally quieter and cleaner than portable devices made for stage use. However, if you use foot pedals or other active controls in your performances, insist on trying your own devices before the engineer convinces you to abandon them. No studio equipment can give you the degree of control you are used to with your own devices such as pedal volume controls, "wahs," and flangers. Especially if you are making a gig demo, a little extra noise will not hurt.

However, if you are doing a master, try substituting the studio equivalents for any devices that operate continuously throughout a whole tune—compressors, noise gates, and the like. To get the same overall sound, you will have to interface your own boxes with these studio units in the same order you use on stage. Ask the engineer if the studio's and your input/output levels and impedances will match. Better yet, bring your effects to a preplanning meeting with the engineer. If the control room is available, the engineer can check their input, output, and noise levels, overall distortion, and tendency to overload or clip.

Buy fresh batteries for everything that uses batteries. And just to make sure, put the new batteries in when you begin the sessions. Get the best you can out of every piece of equipment without wasting studio time.

Audio cables can be the weak link in an entire session. Poorly soldered connections, frayed wires, or rusted plugs can cause hours of delay during a session or, worse yet, ruin the sound of your instruments. The longer the guitar cord, the higher its *capacitance,* an electrical parameter that prevents the passage of high frequencies. On stage you may not hear the 10 kHz component of a guitar's output, but in the studio you need its full range. A lot of what makes some synthesizers shrill or metallic is high-frequency loss, the artificial emphasis (electronic oscillation) of one narrow band of highs, or distortion, any of which can be caused by bad cables. The solution is to buy a set of low-capacitance cables for all of your electric instruments. They do not need gold contacts, an audiophile brand name, or the corresponding high price tag. It is the quality of the wire itself and a solid soldering job that count. In cases where you have several effects boxes in a series between the instrument and amp, use low-capacitance cables for each link, even the shortest. It only takes one bad cable, no matter how long or short, to cause problems.

PLANNING FOR PROBLEMS

Do not wait until the session to repair any problems with your instruments, particularly with acoustic instruments that take time to settle in after they are repaired. Do not waste a second of studio time on things that can be done in advance. To do so will cause an emotional strain between the group and player whose "axe" needs work.

Prepare a list of makes and models of everything you will be using in the studio, and give a copy to the engineer during your planning meeting. The engineer may know what guitars have shielding problems and produce hums and which synthesizers are known for being noisy or having a low output level. The engineer may also suggest modifications you can try before the sessions begin or recommend a repair technician who specializes in bringing problem axes up to studio snuff. If it turns out that the problem cannot be fixed in time for the session, rent an alternate instrument. Whatever the cost, it will be less than the cost of endless studio time you could spend trying to work around an incurable problem, or—worse yet—recutting tracks later.

Of course you should bring extra guitar strings, drum keys, perhaps even a backup copy of any floppy disks for sequencing or sound samples. Since you cannot anticipate every disaster, find out if there are music stores near the studio. Studios are often friendly with nearby dealers and can ask for special favors such as delivering items (for a small fee) or even opening the store for a nighttime emergency. Small emergency expenses will more than make up for a session cancelled because of broken snares. Knowing ahead that the local emergency ward will be open can ease your mind and improve your performances.

BUDGET PLANNING WITH THE STUDIO ENGINEER

To help you plan your studio budget, the engineer has to know your bottom-line goals, the level of sound quality you need, and how much studio experience you have. There is no sense in painting a rosy picture. Be frank and honest about possible pitfalls, weak points, lack of experience, or whatever else might affect the product. Take the engineer's suggestions about rehearsing without vocals, at lower levels, or anything that will help you prepare for possible studio shock. And discuss the artists whose sound you would like to emulate.

With all this information, the engineer should be able to tell you your chances of success or failure. If he or she thinks in light of your budget and goals that studio time will be tight, consider dropping one tune from the must list. If your list cannot be shortened, discuss possible timesaving measures, even at the expense of a little sound quality. The important thing is to bring the engineer into the production, to use his or her mind, hands, and ears to achieve your goals. If the lines of communication are open, he or she can be your best critic and your only objective one. And if something goes wrong, he or she is the only critic who will be able to fix it!

If you plan to record basics first and add individual overdubs and vocals later, get used to playing only your rhythm tracks in rehearsal. Note the proper tempos and stick with them. The tendency when performing basics alone is to speed up or become anxious about the lack of vocals and decoration. In the studio, you must be able to put out the same energy when playing basics that you do while performing the full arrangement on stage because any excess tension or lack of energy will be plain as day on tape.

THE PRODUCTION GRID: A PLANNING AND MONEY-SAVING TOOL

Have you ever started a recording and run out of tracks before putting on the last overdubs? Have you ever recorded an instrumental or vocal part on a certain track and left it out of the mix by mistake? Worse yet, has an engineer ever accidentally erased a part of your kick drum or vocal track, either thinking the track empty or not remembering when a sporadic part or harmony occurs during the song? If your studio experience is like mine, the answers to all of the above (and some other flubs too embarrassing to mention) are yes. And what were the costs, emotional and financial, of such mistakes? Certainly more than we would like to admit.

The production grid is not a panacea for such problems. However, it can focus you on planning your multitrack tape as an architect designs a building, help you log exactly what is on each tape track through the entire song, and prevent accidental track erasures and omission of important recording or mixdown tricks. Best of all, the production grid will save you time and money during mixdown. Recently, for example, grids saved at least $5,000 on the mixdowns of the second Full Circle album (entitled *Myth America*) for CBS. We finished twelve fairly complex 24-track mixes and one remix in less than 50 hours, then chose the best nine for the album. Five thousand bucks is a very significant portion of a jazz album budget, so you can imagine how much might be saved on a major label rock or pop project!

Pre-production by the Grid. The production grid is basically a method for noting what is planned for or recorded on each tape track during each musical section of one complete song. The vertical column of boxes (numbered 1 through 24) at the left serves as an ordinary track sheet. Simply list to the left of each box the instrument or vocal that nominally occupies that track. Directly above this column are four numbered boxes for different recorded takes of the song. What makes the grid so useful is the horizontal "time" axis. This allows you to correlate your plans with the actual tape times (noted via tape counter, SMPTE code or whatever) at which each musical section begins during each take of the basic tracks, and the tape times during which you add ovedubbed parts to each track.

When the overall arrangement for a song is finalized during rehearsals or programming sessions, pencil in all the recording decisions that can be planned before setting foot in the studio. First, inscribe the names for each section of the arrangement on the Form line located above the lines for takes 1 to 4, spreading the section names out to use the full width of the line. For example:

Intro   Verse 1   Verse 2   Chorus   Solo   Bridge   Chorus

Now draw vertical lines down to the left of each section name. You now have two grids of boxes. The upper "take grid" has space to note the tape time or SMPTE numbers at which each section of each take begins, and to write in comments on the quality of various sections of each take. Reactions written here during takes and playbacks will help you identify the best overall take or edit pieces of various takes together, and plan extended or shortened versions of the song for later on. Beneath the "take grid" is a second grid of "track boxes" in which to note the contents of each tape track during every verse, chorus, and so forth.

If you are recording more than one song, plan all the production grids so that instruments used in all the songs are always recorded on the same numbered tracks. This applies for instruments recorded in the basics and during overdubs. This kind of planning minimizes the amount of time spent in resetting the console for cue mixes during overdubs, and during the mixdowns themselves. If you plan to synchronize the multitrack with sequencers to add extra "live" tracks during each mix pass, or if you plan to do automated mixdowns via a floppy-disk-based system, save track 1 or 24 (i.e., the last track, whatever that may be) for SMPTE or MIDI data.

If the automation system stores data only on the multitrack itself, save tracks 1 and 2, or 23 and 24, for the data. Remember too that any track immediately adjacent

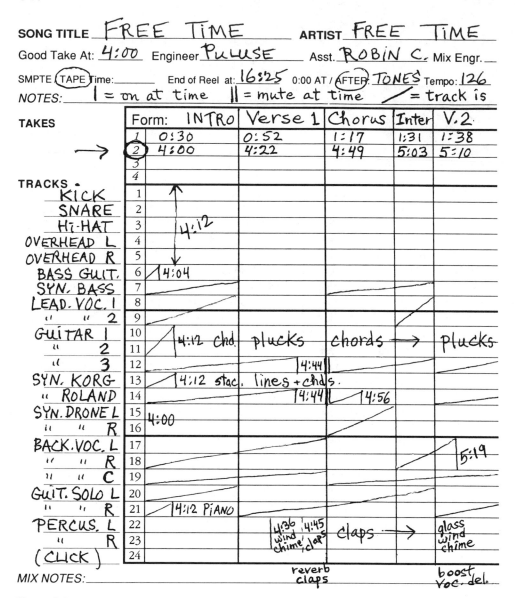

Figure 9.3.   Production grid for the 24-track tape of "Free Time," a pop-rock song

to a track containing SMPTE or MIDI data should not hold any high-level musical transients that could bleed into the data track as crosstalk, potentially rendering the data unusable. A background synth pad or any such smooth sound would be appropriate on a track next to data, keeping the synth's peaks to 0 dBVU, tops.

Planning Overdubs, Insertions and Track Bouncing   If you will need more than the total number of tracks available, and will thus have to bounce some tracks, for example, to double some vocals, plan the layout of the non-bounced tracks so that

PRODUCER W.W./NEWLAND CLIENT BOSTON INT'L.
RCY/DIXON Mix Asst. TOBY ADAMS Studios BKlee A/Syncro

Mix at (Normal) Vari:_____. 15/(30 ips) N/R: ___ Rec. Date 5/85 REEL NO. 2 ✓
muted   short   track done = ✓

Chorus	SOLO	V.3	Chor.	CODA + Fade		
2:05	2:20	2:34	3:02	3:10 —— 3:49		
5:37	5:52	6:06	6:34	6:41 (out 7:28) ←		
					1	24 ↑
			sfz		2	23
			sfz		3	22
	BOOST IN MIX				4	21 ✓
					5	20
					6	19
					7	18 ↓
					8	17 ✓
					9	16 ✓
chords		plucks	chd.	plucks	10	15 ✓
					11	14
plucks			plk.	lines	12	13 ✓
	staccato	lines+chds			13	12 ✓
5:45					14	11
					15	10
					16	9 ✓
					17	8 ↑
				6:48	18	7 ✓
					19	6 ↓
					20	5 ✓
		6:17		6:48 PIANO	21	4
claps	shakers	wood drum shaker	claps	fing. wind c ke cymb chime a cha	22	3 ✓
					23	2
				6:38 6:50 7:12 7:14	24	1
	solo into delays		boost drone	boost Korg Fade at 7:18		

the remaining open tracks are scattered among them, not grouped in one sequentially numbered series. Some multitrack decks cannot bounce material from any track to another immediately adjacent track, so it would be better to have tracks 1, 9, 15, 16, 21 and 22 open after recording basics, rather than tracks 17 through 22. You could then bounce mono signals back and forth among tracks 1 and 9, and stereo pairs among the 15/16 and 21/22 pairs. Clearly, the best way to find out about the studio's synchronization and automation systems, as well as adjacent-bouncing problems, is

SONG TITLE _____ **ARTIST**_____

Good Take At: _____ Engineer_____ Asst._____ Mix Engr. _

SMPTE / TAPE Time:_____ ˙ End of Reel at:_____ 0:00 AT / AFTER: _____ Tempo:_____

NOTES: _____

TAKES

Form:	
1	
2	
3	
4	

TRACKS

1	
2	
3	
4	
5	
6	
7	
8	
9	
10	
11	
12	
13	
14	
15	
16	
17	
18	
19	
20	
21	
22	
23	
24	

_MIX NOTES:_____

Figure 9.4.   Blank production grid to enlarge and use when planning multitrack sessions.

PRODUCER _____ **CLIENT**_____

_____ Mix Asst. _____ Studios _____

Mix at Normal / Vari:_____ 15 / 30 ips   N / R: _____ Rec. Date _____ REEL NO. _____

	1	24
	2	23
	3	22
	4	21
	5	20
	6	19
	7	18
	8	17
	9	16
	10	15
	11	14
	12	13
	13	12
	14	11
	15	10
	16	9
	17	8
	18	7
	19	6
	20	5
	21	4
	22	3
	23	2
	24	1

to ask the engineer ahead of time. By using pencil in all these planning stages, information can be moved to the track line corresponding to the current location of each sound while bouncing and overdubbing proceed.

Once track names have been written to the left of the track number boxes, you will hopefully have some spare tracks (perhaps even stereo pairs) to serve as the "kitchen sink." Any one of these might contain several different sounds, such as a synth line during the choruses, a tambourine part during the solo, and extra background harmonies during the bridge. Pencil in the sound planned for each section of such a track in the "track box" for that section, rather than to the left of the track number. You might simply call a stereo pair, such as tracks 15 and 16, "Sink Left" and "Sink Right" at the left of their track numbers. Similarly, you can write in effects or special treatment that may later be desired during one section of any track. For example, if you want to add a 120-ms delay to the guitar solo, but not the other sections of that guitar track, write this in the track box corresponding to the guitar solo. Use the top and bottom "notes" lines for other info that will insure better takes, overdubs, and mix, for example, click tempos, times when a click might be shut off to allow a freer feel, desired delay times, reverbs, whatever.

Since the form is fairly wide and accommodates long arrangements, the track numbers are repeated in another column at the right to prevent mistakes in notation. The reversed numbers at the extreme right (track 24 at the top, 1 at the bottom) will prevent accidental erasures if you flip the multitrack end for end to create effects such as preverb. For example, it is easy to see that the instrument originally recorded on track 6 will be played backwards on track 19 when the tape is flipped. If track 6 contains the snare drum, the engineer is warned not to put track 19 in record while the tape is flipped. Any amount of planning that can prevent such disasters is clearly worthwhile.

When Tape Finally Rolls. As each take of basic tracks happens, the "take lines" are filled with exact tape or SMPTE times when each musical section starts, and with comments about each section—good or bad—that will help you select a take or sections from which to construct one. Once the best take is identified, circle its number box and rewrite the tape or SMPTE times of each section in pen. All future listening, overdubbing and mixing will be done with respect to these times. At the very least they will minimize the amount of time wasted shuffling around to locate this verse or that chorus. Moreover, you now have exact times for punch-ins and punch-outs on any tracks where overdubs will be entirely contained within named sections of the song. If an overdub begins or ends during a section, note the "in" and "out" tape times of the performance and write these in the appropriate track lines.

Now the fun begins. As recording proceeds I rewrite permanent information in pen. Furthermore, I use a yellow highlighter and green and red ballpoint pens to help prevent erasures and begin assembling mixdown data. When the basics have been recorded, yellow-highlight the numbered track box (in the left column only) of each track with good "keeper" material. This yellow "caution light" warns the engineer or assistant not to erase this track from the top of the tune. For tracks such as drums and bass, or any tracks on which no overdubbing will be done, highlight the numbered track box at the right too. When left and right numbered boxes of a track are yellow, it tells us never to put this track in record again.

Creating Extra Tracks and Planning for Speed-mixing.   For any track containing some good sections not to be erased, and other sections available for later insertions, I yellow in the left number box and the actual sections of that track where the keeper material is, perhaps just one chorus or the solo. This warns against erasure of the good sections of the track and facilitates efficient use of each track as planned, or as new ideas emerge during the session. In this way, it is often possible to put as much separate material on one 24-track tape as some producers might spread out over 46 tracks. If planning ahead can obviate the need for interlocking two multitracks, the dollar savings on 2″ tape and studio time for a major label rock album project could be in the $20,000 to $50,000 range. When all overdubs are finished, the track number boxes should be yellow at the left and right for all tracks used.

Now for the green and red pens. When you are sure of the time at which you first want to hear each track in the final mix, write these "unmuting times" on the corresponding track lines with green ink. Whenever you want to mute a track during the mix, either to eliminate tape hiss during open sections, or to get rid of talking, foot shuffling or unusable musical material, write the mute times on each track line in red ink. If a muted track should pop on again, write in another unmuting time in green, and so forth. For example, if you keep three tracks of lead vocals and decide to construct the final performance from various sections of each during the mix, planning the mute and unmute times ahead will keep you focused on mixing, rather than selecting takes, during the mixdown. You might even draw arrows from the track box for each good section of the vocal to the next track on which another good section begins.

This timing data, together with the green and red markings, serve as a roadmap for the mix session. You will immediately know which tracks have to be brought up in more than one module, perhaps to apply different equalization or processing to various sections of a "kitchen sink" track, or for a short special effect on a track containing only one continuous sound. The complete, color-keyed production grid also enables the engineer to enter all mutes and unmutes into the automation data while you are out of the control room altogether, perhaps working with the musicians, or even taking a well-earned break! Anything you do to facilitate progress in every minute of studio time will save money.

Xerox the blank production grid and enlarge it to 11″ X 17″ for use on your own sessions. The sample grid with data for the song "Free Time" (figure 9.3) maps the actual multitrack tape of this song. This tape is mixed track by track on the second compact disc of the CD package that supplements this text. Use the "Free Time" grid to follow along with the unprocessed tracks or finished mixdown, and to identify each instrument or vocal part as it begins and ends during the arrangement. The tracks are really packed on this production, so "Free Time" a good example of how to stretch 24 tracks to the limit and beyond.

10

DEVELOPING STUDIO EARS AND COMMON SENSE

T HE world of professional recording is changing faster than anyone can follow it. The major complaint I hear from studio engineers and producers is that they cannot learn how to use new equipment fast enough to keep up with clients' demands. A simple example: as synthesizer equipment continues to merge with control-room gear, how much should a good engineer know about synths? Certainly enough to patch their outputs into the board and process the resulting sounds. Perhaps enough to help troubleshoot problems with the MIDI or SMPTE interlock between clients' gear and equipment owned by the studio. For purposes beyond these, let only trained professionals use the synth freely.

TREND AVOIDANCE IN THE RECORDING STUDIO

Musicians must avoid trends in the recording studio by combining a thorough knowledge of their craft with common sense or "good nose." Most important, they must be willing to work hard to achieve results. To those creative minds who have been brainwashed with the false idea that music cannot be made without spending millions, I say that music is at heart an idea, and ideas cost nothing to create. If your ideas are strong enough, you will not need a Stradivarius, Synclavier, or SSL to touch human emotions. Keep in mind what the Beatles achieved on 4-track—with plate reverb yet!

Creativity is the act of turning nothing into something wonderful—fabricating inexpensive, effective audio or visual illusions rather than cash-intensive realities.

116

Greed for gadgets must not replace your drive for human expression. Until you arrive at the top, where Synclaviers come easier, use the best equipment available to you, without carping, and focus your attention on ideas, not fancy packaging.

PRODUCTIVE MONITORING

It can be great fun to *monitor* (play back the takes) at high volumes during recording sessions. After all, most full-size studio monitor speakers will produce undistorted volume levels as high as a rock band generates on stage. However, your finished tape will never be played that loud in the real world, nor will it be played on the same type of speakers. The studio monitors may tell you precisely what's happening below 50 Hz, but the important thing is to know how the tape will sound and feel where it counts—on the bookshelf systems most record company A&R execs have in their offices, on a conventional cassette, and at a volume low enough to allow the listener to take phone calls while listening.

You should conduct critical control-room listening judgments at living-room playback levels. In addition, you should monitor on more than one system, to make sure that your sounds and mix are right on any reproduction equipment. I tend to take a two-pronged approach to getting sounds: First use the large monitors to guide me through patching in various processors and getting a quick approximation of the right quality for each instrument or voice. This allows the engineer to get the whole group up and rehearsing right away, with a good headphone mix. Problems with the very bottom and top end of the frequency spectrum can also be eliminated at this stage.

I normally switch to a bookshelf system or Auratones for fine-tuning. In recent years, variations of Yamaha's NS-10 speakers have become standards for *near-field* monitoring (i.e., using small speakers mounted within five feet of the engineer's position). Placed immediately over the console meter bridge, near-field speakers bypass the acoustics of the control room and bring their own inherent sound to the fore. Instrument resonances that may have escaped your notice on the large monitors will often stand out on a bookshelf system. Beyond this, the lower volume output of the small system will cause less ear fatigue during a long session, which in turn will allow you to make better judgments hours later.

If a project is rock-related—one the listening audience is likely to hear first on radio or in a car—mixing entirely on Auratones is not a bad idea either. In each case, make sure that the studio you book has monitor systems on all three scales: large speakers, bookshelf system, and Auratones. With only one, you can turn out a tape that sounds perfect on that system but has severe problems when played back on anything else.

TUBES, TRANSISTORS, AND INTEGRATED CIRCUITS

The transistor made the development of modern recording equipment possible. Its small size and relatively cool operation enabled lots of components to be put into tiny boxes, without internal meltdown. *Integrated circuits* (known as *ICs* or *chips*) facilitated the next step: the subminiaturization and interface of audio and digitally driven systems, from console automation and interlock to digital recording, mixing, and signal processing. Beyond size and coolth, the finer *solid-state* (transistor and IC-based) systems offer much higher signal-to-noise ratios and less measurable distortion than their earlier tube counterparts.

Tubes were a thing of the past after about 1970, and studios raced to dump all their tube equipment. A decade later, after laboratory bench test comparisons and user-satisfaction studies of tube equipment versus its solid-state counterparts, engineers and producers rediscovered the beauties of tube equalizers, microphones, and compressors. Is this rage motivated by nostalgia, or are there technical reasons that tube equipment may be preferable for certain types of music? Surprisingly, the latter seems to be the case.

First, tube and solid-state devices produce different types of distortion. When a transistor or IC approaches overload, for example, at the onset of a steep signal transient, it produces a high level of *third harmonic distortion.* The third harmonic of any note occurs at three times the notes fundamental frequency and is musically a twelfth (an octave and a fifth) above the note itself, which is its own *first harmonic.* Adding an audible amount of the third harmonics of every sound in a complex signal is dissonant or abrasive to the ear. These distortion products are also perfect fifths, not musically tempered: they sound a bit sharp of normal musical fifth and thus even more grating. The effect is most pronounced in high-level circuits such as power amplifiers. Solid-state circuits for mic and line level signals can be designed with enough headroom to dispense with the problem.

Tube distortion on imminent overload contains mostly the second harmonic, with only a minor component of the third. Since the second harmonic of a tone is its octave, tube distortion is consonant, not dissonant, and thus sounds more pleasing. As a result, in many cases where the measured percentage of tube distortion is much higher than solid-state distortion under similar conditions, the tube distortion is less objectionable. This factor weighs heavily in the design of high-powered guitar amplifiers, where tubes are often used to produce a smoother distortion than ICs. Many amps thus have transistorized preamp circuits and tube power or output stages.

Beyond their less pleasing distortion, the very accuracy of solid-state circuits can give them a cold and clinical sound. ICs have much better transient response than tubes, lower transient distortion, and generally pass signals with a higher degree of faithfulness to their inputs. Yet many instruments, from synthesizers to oboes, create undesirable high frequencies that, when perfectly processed and recorded, produce a less pleasing audio product than when these highs are smoothed out by tube equipment. Synthesizers, for example, generate useless frequencies well beyond 20 kHz as upper partials of square, sawtooth, or triangle waves. If passed on to tape, these frequencies can cause distortion in the audible range, giving the audible highs a harsh, edgy quality.

On the other hand, the close-miking of traditional instruments like the oboe will pick up breath, neck, and phlegm sounds in graphic detail. These also consist of high frequencies, completely unrelated harmonically to the notes being played. Orchestral musicians do their utmost to disguise or mask such sounds and certainly do not want to hear them on tape! Here, too, solid-state circuits may be just too accurate for their own good. A tube condenser mic will smooth out the edgy top end of breathy oboes, sibilant singers, and biting trumpets. When the acoustic levels of these instruments push the mic to its overload point, any distortion in its output will be more consonant than that of the analogous solid-state mic.

The advantages of tube condensers must be taken in perspective, however. For a demo, the difference between tube and solid-state studio equipment is a moot point. Even on a master tape, tube-quality sound can result from careful positioning of a solid-state mic. If all other things about a studio are great, the absence of tube mics would never deter me. I would only let the absence of tube compressors and equalizers affect my studio choice if the intent were to reproduce an authentic 1940s, '50s or '60s sound. To get a real 1960s sound, however, one should record in no more than four tracks and do lots of bouncing too.

DIGITAL VERSUS ANALOG RECORDING

In *analog recording* the waveform is a continuous representation of the original signal, and in *digital recording* the original signal is stored as numerical data that is reconverted to an analog waveform during playback. There may be some listeners whose auditory systems are sensitive enough to hear the steps associated with the sampling rates of various digital record/playback systems, but frankly I doubt it. The vast majority of listeners have long decided that the improved frequency response, signal-to-noise ratio, and distortion specs of digital systems are more than worth the slight, often elusive, thin or edgy quality that some detractors cite as a major problem. Since such complaints were first aired, engineers have learned to mike for digital more carefully than for analog in order to get the same full, rich bass that analog systems produce.

The main argument now is cost effectiveness. Through 1989, the digital equipment required to functionally duplicate the contents of a good 24-track analog recording and mixing studio cost about three to six times more than an analog system. Remember that the increased accuracy of digital recording itself can mandate more expensive consoles, outboard signal processors, and—most expensive of all—much quieter studios themselves to take advantage of digital's 100-dB signal-to-noise ratio.

Does all this expense actually sell more records? So far there is no correlation between digital recording of master tapes and chart position or proven sales levels, except in jazz, classical, new age music, and other so-called secondary sales categories. The reason is that sales of rock and pop are still motivated largely by radio play, and the sound quality of most radio reception and home reproduction is still far below that of the finest LP. Labels are much more anxious to acquire a jazz, classical, or new age master tape if it is recorded or at least mixed digitally. But in rock it is still the musical impact that counts most.

The Society of Professional Audio Recording Studios (SPARS) coined a three-letter code that is now printed somewhere on the rear panel of most CD jewel box inserts. This code tells us whether the recording, mixing, and final mastering of the pressing was done via digital or analog means. A code rating of AAA means that all three stages were done analog, while a DDD indicates full digital preparation.

Obviously, the codes of all CDs end with a D. Any album originally recorded before 1976 will have a code beginning with A, since there were no digital recorders until that date. However, buyers do check SPARS codes, and surveys have shown that a classical recording with an ADD code will sell better than another performance of the same piece coded AAD, when other variables such as a famous name are constant.

Costs aside, many producers and artists feel that analog and digital have separate but equally valuable strong points and resist abandoning analog, even when money is no object. For instance, analog recorders exhibit a smooth overload behavior and distortion characteristics not unlike that of tube equipment. Controlled analog tape saturation gives transient signals like drums a physical punch that is lacking in digital. This effect derives from the fact that magnetic tape takes an instant to respond to the sudden application of an intense field by the record head. Called *hysteresis,* this delayed reaction gives the impression that such transients have been gently compressed by the tape itself. In the end, the choice between analog and digital is a matter of taste. In an interview with *Recorder Engineer/Producer,* Daniel Lazerus picks up on the digital versus analog controversy:

I have done a lot of work in the digital domain—*The Nightfly* is entirely digital [3M multitrack; mix to Sony PCM 1610]—and I've found that there's something missing in recording purely digital. It's almost like you can have something too pure, too clean. You listen to *Sgt. Pepper* or *My Generation* by the Who—those sessions were done on analog two-tracks, or four-tracks, or coupled four-tracks. And there's something wonderful about the analog sound of those records.

You see, there's a way that I like to record, if I can. What I like to do is use an older Neve console, record on an A-800 Studer, use Scotch 226 tape at +6 elevated level, hit the tape very hard, and cut my basic tracks that way. There's a tape compression effect that happens—particularly with drums—and, recorded properly, it's so clean and strong. Then I immediately transfer those tracks to digital. . . . For me, the digital domain works better in the overdub and mix stages.

Engineer Bruce Swedien, who won a Grammy for his work on Michael Jackson's *Thriller* album, reveals his assessment of digital technology to Alan di Perna in a recent issue of *Mix* magazine:

A.P.: You work with both digital and analog?

B.S.: Oh, yes. Digital is wonderful, and I use it a lot; but I have not been able to cut analog recording loose entirely. That analog sound is impossible to deny. So I use my Studer A800, and I also have an MCI 16-track. I record all the drums and percussions on 16-track analog, non-Dolby. I record all of Michael [Jackson]'s vocals on analog, too. I'll do several takes, then composite the vocals to digital.

A.P.: What qualities do you like about digital?

B.S.: What digital does well, it does so dramatically well that there's really nothing to talk about. But one thing that's important to me is this: once I've captured the warmth and beauty of analog recording, I can transfer it to digital, and it will always be there.

A.P.: [About a new Quincy Jones album now in progress] At what point do you generally get involved in a composition that Quincy is doing?

B.S.: It's hard to say, but my input is there right along . . . virtually from the beginning. Quincy will run songs by me and ask me how I feel about them.

A.P.: He'll just show you songs on the piano?

B.S.: Yeah. Or play me a demo from someone else. And he'll say "What do you think of this song? What do you think we could do with it? How could we put our unique touch on it?"

A.P.: How do you generally approach remixes for singles?

B.S.: Well, on anything I do—this isn't peculiar to Michael's records—I always like to challenge the original mix. By the time I remix something I've been away from the song for a while and I've got a fairly objective ear for it. But many times there are songs, like "Man in the Mirror" on *Bad*, that I won't remix. The performance of "Man" was absolutely inspired—the whole recording, right down to the mix.

A.P.: There is something other-worldly about the choir on there.

B.S.: Isn't it unbelievable? I recorded that here in Westlake Studio D, with just two microphones. That song is a perfect example of combining modern recording techniques with a classic stereo choir recording, using a pure X-Y with its resultant acoustical support. It just cried out for that, and the emotional impact, as a result of that acoustical support, is incredible. Multiple microphones would have destroyed the emotion of that moment. You see, what excites me about recording pop music today is that ability to combine natural ambiences with the sort of spaces that could never exist in reality.

A.P.: Do you use the same mix for each release format of a record—vinyl, CDs, cassettes?

B.S.: Absolutely.

A.P.: Aren't you conscious of those different formats and their qualities when you're mixing?

B.S.: Not usually, because the music and the emotion transcend all that.

STUDIO MAINTENANCE

Even the most expensive digital equipment is useless if improperly maintained. In fact, it stands to reason that the more expensive and complex a studio's equipment is, the more maintenance it needs to stay in top form. That is why it is important for you to determine how well a studio takes care of its equipment. Do not assume that because a control room is clean, the console and recorders are well kept.

There are a number of ways to judge a studio's attitude about maintenance. First, if you get a chance to look at the studio schedule, see if there are regular blocks of time set aside for routine preventative maintenance. If not, the studio probably pays attention to maintenance only when devices actually break or fail in service. You might also ask to peek at the maintenance area or room. No studio can stay in shape without a hearty stock of parts and a thorough set of test equipment—from the ubiquitous soldering iron to oscilloscopes and a host of other curative gadgets. A bare maintenance room implies infrequent and summary checking of equipment performances.

Finally, ask for the names of one or two clients who have recorded your kind of music there. Find out whether there was much downtime or repeated breakdowns and malfunctions during their sessions. Ask if the engineer cleaned the heads regularly and checked the recorders with test tapes. More important, if any of these past clients later overdubbed or mixed their tapes elsewhere, did the other studios notice any problems with the original tapes—low levels, improper operation of noise reduction, uneven frequency response in the playback of any test tones that had been recorded by the original engineer?

Such factors are especially important if you are making master tapes, since it is more likely they may be remixed elsewhere. Remember that your entire investment is riding on the maintenance procedures at the studio where you record basic tracks. If something is wrong, it will not be fixable in the mix.

For a sad demonstration of failed maintenance, flip through various cuts on the CD of The Band's second album (called *The Band*), comparing stereo to mono. A complete studio was moved into the group's house for these sessions. Although it is hard to pinpoint what went wrong, it seems the console had phasing problems, while the multitrack and mix machines were variously misaligned during some of the recording and mixdown sessions. In mono, the hi-hat and cymbals on several cuts sound like trash cans because of phasing problems. Some of the vocalists develop instant sinus problems, and one or two instruments seem to virtually disappear, leaving only a wisp of reverb. Yet in stereo, the album works quite well.

Poor studio maintenance does not seem to have affected sales, which only proves that when the music is great, nothing can stand in the way of a hit.

BASIC PROBLEMS IN THE RECORDING PROCESS

T HIS chapter examines some of the flaws in the logic of the system that underlie the entire process of multitrack recording. The way sessions are conducted has evolved from one set of needs and quite a separate set of possible solutions. Moreover, studio engineering is a craft that is usually learned piecemeal, by observation and reading, rather than by an organized period of intense study. Seldom does an engineer have the musicians, equipment, and studio time available to experiment systematically with miking techniques. Rather, an engineer reads that so-and-so got a good bass sound by using one technique, tries the technique on a paying gig, notes the results, and moves on.

Many engineers have never had the time to examine their own medium under the microscope of logic. The pressure of a studio clock numbered in dollar signs urges them to do things automatically, not as they might if there were time to consider the task from the ground up. The chapters in part three can be used like a cookbook. You will find recipes for drum sounds, bass, piano, vocals, and the rest. The compact discs that are available for this volume even give you a taste of many of these recipes, and the booklet a list of ingredients and procedures. If you are in a hurry, you can whip up a decent sound. And if your kit has mechanical and audio problems, you will find standard and home remedies for many of them.

My long-term objective, however, is to impart an ability to think and resolve new problems as they come up; to demystify the science of recording and help you develop a real knack for it; and to understand two crucial facts that underlie the studio work of every great engineer and producer in the industry:

1. the difference between the human ear and the entire collection of equipment called a recording studio
2. the difference between what the human ear *receives* and *per*ceives

Remember that recording is an art of illusion—more like painting than like photography. The only way an engineer can "photograph" a live musical performance is with stereo mikes in row E of a concert hall. In the studio the engineer does not photograph reality but creates it! The finished product—a mixed master tape—is built piece by piece, and each piece is handcrafted from the musical and technical resources at hand. Every technical decision the engineer makes interprets and, ideally, augments the performers' musical and emotional intentions.

Thus, there is no such thing as an objective recording. If you, as a musician, want to achieve specific recorded effects, you must learn to analyze the sounds produced by a wide variety of instruments, know the capabilities and limitations of all the utensils in the studio kitchen, and finally understand the logical and associative processes that enable a good engineer to reach instinctively for the few buttons or dials that will give you the desired sound or feel. In short, you must learn how the engineer thinks. What the engineer does will then follow naturally.

INSTRUMENTS, VOICES, AND SPACES

Until thirty years ago—when an electric guitar was first input with a DI box and heard through headphones—no one had ever heard a musical sound without a room or space around it. For a moment, recall the sound of your favorite instrument. Chances are, even in memory, your mind will add some kind of room sound—reverb, echo, warmth—to the dry sound of the instrument itself. The musical experience is thus intimately tied up with a judgment of the kind of environment in which each listener prefers to hear music.

Furthermore, without realizing it, most listeners have a preferred location with respect to the musical source. Just as various moviegoers instinctively head for the front or rear of the theater, some music listeners like to be near the music—surrounded by it at full volume—while others prefer to stand back and consider it at a distance, like a large painting or sculpture.

For example, a pianist rarely hears his or her own instrument from an audience's viewpoint. If given a choice of two recorded sounds—one for which the mics were placed over his or her own head at the keyboard, another with the mics ten feet to the right of the keyboard (a listener's perspective)—the pianist will often choose the first. Why? Because that is how the piano sounds to the performer: it is the sound the pianist is used to. Most nonpianist listeners, who hear the instrument live and on recordings, choose the second mic position for the same reason. Which position is right? The mics themselves have no judgment capability, nor is there an objective truth about which piano sound is right. The right sound is simply the one that pleases the listener for whom the recording is being made.

Ideally, when recording more than one instrument at a time, we would mike each from a preferred position, as though the others were not there at all. We might want the piano miked at ten feet and the drums tightly miked à la rock. Clearly, this is impossible in any reasonably sized studio, since distant piano mics will pick up considerable leakage from the drums. When all the mic signals are combined, this leakage will produce horrendous interference problems. To a much lesser extent the piano sound will leak into the drum mics and produce similar interference.

This is the central problem in recording groups and ensembles. The need for individual control of sounds is at odds with the way we might otherwise mike each instrument and often with the players' needs for visual and physical communication. We stand to lose great sound and a great performance in the bargain.

Many producer/engineers, including Hugh Padgham who produced *Synchronicity* for The Police and *Face Value* for Phil Collins, feel that today's engineers work at a disadvantage because of the prevalence of close-miking in the 1970s. Many have never recorded full orchestras or even large string sections. Instead, the current trend is toward distant miking, moving mics in or adding punch with close mics if more edge and bite is required. For example, the enormous drum sounds on *Face Value* were created by mics located between 9′ and 15′ from the drum kit.

Many of the tracks for *Face Value* were Phil Collins' 8-track demos, transferred to 24-track for extra overdubbing and final mixing. At least two of the cuts in the finished album were even the rough mixes that Mr. Collins made at home. Somehow, expensive rerecording and mixing of the same songs at the finest studios could not recapture the feel and energy of the tapes made at home. We can be thankful that the artist and producer recognized this and decided to release the better performances, not the better recordings.

Commenting similarly on the necessity of custom synth sounds, Sting has said that he is not very fussy about having special patches. He usually runs through all the factory-supplied patches, selects one that works best for the intended use, and records that without further ado. The important thing is to get on with the music while the musician is focused on it.

CLOSE MIKING

When two desirable goals cannot be achieved, compromise is the solution. In recording, this compromise is *close* or *tight miking*. In theory, the closer we mike any instrument, the less the leakage from others playing in the same space. By the book, every time we move a mic halfway from its initial position to the sound source, the resulting signal should be 6 dB higher (on a VU meter). Thus, if we keep lowering the gain to maintain the same VU level on the desired instrument, each time we move the mic in, the level of other instruments leaking into the mic should decrease by 6 dB. To achieve any desired degree of isolation, just tighten the miking on all instruments until all leakage is below the problem level.

By now, however, we may have sacrificed our preferred listening positions on every instrument. In fact, we might be so close to the instruments that they no longer sound anything like themselves, even to the players! For example, listen to an acoustic guitar or piano from the player's position, then put your head as close to the guitar's body or piano's soundboard as you can get. The most delicate guitar now sounds bigger, boomier, crisper, more metallic. The piano is more percussive, aggressive.

And now you hear every finger-slide and fret noise on the guitar strings, every pedal and damper movement of the piano action. In compromising to solve one problem— leakage—we created three new ones:

1. The entire sound of the room is gone because of our proximity to the sound source.
2. We hear every mechanical noise the instrument makes, noises that are normally lost in the room noise.
3. The mic hears mostly that part of the instrument's body that is closest to it. We are not even hearing the entire instrument.

To correct the first problem, the engineer can use reverb and effects devices to simulate the original room or any other desired performance space. The problem of mechanical noise of the instrument can be partially remedied by processing the mic signal (with equalization, etc.) to sound more like the signal that might be received by the same mic in our preferred position. For the third problem the engineer could use a more highly directional microphone (e.g., super- or hyper-cardioid) and move it back a bit from the source. But that could play tricks with the quality of the leakage from other instruments, such as off-axis coloration. Each of these corrections necessitates secondary compromises, like taking pills to counteract the side effects of other pills: Where does it all end?

The answer depends on two factors:

1. Which of the compromises involved (if any) has side effects that are better for the music to be recorded than placing the mics in their preferred position?
2. How much time is consumed in solving the problems that each compromise creates?

Concerning the first factor, perhaps the piece of music to be recorded is intended to have a light honky-tonk feel, and the added percussiveness of close piano miking gives more of a "tack" piano sound—like an antique upright. The second factor is a very important one for two reasons. First, studio time is expensive, and the more time spent on solving engineering problems, the less time is left for the players to record music. Second, musicians and singers can only maintain their enthusiasm through a limited amount of getting-sounds time. Ideally, they would set up and tune instruments, get a headphone mix (if phones are used), and begin doing takes. The best sounds on earth cannot revive a musical groove that died during the drum miking. The engineer's ultimate compromise, then, is to start recording when the music is ready to be played, almost regardless of the status of any effort to refine each sound to a state of perfection.

LOCAL RESONANCES

Piano and acoustic bass are examples of the if-the-mic's-too-close-you're-not-hearing-the-entire-instrument syndrome. The soundboard of a concert grand is over thirty square feet in area. When the pianist strikes a note, the board begins to vibrate, but not all at once. Since wood has slight variations in local thickness and density, the entire surface can act like a steel drum, with a number of small areas tuned to different pitches but all a part of one large surface. Areas of the soundboard that resonate at the note played will vibrate eagerly, while another area may be totally dead at that frequency.

Such *local resonances* and dead spots make little difference to a live audience because they are blended and smoothed out as vibrations from the entire board meld and travel the distance to the tenth row. However, if an engineer places one mic just a few inches over a hot spot and another over a dead spot for the same frequencies, the response of the resulting so-called stereo piano tracks will be riddled with imbalances, representing only how two small parts on the soundboard react to vibrations over the entire frequency range of the keyboard.

Worse yet is the acoustic bass, which has both body and air resonances. Every enclosed volume of air resonates at one or more frequencies by virtue of its own dimensions and the elastic characteristics of air itself. The larger the volume of air, the lower its resonant frequency, and if it has three different dimensions, each will have a separate resonance. Unfortunately, the internal dimensions of a bass are not large enough to place its primary air resonances below the musical range of the instrument. Similarly, various wooden surfaces of the instrument may resonate at distinct frequencies. Thus, at least three frequencies will be reinforced by air resonances, and another two or more by body resonances. When played as bass notes, all of these frequencies will be louder than nonresonant notes.

Since vibrations spread over the body surface as in the piano soundboard, a good bass can be designed so that body resonances in the front or back plate, top or bottom lobe, partially cancel or phase out some of its air resonances. As with the piano, this self-damping effect will take full effect only at a distance. However, if the engineer places a mic right in front of a hot spot for one or more of these resonances, the damping effect will be lost.

PHASING

A side view of the acoustic-bass soundboard shows us another common recording problem with acoustic sources. At certain frequencies, while one area of the surface is vibrating upward, other areas must be moving down. If we want to record the instrument in stereo and happen to place the two mics right over these spots, the signal from one mic is always out of phase with that from the other, at least at this frequency. If we combine the two mics to get mono, this frequency—and any others for which these positions behave similarly—may be entirely phased out.

For instruments with large soundboards, no pair of close-miking locations will be completely free of this phenomenon. Some pairs may in fact phase out one frequency while radically reinforcing others. I have seen instances where phasing skews the overall recording response of an instrument by 12 dB and more. On the other hand, if the instrument is inherently unbalanced, careful "poor" miking can cancel out the instrument's own problems and restore a good recorded sound quality.

The three-dimensionality of many instruments, even very small ones, derives from local effects and how they play with the acoustic environment. For example, the

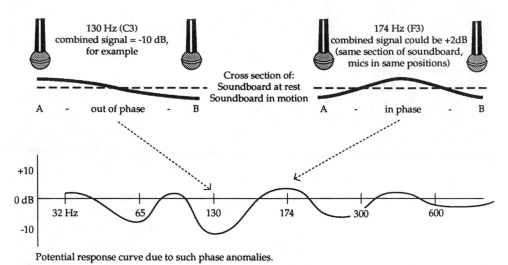

Potential response curve due to such phase anomalies.

Figure 11.1.   Two mics placed over areas of a soundboard that happen to be acoustically in phase at one frequency (174 Hz), then out of phase at another (130 Hz), and the frequency response that could result when the mic signals are combined into mono

sound emanating from a bell may seem to rotate around its source, with certain harmonics panning left and right as the bell continues to ring. This is in fact what is happening. Sound waves travel around the metal surface, sending out resonant frequencies in circular beacons, some tones moving clockwise, others counterclockwise. Because highs travel in straight beams, as these beacons sweep around the source, they also bounce off nearby walls or surfaces, magnifying the "stereosity" of the bell.

In the end, any two mic positions are only as good as their summation. Check stereo miking for phase problems when they are heard in mono. We will discuss assorted resonance and phasing phenomena further in part three.

MULTIMIKING

The more microphones used on a single instrument, or in close proximity on a number of nearby instruments, the more phasing problems. In a drum kit, for example, the engineer obviously intends the snare mic(s) as the principal source for snare drum sound. But the snare is also picked up by the hi-hat mic, the tom-tom mics, and the overheads. Thus, the composite snare sound will be the sum of signals from up to six mics, all at different distances from the snare drum itself. It would be simple if the other mics produced snare signals completely in or out of phase with those from the snare mics themselves. However, the other mics may be at distances from the snare drum that are some fraction of the wavelength of the snare's fundamental overtones. The six-mic composite contains partial reinforcement and cancelation at a whole assortment of frequencies. (Remember that the wavelength of a sound is the distance in air that is encompassed by one full vibration of the sound's frequency.

Thus, with sound traveling at 1,100 feet per second in air, the wavelength of a 200 Hz sound created by a snare drum would be 1,100/200, or 5.5 feet.)

The same is true in a brass section miked by a stereo pair plus close-mics on individual instruments. The close-mics are within a foot of their instruments, while the pair may be ten feet from the entire section. Each sound wave reaches the distant pair later than the close-mic, so it is difficult to determine what phase relationships exist in the final section mix.

For audio purists, there is another problem. When an ensemble is heard by a stereo pair, the relative position of each instrument from left to right is clear and consistent. However, multimiking places the listener's ears in a number of different places at once. If the engineer is not careful to pan the individual mics into the same L/R positions at which each instrument appears in the stereo pair, there will be more than one apparent position for each instrument, a smeared stereo image of the entire ensemble.

CLOSE MIKING AND THE ORDER OF SIGNAL-PROCESSING DEVICES

Picking up mechanical sounds made by the instrument is the other side of the close-miking problem. In a live performance, these sounds are masked or covered by ambient and audience noise. In the studio, compression of close-miked sources tends to increase the relative level of breaths, valve, fret, key, action, or pick sounds. Beyond this, close-miking picks up the continued ring or release (in envelope terms) of percussions from drums to piano and plucked instruments from guitar to harpsichord. Fortunately, all these undesirable side effects point the way toward a sensible methodology for applying processing to close-miked sources.

So far we have identified two types of unwanted sounds: those that precede and follow the desirable part of an instrument's sound and those frequencies that are unnaturally reinforced or canceled by close-miking (such as local resonances). Since the signal-to-noise ratio of tape is the weakest link in the entire recording chain, it is best to get rid of both these problems as soon as signals enter the console. First apply destructive processing, then add your constructive processing to taste. The same logic applies in cooking: the chef cleans a chicken and discards waste before dressing and cooking it!

Resonances can add many decibels to the signal level of a sound, so if objectionable resonances are present, the first signal processing device should be a parametric equalizer. We can find and dip resonances with narrow bandwidths, as discussed earlier. The resulting usable signal can then be boosted to take full advantage of the S/N ratio of circuits that follow, and of the tape itself. Next, we should apply noise gating to reduce or eliminate mechanical sounds between good notes. The pluck of a string or a percussive hit are sounds that can be lessened by selecting an attack time slightly longer than the envelope attack of the instrument itself. Release problems can then be treated by careful setting of the hold and fade times (or whatever these parameters are called on the noise gates at hand). The decibel reduction applied to both of these is determined by the floor or range control.

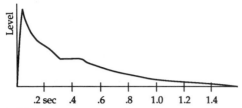

A. The raw tom-tom sound envelope.

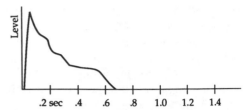

D. The drum's envelope after noise-gating which shortens the tom's ring. Some of the changes in the decay section are due to destructive parametric EQ applied before gating.

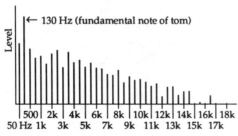

B. The envelopes of three selected frequencies from the original raw sound. Note that higher frequencies fade to zero level quicker than lower ones in this drum sound.

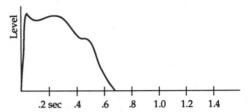

E. Same, after compression for a fuller sound.

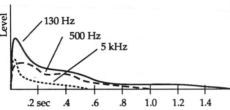

C. Graph of the relative amplitudes of various frequencies present in the original tom tom sound, measured over the complete 1.6 second envelope (A).

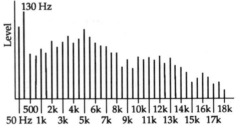

F. Graph of frequency content of the compressed signal (E), after final in-board EQ to feature the attack and fundamental of the drum.

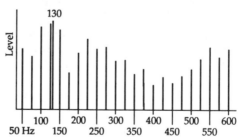

G. Expanded version of F. showing the levels of frequencies from 50 Hz to 600 Hz in more detail. Note the narrow dip at 175 Hz a narrow-band resonance eliminated via parametric before gating, and the broader dip around400 Hz, introduced by in-board EQ in F.

Figure 11.2.   One note played on a tom-tom showing changes made to the envelope and/or frequency content after successive stages of processing

The resulting sound is cleaned of waste. Now it can be compressed and equalized (if necessary) in preparation for recording. However, once resonances are gone, many sounds need no compression. This is particularly true of acoustic guitar and bass and other hollow-bodied instruments, even an electric bass. Dipping one or two resonances can balance the response of the entire neck or fretboard. The same is true of amplified guitars, where the body of the speaker and cabinet can wildly boost some frequencies and cancel others. Even if the instrument now needs no equalization, a little brightening during recording will eliminate the need for a treble boost during mixdown, thereby helping to fight tape noise in the bargain.

By processing in this order, the signal level that goes to tape will be entirely usable in the mix. You may even be able to dip highs at that stage. The best possible S/N ratio is therefore preserved right through to the final mixdown, an important consideration when CDs and DATs continue to spoil listeners who once accepted tape noise as a part of recorded music. We will see exactly how this logic helps with specific instruments in part three.

RECORDING DECISIONS

One of the biggest flaws in multitrack recording is a user rather than a system problem. Because there may be 24 or more tracks, engineers encourage producers and artists to defer final decisions about music and sound until the mixdown session. Should you play each instrument straight through the arrangement, put in optional fills, a flange on the synth track, a delay on this chorus of the lead vocal? As a musician and producer, I strongly advise that you make these decisions before recording and put most or all of the effects you want right on the multitrack. The mixdown is the weakest link in the chain. Everything in it has to be accomplished in real time. Worrying about details will take attention away from the overall feel, and feel is what a first-time listener must have. If the build, feel, groove, and right emotional quality do not come through loud and clear, the right flanging or DDLs on this or that track will not matter at all. Think "forest first"—then paint in the trees, if there is time!

The cost factor is also a major consideration. It is often a simple operation to add an effect during recording, even if it requires manual gain-riding by the engineer or a member of the group. In the mix, the effect may require an extra module. How many are there? How many extra mix passes will it take to mute/unmute and blend the effect in properly? Time is money. Beyond this, I believe it is good artist training to make irrevocable creative decisions and live with them. It sharpens your wits and forces you to think precisely about why you want each effect and to consider whether it is worth the extra time and trouble to achieve it.

ADDING EFFECTS

There are three good reasons that you should refrain from subtlety in the amount of reverb and effects you add to your tracks and the mix.

1. Listening audiences are jaded by the heavy and elaborate effects used in many pop and rock releases. Like someone whose palette has been blunted

by a heavily spiced appetizer, they may entirely miss subtle spicing in the main dish, even though a gourmand would praise the artist's admirable restraint. Producers are gourmands, but they buy few records. Critics, like the public, have been getting more than their share of "jalapeño" engineering. If you want a texture or sound noticed, do not be sparing.

2. As an artist, you know every effect you are adding to the music: when it begins and ends, what created it, and why it is there. The audience has no such prior knowledge and furthermore will not be listening first for little touches. If you want these effects to have an effect on the listener's first impression, you must bring them up higher or louder than satisfies your own taste, just to make sure they are noticed.

3. The average listener's living room is not a studio control room. It has its own reverb and a lot of ambient noise masking subtle components in the mix and neighbors who prevent the listener from playing the music loud enough to hear them. It seems strange, but you have to fight the flaws in the listening environment with a heavy hand on the spice rack during mixdown.

Again, adjust reverb and effects levels by listening to your mix in mono and over Auratone or other small speakers. Since these speakers have limited frequency response and cannot be played at studio levels, elements that are too subtle will not be heard at all on them. Moreover, monitoring in mono simulates how your record will sound when listeners are not seated right between their speakers. Think how often you listen to music from the next room or from an off-center chair or sofa, where stereo effects are minimized.

You can now see that the recording studio is a very deceptive environment. The sound quality it provides is both an asset and a liability in making creative decisions that will convey the fullest potential of your music. Let each mic, module, and signal processor make a clear and audible statement in the less-than-perfect acoustics of the urban living room. In this way, recording art must imitate life, because in the real world, the reverse is quite impossible.

Part III

RECORDING INDIVIDUAL INSTRUMENTS AND SECTIONS

INTRODUCTION

Some instruments walk into the studio ready to be recorded. They sound wonderful and need little if any signal processing before taping. Unfortunately this is not true of most instruments. In the following chapters I have assumed the worst, that everything possible is wrong with the instruments discussed. That is why you will read about seemingly endless sequential processing: notch filter, then gating, then compression, then re-equalization, then reverb. In the worst case you might need to do all this and more to get a usable sound from any one mic or input.

Only by revealing all the possible problems and suggesting solutions can I give you a feel for how to listen to a raw sound, recognize its strengths and weaknesses, then instinctively reach for the one, two, or six devices that will turn what you have into what you want. Your instinct is probably suspect if you wind up using several devices on every mic in the session, but do not be afraid to try anything that might logically pull a sound in the right direction. If your trick does not have the desired result, admit it and throw away the five minutes it took to try. Even then the time is not wasted, because you have added a new trick to your toolkit for some other session. Remember that beyond this particular session lies the rest of a career!

Bear in mind as well that there is no "right" order, either for setting up mics and getting various sounds during record or for processing tracks and building the final mix. The chapters on individual instruments are roughly in the order I prefer to process and perfect individual sounds during mixdown. Normally, I get a rough drum and bass sound first, then add the lead vocal or instrument, perfecting its sound and optimizing the blend of the drum and bass structure with the actual melody or song.

To that basic blend I add various single instruments and sections, beginning with those that are most important to the specific song and ending with the decorative touches. In no case do I change the vocal or lead sound very much to accommodate a rhythm or backup sound. Rather, the level and sound of each accompanying sound should help support and highlight the lead. If the piano rhythm part needs to be highly compressed and sound a bit thinner than in real life, so be it. There is no loyalty to individual sounds, only to the betterment of the entire recording. Very often, when the sounds all work properly with the lead vocal or instrument, the listener will believe that each sound is perfect on its own. The right compromise persuades the untrained ear that no changes were ever made.

You may think, "Why go into certain engineering topics in such detail? After all, I won't be engineering my own session." I firmly believe that musicians can really understand the deepest and most intuitive truths about good recording—without math and physics—if they are willing to exercise their logic and use their ears objectively. The fact that engineers approach the same subject matter through more rigorous math tells me only that most engineers have more technical than musical backgrounds and that they are paid to operate the studio equipment. They must know its inner workings as well as you know your guitar or drums. In terms of getting good sounds, however, either the intuitive or the technical approach can bring you to the goal. The real magic is in recognizing what each song or production needs.

Lastly, if you read the entire book, you will find reviews and expansions of many topics already covered. As a musician, I know how I read, and I assume that drummers will not automatically plow through chapters on woodwinds and vice versa (although there is much to be gained by doing so!). Even if you do make it to the end, it will probably be in many short readings—here a chapter, there a few pages. In this light, some ongoing recentering is necessary. When you come upon a familiar topic, do not skip ahead; it usually reappears in a new context, with at least some new light thrown on it. In a world that bombards you with so much data, the important things bear restating.

12

DRUMS

$\mathbf{E}$VEN if you do not play drums, read this chapter. Many of the basic concepts, techniques, and tips of good recording are most graphically illustrated with the drum kit. Although these principles will be used in later chapters, the underlying logic will be demonstrated only once. In addition, this chapter contains data on studio microphones and other equipment that will be useful to all readers.

Again, these chapters are written as though the reader will engineer his or her own recordings. If you are indeed able to work at top studios with seasoned engineers, you may not need to comprehend problems and processes in such depth. However, no one works in a vacuum. Creative ideas often spring from understanding how others approach their crafts. I hope some of what follows will turn on lights and foster tighter working relationships among those on both sides of the control room window, who must strive together for that magic sound, take, or mix.

BASIC PROBLEMS

The drum kit is the most complex of instruments to record, if for no other reason than because it actually consists of between seven and twenty separate instruments in close physical proximity. In an effort to maintain separate control of the level and sound of each drum and cymbal, the engineer encounters every problem we have discussed and more. Setting up, miking, and processing drums can take half the total setup time for a complete session. By applying a little common-sense analysis and a taking a few precautions, you can help minimize setup time and guarantee a solid sound every time.

The best single tip I can give is this: do not make the job any more difficult than necessary. Think of how the drums function in your music, and plan the simplest possible setup to make them work. For example, a small jazz drum kit consists of kick (bass) drum, snare, one rack tom, one floor tom, hi-hat, ride, and crash cymbals. Buyers of traditional and progressive jazz records are not used to the same kind of tight-miked, highly compressed sound that is expected in pop or rock records. Moreover, jazz drummers are often more concerned with texture and dynamics, and with keeping the feel of a unified set, than with maximum separation and punch on each drum.

The best and most objective miking for the jazz sound is a simple spaced pair of overheads—omnis or broad cardioid. This makes sense because, except for the kick, all the drums and cymbals face upward. If the cymbals are up on high stands or booms, and thus closer to the mics and artificially loud in the blend, cheat the mics back a bit. The only other absolutely necessary mic is on the kick drum, and this is mainly to pick up light hits that might otherwise get lost in the drummer's cymbal work. If the snare needs more punch, the engineer can creep in a close mic on the top skin and blend it into (not dominate or override) the snare sound from the over-heads. No noise gates, no compression, just the unaltered sound of the kit and the performance. While there will be leakage from other instruments in the studio, and considerable room sound in the drum tracks, and while we will not be able to flange the toms in the mixdown, we will capture the ensemble sound of the drum kit exactly as it sounds in real life—and in just a few minutes. The rest is up to the drummer.

I cite this example to dispel the impression that miking drums takes fifteen mics, twenty processors, and a PhD. A decent sound is easily achievable for almost any genre of music, but more than this takes a bit of creative deception. The most common complaint about studio drum recordings is that they just do not capture the sound of the performer's kit. This complaint is mistaken because, more often than not, the kit sounds fine on tape: what is really missing is the room sound, the physical impact of a set played at live volume, and the sweat and energy the drummer puts out while playing.

Drums Without Rooms. Musicians generally like the way their instruments sound live. They select and buy instruments based on their sound in a showroom and adjust them to sound good in the rehearsal room or live on stage. Rarely, if ever, does the musician hear only the instrument, without the added sound of a room. Let us examine the components of a snare drum heard at various distances (figure 12.1).

The drummer whose ears are three feet from his snare hears the direct sound first, then early reflections from the floor, ceiling, and four walls, each spaced from 3–30 milliseconds (ms) after the others. Since the speed of sound in air (at 70°F) is about 1,100 feet per second, every foot the sound travels from its source to the drummer's ears delays the bounced sound about one millisecond. You can calculate the contributions of early reflections to the sound of your kit in your own rehearsal space. Because the ear cannot distinguish sounds separated by less than about 30 ms, this short burst of early reflection repeats is perceived as part of the drum's inherent sound and seems to prolong its initial impact.

With a mechanical beater capable of duplicating a snare hit, test equipment, and an *anechoic chamber* (a room lined with thick sound-absorbent material so that no sound bounces back from walls, floor, or ceiling), we might find that a certain drum's transient (the initial attack and decay of its envelope) lasts 23 milliseconds and measures 105 dB SPL (Sound Pressure Level) at 3 feet. Back in the rehearsal room, the perceived transient from an identical hit might last 52 milliseconds and reach 112 dB SPL. Remember that every 6 dB increase corresponds to a doubling of the resulting signal voltage and level. That same 6-dB increase multiplies the acoustic power gener-

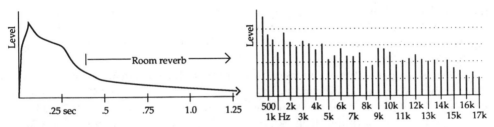

A. Envelopes (left) and frequency response graphs (right) of a snare drum signal with the mic at 20 feet. The frequency content is an average over the length of each drum envelope.

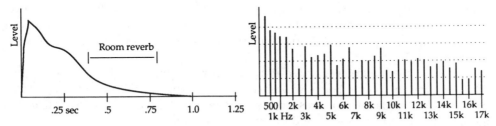

B. Envelope and frequency response graphs of a snare drum signal with the mic at 2.5 feet.

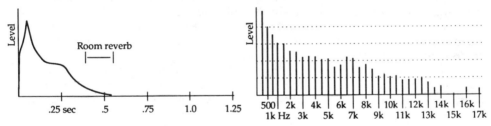

D. Envelope and frequency response graphs of a snare drum miked 3 inches from the top head.

Figure 12.1.   The envelopes (left) and frequency contents (right) of a snare drum, as heard from three distances in a live room: A. 20 feet, B. 2.5 feet and C. 3 inches from the top of the head. Note the sound of the drum itself dies after about 0.4 second, and the closer the mic (keeping peak signal level even for each location), the sooner the reverb diminishes beyond audibility. Also, while the mic hears plenty of highs from the snares at 20 and 2.5 feet, at 3 inches the mic hears mostly the top skin with decreased response starting at 2 kHz, and very little at all beyond 8 kHz.

ated by each hit (in watts of energy) by four. The early reflections have therefore doubled the length and more than quadrupled the apparent volume of the drum's transient.

Why do we lose these room components with close miking? Each time the distance between a mic and its source is halved, the resulting output signal goes up 6 *decibels* (dB). The difference between the snare's level at 3 feet and at 3 inches will be about 3.5 units of 6 dB each, or 21 dB (6 dB each for moving from 3 feet to 1.5 feet, 1.5 feet to 9 inches, and 9 inches to 4.5; and another 3 dB or so in moving halfway from 4.5 to 2.25 inches). Yet the actual volume or SPL of the room reflections is about the same at all of these mic positions. To maintain the same mic output level, we reduce the console gain by 21 dB when miking at 3 inches and thus take the relative volume of the reflections in the signal down by the same amount, 21 dB! They might as well not be there.

For comparison, think how much further the audience is from the whole drum kit than the drummer. At 30′, early reflections and overall drum reverb may make up 80% or more of the entire drum sound the audience hears and are thus an even more important component of the drum sound than they are to the drummer. In concert sound-reinforcement, close-miked and amplified drums are still projected from speakers that are fairly distant from the audience. The resulting sound (often to the annoyance of the sound crew, who would like to deliver studio quality) is still subject to the same room effects that characterized the unamplified drum set, such as early reflections and reverb. Amplification alone cannot overcome inherent problems with room acoustics.

Back in the studio there are several ways of restoring or re-creating the overall effect of early reflections. For now, we will continue uncovering problems. Later we will see that many familiar drum sounds are defined by the specific problems that are ignored, those that are solved, and the way they are solved.

[For award-winning engineer Al Schmitt,] The most important aspect of recording any instrument is to get into the room and listen to the musicians play. Then go back into the control room and try to duplicate that as quickly as possible. People like Steve Gadd or Jeff Porcaro . . . have their kits tuned the way they want them. My job is to get them that sound on tape.

I try for a complete, overall drum sound. The only time I worry about leakage—like the cymbals leaking into the tom mics—is if the composite sound isn't good. Then I'll try to figure out where I need more separation, a different mic, or whatever. Otherwise I go by the overall sound in the monitors.

The drums are usually recorded on four tracks; kick on one track; snare on another; and then the overheads, toms and hi-hat on two other tracks for a stereo field. I try to get my mix and my blend during the recording. I set up my drum sounds as if I were playing [the kit]. . . . The kit is spread out from the hi-hat on the left, to the floor toms on the right.

When I'm mixing the first thing I'll do is get my bass sound, and then throw up the kick to get them both working together. . . . I don't use too many effects on bass drum to separate it from the bass guitar. I may use a tiny amount of equalization, but not very much. If I have to overequalize a track—more than 4 dB up or down—either the microphone is in the wrong place, or the wrong mic is up there. It's so important to develop proper mic techniques, and not to depend on the electronics.

Vibrating Membranes: Local Resonance and the Proximity Distortion of Frequency Response. The head of a drum under uniform tension from all tuning pegs, like the surface of water in a bucket, can be deflected from its rest position in numerous ways. And like water itself, a drum head propagates sound waves from the point at which it is struck across its entire surface, the waves then bouncing back off the rim like those returning from the rim of our bucket. If struck in the center, the head will be deflected uniformly down in a single curve, then return past rest position in a single upward curve, and so on. This simplest of possible deformation is called *first-*

mode vibration. As you might expect, a high proportion of the sound energy that is generated is at the head's fundamental pitch, i.e., the musical note to which it has been tuned.

   If struck one-sixth the distance across the head, the drum head will vibrate in its first and second *concentric modes,* the resulting sound containing a second, higher pitch along with the fundamental. The third and fourth concentric modes produce still higher pitches when the head is struck one-tenth and one-fourteenth of the way across its diameter, respectively. The pitches from this odd series of locations are not related harmonically. Instead, they depend on the tension, elasticity, and density

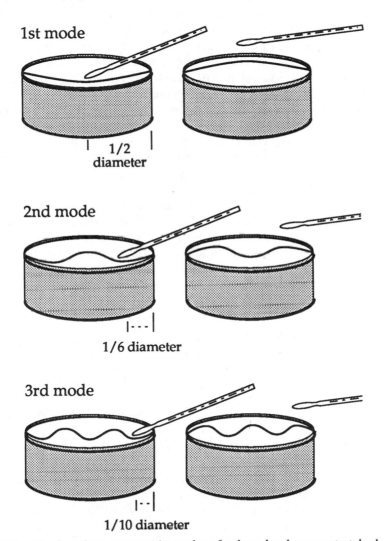

Figure 12.2.   The first three concentric modes of a drum head or any stretched circular membrane. The initial shape of the drum head after the strike is illustrated on the left, its shape after passing back through rest position is on the right.

(weight per unit area) of the head, as well as on the volume of air enclosed within the drum, which either resonates with or resists the frequencies corresponding to the various modes.

For each mode, certain points on the head vibrate vigorously at the corresponding frequency, while others remain relatively fixed. These vibrating and fixed points are called *antinodes* and *nodes,* respectively. The antinode of the first concentric mode, namely the center of the drum head, will be a node for the second, fourth, and all even-numbered concentric modes. Conversely, the antinodes for even numbered modes will be nodes for the odd modes.

Now we discover another complication—a separate series of pie slice–shaped vibrational modes. Just as waves from a stone dropped into a bucket travel around the perimeter, so vibrations in membranes such as drum heads can race around the head near the rim, engendering pie-shaped resonance modes at new pitches totally unrelated to those resulting from the concentric modes just mentioned. These resonances are accentuated in large, thin drum heads (such as floor toms and tympani), especially when the drum is struck way off-center or when tension over the entire head is slightly uneven. Together they are a drummer's tuning nightmare, generating wavering, multipitched ringing tones in the sustain and decay of the drum's envelope.

For a listener or mic relatively far from the drum, the combined modal vibrations meld into one sound. Low-level ringing in the sustain or decay of the drums vanishes into the room noise of a live performance. However, a close mic just above the rim hears everything. And since the mic may be near a variety of nodes and antinodes for different concentric and pie-shaped modes, some local resonances will be reinforced, while others will be completely eliminated in the mic's output. Moving the mic just an inch can readjust the miked sound, emphasizing pitched resonances that you want and subduing less desirable ones. If time permits, try a variety of mic positions to get close to the right sound. Experimentation is preferable to deciding right away on a mic position that might force you to resort to heavy signal processing in order to drag a good sound out of a flawed signal.

The extreme sound pressure at the drum mic's diaphragm is another source of problems. A rock snare drum played with the butt end of the stick can produce transients well over 150 dB SPL at 2″ above the rim. Mic diaphragms are hard-pressed to follow such explosive sound waves accurately; these waves can simply stretch a diaphragm beyond its elastic limit, producing incurable distortion. Even mics designed for high SPL sources may have frequency responses shifted heavily toward the highs, resulting in a thin, metallic sound that lacks body. In general, do not close mike drums with microphones whose rated maximum SPL is under 140 dB. Unless your drummer plays lightly, you are likely to have distorted sound coming into the console—distortion that is uncorrectable later.

For handy reference on the maximum SPL that specific mics can handle, and other specs, see the comprehensive chart of manufacturers' specs on studio mics. This chart will be useful for this and every chapter that follows; refer back to it as necessary. Esoteric and antique tube mics are not included here because spec sheets and accurate data on them are hard to find, and these types of mics are usually found only in the more expensive mastering studios, whose engineers should know when to use them and when to refrain.

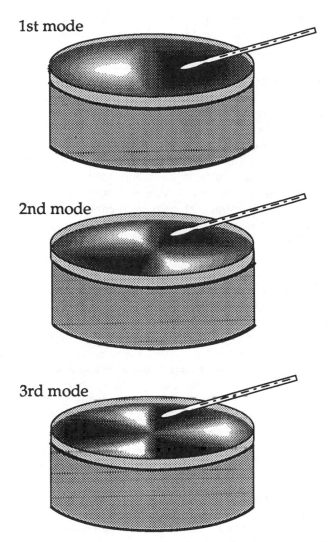

Figure 12.3. The first three "pie-sliced" modes of a drum head or any stretched membrane. The darker areas indicate compression nodes (down from rest position), the lighter areas indicate rarefaction nodes (up from rest position).

Internal Resonances and Tuning Problems.   The ultimate sound of a drum depends on more than just the head tuning. All drums contain a fixed internal volume of air. This air has a primary resonant frequency, with lesser resonances at the second, third, and fourth harmonics of this *fundamental* (one octave, a twelfth, and two octaves up). In addition, the drum shell, whether metal, wood, or plastic, will have one or more body resonances whose frequencies depend on its dimensions, thickness, density, and overall weight with hardware. The shell resonances may not be at or near the same frequencies as the air resonance(s).

To complicate matters even more, most double-headed drums have air vents and damping mechanisms. Because they couple the air inside the drum with the air outside, vents effectively increase the volume of air resonating and thereby tend to lower the internal air-resonance frequencies. Dampers, on the other hand, tend to raise the pitch; their constant pressure creates permanent nodes and antinodes at certain frequencies. Finally, the proximity of one drum to another, with two or more drums often physically connected by their mounting hardware, causes one drum to resonate when its neighbor is struck.

All of these resonances make drums a complex animal to record. However, if your set, by virtue of its drum sizes and construction and the lucky absence of conflict among its resonances, produces a clean, clear, and distinct sound live, you should be able to capture that sound in the studio. We will take it drum by drum, from the bottom up. Assuming the worst in each case, even after thoughtful mic placement, I will show what can be done by first applying destructive processing to eliminate unwanted portions of the mic's output signal. Then we will apply corrective processing—either to highlight the best parts of the signal or to make up for the loss of early reflections. Finally, we'll discuss special effects, which can be added directly to the corrected signal or generated from a duplicate of it and manipulated through a separate console channel and associated electronics.

Before a single mic is set up on the drum kit, tune the entire kit to your complete satisfaction. Since getting a good sound mandates chasing and eliminating some internal resonances in each drum, it makes little sense to introduce electronic processing before the set has been fine-tuned. Remember that any two drum heads tuned near the same pitch will vibrate sympathetically when either is struck. While identical pitch between top and bottom heads of any drum will give a pure, round tone, pitch isolation of one drum from another will make the engineer's job easier. It is especially important to prevent the bottom snare head (and metal snares mounted on it) from vibrating when the toms, kick, timbales, or other drums are struck. Whatever tuning you prefer, pitch isolation minimizes recording problems, and problems take time (and money) to solve.

In general, the drummer should settle on a precise sound before fiddling with mics and processing. Preserving a live sound that is right for the music is much easier than creating it through electronic manipulation. Remember too that what sounds right to the drummer does not sound the same to an audience. Listen to the kit from the drummer's viewpoint to get a proper idea of what you want to re-create in the control room. Approaching the task this way can make the selection of mics and processing automatic—an instinctive reaction to what you hear over the drummer's shoulder.

THE KICK DRUM

Microphone Selection, Mounting, and Placement. In most rock and pop records, kick and snare drum are the two loudest components of the finished mix. For this reason alone, the quality of these sounds is very important to the overall feel and to the success of the record.

Microphones Commonly Used in the Recording Studio

Make and Model		Output dBVU*	Freq. Resp. Hz-kHz	Max. SPL dB**	Pad dB	Low Filter Hz	Features / Common Uses
DYNAMIC, Omnidirectional							
Beyer	M 101	−59	40–20	138	no	no	Low cost, used for RTA†
Electro-Voice (EV)	635A	−55	60–15	medium	no	no	Sturdy, low cost/ambience, voice
	RE-55	−55	40–20	medium	no	no	Flat response, sturdy/all-purpose ambience, stereo pairs
CONDENSER, Omnidirectional							
B&K	4007	−59	20–50	medium	no	no	Very flat response/vocals, piano
Crown	PZM-6LP	−70*	50–15	medium	no	no	Requires 24 V., hemispherical response
TRAM	TR 50	−55	40–18	126	no	no	Lavalier,‡ requires battery or 48 V.
DYNAMIC, Unidirectional							
AKG	D 12 (or D 112e)	−74*	35–16	high	no	no	/Kick drum, bass, and loud lows
Beyer	M300n	−58	50–15	medium	no	yes	Mid-highs boosted/live vocal
	160N	−59	40–18	high	no	no	H.,†† ribbon, good side and rear rejection, small/snare, cymbals, ambience
	M88n	−51	30–20	high	no	no	H.,†† highs boosted/drums, vocal, instrument amps
Electro-Voice (EV)	D308	−53	40–17	141	no	no	Pivoting mount/drums, vocal, brass
	RE-20	−57	45–18	high	no	yes	Good rejection/drums, vocals, amps
	RE-15 or 16	−56	40–17	high	no	yes	H.,†† bright sound/brass, reeds, vocals
	D-757	−50	30–18	high	no	yes	Rugged, flat response/vocals, percussion

Make and Model		Output	Freq. Resp.	Max. SPL	Pad	Filter	Features / Common Uses
Fostex	M 55	-47	70–18	medium	no	no	/Vocals
	M 77	-56	40–18	high	no	yes	/Bass, amps
Sennheiser	MD421U	-53	30–17	high	no	variable	Good rejection/drums, amps, vocals
	MD441	-65*	30–20	high	no	5-Position	S,†† brilliant switch/vocals, piano, percussion, overheads
Shure	SM 57	-56	40–15	high	no	no	Good rejection, rugged/all-purpose

CONDENSER, unidirectional (cardioid and variations):

Make and Model		Output	Freq. Resp.	Max. SPL	Pad	Filter	Features / Common Uses
AKG	C460 with CK-1 or CK-5 capsule	-60	20–20	138	-20	50/70/150	Requires 48 V./piano, acoustic guitar, percussion, overheads
	C451/CK-1 or 5	-40	30–20	high	no	on EB model	Requires 48 V., flat Response all-purpose
Audio-Technica	C 535	-62	20–20	132	no	100/500	Requires 48 V., low cost
	ATM-31	-55	30–20	141	no	no	Requires 1.5-V. battery, low cost/amps, brass
Neumann	KM 64	-39	40–20	120+	-10	no	Requires 48 V., small/snare, hi-hat, acoustic guitar, percussion
	KM-fi	-44	30–20	130+	no	no	Requires 48 V., Lavalier‡/winds, strings, hi-hat, acoustic guitar
Shure	SM 81	-65*	20–20	134	-10	2-Position	Requires V. great response/piano, sampling vocals, percussion
Sony	ECM 23F	-56	30–20	130	-8	low	1.5 V. battery/acoustic guitar, percussion

DYNAMIC (Ribbon), bidirectional:

Make and Model		Output	Freq. Resp.	Max. SPL	Pad	Filter	Features / Common Uses
Beyer	M-380	-46	50–20	medium	no	no	/Percussion, ambience, sections
Fostex	M 80	-52	50–18	medium	no	no	Mellow sound/vocals, speech

DYNAMIC, multipattern:

CONDENSER, multipattern:

Maker	Model	Output	Freq.	Max SPL	Pad	2-Position	Notes
RCA	77-DX	−53	50−15	medium	no		Omni- and bidirectional, cardioid, smooth/brass, reeds, 1940s sound, vocals
AKG	C414	−64*	20−20	138	10/20	75/150	Req 48 V., omni, bi, car., H.,†† great response/piano, all-purpose
	C740 "Tube"	−50	30−20	128	10/20	2-position	Warm sound, low noise/vocals, piano
Neumann	KM 86	−42	40−20	120+	10	no	Requires 48 V., omni, Bi, car./vocals, tom-toms, winds, brass
	U-87	−38	40−16	120+	10	3-position	Requires 48 V., omni, bi, car./vocals, drums, sections, all-purpose
	U-89	−38	40−18	134	10/20	3-position	Requires 48 V., omni, bi, 2 car., H.,†† bright sound/vocals, all-purpose
	U-47	−42?	40−18	med	10	yes	Warm sound/vocals, brass, bass

The above specs are taken from the latest available manufacturer data sheets and brochures. Be aware, however, that various companies use different measuring standards and reference levels.

*There are at least three scales by which output (and sensitivity) are measured, making it difficult to make relevant comparisons. Usable output will be no less than the values given but may be greater by up to 12 dB in a few specific mics, identified above by an asterisk.

**These are figures without the internal pad (if any). Using the pad will give a higher SPL but not necessarily the same number of dB by which the pad reduces output level. To confuse matters, some manufacturers such as Neumann specify *maximum SPL* for the level that produces 0.5% harmonic distortion at the output, yielding deceptively low max SPL ratings. Most companies designate max SPL at the 3% distortion level, usually 8–10 dB higher than Neumann's max SPL rating. Where no specific numbers were available, medium designates an SPL of about 135–140, high more than this.

†RTA = real time analysis, a process for measuring the overall frequency response delivered to the engineer's position, taking both the monitor speakers' output and the effect of the control room acoustics into account.

††S. = Super-cardioid, H. = Hyper-cardioid

‡A lavalier mic is worn on a cord around the musician's neck.

145

The raw kick drum, whether single or double-headed, creates a dense cluster of low frequencies (from 25 Hz to 400 Hz) at very high volume (up to 150 dB SPL if played hard with a wooden beater). This is the toughest problem any close mic can face. For technical reasons, it turns out that dynamic mics handle this situation best, and among these many engineers prefer the Electro-Voice RE-20 and Sennheiser MD421U. These are both highly directional, and their adjustable internal filters reduce the preponderance of extreme lows that are generated by a rock kick drum. The 421U also has a helpful peak in its midhigh frequency response between 3 and 6 kHz. The AKG D 12E and Shure SM 57 are also popular for kick drums, though some engineers are now switching to PZM mics, which are naturally very bright. Although other mics could do a fine job, many engineers prefer to start with a known solution, then change to something else if the sound is not right.

Concerning single versus double heads, rock demands precise and audible transients on all drums. Because of the large internal volume of the kick, as well as the large diameter and weight of its heads, a front skin (nearest the audience) takes some time to react to and begin vibrating with the hit of the beater on the rear head. This double transient reduces punch, so most rock and related recordings demand a single-headed kick or one from which a large area of the front head is removed. In this case, the mic can be placed in front of, at, or behind the front head, that is, inside the drum.

Centered immediately in front of or at the hole in the front skin, a mic is subjected to the highest air pressure, since all the compression inside the drum is forced out the front hole. If the front-skin hole is small, the resulting breeze can overload the most sturdy dynamic. Because the center of the front hole is the antinode of the rear head's first mode, receiving sound generated by the entire area of the head, its signal will contain the most balanced cluster of lows. A cardioid mic inside the drum will pick up more of the beater hit but can suffer from the local resonance syndrome discussed earlier and may hear only the frequencies whose antinodes are directly in front of the mic's diaphragm.

Aiming the mic in a particular direction can bring a couple of bonuses. First, positioning the mic at an angle other than perpendicular to the heads can reduce the sound pressure to which the diaphragm is subjected at the very lowest frequencies, helping to prevent distortion and eliminating the preponderance of lows in the output without filtering it. Also, by aiming the mic away from other drums (toward the drummer's right), extra isolation will result that can reduce the need for gating and improve the sound of the entire kit. I begin most sessions by suspending the mic inside the drum, a few inches off center, with the diaphragm perhaps 4″ to 6″ from the beater head, aimed toward the floor tom, and slightly down, to avoid leakage from the snare and rack toms immediately above it.

Because the kick generates so much acoustic energy, it is important that the mic be mounted on a heavy stand that rests on a solid surface (on the main floor of the room, usually a concrete slab), not on a wooden drum platform that can send mechanical vibrations through the stand to all the drum mics. Lacking a concrete floor, set the mic stand on top of a folded sound blanket or other absorbing material that keeps floor-transmitted vibrations away from the stand. Remember to check the mic position between takes or songs: a little slippage can defocus your kick sound. A shock mount is not necessary, but the mic clip, mounting, and/or boom arm should be tightly attached, with no loose or rattling parts.

Damping, Padding, Pillows, and Blankets. While noise gates may later help limit the duration of each kick, they cannot influence internal characteristics of the drum's sound envelope. For most rock and pop tunes, a kick drum's internal damping is insufficient. It is thus common to install damping inside the kick, both to control boomy lower midrange frequencies and to highlight the transient created when the beater hits the rear head. There are no rules about what is best to use, but be careful that you place a couple of heavy weights on top of the pillows, blanket, or parka wedged against the rear head. The sheer force of the beater and the enormous acoustic pressure within the drum will quickly move anything that is not weighted down, and halfway through the take your damping may be gone. One or two mic-stand bottoms, unscrewed from the vertical tube, are heavy enough to do the trick.

Do not resort to resting the mic on or taping it to the damping material, however. The damping vibrates through its direct mechanical linkage with the shell and will transmit these vibrations to the mic through its shell, rather than through air to its diaphragm, which is how the mic is designed to work.

Destructive Equalization and Noise Gating. Remember that kick drums, like all large instruments, are designed to be heard at a distance, where all their frequencies have melded. No matter how you mic a kick drum, be ready to apply narrowband, destructive parametric equalization. Depending on the drum size and shell type, and the overall evenness of its tuning, you may expect to find one or two frequencies accentuated in the close-mic signal. In general, these frequencies also ring the longest, giving the drum an uncontrolled, flabby bottom end or "dongy" midbass.

Use the parametric equalizer ("eq") to sweep the lows with a bandwidth of 0.2 octave or less, boosting to locate resonances. Then use one or two bands to take out up to 10 dB at each resonance—enough to restore a tight bottom end with balanced response. If the drum needs more attack, use another parametric band to find the best frequencies in the beater hit, and boost these. The 1 kHz range is good for hard rock, and 2 to 3 kHz are best for R&B and dance music. If removing the resonance leaves the drum sounding a bit thin, you can boost the entire low end in the console after adjusting the dynamic range.

Even after removing resonances, the kick sound may ring too long, obscuring clarity in the bass guitar or in an acoustic or synthetic bass. To correct this problem, patch in a noise gate. Its threshold must allow every note played on the kick to pass through, so ask the drummer to play the softest kick hits to be used in the session and set the threshold a few dB below this level. Exact numbers are unimportant. The attack of the gate should be adjusted so that the beater is heard, but it should not be so short that you hear the electronic click of the gate opening with each kick.

As explained earlier, the floor to which the gate reduces its output level when closed also has an effect on the audibility of the gate click. If you set a − 10 dB threshold and a 60 dB floor (or "range," as Kepex calls it), the gate has to open 50 dB to allow each hit through. Very low floors increase the audibility of the click and may be unnecessary for the desired separation and clarity of kick hits. For this reason, I

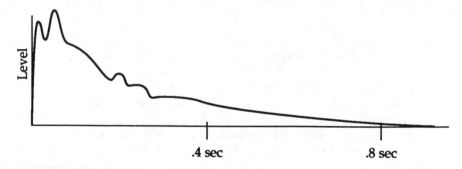

The envelope of an unprocessed kick drum.

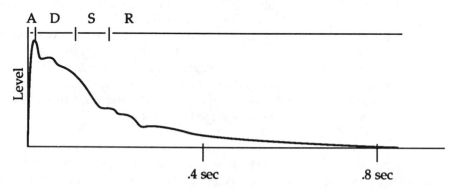

After destructive eq for resonance removal.

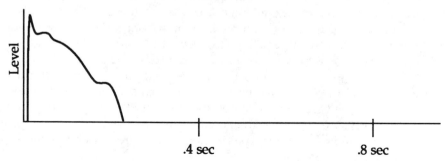

After noise gating appropriate to synth pop.

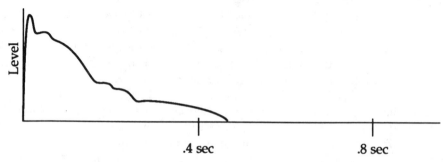

After noise gating appropriate to heavy metal or hard rock.

148

generally select a 25 to 30 dB floor. Remember, you can always gate more later, but what you remove now is gone forever.

The right hold and/or fade times of the gate depend on the kick's musical function in each tune. Most pop records employ the kick as a timekeeper or marker, with fairly short hold/decay. In contrast, hard rock and heavy metal records often depend on the sustained weight of an extended kick drum, which can be held via compression and other processing for a full sixteenth or eighth note. In any case, with unwanted frequency and resonance components removed, we can move on to constructive processing.

A special note on jazz kick sounds. Whether you want the objective two-mic drum sound described much earlier or a more rockish kick sound on a jazz record, you must give the drummer room for dynamics. This means you may have to set the threshold of your gate so low that other drums leak onto the kick track. There are three possible solutions. First, live with the leakage. Second, use a more directional mic or move the original kick mic anywhere you can find better acoustic separation from the other drums. Just make sure you can live with the change in kick sound or repair it in the control room. Low-level kick hits have proportionately less high frequencies than loud hits. Do not be afraid to use the opening gate click itself to increase the clarity of low-level kicks. If the click, rather than the beater, is audible as a spurious electronic sound, increase the gate's attack time a touch or raise the floor or range. If you are worried that the click will sound artificial, record a snippet and check this effect with the rest of the arrangement before printing it to tape.

The third (and quite baroque) solution is to create a frequency-dependent noise gate by feeding a duplicate of the kick signal through a parametric eq and into the control channel or keying input of another noise gate. Then, locate one frequency range that is present in the kick and no other drum, boost it, and dip everything else. The gate will now open only when that unique kick frequency sounds. Obviously, you must set this gate's parameters to allow every kick hit through. It is amazing to what lengths one must sometimes go to give the impression that nothing was done at all.

Constructive Processing: Compression and Console Equalization. Compressing a kick drum right after noise gating may seem absurd, but remember the behavior and importance of early reflections in drums. As illustrated earlier, the attack/decay portion of the envelope of an unprocessed kick drum can last up to 60 or 80 milliseconds (ms). Although this seems long in comparison with the 20-plus ms attack/decay portion of a snare hit, remember that each full cycle of a 40 Hz wave takes 25 ms (1 second = 1,000 ms). Divide that by 40 to see the significance of the problem. Only three or four full cycles of a kick drum's fundamental pitch are heard in each hit, and much of this occurs in the decay phase. With little room reinforcement to strengthen the decay, compression is usually necessary to keep the bottom end of

Figure 12.4. The envelope of a partially damped kick drum as heard by an internal close mic: narrow band eq removes ringing peaks after the initial transient, smoothing out the drum's decay and sustain. Then noise gating is applied to shape the release differently for synth pop and rock/metal styles, respectively.

rock and pop kicks tight and pumping. The type of compression depends on the music itself.

Very short attack (2 ms or less), especially with a high compression ratio (maybe 8 : 1 or greater—almost limiting), will flatten out the envelope of the drum altogether. Each resulting kick hit will begin with a high-frequency beater hit (1 to 3 kHz), followed by a continuing puff of lows, which in turn die when the noise gate shuts down. This type of kick sound works well with midtempo straight-ahead pop or lighter dance rock because its level is very consistent and the beater hits are crisp, clear, and unobtrusive. However, with such high control, this sound can be mistaken for a drum machine kick.

For a punchier sound with equal weight and clarity, lengthen the attack time to 5 or even 10 ms. The beater hits now poke through at a higher level, enabling you to bring down the overall kick level (and thus the part of each hit containing the sustained lows) in the mix. Of course, for each hit to be audible, the compressor release time must be shorter than the interval between consecutive kick hits. Properly done, this sound is great for energetic up-tempo pop, country, R&B, or any record in which an unusual kick pattern must cut through without becoming too heavy.

The thunderous kick sound heard in hard rock and heavy metal results from a high compression ratio, fast attack, and a fast release (30 ms or less). While the beginning of each kick is highly controlled, the short release can actually cause an increase in volume as each hit sounds, especially if the release time of the compressor is less than the fade time of the gate. Try drawing the envelope as an aid to visualizing the effect and imagining its sound. While the kick's highs will fade out after about 10 ms, its unnatural or *reverse envelope* (getting louder after the ostensible decay) keeps the lows out front in the mix until the gate shuts down.

A word about specific compressors. Units like the UREI 1176, which are great for vocals and other very fast attack applications (under 1 ms), do not work well on a kick drum. Instead of following the drum's envelope, these compressors may actually try to follow the individual waveforms of each low-frequency vibration. Unless used with extreme care or for special effect, such compressors take the weight out of low-frequency signals.

Again, final equalization depends on the type of music. A pop kick does not need a lot of real lows for two reasons. First, many AM radio stations, whether mono or stereo, still roll off everything below 60 Hz to prevent speaker-flap on listeners' portable and car radios. Second, the high compression added by most AM stations makes a heavy kick drum too ponderous. Such AM roll-off and compression help project the broadcast signal the greatest possible distance from the transmitting antenna, thereby reaching the largest possible audience.

Many engineers making pop records automatically boost the kick around 70 to 100 Hz, dip it heavily in the 400 to 600 Hz range (to prevent conflict with the body of rhythm instruments and vocals), and boost it somewhere between 1 and 2 kHz. In contrast, a boost in the 2 to 4 kHz range produces the characteristic "tick" of European dance or disco records. Most drum machine kicks have a sharp peak between 3 and 4 kHz. Oddly, kick sounds have a strong effect on how people dance to a record. A "Euro-" kick encourages floaty, tip-toes dancing, while heavier kicks seem to induce earthier steps.

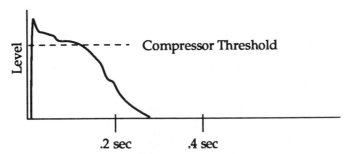

After compression appropriate to pop/rock, using a
fast attack, medium ratio and medium release.

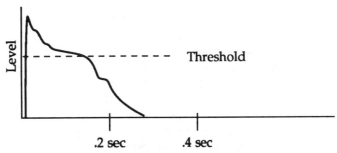

After compression appropriate to dance/R&B, using
a slower attack, higher ratio and medium release.

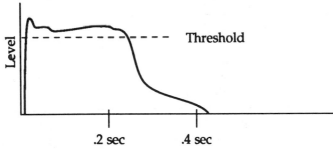

After compression appropriate to heavy metal, using
a fast attack, high ratio and fast release.

Figure 12.5.   Envelopes of 3 styles of compressed, gated kick drum. The faster the attack,
the more the initial transient is smoothed out. The higher the ratio, the flatter the decay
section of the envelope. Remember that, in each case, the compressor continues to operate
only during the portion of each kick where the incoming signal is above the user-specified
threshold level.

Hard rock, which requires that guitars and other rhythm instruments have a heavier sound, demands a dip in kick response in the 200 to 300 Hz range. The lower the frequency of the high-end boost, the meaner the sound of the drum, although boosting much below 1 kHz will give a boxy, hollow kick sound. Remember, too, that other drum mics—the overhead mics and any others that are not noise gated—will contribute to the kick sound. The composite kick sound is what counts, so polishing the kick sound before auditioning the rest of the set may prove a wasted effort. I prefer to spend just a few minutes roughing out the kick sound, then come back to it for fine-tuning after preparing the desired lead vocal and rhythm bed sounds. After all, the melody and chords are the song, and the kick has to complement these elements.

Special Effects.   Except in short sections of rap and other dance genres, special effects are rarely used on the kick drum. Because the kick defines the rhythmic structure of most dance and rock tunes, producers and artists have been reluctant to detract from its natural punch by using delays, flanging, and chorusing. Used in moderation, such effects would probably be obscured by the low frequencies in the direct signal and bass instrument, anyway. Until Sting's 1986 *Dream of the Blue Turtles* LP, even using reverb as an intentional effect on the kick was avoided. Someone finally noticed that digital reverbs handle lows fairly well, while many plate and spring systems overload when low frequencies are input at high levels.

I feel that the kick should seem to be in the same acoustic space as the body of the music. A little reverb can help to produce this feeling, even if more is used on snare, rhythm instruments, or vocals. The more live the intended sound of the record, the more kick reverb is appropriate, even necessary! However, for dance records specifically intended to be played at high volume in clubs and discos, using reverb on the kick may only compound the acoustical problems that already exist in the clubs. For these records a tight and dry kick drum is usually best, although many rap and so-called "house" records are setting new trends with processed kick sounds.

A word on monitoring kick drum sounds. Studio monitors driven by hundreds of watts per channel can handle the lows in a heavy kick sound. However, if the same kick causes Auratones (and probably car speakers) to flap uncontrollably at a volume where rhythm instruments and vocals sound fine, then there's too much bottom end on the kick. However solid they sound through the big monitors, trim the lows a bit. Otherwise, listeners will probably turn down your record when it is broadcast, which is not a good omen for sales.

Externally Keyed Sounds.   There are times when even the best-sounding kick drum, with all the right mics, just does not have the weight or particular sound you need. In that case, it is possible to use each real kick hit as a *trigger* to open up a second noise gate. Simply feed a multiple or duplicate of the processed kick sound into the keying input of a second noise gate and a second sound (whatever program is fed into and through the program channel of the gate) will occur with each kick hit.

To fatten up a thin kick, you might use a synthesizer to generate a continuous output of closely grouped low frequencies. Fed into the program channel of the second gate, a burst of the synthesized lows will emerge along with each kick hit, with whatever attack, fade, and floor you set on the second gate. These synth lows can then be combined in the console and sent to the same track with the deficient kick drum. Or for a comical effect, you could arrange for each original kick hit to trigger a sampling synth to output the sound of a gong, spring, a frog croaking—anything you feel will produce or enhance the kick sound you want.

However, be careful with the amount of keyed external sound you add to the miked signal. It cannot be reduced or removed later. For that reason, I often suggest that the keyed signal be recorded on a separate track of the multitrack tape, to be bounced together with the real kick drum when the combo can be heard in context of the whole arrangement, even including vocals.

It is also pretty common these days to use drum machines and a variety of sampling synthesizers to have one or more drums from a real performance trigger presampled drum sounds made by famous drummers. This process needs little comment here. The engineer at your session need only set up a unidirectional mic and noise gate on each drum to be replaced. The synthetic drum generator only needs to know when, and at what level, the real drummer hits each drum. The quality of sound heard by the live mics on these drums is totally irrelevant. If you intend to replace real with canned drums, let your engineer know well before the session to make sure you and the studio have all the necessary devices and cables and to save the time and expense of getting high-quality live sounds that will never be used in the final multitrack or mix.

THE SNARE DRUM AND HI-HAT

Wallets, Dampers, and Taping.   Many engineers contend that the snare is the most important sound in a record. Others, who would never admit it publicly, prove the point daily by spending more studio time and money on snare sounds than on the sound of lead singers and soloists. However, if forced to compromise either on the snare or lead vocal, I always defer to the best possible sound on the melody line. After all, the melody is the song, not the snare.

Nevertheless, the snare drum's prominence in rock, pop, R&B, dance, and even country records gives it a major role in setting the feel of these records. An improperly miked or processed snare will take the bite out of a hard rock song or give the smoothest ballad a harsh, grating undertone. Again, because the snare is picked up by overheads, hi-hat, and other ungated drum mikes, the composite snare sound is what counts, not just the sound going to a snare track. The snare cannot be fixed in the mix—not without ruining the rest of your drum sounds.

All that we know about the modes of drum-head vibration and the effects of vents and dampers is doubly true of the snare drum. Every snare has two heads: a top head on which the drummer plays and a bottom head beneath and against which the metal snares are mounted. The bottom head vibrates sympathetically whenever the top head is struck or brushed. It also vibrates in response to other drums being struck, and most vigorously if those drums are tuned to the same pitch as the bottom head of the snare. This is why it is advisable to avoid pitch duplication when tuning the entire set.

Close miking accentuates every nuance of a drum's sustain and decay. While noise gating allows you to set the ultimate envelope length of each drum hit, it does little within that envelope to stifle early ringing and local resonances. The traditional cure for these problems in a snare, laying or taping a leather wallet or billfold on the top skin, may overdeaden the sound. Tight snares are good for uptempo pop, but unless the heads are tuned quite low to deliver extra weight and sustain, the wallet doesn't work well for hard rock, R&B, and the heavier genres, even ballads. You just wind up adding delays and effects to re-create part of what the wallet removed.

Internal dampers, because of their small surface area, often deaden the drum without removing pitched resonances. Moreover, the drum heads now available with two bonded layers, or a narrow outer ring of thicker damping material bonded to the main surface (Remo Pinstripes and other makes), are great for live performance but too dead for most recording applications. Once such a head is in place, the effect is nonadjustable and irreversible. The best and most versatile cure is simply a few square inches of duct tape (double or triple thick as necessary) applied to any areas near the rim where a pitched resonance is apparent when you tap the head lightly with a drum stick.

You may wind up with several tape patches in a random pattern, but they will usually kill the worst rings and resonances. Just remember to remove the tape after each session, since the tape will be needed in different positions every time you retune. In addition, if you leave it in place too long, the adhesive will weld itself to the head and leave a gummy residue.

A newer and better solution for reducing resonances and ringing are Zero Rings, made by Noble and Cooley. These thin plastic circles fit just inside the top snare rim, covering only the outermost inch or so of the head itself. While these shorten resonances almost like a noise gate does, it may still be necessary to eq them out as described in the following paragraph. If Zero Rings are unavailable, you can make something almost as effective from a worn out drum head, using scissors.

The bottom head almost always needs to be damped, and the internal types are perfectly satisfactory. Lacking these, tape a wad of rolled-up felt or gauze padding to the head on one or both sides of the metal snares, as necessary to achieve the desired deadening effect. Tuning the head down a bit can also get rid of a frequently encountered 200 Hz resonance (about G or A below middle C) in snare drums and give them extra weight. As often as not, the bottom head projects cleaner and more usable sound in the 100 Hz range, exactly where the top head is most difficult to separate from rack toms just inches away. Thus, you can emphasize the low end from the bottom head in the two-mic blend, rolling off lows in the upper mic and, with them, tom-tom leakage.

Miking the Snare. In the past two decades the trend has been toward more and more mics on the whole drum kit. Although this approach multiplies the phasing problems among mics, it does let the engineer build the drum sound incrementally. Keep in mind, however, that every additional mic takes time to set up, adjust, process, and blend in with others. Once this time has been spent, few engineers would consider whether the kit sounded better five mics ago!

Nevertheless, in rock and related genres, separate mics are generally used on the top and bottom snare heads. In one way this makes complete sense. If the snare drum shell is 6″ deep, and both heads sound at about the same volume, then a mic three inches above the top head will be nine inches from the bottom head. According to our relationship of distance and volume, the bottom skin and snares, being three times as distant from a top mic, will sound about 9 dB lower to the mic. No amount of compression or equalization can make up for this basic imbalance.

Remember that the drummer hears the summation of direct sound and early reflections from both heads. Most room surfaces bounce midrange frequencies much more efficiently than extreme lows and highs. Since the sound of the metal snares is concentrated precisely in that 1 to 4 kHz range, the room will appear to boost the relative acoustic level of the snares in the composite sound. A top-head mic will barely hear these early reflections. This loss, combined with the bottom head distance factor, often results in a dead, tom-tom-like top-mic sound bearing little resemblance to the live sound of the snare and devoid of the "crack" that most drummers like and records need.

Whether you use one mic or two, here are a couple of hints that can improve the snare sound. First, in most drum kits it is almost impossible to position a single top-head mic vertically near the far rim of the drum (drummer's point of view). There is just no space between the toms and cymbals. This turns out to be beneficial: if you use a super- or hypercardioid mic aimed straight down, you are miking only one small area of the entire snare head, and local resonances will dominate its overall sound; it is best to aim the top mic more parallel to the top skin, so that the maximum area of the head is on axis. Better yet, aim the mic diagonally from above the far top rim toward the bottom rim nearest the drummer's seat.

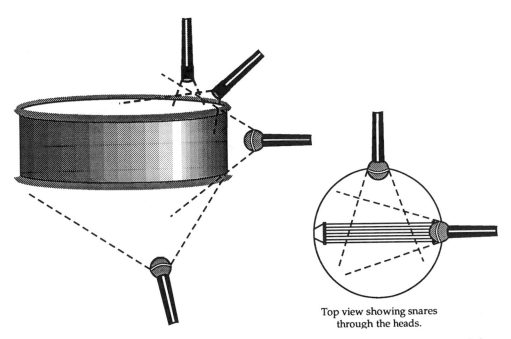

Top view showing snares
through the heads.

Figure 12.6.   Top and side views of a snare drum showing common mic positions and the on-axis angle within which high frequencies will be picked up (if a cardiod mic is used).

Next, unless you need to disengage the snares during a take, with the snare release handle in easy reach, turn the entire drum so that the metal snares are in line with the mic axis. In this way, the mic will see the entire length of the snares, rather than a short section that intersects its area of maximum sensitivity. In general, learn to think of instrument and mic positioning as your first tool in sound improvement. Anything you can do to coax the sound you want into a mic position you are stuck with or to keep undesired sounds off mic will reduce the number of problems that must later be fixed by signal processing. Where processing is concerned, less is more.

One way to balance the snare sound is to place a less directional (even an omni- or bidirectional) mic a few inches from the vertical center of the shell—equidistant from top and bottom heads. While it is not aimed directly at either head, the mic picks up equal (though indirect) sound from both. If you adopt this procedure, just make sure the drum's air vent is not puffing directly at the mic diaphragm.

Concerning specific mics for top and bottom snare heads, many engineers prefer to use dynamics, simply because of the extreme SPL levels (150 or more dB) present near both heads. Among these, the Sennheiser MD 421U is again popular, and so is its big brother, the 441. Both of these are considered bright mics, with a boost in frequency response around 3 to 5 kHz. Both also have variable bass roll-off (shelf reduction) controls, and the 441 has an extra "brilliant" switch that shelf-boosts 5 kHz and up about 6 dB. Shure SM 57 and 58s are also popular for top and bottom heads, although they have no internal response adjustments or pad. Electro-Voice's RE-15 and RE-10 have steep low roll-off filters that lessen kick drum leakage when used as bottom mics. Their smooth high end helps blend the scratchy, metallic bite of the individual snare windings.

Although I rarely use condenser mics to close-mike drums, some engineers swear by the Neumann KM 84 for the top snare head. Despite its manufacturer ratings, which do not indicate high maximum SPL levels, this mic gives a tight, explosive snare sound. If the drummer plays very hard, however, the KM 84 sometimes overloads. When the diaphragm is stretched beyond its elastic limit, the internal pad will not help. Shure's SM 81 condenser, although brighter-sounding, is also susceptible to failure at high SPL levels. If the mic you select has an internal pad, use it. But avoid using a low roll-off filter that dips anything above 100 Hz. Remember, too, that all cardioid-family close mics produce exaggerated low response due to the proximity effect. This alone mandates corrective high boost and/or low cut with all close drum mics.

In an interview with *Mix* magazine editor David Schwartz, engineer Roger Nichols discusses his approach to miking drums:

I've been using fewer microphones on drums. I would use a mic under the snare drum to get more snares, because the crispness of the snare is one of the first things to get lost in an analog recording, but I don't do that anymore.

One of my favorite new mics is the AKG "Tube." I like tube mics because they are nice and warm—they accentuate the even harmonics, as opposed to digital or transistorized equipment that seems to accentuate odd harmonics. . . . I used [the AKG] for vocals on the Frank Sinatra album with L.A. *Is My Lady* on it, and on John Denver's *Dreamland Express* album. I've heard people tell me that they don't like the microphone because it's too noisy. . . . If you can't turn off the phanton power in the console, it "fights" with the power supply in the microphone, and there is some noise.

I usually use a Shure SM 56 on snare; my favorite kick drum mic is still the Electro-Voice 666, which used to be a garage band vocal mic in the '60s; U87 on tom-toms; a little Sony electret condenser mic on the hi-hat; and AKG 414s for overheads. My overall philosophy is that the microphones are the least of the problem: usually when I go into a studio, I let the second engineer pick whatever microphones he wants to use.

I'm a firm believer in changing the sound at the source—changing a snare drum, drum heads; the bass strings or bass—before I'll touch the eq or use anything external. If you get the source sounding good, and it sounds good in the room, just put any professional microphone in front of it and you're 80% there. If you start with everything perfect, then it's easy to make little changes, and the mics are not so important to differences in sound quality as people want you to believe.

Mini-Baffles and Other Acoustical Tricks.   The snare drum consists of a hard, cylindrical surface (the shell) with two taut heads intersecting it. The toms, located within inches of the snare, are constructed quite similarly. Ride and crash cymbals are metallic and resonant; they are large reflective surfaces mounted about a foot above the drums. Everywhere you turn, the sound of one drum bounces off the others and the cymbals, and vice versa. Thus, it is difficult to get any real separation between the sound entering three to six mics that are only inches apart within about two cubic feet of air space.

One solution is to devise ways of keeping the bounced sound of each drum from reaching mics that are intended to pick up only one member of this cluster. I have an assortment of small pieces of thick felt, perhaps 6″ or a foot square. After placing mics on the top snare head, rack tom(s), and hi-hat and listening to their direct sound, I wrap a piece of felt loosely around the front of each mic barrel and tape it in place, creating a broad cone (one to three layers) that keeps out off-axis highs. In emergencies, the open end of this conical baffle can extend perhaps an inch beyond the mic barrel. Highs from a crash cymbal directly above the snare mic, for example, will be absorbed by the cone and reduced by perhaps 10 dB.

There is, of course, one possible adverse side effect to this trick. The directional characteristics of many mics are created through the interaction of direct sound and the sound entering the barrel through the side and rear ports. If these ports are covered by the felt or any tape, you can lose some of the basic qualities for which the mic was selected in the first place. Thus, mount your cones carefully, and only if you feel the extra isolation is really necessary. You may need a cone only on the snare or a rack-tom mic, for example. Keep your ears open for undesirable side effects—a boxy midrange or a shrill, metallic quality in the high-end output of any mic that sounded fine before it was coned. In this event, use only a small flap of felt taped above the mic to reduce the primary source of leakage. I recommend listening to the unconed mic signals first due to these possible side effects; you might even record a bit of drumming through them for comparison. An unavoidable adverse side effect of the felt treatment is that it takes time. Make sure the situation warrants it before trying it.

The Bottom Mic.   A mic on the bottom snare head has one advantage: it is aimed upward. In theory, if the heads are tuned similarly, both mics will pick up the drum's fundamental frequency, but only the bottom mic can be positioned near the center of the head, near the antinode of mode 1. If the low frequencies are more solid through the bottom mic, feature them in its output. However, only the most directional mic will be able to reject the added kick leakage caused by proximity to the rear head and beater.

Rarely are condenser mics used on the bottom head. Condensers have such detailed high-frequency response that they seem to separate the sound from each winding of the snares, an inherent problem with any close mic in this application. In addition, a condenser looking up through both snare heads will pick up more cymbals than a similarly positioned dynamic. For both these reasons the SM 57 and 58 series and RE-15 are bottom-head standbys. Aiming them diagonally along the snares and up toward the drummer's chest will maximize snare pickup and minimize cymbal and other leakage.

In any case, if top and bottom mics are used, you should combine their signals in the console, sending the blend to a single tape track. To minimize kick leakage, the low roll-off of the console should be used on both snare mics. You should decide whether the electrical polarity or phase of the bottom mic signal needs to be reversed with respect to the top mic. Many engineers do this automatically, since logic dictates that both heads move down when the drum is struck, causing a rarefaction of air at the top mic's diaphragm and a compression at the bottom. (Remember, the bottom mic is pointed essentially in the opposite direction.)

After setting both mic signals at equal levels in the console, listen to the combination "in" and "out of" phase. If one relationship between them clearly gives more bottom and punch to the drum, that is the relationship you want. In many cases, however, the acoustical relationship between the sounds reaching the two mics is neither fully in nor out of phase but somewhere in between, and it may be different at various frequencies, too. It's your choice which combination of signals best suits the feel of the music. Use your ears, not rule or custom, to make your decision. If each combination has a different emotional implication, select the one that supports the intended emotion of the song you are recording now.

Destructive Processing. You may need to apply narrow-band parametric equalization to find and eliminate resonances. In the top mic, there is usually one somewhere around 200 Hz, only a few Hz wide (from 195 to 205 Hz). Some snares have little body below this resonance, so be careful about dipping it too much. On the other hand, this resonance can have a definite musical pitch (between G and A below middle C), one that may work with or against the song at hand. A resonance pitched very close to the tonic of the song can help unify its feel, while one pitched a tritone (flatted 5th) away may cast a discordant, uneasy feel over the entire track. The tonic resonance can subtly reinforce consonance in a happy song, while a discordant snare resonance will complement tense or angry lyrics well.

If you do find some good weight in the 100 to 150 Hz range, you may use a second band of the parametric to boost it. These days trends are toward fatter snare sounds, so a lower band more than adequately replaces the resonance you are removing less than an octave above. After this, go hunting for another ringing or metallic resonance in the 300 to 800 Hz range. As in the kick drum, snare resonances tend to ring longer than the drum as a whole. And being pitched, they are quite obtrusive and difficult, if not impossible, to remove during a mix. In piccolo snare drums, all

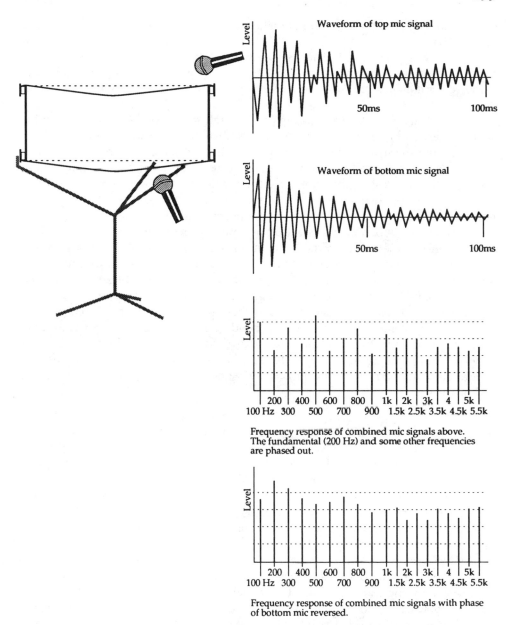

Waveform of top mic signal

50ms 100ms

Waveform of bottom mic signal

50ms 100ms

200 400 600 800 1k 2k 3k 4 5k
100 Hz 300 500 700 900 1.5k 2.5k 3.5k 4.5k 5.5k

Frequency response of combined mic signals above.
The fundamental (200 Hz) and some other frequencies
are phased out.

200 400 600 800 1k 2k 3k 4 5k
100 Hz 300 500 700 900 1.5k 2.5k 3.5k 4.5k 5.5k

Frequency response of combined mic signals with phase
of bottom mic reversed.

Figure 12.7. Cross-section of snare drum showing the motion of both heads immediately after being struck. The signals from the two mics can be out of phase at times, as shown. Specifically, at the instant of impact, both heads move down, lowering air pressure near the top mic, raising it near the bottom mic. Thus the top mic's waveform begins with a negative peak, the bottom mic's with a positive peak.

the potential resonances will occur at higher frequencies, perhaps 270 Hz and 1 kHz, for example.

In the event that kick leakage is still objectionable, use a third parametric band to find the worst frequency and reduce it to an acceptable level, unless of course this is the very frequency the snare needs for its own weight. If so, gating may save the day.

A noise gate can be used to limit the overall length of each snare hit and to keep leakage from nearby kick, toms, and cymbals from showing up on the snare track. Because the snare drum itself contains lots of highs, the opening click of a gate will usually not be heard, even if you decide to use a very short attack time and 70 dB floor. Nevertheless, I prefer milder gating, with a 30 dB floor or so. Too much separation between drums and you lose the feel of a kit. And as we know, you can regate in the mix, but ungating hasn't been invented yet.

I rarely apply parametric equalization to the bottom mic, but it is possible to treat egregious resonances in the lower head with a parametric. Do not presume, however, that these resonances will be at the same frequencies as those in the top head: damping and the pressure of the snares themselves will doubtless have an effect on bottom-skin. If lows from the bottom mic are indeed cleaner than those from the top, use the parametric to locate and boost these so that, in your preferred blend of both mics, the combined bottom end is solid, full, and musically inert (devoid of pitched resonances). I tend to mistrust my ears if what seems to be the right eq in either mic involves more than 8 to 10 dB of boost or dip in any range. That is a serious amount of eq, especially if the snare sounds okay in the room before miking and processing.

Crisis Keying.   If the snares rattle a lot when other drums are struck, you may want to noise gate the bottom mic, keying it with the output of the top mic. This way, only a hit on the snare itself will allow the bottom mic to be heard. If the gate still opens through sympathetic vibration with similarly tuned drums, make a multiple of the top snare mic signal, find some frequency from this mic that is unique to the snare drum (perhaps one of its unwanted resonance peaks), use an equalizer to eliminate everything but that frequency, and use it to key the bottom snare mic gate. Providing no other drum sounds at the keying frequency, you will hear the bottom snare mic only when the snare is hit.

Obviously, all these tricks cannot be tried on a demo budget. Nor (thank goodness!) have I ever had to use them all at once, even on the most careful album project. However, knowing the full range of potential problems and starting solutions will help you develop a good feel for studio recording. After a while, you will recognize a problem and instinctively reach for the right device(s) to solve it. You may even be able to guess frequencies, bandwidths, dB settings, and the like quite accurately before hearing how these devices affect the sounds at hand. At this point, studio craftsmanship and artistry begin to merge.

In fact, it is helpful to remember a few specific pitch/frequency relationships. Middle C is about 260 Hz, A below it is 220 Hz, and G about 200 Hz. D and E above are 290 Hz and 325 Hz, respectively. With these in mind, you can guess that a snare pitched at $C^{\#}$ has a resonance at 275 Hz. One that sounds at $G^{\#}$ resonates at 210 Hz, and so on.

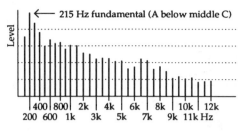

A. Mic signal of a snare's top head, unprocessed.

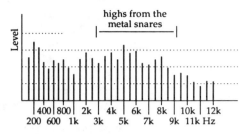

D. Mic signal of the same snare's bottom head.

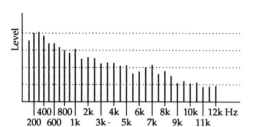

B. Top mic signal (A) after narrow-band resonance removal, reducing awareness of the fundamental.

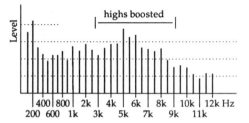

E. Bottom mic signal after in-board eq.

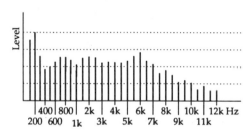

C. Top mic signal (C) after in-board eq. Bands around 400 Hz and 1.2 kHz are dipped, while a broad boost is applied around 6 kHz.

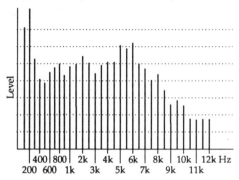

F. Combined mono signal from both mics.

Figure 12.8.   Frequency content of top and bottom snare mic signals before and after various eq steps. In the final composite sound (F), the 100-300 Hz band is boosted for punch. Within this band the 215 Hz top skin resonance was removed in B. The boosted 2 kHz range lends an aggressive "crack," and real highs from the bottom head enable the drum to cut through the densest rock or metal arrangement.

By now you should have a blend of two mics that captures the punch and crispness of a fine snare drum without leakage from, or much snare rattling cause by, the other drums. If something is still missing, you can use the snare sound to key in a synthesized filler sound or even a replacement snare from a TC unit or other canned source. Remember, however, that it takes a couple of milliseconds for the trigger to supply each replacement snare. Even this short delay can subtly change a song's feel.

Compression and Console Eq.   Two basic types of compression are used for snare drums. If the record needs a smooth, slick cruising or driving feel (which I call

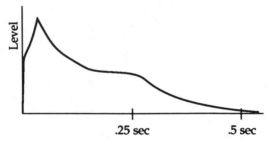

Uncompressed snare drum signal.

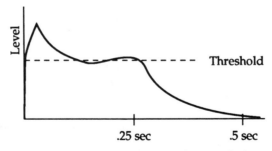

Snare signal compressed for that "horizontal" feel.
Fast attack, medium ratio, medium release.

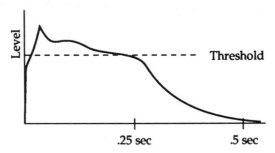

Snare compressed for a punchy, bouncy feel.
Slower attack, medium ratio, very fast release.

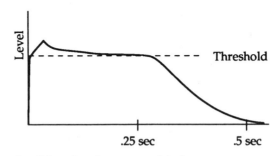

A solid rock or heavy metal feel.
Fast attack, high ratio, slow release.

62

Figure 12.9. The envelope of a snare drum showing three different styles of compression described in the text.

horizontal), use a short attack (under 2 ms), high ratio, and a long release (1 second or more). By tightly controlling each transient, you can ride the snare as high as necessary in the mix without the attack poking through the mix and causing an over-load in the LP mastering or broadcast. If the record needs a high-stepping, bouncing feel, use a long attack (5 to 15 ms), a low ratio, and a short release (under 0.2 sec-onds). Each snare transient will then pop through the musical blend and be signifi-cantly higher than the average level of the mix. Moreover, you can get the short re-lease to produce the same kind of volume expansion at the end of each hit that is found in heavy metal kick drums. The extra lift is more felt than heard, but it definitely lends what I call a vertical quality to the finished mix.

A final console eq is best left until after you have fine-tuned the vocal and other lead musical sounds. Male vocals generally require a heavier snare to complement their weight, while higher female voices may be overwhelmed by too heavy a drum sound. Most two-mic snare sounds still benefit from dipping of the lower midrange (in the 300 to 600 Hz range) and perhaps a gentle peak somewhere in the top end. Tune these mics so that they support the entire rhythm section without obscuring the lyrics.

For the moment, get a quick overall eq that works with the kick and move on. The snare, kick, and toms can all be recorded to tape so that the loudest hits register +12 dB on peaking meters or just a touch over 0 dB if you are using VU meters. With most professional tapes, you will be at or near *saturation* (the level at which the oxide is fully magnetized), but many producers feel this overdrive adds punch, excite-ment, and a kind of natural compression. Obviously, levels much higher than this will result in a crunchlike audible distortion.*

Re-creating Early Reflections. Genuine early reflections smooth over such flaws as the raspiness of a bottom snare mic and the crackle of hardware throughout the drum kit. If they go unchecked in recording, these flaws can later steal attention from more important high-frequency information like vocal sibilants and percussions. To re-create that smooth crack of the snare, feed the bottom mic (or possibly the blend) into a real plate reverb (not a digital version) set for about half a second reverb time and bring the plate's output back into the snare blend just enough to mask the roughness. (With an exceptionally bright top or side mic and some eq on this reverb, a bottom mic may be unnecessary.) The reverb will seem to be a part of the snare sound, extending and smoothing out the overall envelope.

During a final mix you may want to use the plate for something else, so print minor touches like this right onto the multitrack tape. The more you postpone cre-ative processing decisions until the end, the less likely they are to get done, through limited equipment and time, memory lapse, or all three.

In mastering, effects such as distinct delays, repeats, gated reverb, and such are rarely recorded directly onto multitrack tape. Instead, these are usually added during

---

*All of my suggestions for maximum tape levels on various instruments are referenced to the current U.S. test tape standard of 320 nanowebers (a measure of absolute magnetic field strength). If your engineer cringes at the idea of cutting tracks near saturation, follow his or her advice. Engineers know their equip-ment best, and it is entirely possible that their studios use another standard reference level.

mixdown, when the proper proportion and sound of each is easier to judge. For demos, however, shoot from the hip and make sure every effect is heard clearly. Do not get too fussy about details. Small errors in level will not ruin the tape if the material and performance are strong.

Hi-Hat Miking.   Fortunately, hi-hat miking is a fairly simple matter once you determine what sensation you want from the hat. If harshness is a part of the emotional or musical theme of the song at hand, use a cardioid condenser mic (Neumann KM 84, Shure SM 81, or equivalent) boomed in above the open hat and angled toward the drummer's left, beyond the rest of the kit. Because of extraordinary detail in its high-frequency response, the condenser will accentuate the upper harmonics and partials and give the impression that you can hear the stick or brush in contact with each circular grinding of the upper hat cymbal. This positioning will prevent the mic from picking up highs from cymbals above or from adjacent drums. Without fail, use any internal mic pad and low roll-off, and keep your ears open for distortion anyway.

On the other hand, if you want a smooth, silky *tsssp* of highs from the hat, use a dynamic (the AKG 441, Beyer 160, and Electro-Voice RE-15 are common first choices) in the same position. In either case, the mic should be no closer than 4″ to 6″ above the open hat. The foot pedal can lift the top hat cymbal two inches or more. Thus, closer miking will render open hits much louder than similar hits played on the closed hat. At such small distances, a couple of inches can mean a difference of 6 dB or more at the console. Again, a felt cone or flap can be employed for increased rejection of highs from other nearby sources.

Although some engineers gate the hi-hat to minimize leakage from other drums and then compress the hat to bring each hit out loud and clear, I prefer to use console equalization to achieve separation. There is little usable sound from a hat below 500 Hz, and even that range often clashes with ride and crash cymbals anyway. We can use the low cut and take out everything below 500 Hz. With proper mic positioning, this should reduce drum leakage to an acceptable level when the hat mic is heard in the context of the entire kit.

If you must have a squeaky-clean hat track and the snare is still bleeding into the hat mic, make a multiple of the hi-hat signal and introduce a graphic equalizer between it and the keying input of a gate on the mic's signal. Removing everything below 2 kHz from the keying eq will prevent the gate from opening at all in response to mid and low frequencies, such as those from the snare, toms, or kick.

Drummers often phrase their hi-hat lines with volume variations that are important to the feel of particular rhythm tracks. Compressing during recording will flatten this phrasing out forever. I prefer to compress the hat during mixdown, if at all. For an out-and-out dance record, though, limiting is a must, if only to rescue the tweeters (and patrons' ears) during high-volume playback on the dance floor.

After this, a boost above 8 kHz will add a silken quality to the dynamic mic signal. The resulting hat signal can be recorded onto a separate track or blended in with the overheads. It really depends on track availability, the possible necessity of a repeat, delay, or other effect on the hat in the mixdown, and so on. For most rock, pop, R&B, dance, and related styles, a separate hat track helps a lot. In any event, because dense highs from the hi-hat mic will overload tape at relatively low levels, do not let peak levels during an open hi-hat roll exceed $+8$ dB on tape. Equivalent VU readings may register no higher than -6 dB on solid staccato hits or perhaps -2 dB VU on the loudest smash.

TOM-TOMS

Most drummers like toms to have a single, pure tone with lots of body resonance—a smoothly tapering sound envelope free of secondary rings and resonances that creep in as the drum fades out. The first step to achieving this sound is a perfect tuning of the live toms. Next, for a smooth decay, the mounting of each tom must be as free as possible; the drum's shell should not be directly clamped or bolted to any other drum. A hard mount transfers vibrational energy away from the individual drum and dissipates it in attached stands, other drums, and the floor. Among various commercially available isolation systems, RIMS brand hardware (made by Purecussion, Inc.) provides the best physical isolation that I have encountered.

Generally (except for single-headed Rototoms or the curved-shell toms designed for maximum live projection), drummers leave both heads on, tuning them identically in each tom and using the internal air resonance to optimize the duration of the drum's envelope.

Once the desired sound is there live, we can begin miking and processing. One good omen for controlling cymbal leakage is that tom-toms emit little above 6 kHz. However, their SPL level is again very high, so dynamic mics are a natural starting point. The 421U is a standby because of its mid-high boost and continuously variable low roll-off: SM 57 and 58s are my own next choice. Electro-Voice RE-15s, also less bright, respond well to high-impact sounds, and their extreme directionality helps to limit leakage from all nearby sources, especially cymbals. Why many engineers use the Neumann U87 for floor tom remains a mystery to me. Even with the pad, it can overload, and the mic's superb response (and high cost) seems wasted in an instrument rarely struck and lacking any output above 8 kHz.

In many setups the only way to get a microphone near the top head of the rack toms (without getting in the way of the drummer's sticks) is to aim the mics at the drummer's belly, along the rack toms' head surface, or diagonally down through the drum. As with the snare, diagonality gives the richest and most balanced sound and the fewest local resonance problems. Unfortunately, the rack tom mics are also pointed right at the snare drum, with all the attendant leakage and phasing problems with respect to the snare mics. Even with gating, the snare may be loud enough to open the tom gates, thereby destroying its own sound.

One solution is to use an *X-Y pair* on two rack toms. If there are three, add a Z mic aimed across the third tom and away from the snare. The X-Y pair, with diaphragms one over the other, each aimed at one tom and 45 degrees or more away from the snare, has the added advantage of being coincident with respect to both toms. Low frequencies from each rack tom reach both mic diaphragms in phase, eliminating any low-frequency phase difference and preserving the full weight and resonance of both toms.

Because these lows act additively, the level of each drum's fundamental is duplicated on the two channels or tape tracks to which the separate mics are sent. You can then roll off lows from each mic by about 6 dB while retaining the same overall weight in each tom, reducing snare and kick leakage in the bargain. At the same time, highs from each tom remain discreet, directing a listener's attention to the stereo panning position selected later for each tom. However, since lows from the snare also accumulate additively in these coincident mics, you may need to patch in a pair of parametrics, locate the snare fundamental, and dip a narrow band around this frequency (say 0.2 octave) before sending the tom mics to tape.

If the drum setup makes it impossible to deploy an X-Y configuration, use a spaced pair on dual rack toms and take advantage of a handy trick. Spread the pair as far apart as possible on the toms and flip the phase of one of the mics, preferably the mic on the tom tuned lower. Because the distance from snare to either of these mics is about equal, any snare fundamental reaching both mics will be out of phase between them. Even if the tom tracks are later panned broadly left and right in the mix, the bottom end of each tom will be unaffected, while snare leakage will be partially phased out or cancelled when the record is heard in mono or if these mics are panned near each other in the mix.

If there is more than one floor tom and you desire separate control or panning positions on each, another X-Y pair of dynamics will serve best, again sharing the burden of the low frequencies among the tracks or channels to which each mic is sent or later panned. If you wish to increase the apparent left/right separation of rack or floor toms, install felt cones or flaps. These will reduce leakage from cymbals above and around and ensure that each of the X-Y pair picks up highs only from its on-axis tom.

My own *tracking* preference (the way various mics are grouped and sent to tape) is to submix all tom mics down to two tracks of tape, each panned where it will be needed in the final mix. Since toms are used far less than the kick and snare in most songs, there is little reason to dedicate a separate track to each tom. You may later have to *bounce* them (rerecord the contents of one track, or a blend of several, onto another) all together anyway. This wastes precious studio time and introduces a measure of uncertainty about their phase relationships with other drum tracks because not all multitrack machines and processing devices maintain the initial phase of signals from their input to output or vice versa.

Panning Consistency and Stereo Imaging.   The toms are really our first opportunity to think about stereo in the complete kit. Because of the prominent level needed on kick and snare, both these drums are usually panned to the center position in the final mix. But what perspective do you want for the rest of the kit? The drummer's perspective, with hi-hat far left, floor toms far right? Or, oppositely, the audience's perspective? There are no rules here—but once you decide, treat every pair of stereo drums tracks (toms now, overheads later), and each single mic (e.g., on floor tom or hi-hat) from the same perspective.

If, for instance, the toms are assigned to tape tracks 5 and 6, with the floor toms on 6, make sure that you maintain the same positioning of the toms in the tracks that record the overhead mics. If the latter are sent to tracks 7 and 8, assign the overhead mic pointed most nearly at the floor toms to track 8. When you later split

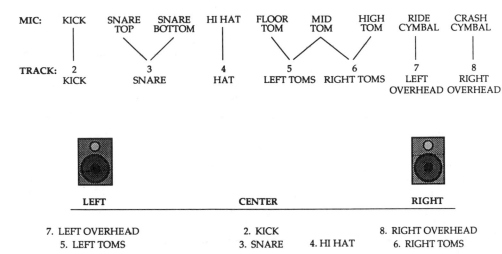

Figure 12.10. Drum mic assignments to each of seven tape tracks (top) and their panned positions in the final mix (bottom). In this configuration, the drums are heard from the audience's perspective, as the kit is viewed in Figure 25.1 (top).

each numbered pair of drum tracks during the mix, a coherent image of the set will result automatically. The overhead mics dictate the overall L/R image: you have to pan the individual drums tracks into about the same position at which each source appears in the overheads. Without this precaution, each drum will appear at two or more L/R locations, draining its punch and smearing its image.

Processing.   Properly tuned and suspended, toms need little processing during recording. Unless snare leakage is a big problem, in-console eq should be adequate for destructive and constructive shaping of the response. A low-cut filter on the console will diminish kick leakage. If the console has parametric eqs, and if the tom sound itself is not in need of an additional low-end boost, you may use the bottom band of the eq to locate precisely the loudest frequency range in the kick leakage and dip it further. Next, locate the range of highs that brings out the kind of skin sound you want. The 4-to-5-kHz range affords a hard edge that adds aggression to hard rock tunes. Boosting to 6 or 8 kHz gives a more delicate feel.

As with the entire kit, a dip somewhere in the low-mids usually removes the cardboardy or boxy sound that often comes with close miking. Exactly where depends on how loud you want the toms in the mix and what else they have to cut through. If other rhythm instruments will be very dense in the 500-Hz-to-2-KHz band, try dipping the tom mics just below this, say between 300 and 400 Hz, leaving plenty of tom highs to cut through the already-crowded band above. But if the instrumental bed will be more weighty than bright, dip the toms in the 500-to-900-Hz range. Logic might nudge you toward dipping the toms where the rhythm instruments are hottest, giving the toms a clear band in which to sound, but heavy toms will trivialize a light arrangement, and light toms will sound wimpy in a heavy one.

Gate after equalization, if at all, bearing in mind that the toms will also be heard through the overhead mics. The principal job of the gate will be to reduce leakage from the kick and snare. Thus, you may find that the threshold has to be set fairly high, not far below the level of the toms hits themselves. When the gate closes, you will doubtless hear it, but this side effect is usually inaudible when the overhead mics are brought into proper perspective. If the gating is still obvious, raise the floor and/ or slow the fade until the gating is just barely perceptible. A touch of reverb will mask the rest of the problem unless there is a drum solo somewhere in the song's arrangement.

Although compressed toms have an ear-filling punch, I would not compress during record unless the overall arrangement is very dense. In a dense arrangement, the toms will have a hard time cutting through and maintaining enough sonic weight. In this case a compressor attack of about a 5-to-10-ms, 5 : 1 ratio, and medium release time (0.5 to 1.0 seconds) will preserve maximum acuity on each hit and maintain full resonance and sustain on each tom hit. A shorter release of 0.1 second can give a reverse-envelope effect (where volume increases briefly during the sustain of each hit) that calls attention to single tom hits. However, the same effect on a complex tom fill will garble the individual hits and distract the ear from the rhythmic function of the phrase.

Avoid compression unless you are sure it is necessary—remember that you can always compress later during the mix. Expansion of overcompressed toms is not very satisfying because no expander can re-create the natural envelope of the tom once an overzealous compressor has flattened it like a pancake. Whether or not you choose compression, do not be afraid to cut the toms hot on tape, peaking at +12 dB or at +2 dB on VU meters. The natural compression of mild tape saturation can add weight and punch, while the minimal top end of the toms cannot easily cause audible distortion.

I am not a fan of cutting special effects directly onto the tom tracks. If you definitely want some flanging, a special reverb effect, or whatever, and if you think this processor may not be available for these tracks during the mix, by all means blend it right into the tracks. However, set the level and sound of the effect only when you hear the entire band rehearsing the rhythm tracks. Setting effects levels while listening only to the drums, one tends to put in less of the effect than will eventually be necessary to hear it through all instruments and vocals in the final mix. In short, do not be shy—where an intermittent effect is concerned, too much is better than not enough.

DRUM KITS AND CYMBALS

Overhead Mics.   There are several methods of overheard miking, each with its benefits and problems. Before deciding on the types of mics and their configuration, think of how the drums should function within the finished musical context and how the tape is likely to be reproduced. Condenser mics make good overheads for music with an aggressive edge, from hard rock to R&B and dance. Their unmatched transient and high-frequency response accentuates every sharp edge in the drum part and delivers the metallic spectrum of cymbals almost verbatim. For more laid-back styles, from mellow jazz and new age to pop ballads, dynamics or ribbon mics can deliver an atmospheric overhead sound, with silkier highs and less jagged edges, and—depending on positioning—an expansive quality.

Among condensers, Neumann U87 or KM89s are generally the mics of choice, with AKG 414s and various Sony models as close runner-ups. Of these, the Neumanns are the brightest, the 414s the mellowest. They all feature variable pickup patterns— omni-, bi-, and one or more unidirectional options. The right choice of mic and pattern depends on the room height available above the kit, the size and construction of the drum booth or platform, and the feeling of acoustical space desired in the recording. If there is little room to raise the mics more than 6 feet above the floor,

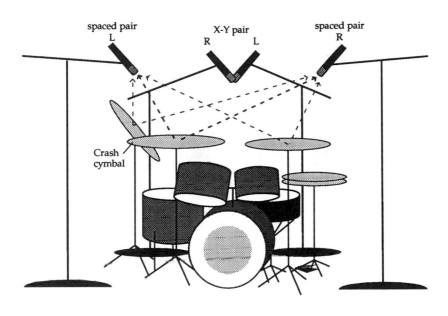

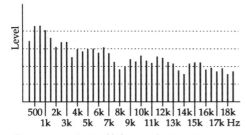

Frequency content of left spaced pair mic responding to a loud crash cymbal.

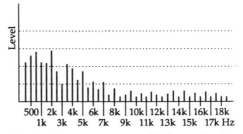

Combined frequency content of both spaced-pair mics (blended into mono) responding to the same crash.

Figure 12.11. Spaced and X-Y mic pairs mounted over a drum kit. Note that the right mic of the spaced pair is much farther from the crash cymbal than the left mic. When the spaced pair signals are combined, frequencies above 2 kHz are severely attenuated by phase cancellation. This underscores the importance of checking the mono blend of spaced pairs when setting the mic positions.

or about two feet above the tallest cymbals, select omni if only to make sure the mics hear the entire set. The only workable configuration in that case is a pair spaced at least two feet apart.

Because it is analogous to separating your ears by several feet, stereo separation of spaced-pair mics seems exaggerated. But the distance from any off-center sound source to each mic is different, so that various frequencies may be canceled out when the overheads are blended into mono, as in AM radio, television reception, and movie soundtracks. If the drum booth is taller and allows you to raise the overheads to 7 or 8 feet, you can select cardioid and hang a coincident X-Y pair above the drummer's head, one mic aimed left, the other right. This produces a more natural stereo, with no hole in the middle and without phasing problems that result in lost frequencies when the mics are heard in mono.

Among dynamic overheads, Sennheiser 460s and 441s, Electro-Voice (EV) RE-55s and Beyer ribbon models are used widely. The 441s, with both a treble boost switch and low roll-off, may reduce the need for extreme console equalization. The RE-55s are omni and thus useful only in spaced pairs. PZM mics are also gaining popularity as overheads. These can be stand-mounted or taped directly to the ceiling or walls of the drum booth. To my ear, wall- or ceiling-mounted PZMs give a broad stereo sound with a feeling of space, though the sound is somewhat more diffuse than that given by *boom-mounted mics* (mounted on a telescoping support arm), probably because the walls or ceiling are farther from the drum kit. Suspended in midair, there is little difference between the sense of space given by the PZM and the standard omni mics.

Processing.   So far, we have tried a lot of processing on the kick, snare, and tom mics, all to increase the separation among them and maximize the useful portion of their signals that goes to tape. As a result, there is little to glue their sound together and give the illusion of a complete drum set. Drum machines, with completely separated outputs for each drum and cymbal, represent the endpoint in a twenty-year engineering crusade to reduce the drum set to a group of individually manipulable sounds. The overhead mics represent your only opportunity to capture the entire set of live drums in natural stereo, with the natural imaging of each drum and cymbal in its own place and at its true relative volume.

For this reason, I suggest you process the overheads as little as possible. No gating, no compression—just some console eq. In most mixes I rely on individual drum tracks for the punch and bottom end, using the overheads to unify the set and define the space around the drums. Thus, use the console's low roll-off, and perhaps a shelf equalizer to lower everything below 300 Hz or so before sending overheads to tape; no need to print low-frequency information you will only shelf-dip in the mix. I also generally shelf-boost everything above 6 kHz by 3 to 6 dB, depending on the mics used, for extra silkiness. If the result proves too bright in the mix, I can get rid of some tape noise while bringing usable highs back into perspective.

As with hi-hat, set the level so that the loudest cymbal crashes peak at $+8$ dB or so. On VU meters that corresponds to about -3 dB, or perhaps a tad more. Higher levels of dense highs will lead to tape saturation and distortion. In addition, I usually find that the level a drummer gives you during setups will increase by about 3 dB during actual takes of the song. Better safe than sorry!

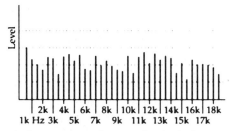

A. Response curve from overhead mic above a
   22" ride cymbal

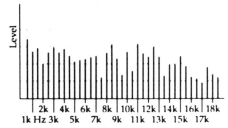

B. Response curve from a mic underneath a
   22" ride cymbal

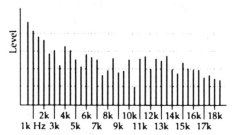

C. Response curve from overhead mic above a
   16" crash cymbal

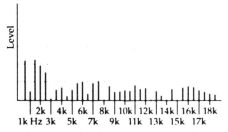

D. Response curve from a mic underneath a
   16" crash cymbal

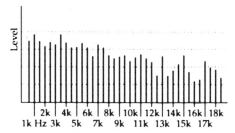

E. Response curve from overhead mic above an
   18" chinese crash cymbal with cracks.

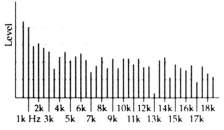

F. Response curve from a mic underneath an
   18" chinese crash cymbal with cracks.

Figure 12.12.   The frequency content of various cymbals as heard by an overhead omni mic
3 feet above the kit (left), and the same mic 6 inches below the outer edge of each cymbal
(right). Snare, tom and hi-hat mics positioned near or beneath the edges of cymbals pick up
grossly colored cymbal sounds as in B, D and F. These stray cymbal signals can ruin the full
cymbal response delivered by properly placed overheads as in A, C and E. This problem
underscores the need for isolation among mics and/or noise gating of the drum mics below
the cymbals to reduce leakage in the composite drum kit sound.

Cymbals.   Heard in the context of a full drum kit, cymbals may seem to generate only frequencies above 2 kHz. In fact, however, the lowest mode of a 20″ ride
cymbal may be as low as 50 Hz, with a dense series of higher modes generating
frequencies up to and beyond 20 kHz. Fortunately the output levels of higher frequencies far outweigh the lows; otherwise cymbal leakage would keep us from achieving
a tight and punchy recorded drum sound.

In essence, a cymbal is a rigid metallic membrane, so rigid that it needs no outer support or rim to maintain its shape and internal tension. When struck at one edge, the near half of its surface is deflected downward, causing a first pie-mode reaction as the wave travels across the surface, deflecting the far side upward. The speed of sound in metal is extremely fast, which means that the far side moves up at virtually the same instant that the near side is moving down. The net result is an almost total acoustic phase cancellation of of the lower modes at a distance.

A mic placed 3' above the center of a cymbal thus hears little of its lower modes. However, a mic placed directly under one edge picks up lots of lows. As you might suspect, snare, rack, and floor tom mics hear a lot of undesired cymbal noise. Worse yet, the leakage through each has a slightly different phase relationship to the cymbal sound heard by the overheads. With all mics balanced in the console, the resulting cymbal sound can produce nasty ringing peaks and a very indistinct L/R image of cymbal positions. Such problems underscore the importance of positioning the close mics on drums for maximum isolation and of shielding them as much as possible from cymbal leakage.

The real problems with cymbal sounds begin in the 1 to 3 kHz range. The heavier or thicker the cymbals used, the higher their output in this range, and the longer it sustains, masking clarity in the snare and toms. Some of this upper-midrange ringing can be nixed by applying a few patches of masking or thicker tape to the cymbals, usually near the outer edges (but not right where the drummer strikes them). For best recording of rock, jazz, or even metal, use thinner cymbals than those played on stage. The lower and middle modes of thin cymbals die out rather quickly, since the cymbal's mass and rigidity cannot sustain internal vibrations much under 500 Hz. We will observe the same behavior later in the thin or less rigid soundboards of certain stringed instruments.

Overhead mics hear a balance of everything the drummer plays. Moreover, they deliver individual drum highs that are not present in the close-mic signals because of the proximity-effect bass boost and the fact that the top snare mic is so much closer to the top skin than to the snares. In theory we should be able to use the overheads to brighten the kit. However, the high 1 to 3 kHz output of the combined cymbals can prevent brightening. Instead, we might wind up dipping the upper midrange from the overheads and reaching for highs from the close mics. Resolving this "cymbalic" conflict calls for many of the miking and processing techniques already discussed at such length.

Apart from DI work, Alan Parsons has tended to develop a standard approach to microphone technique. In an interview with *Studio Sound*, he says:

On drums, it's a [AKG] D20 on bass drum, KM84s on snare and toms, and a pair of 4038s on top, with no hi-hat mic. The hi-hat always appears when you put lots of top on the snare. Sometimes I'll go through three board equalizers to eq a snare. Most of the mics I use are Neumann—all the condensers are. I place the 4038s quite high—about 4' above the cymbals.

In a pop recording the drum set should be treated as a combination of instruments, [engineer Bruce Swedien believes,] because many of the desired effects have to be emphasized electronically. If the effects were heard in a natural acoustic balance, much of this sound would be lost. Multiple miking on the drum set is the only answer.

I mike the overall set with a pair of high-quality condenser microphones about 6' in the air in a stereo configuration. . . . A good choice for overhead is the Neumann U-87 in a cardioid pattern. If the drummer has really good quality tom-toms which are tuned to specific tonalities, usually a Neumann U-87 or KM-84 will work well placed about 8 to 10" away. If the drummer has tom-toms with very little low-frequency content that need a lot of help, the mic is generally placed closer, to make use of the low-end proximity effect.

For bass drum I use a Sennheiser MD421, AKG C412, or an EV RE-20. I also use a specially made bass drum cover with an elastic around it and a slot in the middle for the microphone.

On the snare I use a mic technique that I developed many years ago in Chicago for recording rhythm and blues records, where a hard drum sound was necessary. My current choice of microphone for the snare is the AKG 451, with a cardioid condenser capsule and a 20 dB pad. I mike the snare drum from the side about 8 to 10" away from the shell of the drum, being very careful not to position the mic anywhere near the air hole on the side of the shell.

On the sock cymbal or hi-hat I use two types of microphones, depending entirely upon the sound. One choice is the RCA 77DX ribbon mic, and the other is the AKG C451 (occasionally I'll use a Shure SM57 dynamic).

While recording drums tracks I never use any limiting or compression, and very little equalization. The only drum mic on which I would use any eq would be the kick, usually boosting it about 2 to 4 dB at 1.5 kHz, and maybe a 2 dB peak at 100 Hz. On the sock cymbal I will usually use a high pass filter set at 100 Hz.

[For Phil Ramone, in an interview in *Mix* magazine,] drum booths in a lot of studios are so dead that I have to fight to get the drums to come alive. So I use a large isolation room for the drums as much as possible, with variable acoustics on the walls and glass and wood. I set the room up to have a resonance so that drums actually sound like a set of drums.

Generally, there are two mics that I like on the snare. I'll either use a Sennheiser 441, or if I'm doing a fat rock-and-roll kind of thing, I'll use a Sony C-37, close miked and padded down at the preamp so it doesn't overload. It's dangerous to use a condenser mic in that proximity, but it does have a way of hitting you right in the lower gut.

On the kick drum I generally use an old Electro-Voice 666 that seems to work real well. For the hi-hat, depending on what I'm using on the snare, I'll switch off between the Sennheiser 441 and a Shure SM 57. I use Beyer 160s on the tom-toms, hung, and aimed from the drummer's point of view looking out at the drums, not the other way. Overheads are usually a pair of Sennheiser 435s. As long as the tom-toms are balanced, I'll sometimes use just one mike for the overheads. You can get just as much spread with less phase problems, and you'll avoid those hollow holes that can make the drummer sound like he's in a tub.

In the A&R [Studios] drum booth there are metal railings so the mics can be suspended with pipes and goose necks and be positioned out of the drummer's way. It's important to take whatever steps are necessary to keep the drummer from beating the mics.

It may seem that days have been spent getting a good drum sound. In fact, many a group has devoted a week or more to setups for one or another of their hit albums. So how can you possibly get a decent drum sound in an hour? Fear not: you will probably never encounter all these problems and variables in a single session. It is important to plow through them all here to demystify what is on the minds of engineers with whom you work; to encourage you to communicate with engineers and producers in emotional, dramatic, musical, and technical terms, not just the latter; and to introduce you to the kind of creative audio thinking that will enable you to develop your own studio sound and techniques.

Drummers should not stop here, however. There is much to learn from the chapters that follow. We will continue investigating the properties of vibrating membranes in the piano chapter, the sonic behavior of enclosed air masses in later discussions of organ pipes and woodwinds, and ringing phenomena such as bells and chimes in the chapter on tuned percussions. After all, a large organ pipe is the tube from which drum shells are sliced, and a bell is nothing more than a deep-dish cymbal.

13

ACOUSTIC AND ELECTRIC BASS

ACOUSTIC and electric bass are the musical foundation for the melodic and chordal structure of many recordings. While their frequency range extends from below 30 Hz to well over 10 kHz, almost all their acoustic energy is concentrated below 500 Hz. Nominally, the lowest E of a standard bass is tuned to about 40 Hz. However, most basses emit a short burst of even lower frequencies when each string is plucked. It simply takes a short time for the energy of the pluck to disperse throughout the string and kick it into uniform vibrational motion. Because this transient gives punch to both electric and acoustic basses, it is important not to roll off the extreme lows too steeply.

BASIC PROBLEMS

In addition, although the highest harmonics and so-called rosin sound of bowed or plucked acoustic bass are not actually necessary to hear the bass notes being played, these upper partials open up the instrument's sound, giving an airy quality that can grab the listener's attention even through very dense rock and orchestral arrangements. Together these factors makes the bass a difficult instrument to record well, and each type has its own problems.

Just as drums serve different functions in jazz, pop, heavy metal, and other musical genres, so the electric and acoustic bass play a number of dramatic roles. Because the bass is as prominent as drums in most mixes, it is important to consider what type of bass sound best suits each piece you record. Should it be full and sustained, following and reinforcing the rhythm of the kick drum and supporting the chords and melody with a continuous cushion of lows? If so, it might be best to deemphasize the low-frequency transient to let the kick drum attacks cut through clearly and define the rhythmic structure.

Will the bass itself play a more rhythmic role, defining a counter rhythm to the kick drum or snare? If so, every pluck on the bass should have the punch and weight of the kick. This approach mandates a boost of whatever frequency bands bring the exact timing of each pluck to the fore. A song may also require that each bass note be the same level, with a quick decay to dead silence when the string is muted, or just the opposite—high dynamics with continuous low-frequency information bridging even the gap between notes.

Although the type and order of processing can do a lot to change the sound and feel of the instrument, the best way to get the sound you want is by using the right bass and keeping it in top shape. Whether your bass is acoustic or electric, you may have to change strings prior to a session, either to even out the level and/or sustain of various notes and ranges or to increase the output of upper partials. As with drums, do this the night before the session, so that the new strings will hold pitch without having to be constantly retuned between or even during takes.

The output of an electric bass also varies with the distance between each string and the corresponding magnetic pole piece in the pickup. Adjust this at home, by ear, and/or VU meter, balancing output response so that notes played evenly on the fifth fret of each string (a musical 4th above open tuning) decrease in volume by 3 dB or so from the first (lowest E) to the fourth G string. Overall, output level should decline about 6 dB over the two-and-one-half octave diatonic range from the open E string on up. A properly scaled bass may need no compression during recording or mixdown. Beyond this, the characteristics of acoustic and electric bass diverge.

ACOUSTIC BASS

Several sizes of string bass are available, varying from one slightly larger than a cello to the mammoth 5-string double bass developed in response to the demand for thunderous lows in romantic orchestral repertoires, particularly Liszt, Strauss and Wagner. Some musical scores include a low A that sounds at 27 Hz! In addition, the bass can have a dynamic range of over 30 dB, from the softest *ppp* to a full *Sfz,* both when plucked and bowed (bowing is designated *arco* in scores); in some ranges, low-frequency transients are nearly as steep as those in the kick drum.

How Sound Is Produced and Amplified. Sound in the acoustic bass is produced when the vibrations from a plucked or bowed string travel through a bridge to the front surface or plate, which then disperses these vibrations to the entire wooden body and the contained volume of air. By vibrating sympathetically with various fundamental frequencies sounded by the strings, the body and enclosed air couple or transfer the strings' energy to the surroundings. Thus the entire bass is essentially an *acoustic amplifier.* Unlike a cylindrical drum shell, the body of a bass is irregularly shaped. Its wooden belly (front) and back plates are hand-shaped, with varying thicknesses and curvatures. Together the resulting irregularities generate modes of vibration far more complex than those of any drum.

The first mode, in which the body and contained air amplify the very lowest notes, occurs when the entire front and rear surfaces flex in a single arc. Since the body is divided into two vertical chambers or lobes, a larger one beneath and a

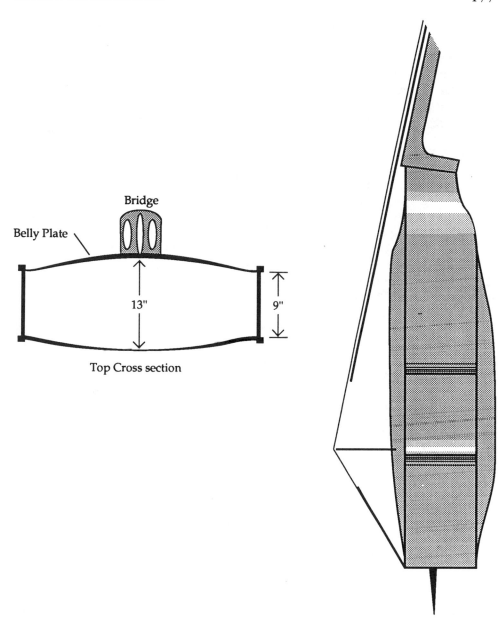

Figure 13.1.   Side view and top cross-section of a "fat back" acoustic bass, showing the varying thickness and curvature of the wooden surfaces. Since the belly plate bears the full force
of the strings' tension through the bridge, it must be thicker than the rear plate. Each can
thus resonate with and reinforce different frequency ranges. Similarly, the varying depth
(about 9″ to 13″ in this example) helps to project a broad band of midrange and upper
harmonics. If the plates were flat and parallel, one frequency would be amplified rather than
a whole range. The same logic applies to the varied interior heights and widths enclosed by
the upper and lower lobes of the body itself.

smaller one above the f-holes, the plate surfaces over each of these has characteristic local modes and resonances that amplify two separate higher-frequency bands. Furthermore, each subplate itself has smaller areas that resonate at even higher pitches, like the individual notes of a Jamaican steel drum.

The air mass inside the bass has three primary average dimensions (the thickness, for example, varies between seven inches and over a foot), each with a characteristic resonance in a narrow band of frequencies whose wavelengths are four times that dimension. (For a discussion of resonating air columns, see chapter 18.) A double bass whose body is nearly 4.5 feet high, 2.5 feet wide, and 10 inches deep will have primary air resonances at about 65 Hz, 110 Hz, and 320 Hz, with lesser peaks an octave above each of these pitches.

It is the combined primary modes and local resonances of various surfaces and local subvolumes of air that enable the instrument to amplify the entire range of frequencies generated by the strings. However, no bass amplifies all these notes evenly. Even the finest instrument, if played with constant bowing pressure, exhibits a 3 to 6 dB range of volumes on various notes. The acoustic amplification of lower harmonics of these notes is often even more erratic, with ringing, pitched midrange resonances and dead spots at various upper frequencies.

The neck of an acoustic bass is supposedly motionless with respect to the body. However, lab tests show that when a string is plucked hard, the neck does indeed vibrate front to back at one or more pitches that are related to its length, weight, stiffness, and the type of attachment to the body at the end block. Obviously, these resonances will amplify certain played frequencies. Tests aside, however, the speed with which plucked notes decay tells us that vibrational energy is quickly dissipated through imperfect mechanical linkages all over the instrument. In comparison, plucked notes on a solid-body electric bass sustain for up to 10 seconds.

Vibrating strings themselves behave as you might expect from our discussion of membranes. *First-mode vibrations* result if the entire string moves in one arc, with a single antinode at the center and nodes at the bridge and nut. The second mode has two equal arcs, each half the string length, with an additional node at the middle. The third mode has three arcs and four nodes, and so on. The relative volume of each mode in any note played depends, quite logically, on where the string is bowed or plucked.

If the string is plucked at its center, the fundamental and its odd-numbered harmonics will be preferentially generated, corresponding to 1/3, 1/5, 1/7 . . . the string's length and sounding at 3, 5, 7 . . . times the fundamental frequency. Played at one quarter the length, even-numbered harmonics will be heard in better balance. Plucking closer to the bridge generates less of the fundamental and a more even blend of all upper harmonics, since the player excites ever-higher vibrational modes of the string.

Arco Bass. Whenever a string is bowed, a group of nonharmonic upper partials and mechanical sounds is generated by the scraping action of the bow. Each "tooth" of the horsehair in a sense replucks the string in rapid succession, the speed depending on how fast the bow is drawn by the player. In a bass, these highs extend over 10 kHz, though at relatively low volume and acoustic energy. In a violin they are proportionately louder, extending far past the 20 kHz limit of human hearing. The

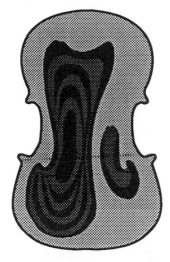 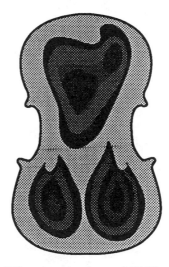

Vibration modes at 540 Hz.   **Vibration modes at 800 Hz.**

Figure 13.2.   The belly plate of an acoustic bass, as seen by an inferometer. This device allows us to see the areas of the wooden surface where energy is emitted when specific frequencies are sounded (either as fundamentals or harmonics). Light gray areas are stationary, i.e. anti-nodes, while the oddly shaped dark areas with concentric innards are vibrating. The more concentric interior figures in each area, the more vigorous the vibration. Note that due to uneven thickness of the plate in this instrument, 540 Hz vibrations (about C5) are emitted almost entirely from its left side. In contrast, 800 Hz (near G5) is radiated by three smaller areas (one in the top half of the plate, the others located symmetrically below) separated by anti-nodal lines.

pitches within the cluster of highs are relatively constant, regardless of the note played, although the volume of the entire cluster depends on where the string is bowed. Sometimes edgy, other times silky, this rosin sound is an important component of the sound of all real strings.

When a string is plucked, it can vibrate in any direction (360 degrees) around its rest position. Bowing, however, forces the string to vibrate mostly in one direction, back and forth parallel to the bow itself (and belly plate). Since the bridge vibrates more sideways than up and down, the front plate receives less energy at the fundamental and lower harmonics. Bowed bass thus has a brighter tone than plucked bass, with an obvious increase in the proportion of rosin tone in its output. For this reason, make sure you set recording eqs so that bowed notes are not too harsh or bright. It is often difficult to find a happy audio medium between good plucked and bowed sounds if both are used within a single song.

Body Resonances, "Pluck Tone," and Destructive Equalization.   The engineer is lucky if the enclosed air and wooden body of a bass resonate in separate frequency ranges, spreading the overall response peaks over a broader frequency band. For a typical full bass, the lowest air-mass resonance might be somewhere between 65 and 90 Hz, although the interaction of upper and lower lobes can spread this out over the better part of an octave.

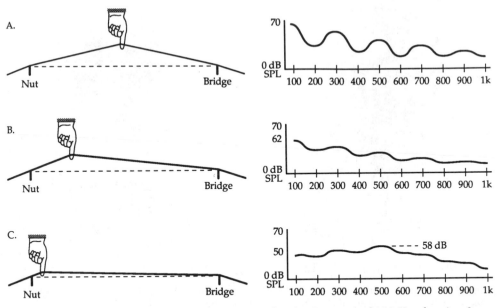

Figure 13.3.   A side view of a vibrating string with a fundamental of 100 Hz, showing 3 possible "plucking points" and the relative level of the first ten harmonics in the resulting sound. Each point is plucked with the same force. In A., the fundamental (100 Hz) and odd harmonics (300, 500, 700 Hz, etc.) are accentuated. The closer the pluck to the nut (B.) the more even the resulting level of all harmonics. When plucked very near the nut (C.), higher harmonics are actually louder than the fundamental. (Note: the graphs are averages to illustrate the point, and not precise frequency response curves.)

The wooden body, however, can have two or three sharp peaks, perhaps +6 dB each in a band no more than 2 to 4 Hz wide (4 Hz spans a musical semi-tone in the 100-Hz range, or two semi-tones, in the 50-Hz range). In addition, there will be a characteristic frequency at which the whole neck/body/string system resonates when a taut, muted string is plucked. This narrow-band transient *pluck tone* is generally between 30 and 60 Hz. The most important problem for recording is that you can hear all these resonances clearly about a foot in front of either f-hole. Farther away, in the tenth row, they blend together smoothly, as do the resonances in various areas of a piano soundboard.

Miking.   Mic selection should be based on the sound of the specific bass, how much of each resonance is desired, and the acoustics of the studio or booth in which the bass is played. Most engineers prefer condenser mics for string bass, no matter how played or at what volume, because of their variable patterns, superb transient response, and crystal-clear response in the 5-kHz-and-up range. The latter gives the listener the impression that he or she can hear the bassist's fingerprints as they brush against the windings of each string.

For close miking a bass, the Neumann U-87, KM-89, and U-47 (tube or transistor version) are the most popular models. These mics have a crisp high-end response that can give a strident quality to violin and viola, but the extra brightness helps the bass cut through heavy instrumentation. For a mellower tone, use the AKG 414 or C-451 with omni or cardioid capsule. If the condenser is just too crisp for your taste, or if you want a rounder, less intimate sound, try a Sennheiser 421U or 441 or EV RE-20. Both Sennheisers have variable low-end roll-off that helps defeat the proximity effect, while the 441 also has a high-end shelf-boost switch. The full-sounding RE-20 gives a more traditional plucked jazz bass tone.

Mic pattern and position can be tricky. At a distance, the peak and local resonances emanating from lobes, plates, and holes blend to give the instrument its characteristic "fullth" (prominent lower midrange). To minimize imbalances when close miking, have the bassist play his or her part at normal volume and listen to the instrument about a foot in front of, above, and below each f-hole: there's no guarantee that left and right sides of the instrument sound alike from this close. Ideally there will be at least one so-called *"sweet spot"* where the response is fairly even for all notes and strings and where the air, body, and pluck resonances are not too prominent. Refer to chapter 10 for a discussion of isolation booths and how they can adversely interact with the bass itself.

If leakage from other instruments is not a problem, set the mic to omni (or switch to an omni capsule if you are using the C-451) so that it hears the largest possible area of the bass. This also helps control proximity boost. On the other hand, cardioid does have one advantage: if your sweet spot turns out to be very near the part of the strings that is plucked or bowed, you can turn the mic axis away from the excess mechanical noise emitted here. Even using omni, though, you could hang a small piece of felt between the mic and the source of these mechanical noises.

Stereo Miking and Recording. Common sense and convention in mastering LPs say that, like the kick drum, the bass should be recorded mono and panned to the center in the mix. This technique does maximize punch and eliminate potential low-end phasing problems between the left and right stereo tracks or channels of an LP. However, recording the acoustic bass in stereo has several advantages. First, two mics in different positions will hear a larger surface area of the instrument, and thus reduce or at least spread out local resonance problems over a wider frequency range. This is especially helpful if you are forced to use a cardioid pattern on both mics because of leakage problems.

Second, any left/right movement or turning of the instrument during the performance will show up on tape, which can help the listener focus on the bass through the rest of the arrangement. Third, stereo bass sounds great: it has a wonderful airy quality that cannot be reproduced during mixdown by fancy processing of a mono bass signal.

Use a matched pair of mics, and look for two sweet spots. They do not have to be symmetrical, left and right of the strings. Nor do both mics have to be exactly the same distance from the instrument, so long as their signal levels are about equal. In fact, on larger basses, I would look for one spot in front of the upper lobe and another down below, maybe even both on the same side of the strings. This way you are sure to take advantage of the different resonances of each cavity within the instrument.

One caution: beware of phasing. Switch your monitors from stereo to mono a few times while the bassist plays. If there is an objectionable drop in level or dulling

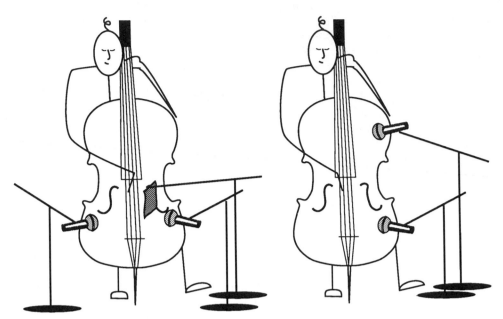

Figure 13.4. Two stereo mic set-ups for acoustic bass. Note the felt mini-baffle in place at left, to minimize finger noise received by whichever mic of the symmetrical pair hears more of the player's finger slaps.

of the midrange in mono, solo each mic. Leave the mic that sounds best where it is and move the other a few inches in various directions until the problem is minimized. You cannot move mics during a mix, and again, no amount of processing will correct phasing problems once they are on tape.

In any case, unless you really do not care to feel the space around the bass, avoid using ordinary lavalier mics attached to the bass itself. Although some engineers swear by a *lavalier mic* (a small mic intended to be worn around the neck or clipped to a person's clothing) wrapped in cloth and taped just under the bridge, this sound seems too tight, almost electric, to me. The full three-dimensionality of an acoustic bass derives from the way it transfers or couples lows to the surrounding air. To circumvent this process for a few decibels of isolation sacrifices part of the instrument's personality.

The Pros and Cons of Bass Pickups.   On stage, a pickup is really a must. The high level of ambient low frequencies in most halls and clubs, together with the need for room-filling bass-amplification levels, leads to a loose or flabby bottom end with a tendency toward speaker-blowing feedback if you rely on mics for the bass. Then, too, pickups such as the Fishman, Underwood, and Barcus-Berry are quite good these days. Their response is even from bottom to top, although no single pickup can give an impression of the physical size of a bass. Nevertheless, when leakage is the problem in the studio, a pickup can save the day.

Since the pickup itself is a *contact mic* (receiving its signal through vibrations of the mic body, not via the air), rather than a magnetic sensor as in electric guitars, it should deliver a signal free of RF interference. Make sure you use a low-noise, low-distortion direct box such as the Countryman, Axe, or a Simon Systems unit, if available. Preamp boxes designed for onstage use are generally too noisy for master recording applications, at least on acoustic bass.

However, pickups do have inherent problems. First, they are hard-mounted to one spot on the bass (usually on or near the bridge), which has its own local resonance—not necessarily one you like. In addition, because the pickup is physically a part of the instrument, it hears mechanical noises and accidental bumping of the body more than a normal mic. Since the pickup hears only the wood-transmitted vibrations, you will lose any special bowing or string sounds the bassist may interject for added effect.

My own recording preference for a mono bass track is to blend the mic and pickup sound. Like any direct signal, the pickup has a purer, more focused sound. Also, because it is hard-mounted, the pickup will maximize the sustain on each plucked note. As with any two sources, the mic and pickup may not be in phase with each other. Actually, different frequencies will probably have separate phase relationships, anywhere from full coherence to cancellation. While the bassist plays, switch phase in the board and choose the setting that gives the fullest sound with the mic/pickup blend of choice.

If time and tracks allow, my all-time favorite acoustic bass sound involves blending some of the pickup signal into the center of the stereo mic setup described earlier. Although this does require two great mics and three modules of the board, the resulting sound is clear enough to bring out melodic bass figures well, and it gives an illusion of space that holds attention in bass solos—all this without boosting the instrument abnormally in the mix.

Processing.   Most engineers reach for a compressor the moment a bassist begins playing. They do so for three reasons. As cited earlier, some acoustic basses have output variations of nearly 10 dB among various notes or ranges. Second, acoustic bassists like to use the full dynamic range of the instrument itself, which is well over 30 dB. Third, plucked acoustic bass notes die out completely in less than three seconds. While this is not a particular problem when recording, listening audiences are accustomed to the sustaining and supporting role of the electric bass in rock, jazz, and other recorded genres. Because we are addicted to that sound, we try to make the acoustic bass function in the same way.

I prefer to correct imbalances in the instrument's output by using parametric equalization. The first graph in figure 13.5 shows the relative output of each chromatic note for 2.5 octaves starting at low E on a typical string bass, with all notes plucked with the same force. You can see two sharp air and body resonances and two broader ranges of acoustic emphasis. Application of four separate bands of parametric eq to this erratic output restores chromatic response to within tolerable bounds.

Of course, if the bassist plays with exaggerated dynamics, reach for the finest compressor in your rack, a Urei 1176LN or equivalent. The Urei is particularly good because it has a very smooth attack adjustable to under 100 microseconds, because it does not overshoot on louder notes, and because its release curve works well with the sustain and accelerating release curve of many acoustic instruments. The resulting compression, when properly adjusted, is hardly audible, even in the solo signal.

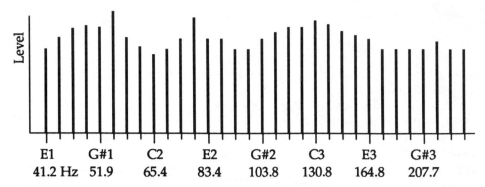

Relative volume of chromatic notes played on an acoustic bass, each note plucked with equal pressure.

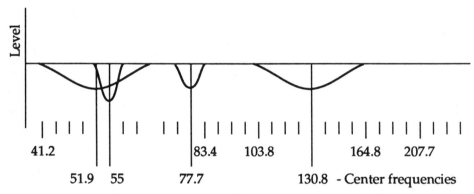

An equalization curve that will restore more balanced response.

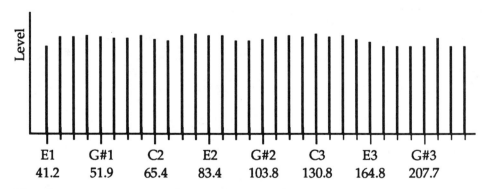

The chromatic response after eq, showing that compression is no longer necessary.

Figure 13.5.   Graphs of the relative volume of the notes of a given bass and the eq curve that will restore even volume to the instrument. While it is neither prudent nor possible to restore a totally flat response using many parametric bands, one or two narrow dips at 55 Hz and 78 Hz will reduce air and body resonances in this instrument, taking the "lumps" out of its low end sound. The broader dips around 52 Hz and 131 Hz lead to smooth output (bottom).

The proper attack time for acoustic bass is inversely proportional to the level of body resonances and the aggressiveness of the player's plucking. Lots of player attack mandates short compressor attack. Be careful, however, that you do not go too short. A half-cycle of 40 Hz (one hill or valley in its waveform) lasts about an 80th of a second, or 0.015 second. A compressor whose attack time is set to much less than this, say 0.002 second (two milliseconds), will mistake the individual peaks of each cycle for the volume envelope of the sound (we discussed this phenomena in chapter 12 as kick drum compression). Very low notes will be unnaturally suppressed by the resulting intermodulation distortion sounding strangely garbled, while higher ones are properly compressed (see figure 13.6).

To avoid such imbalanced compression, have the bassist play loud, staccato low notes when setting the attack time. A good starting point is 3 to 5 milliseconds. On the Urei, this corresponds to the longest release time available (the dial is not labeled in ms). Release time depends mostly on the amount of sustain in the individual bass. The notes of a fast-walking bass line can be spaced closer than 0.25 second. Because uneven output may naturally suppress some of these notes, I generally use a release well under 0.5 second—as short as I can get away with without hearing too much finger slapping and damping or hearing the compressor breathe.

Since it is impossible to remove compression later, undercompress a bit. A low ratio, say 4 : 1, will preserve some sense of dynamics, even in extremely loud passages. Ask the bassist to play the most aggressive part of the tune, and set the compressor to ride this passage continuously—6 to 10 dB of gain reduction is quite normal. However, in the quieter sections, do not worry if the compressor never kicks in at all, as long as the bass sound has the body you need.

Reverb. Most engineers shy away from using reverb on bass, especially while cutting basic tracks. The very attempt to put an electric bass in some kind of reverb-generated space may seem unnatural. Yet what audience ever hears an acoustic bass without natural room sound or reverb of one kind or another? Rather than avoiding reverb when mixing, find the kind that reinforces the role the bass plays within the specific music at hand.

If you want more sustain on the bass without applying excessive amounts of compression, try adding a touch of short plate reverb, between 1/2 and 2 seconds (depending on the speed of the bass part). Without a predelay, this plate reverb will sound like part of the bass notes themselves, a smooth extension of what is being played rather than an acoustic response to the bass. In the 0.5-second range, plate reverb can help to mask the mechanical sound of the player's fingers (a string being pressed against the fingerboard, strings being muted, etc.). Between 1 and 2 seconds, the reverb will add a smooth, languid quality to the notes, especially if the highs are equalized out of the reverb return.

A touch of chamber, room, or hall reverb will put the dry bass in an architectural space, especially if you introduce a little predelay to imply a distance between the instrument and the walls. If the intent is to place the whole band in one space, use the same reverb unit already in use on the drums. (Musical and "energy" effects of various predelay times will be discussed fully in chapter 25.) Low-frequency material, working with effects that define space, can set the stage for a wide variety of moods and emotions in the finished tape. You may be wise, however, to add reverb and the

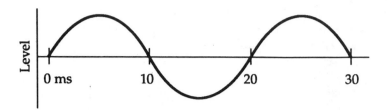

The first one and a half cycles of a 50 Hz note played on a bass guitar, before compression.

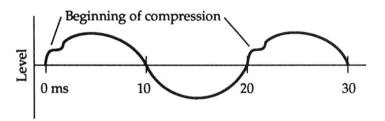

The same signal after compression with an attack time of 1 ms, corresponding to about 1/20th the full wavelength of 50 Hz. Waveform distortion is caused because the compressor sees each positive half-cycle "hump" as a new envelope.

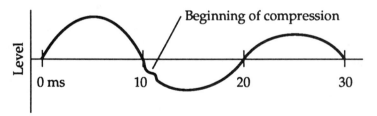

The same signal (top) compressed with an attack time of about 12 ms. The compressor now sees and reacts properly to the whole bass envelope, reducing the level of each half wave smoothly after kicking into action at 12 ms.

Figure 13.6.   Graphs of a low frequency wave from the bass showing the effect of too short an attack time riding the waves.

other effects described below during mixdown, unless you are absolutely sure, before recording basics, that they will be necessary.

Digital Delays and Flanging.   If you need a more energetic bass rhythm, without adding the same to drums and the other rhythm tracks, try a DDL on the bass, with delay time set to a rhythmic interval in the song. But beware that a delay line, unlike a reverb, creates a single verbatim repeat of the original signal. If the delay time is equal to the half-wavelength time of a certain frequency (meaning the direct and delayed signal are out of phase), the delay will partially or fully cancel that frequency in the mix if volume of direct and delayed sounds is equal.

A frequency of 50 Hz (the lowest G), whose half-wavelength time is 1/2 of 1/50th second, will be canceled if mixed equally with the same signal delayed by 10 ms. In addition, a delay of 10 ms will cancel any two frequencies for which 10 ms equals 1.5, 2.5, 3.5, 4.5 ... full cycles of the note, or about 160, 265, 375, 480Hz, and so on. A complex sound with this series of harmonically unrelated pitches notched out produces a rather abrasive *comb filter* effect—not something you always want. (The term *comb-filter* applies to an acoustic or electronic effect in which the frequency response of a sound or signal is artificially altered so that it has a series of alternating boosts and dips.) Beware of using delays smaller than 20 ms or so with any instrument, not just bass.

Flanged acoustic bass is not a natural sound, and many purists refuse to discuss flanging in the same breath as the acoustic bass. Nevertheless, gentle flanging can produce a liquid, miragelike quality, especially if the rate or speed is low (0.2 to 0.5 second) and depth relatively high, say 30% or more. If the piece calls for an ethereal feel or ambience, or if the unflanged bass needs something extra so that it stands out in the upper arrangement, a small percentage of flanging mixed in with the direct signal or fed into the reverb instead of the direct signal can give a more full stereo sound and simulate the mellow warmth of low horns subtly added to the mix.

For an effect of even more space, feed the dry bass into two flangers using different rates and depths, bring each back into a separate module, and feed all three signals to a pair of tracks with the dry bass in the middle. Stereo chorus boxes used onstage produce much the same effect, but they usually create far more noise in their outputs. If you must use them, it is better to bring their outputs into a console through separate modules and blend these with the clean direct signal in the control room. The worst bands of noise can then be dipped with inboard equalization.

A very tubby bass can be lightened and brightened by adding just a touch of the same instrument moved up an octave via a Harmonizer or pitch transposer. Too much of this effect produces a giddy "Chipmunk bass." On the other hand, to create a perfectly even staccato or walking-bass feel, a noise gate with hold and fade set properly may appear to "sequence" the notes as though they were synthetically derived. Use this or any effect for one or more sections of a tune, for a change of feel, a momentary laugh, or whatever.

Beyond this, effects begin to take away the punch and solidity of the bass—two of its most important qualities. Too much decoration weakens the structure, unless it is perceived as a totally separate element. For instance, each bass note can be used to trigger a synth to generate a second bass instrument, then control the envelope of that new sound. Because synth bass is not a naturally occurring sound, you can process it all you want without degrading the acoustic bass itself. In general, however, I would cut the basics and print all such triggered effects on a separate track. It would be nearly impossible at this early stage to guess which effects will sound right in the final mix.

Recording Level. Recording level for acoustic bass is a touchy subject. The same saturation compression that many people like on kick drum or electric bass sounds unnatural on acoustic, so I advise holding the VU level to +3 for all but the few hottest transients. Because of the relatively slow attack of acoustic bass, peak meter readings may be only 6 to 8 dB higher than this, rather than the expected 10 to 12 dB. If you have any doubts, try recording the same musical phrase at three different levels and listen to a playback to determine the point at which noticeable overload or saturation compression creeps in.

ELECTRIC BASS

Electric bass is another animal altogether. In theory, the instrument's solid body and neck are mechanically inert, merely holding metal-wound strings in place above magnetic pickups that sense the strings' vibrations and generate an output voltage. No ugly body or air resonances, no rosin tone, just pure bass sound . . . in theory! The complex tone-generation system of an acoustic bass gives it more fullth and emotional impact, but the very simplicity of the electric bass engenders unique recording problems.

How the Output Is Generated.   Each bass pickup contains one or more magnets, with pole pieces positioned under each of the four or five metal bass strings. When a string vibrates, it cuts through the field of the magnet, inducing an electric current in a very fine wire coil wrapped around the internal part of each pole piece. The voltage generated is proportional to the magnet's strength, the number of windings, the mass of the vibrating string and its deflection from rest position, and a few lesser factors.

Since the pickup hears only the vibrations of the part of the string directly above it, most basses have two pickups, one near the bridge (to detect the upper harmonics or vibrational modes of each note, giving brighter tone) and the other closer to the center (emphasizing the first-mode fundamental and lower harmonics). The distinctive sound of each bass is determined by its pickup design, the internal electronics that control tone and blend the output of various pickups, and the type of strings used.

Round-wound strings, since they flex rather easily, can produce steep transients and lots of upper harmonics, as well as a bright sound with long sustain. As in a guitar, however, unavoidable finger slides over the windings are perfectly audible. In contrast, less flexible flat-wound strings give a fuller tone with less highs and fretboard noise and much gentler transients.

A poorly shielded or improperly grounded pickup will receive stray electromagnetic fields from nearby power lines and motors, fluorescent lamp starters, and radio or television station antennae and output them as RF interference in the bass signal. For studio recording, use "humbucking" pickups (EMG and Duncan brands are among the best, some models including internal battery-powered preamps). Proper ground connections of all conductive parts, mandatory for all studio recording, will also help to reduce interference. Without these precautions, the player can introduce ground loops through the salty perspiration of sweaty fingers.

Remember to use a low-capacitance cable from bass to DI and/or its amp. This done, any small amount of residual interference or leakage should be drowned out if the pickup output is high enough. If RF interference persists, the engineer can try switching DI polarity, lifting the ground entirely, or both.

Fortunately, the mass of bass strings does produce a high output, but that can generate still more problems. Electric bass can develop a continuous output on sustained notes of better than 0.1 volt, with the transients of slapped notes approaching 1.0 volt. Unless trimmed, such transients easily overload most DI boxes and in-console mic preamps. The Countryman and Axe DIs are less prone to overload than many, though any unit with a hefty transformer should do the job equally well. The AC-powered Simon Systems DI box has completely separate paths for power and program signals and provides additional RF rejection and very fine transient response.

If your bass has an internal, battery-powered preamplifier, replace the batteries before every recording session. In addition, the preamp's output can be even higher than mentioned, sometimes at full 1-volt line level. If so, be very careful not to overload the mic input of the console input module. Even the input trim may have limits on how far it can reduce a signal. If you have to run the mic trim all the way down to prevent overload, try running the bass straight into a line input at the console patch bay.

Oddly, the pluck tone on some electrics is even more prominent than that on an acoustic, since every physical object or system under tension has a resonant frequency, including a fully strung solid-body bass. The slightest weakness in the neck-to-body mechanical linkage will accentuate this resonance, and the magnetic pickup will output it at high volume, no matter how low its frequency. Although 20 Hz is well below the frequency response of most instrument amplifiers, and a full octave below the low E of the bass, a burst at this frequency can overload the input stages of preamplifiers, DI boxes, and consoles, causing interference or distortion in the higher notes that are actually played.

Distortion in low frequencies appears in two primary forms, both of which are difficult to detect and which increase in proportion to the signal or actual listening level of individual notes. *Doubling* is a form of harmonic distortion, in which the output signal contains the original pitch and another note one octave up (the second harmonic, which is double the fundamental frequency). Speakers unable to reproduce very low notes generally double them, and the phenomenon can also occur electronically. Oddly, doubling can add a certain warmth not present in the original sound. If you like this sound, use it, even if it is distortion by definition. In many cases, however, the amount of doubling is wildly different from note to note, rendering the effect uneven and obtrusive.

The second type of distortion is heard as a fluttering quality on loud notes that sound fine at lower volumes. In this case an inaudible sub-bass pluck tone or resonance is modulating or interfering with the musical fundamental of the note being played. If the continuous signal level is too hot, this IM *(intermodulation)* distortion* will give the bass a mild case of "tuba tone." To imagine how IM distortion sounds on a bass, say you are playing a low C (about 65 Hz), but there is a subsonic pluck burst at 20 Hz with every note. You will not hear the 20 Hz, but you might hear a note that is the difference of the two frequencies: 65 minus 20, or 45 Hz. This will cause momentary beating with the C every time the note is played. A different so-called *resultant* will occur with every new bass note played. The simplest solution is to turn down the output of the bass until the loudest, lowest notes

---

*When two pure tones are input to a circuit simultaneously and the output contains one or more new or spurious tones, the spurious products are IM distortion.

are clean and solid again. When you have determined this distortion threshold, mark the max level setting right on the bass, and compensate for lost signal level at the console I/O trim control. If the bassist plays louder during real takes, ask him or her to reduce the instrument's volume control setting again until acceptable console meter readings are restored. Leave the console input trim alone.

Some bass pickups are solid cast, without individually adjustable pole pieces. While such a pickup may have a wonderful sound, it prevents proper *scaling* or individual adjustment of the relative volume of each string. Adjusting the bridge height for each string may help but can produce fret buzzing if you go too low with the bridge or make fretting very difficult if a string is raised. Obviously, any corrections you make in your pickups or fret height for recording will also improve the bass sound on live gigs.

The internal tone or treble controls on most basses (and electric guitars) are merely passive attenuators. Without active electronics, they can only suppress highs coming from the strings and pickups themselves. Thus, always turn the instrument's treble or tone control to its brightest position, regardless of the sound you want on tape. To minimize noise and interference, it is best to generate a bright signal at the instrument and tame it at the instrument amp and/or console.

Finally, do not be afraid to record bass hot on analog tape. VU levels up to +5 dB will do no harm on Scotch, Ampex, or Agfa mastering tape, and the tape's own tendency to saturate can give the effect of gentle limiting. Remember, too, that bass is usually one of the upfront trio (the others are drums and lead vocal or instrument). Brightening the bass in the mix boosts tape noise too, so the more level and highs on the master tape, the better—within reason, that is.

Signal Processing.   The low-cut filter of many console modules (rolling off sharply below 40 Hz) may thin out the very bottom end of the bass. However, its steep *slope* (the number of dBs roll-off per octave below the filter's turnover frequency) should prevent the pluck tone from reaching the input preamp, thus precluding overload. When the player has scaled the instrument as evenly as possible, use bands of a parametric eq to smooth out the instrument's output through its bottom two octaves. A progressive 3 dB decline in volume from the low A (5th fret of the E string) to the C at the 5th fret of the fourth string is optimal. Narrow-band peaks and resonances can be reduced via bandwidth settings of 0.2 octave or less.

Many engineers automatically reach for a compressor to achieve proper scaling. But the equalizer can achieve much the same effect without altering the dynamics of the performance itself. However, if lots of punch and sustain are what you want, do not hesitate to compress next. As with the acoustic bass, too short an attack time can actually ride the low-frequency waveforms and erode solidity. A bass whose scaling is fine without equalization can be compressed first, with console equalization added after the compressor to reshape the midrange and highs.

Although electric bass has steeper transients than acoustic, I generally start with an attack in the range of 4 to 8 ms, a little less if the instrument has round-wound strings, a little more if smooth or flat-wound. The right compression ratio depends on how well the instrument is scaled and on the consistency of the player's volume. If the instrument's scaling is even and the player's changing dynamics are important to the song, start with 4 : 1 and creep up as necessary. If the player has an enormous dynamic range or switches from normal to slap playing quickly, a 10 : 1 ratio (essentially limiting rather than compressing) may be necessary. The compressor need not squash every note; you can always add more compression during mixdown.

Release time depends on the instrument's inherent sustain and the speed of the part. For a very uneven bass and performance, or to inject some nervous energy into a too-smooth part, try a 0.3 second release or less. Remember that fret and fingerboard noises will be accentuated by a fast release. For added smoothness, go with 1 second or more, remembering that grace notes and other nuances may be lost while the compressor is recovering from each loud note.

Here is a bit of advice regarding funk and other slap-bass parts. Controlled overload is a part of what gives slap bass its knife-edged high-frequency transient. Onstage this takes place both within the bass pickups and at the input stage of the amp, giving the instrument extra presence or cut. When recording a slap bass direct into a console, the signal may generate a narrow-band ringing peak that sounds like feedback in the 2 kHz to 3 kHz range. If your slaps seem harsh and grating rather than bright and crisp, locate this peak by sweeping the upper midrange with a narrow band parametric, and remove it during record. For some reason, trying to remove these peaks during playback or mixdown seems to dull the bass sound and wash out the slap effect.

Headphones and Musician Placement in the Studio. Bass is a physical instrument. In most live gigs, bass is sensed as much through the floor and structure of the room or stage as by the ears. Thus, listening to bass through headphones gives only half the normal experience. To make up for the difference, many bassists ask for outrageously loud bass in their cue mix—much too loud for the other band members. Instead, seat the bassist near the drummer for good visual contact and give the two of them a bass-heavy cue mix (using separate cue or auxiliary sends) and the rest of the band a more balanced version.

Recording Amplified Electric Bass. There are three good reasons not to bother setting up and miking a bass amplifier. First, it may take 15 or 20 minutes to mike and baffle, then to adjust and process the signal. Second, low frequencies cannot easily be contained by baffles, so amplified bass in the studio will leak into most other mics and force you to spend more time isolating everything else. Third, even the best-sounding amps often have noise or hum problems that are impossible to eliminate.

However, amplified bass affords a more physical sound than direct bass. The interaction of tube amps and speakers in particular provides a warm, ear-filling, tactile feel that cannot be imitated with DI and electronic processing. This effect is best (and leakage worst) when the amp is run at high volumes. The amp appears to smooth out and limit the sound as you might otherwise do in the control room. If this is the sound that your music needs, live with the problems, or (my own favorite solution, if time permits) blend the best parts of the direct and amplified bass through separate modules.

To cope with the high acoustic power emanating from a bass amp and to minimize noise and RF problems, most engineers prefer cardioid dynamic mics like the Sennheiser MD421U or 441, or EV RE-20. However, any large-diaphragm condenser like the Neumann KM 87, Beyer MC 740, AKG 414, and the Tube should also work

come as familiar to the ear as the factory-programmed patches on a DX7, Juno 60, or D-50 synthesizer.

Overall, although effects can be ear catching, beware of trading structure and solidity in the bass sound for mere decoration. If you must track such effects (record them onto the multitrack tape) during the basics and are in doubt about where to use an effect, or how much of it to blend in, record the effect on a separate track for later bouncing. You cannot restore natural body to an overprocessed or washed-out bass signal, nor can you later use the wreck to key in and substitute a new bass sound, as you can with drums. When recording bass, apply all effects sparingly.

14

VOCALS

THERE are many types of leads in recordings, but all serve the same function: to deliver the actual melody, tune, lyrics—the song itself. If you only have enough time in a session to get one sound perfect, certainly it should be the lead vocal. It is the lead that each listener will remember from your song.

The lead must be easily heard through the mix, and nothing—rhythm tracks or their arrangement, sections, sweetening, percussion—should distract the ear from hearing the lead. Even a brilliant recording and mix cannot preserve and defend the lead if the arrangement is cluttered; if fills, riffs, and lines are written or phrased to conflict with it; or if rhythm patterns work against the phrasing or scan of the melody and lyrics. While advice on writing and arranging is beyond the scope of this volume, I cannot emphasize too strongly that well-written and arranged compositions need little decoration to make their point.

LEAD VOCALS

In 1984 I was asked by two friends (who own a large studio in Athens, Greece) to do a guest mix. Flattered, I gingerly sat down at the Neve console and put together a rough blend, eq'ing as I went. The tape was well recorded, but the lead vocal (a baritone) seemed a bit muffled. As I reached for that eq, the producer slapped my hand and popped the eq switch off in one sure stroke. The lead vocal, he informed me, is never altered in the mix (and rarely during recording).

Later, in a fatherly talk, he explained that the lead voice or instrument is the reason the recording is being made. It is the featured sound. One must pick the right mic for it and record it flat, and one cannot tamper during the mix to make it work with rhythm tracks, drums, or anything else. On the contrary, everything else should be adjusted to feature those qualities of the lead that make it special in the first place.

Mic Selection. When working with a singer for the first time, I ask him or her to sing a few bars over my shoulder as though my ear were the mic. Is the voice mellow, bright, sibilant, loud, thin? How do its qualities work with, or against, the

195

song itself? Is his or her voice too dark for such a cheery lyric? Does his or her nasal quality undermine sincerity in this doleful ballad? How can I make the voice as angry-sounding as the song itself? The answers to such questions determine the right mics to try.

Set up three mics, right next to each other, that might work well, play them all into separate modules, and even out their in-console volumes for a fair comparison. Go so far as to record a verse with each mic (flat) and ask the vocalist to render a control room opinion. I insist on this procedure because most engineers, as well as clients, automatically reach for a Neumann U 87 or 89 or the most expensive mic in the house for lead vocals. However, the Neumann is simply not the best mic for every singer.

Condensers work well on vocalists who have controlled sibilance. Specifically, the Neumann is the starting choice for a full or mellow voice. It will brighten and clarify the lead and ensure that the lyrics are intelligible. For an already-bright tenor, try an AKG 414. This is my first choice when there is no time to compare various models. The Neumann U- or KM 47s have much the same quality, as does AKG's MC740, although at twice the purchase price of the 414. For extreme smoothness in a condenser, the Neumann U-67 is well respected, but few studios have this venerable tube model.

Sibilant voices demand dynamic or ribbon mics rather than condensers. Brighten a mellow singer with the Sennheiser 421U or 441, and soften a piercing voice with the EV RE-15 or any of the Beyer ribbon models (the D160, for example). I have even seen cases where a TRAM (a lavalier designed specifically to record dialogue in motion pictures) turned out to be right for the singer. Just as an inexpensive shirt can be the right shade that brings out the wearer's complexion, so an inexpensive mic can be the right choice for some singers.

If the vocal is recorded in the same room as the other instruments, or if you want a very intimate sound, cardioid pattern (if available) is a must. However, if you have no leakage problems and want a big, open sound that will dominate a dense or bright arrangement, omni is my choice. If you have narrowed the mic selection down to two good candidates, let this factor determine your final choice.

Except for operatic basso voices, most human voices emit little below 125 Hz. However, much of the content of room tone, A/C noise, and undesired vocal plosives (the burst of air resulting from words beginning with p, b, and sometimes d and t) is below 80 Hz. Thus, if the chosen vocal mic has a low-frequency roll-off filter, use it. Otherwise, if you later compress the vocal, background rumble will rise between each line of lyrics.

Be careful to check that the mic's filter affects only frequencies below 100 Hz. Those in most condenser mics are fine. Some even have the exact roll-off frequency printed on the mic (selectable 75 or 150 Hz in the AKG 414, for example). If a continuously variable filter is marked *M/S* (for Music/Speech), use it sparingly. Usually designed for television or radio use, these mics, such as the Sennheiser 421, begin rolling off as high as 500 Hz. Before using one, check it by ear, or use the low-cut filter in the console instead. Using both, however, will doubtless steal vocal weight or so-called chest tone from a male singer, especially a basso.

There is a movement toward the recording of lead vocals in stereo, using two mics and two tape tracks. In theory we can identify good reasons for doing so. Stereo can surround the singer with a real space and lend an airy quality to the vocal, allow movement of the vocalist within the stereo image, and permit the use of separate processing or effects on the two tracks. However, for any type of demo such details are totally unnecessary. Moreover, one must use two identical and identically adjusted equalizers, noise gates, de-essers and compressors to process the stereo vocal during mixdown. Even when such paired processors set precisely alike, a jarring imbalance can occur if the singer moves too far off center. The ear will immediately sense such audio problems in a recorded voice, while they may go unnoticed on a sax or guitar lead recorded by the same stereo method.

Mic Placement, Mountings, Windscreens, and Accessories. Except in classical recordings, we are used to hearing tight-miked vocalists. It is far easier to distance a singer from the mic with reverb and processing than to tighten up a vocal miked at too great a distance. In general, my starting rule is to place the mic one full hand-stretch (8 to 10″) from the singer and perhaps 4″ above his or her mouth. The human voice projects upper midrange frequencies in the 2 to 3 kHz range (those that maximize intelligibility) about 30 degrees upward from the mouth. A mic placed a foot in front of the singer should therefore be mounted at his or her eye line, axis toward the mouth. He or she need not sing upward into it. Moreover, this position will help to prevent overloading of the capsule by the wind blasts of vocal plosives, and it will keep percussives from popping, even without the use of a windscreen.

All windscreens, by the way, absorb a bit of high frequencies, so use one only when exaggerated sibilance is a major problem. An alternative that does not absorb highs is a wire ring (6 to 8″ in diameter) with two or three layers of a nylon stocking stretched over it, mounted between singer and mic. Handmade versions may look a bit crude, but they work fine. Beyond this, a shock mount or other mic suspension will prevent foot shuffling and accidental bumping of the stand from ruining a take. But so will perching the mic stand on a couple of layers of a sound blanket. Unless the singer screams while swallowing the mic, an attenuation pad should not be necessary.

Vocal Booths. Vocal isolation booths have their good and bad points. If the lead vocal must be recorded while a rhythm section is playing, you have little choice except to use the booth. However, beware that small rooms have inherent acoustical problems that cannot be processed away. Foremost among these are resonances having to do with the booth's physical dimensions, especially if the booth is rectangular. Frequencies whose wavelengths are twice and four times each dimension will be strongly reinforced; lesser reinforcement occurs where the dimensions equal the corresponding wavelengths. As demonstrated earlier, the series of frequencies for which booth dimensions equal 1.5, 2.5, and 3.5 wavelengths will be partially phased out or canceled.

A sample worst case would be a booth 4′ X 4′ and 8′ high. In this case 140 Hz and 280 Hz will be doubly boosted by each of the 4′ dimensions; 70 Hz. and 140 Hz will be boosted by the 8′ height. The reinforcement will be hottest in the center of each dimension, up to 10 dB at 140 Hz in this example. A booth 8′ X 8′ will have just as heavy a boost at 70 Hz, causing havoc with an acoustic bass. Thus, avoid placing the mic in the middle of the booth, especially halfway between the floor and ceiling.

Instead, try placing it perhaps 1/4 to 1/3 the length of each dimension from the corresponding wall or ceiling, with the mic axis aimed and vocalist singing along the longest available dimension. If this puts the singer in a very uncomfortable position, live with some resonances. If the studio's console has a sweepable tone generator and the booth has monitor speakers, you can find the resonances and holes by sweeping from 50 Hz to 500 Hz, noting frequencies with significant peaks by watching the in-console I/O meter showing the vocal mic's output. The very worst midrange irregularities can be dipped or boosted with a parametric eq. Since highs are less subject to booth acoustics, do not worry about the high-frequency response.

Mechanical Problems and Tips on Solving Them.   Any hard surfaces near the vocal mic can reflect sound and, by virtue of their physical distance from the singer and mic, will reinforce or cancel certain frequencies, creating an acoustic comb filter. Any frequencies for which the difference in distance direct from source to mic and source to surface to mic is half a wavelength (or 1 1/2 or 2 1/2 wavelengths) will be partially canceled, while those for which that difference is 1, 2, 3, or any number of whole wavelengths will be reinforced.

A music stand or even hand-held sheet music located as shown in figure 14.1 will reinforce around 600, 1,200, and 1,800 Hz while canceling about 300, 900, and 1,400 Hz. Depending on the vocalist's range (e.g., bass or soprano) and tonal qualities, this altered response may generate a harsh, nasal, midrange twang or give a hollow, seemingly phased effect.

Solutions to this problem include adjusting the position and angle of the music

Figure 14.1.   Side view of a singer, a mic and music stand. Some vocal frequencies are reinforced, others partially canceled by the sound that bounces off the music stand and into the mic. The direct mouth-to-mic distance is 1 foot, the path reflecting off the music stand is 4.5 feet.

stand so that there is no direct bounce of the source back to the mic and placing some thick felt or padding over any parts of the reflecting surface that the singer does not need to see. Remember too that sheet-metal music stands ring at some frequencies, usually in the 1 to 2 kHz range. Without some padding to mute them, the mic may pick up these mechanical resonances loud and clear. Again, no amount of processing will cure these problems in a mix, so develop a good ear for them while recording.

Making the Singer Comfortable. If the vocalist is used to working with a hand-held mic and has trouble emoting without something in hand, by all means give him or her a dummy mic, but make sure that it causes no mechanical noises while being wielded during takes. On the other hand, if the vocalist cannot emote while standing perfectly still, move him or her back another foot from the mic, set the mic to omni, and let him or her move. Many singers gesticulate wildly, contort their faces, and otherwise flail about while delivering emotional performances. The added emotion will more than make up for a slightly looser sound.

Some vocalists are uncomfortable without a guitar or "axe" slung over one shoulder or at their fingertips. There is no harm in helping them re-create the excitement of a live performance as long as you can separate mechanical instrument noise from the vocal you want on tape. For example, the flat surface of a well-padded music stand placed horizontally between the vocal mic and the guitar will prevent the jangling of strings from being picked up.

Or the singer may just have a case of studio fright, caused by the unfamiliar location or atmosphere or by being the only person on that side of the glass. Perhaps he or she would feel less self-conscious if a tall baffle prevented those in the control room from staring during takes. Whatever the problem, technical or psychological, be creative and accommodating. Be aware of any factor that will prevent the vocalist from giving his or her best performance, and devise ways to get that performance on tape as quickly and cleanly as possible.

In an interview published in *Mix* magazine, Phil Ramone discusses his approach to recording vocals:

I usually go through several different brands of microphones before finding the one that both the artist and I are happy with. When we find the one that sounds good, it's marked and then set aside so that it is only used for that artist and for that session. This is important to me and my artist because, even though two mics may have the same manufacturer and model number, each microphone will still have its own slightly different characteristics.

With Paul Simon, we changed mics several times during the course of four albums. We started with a Neumann U-87, then went to a Sennheiser 435 for a while. Most recently we've been switching off between a Beyer 260 and an AKG 414. Paul's vocals are very sensitive, so we need a pretty high gain mike, and at the same time, we need one that doesn't have much pattern distortion since Paul tends to move around the mic quite a bit as he's working. Sometimes he cuts his vocals right in the middle of the room with the other musicians, and I have to do my best to come up with a pattern that will allow that vocal to be used in the mix, if necessary.

When we recorded Phoebe Snow we alternated between a Beyer 260 and a 160. Billy Joel used the Beyer 260 exclusively and never left the piano. All the vocals are as is. The whole performance of his albums are live.

Control Room Processing. Most of us hear human voices day and night and are thus quite sensitive to what sounds natural and what does not, especially in terms of vocal processing. If your tendency is to patch in a noise gate, de-esser, equalizer, and compressor, hang on. Resort to gating only if a tighter pattern, baffles, different mic position, and other alternatives do not cure leakage or excessive room noise.

If you do gate, make sure the threshold is just above the leakage or noise level, the floor or range is just low enough to improve the situation without leaving dead air between vocal lines, and the attack and fade gentle enough (about 0.1 second and 1.0 second by the dial, respectively) so that you do not hear the unit popping open and closed. Incidentally, human breathing is an important part of a vocal performance, so if you must gate, try not to lose breaths entirely by setting the floor too low.

Dense high frequencies can easily overload tape, so de-essing should be next on your hit list. The human voice has an enormous dynamic range (close to 100 dB!), with steep transients on initial sibilants and some consonants and plosive sounds (*p, b, d, t,* hard *c,* and the like). However, vocal transients (unlike those in drums) are not the principal or finest attribute of most singers. For vocals, de-essers and compressors should have extremely fast attack, under 500 microseconds (which equals a 1/2 milli-second) if possible.

Orban and Allison de-essing units are quite good in this respect, with a smooth, almost inaudible action. However, they afford little control of the relative amount of compression applied to each range of the highs. If the studio has no de-esser, impro-vise one by patching a multiple of the vocal signal into a graphic eq, and that into the control channel of the fastest-attack compressor in the house. The Urei 1176 is my personal favorite and that of many top engineers.

You can now control the amount and frequency range of the de-essing by boost-ing various frequencies above 5 kHz (by up to 15 dB as necessary) and dipping lower frequencies until this one compressor takes care of sibilance and dynamic range prob-lems. Wherever the singer has a peak (perhaps around 200 Hz if a baritone or 2 kHz if a piercing tenor), leave the corresponding control on the graphic at 0 dB for starters. Dip any ranges that need to be emphasized rather than compressed com-pletely out on the graphic. Remember, the more you boost any band, the greater the compression and more gain reduction that will be applied there, and vice versa.

Since dynamics are important to every vocal performance, a low compression ratio of 4 : 1 should generally be used, with passages sung at full volume causing an average gain reduction of perhaps 4 to 8 dB. A full-throated scream may cause more than 20 dB of reduction, while softer passages are not compressed at all. On the other hand, if you want a forced, pushy vocal sound (the norm in heavy metal tapes), do not hesitate to lower the threshold until everything is being squashed. The numbers given here are only suggested starting points. Who cares if your gain reduction is "normal" if you do not like the sound?

To accommodate instantaneous changes in vocal level, the release time should be fairly short, say 0.5 second or so. Longer than this and you may lose the beginning of a soft lyric following a loud one. Shorter than this and the breathing of the compres-sor itself will become an obtrusive distraction. If you want a nervous quality in the vocal, lower the release time even further, but be prepared to hear every breath and lip smack in graphic detail. On the other hand, if the vocal is rather languid, and smoothness is what you are looking for, go up to 1 or even 2 seconds on the release.

Equalization.   There are three main factors to consider when equalizing lead vocals: continuity of the voice from song to song, the sonic quality necessary for proper emotional impact on each song, and the degree of weight, power, or dominance that the lead should have in the total recorded sound. It would be very disconcerting if the singer's voice varied wildly from one selection to the next. Yet as each song calls for different emotions, the singer automatically varies the frequency content of his or her voice by controlling both volume and vocal apparatus to the desired effect. A bit of prudent equalization can emphasize these efforts and make the point perfectly clear to the listener.

If the singer's voice is very mellow and the song calls for anger or aggression, add midrange in the 1 kHz to 3 kHz range to give the voice a brassy, guttural edge. If the voice is very bright and the song calls for intimacy, add midbass around 200 Hz and highs in the 8 kHz to 10 kHz range for a chestier feel and the crispness of a whisper. You might get a gentler version of the same effect by dipping the midrange around 1 kHz.

There is more than one way of achieving any desired overall equalization. For instance, if you need two shelf boosts, one of frequencies below 300 Hz and the second of frequencies above 2 kHz, you might dial these boosts directly. Or you could use a parametric eq to dip a three-octave-wide band centered at 800 Hz. Which method is better? Many equalizer circuits create boosts by causing the chosen frequency to resonate electronically. The greater the boost, the more this resonance can lend a harsh or forced sound to the signal. Thus, the 800 Hz dip should afford a smoother overall sound than the dual shelf boosts. If you want to add an aggressive edge to the original sound, boost away. But if you simply want to reshape the sound's frequency content, dips give a much gentler sound.

All this presumes, however, that the arrangement and instrumental sounds will permit the voice to be heard clearly when you equalize it for its best solo sound. Choosing the proper record eq thus depends on knowing the number and kinds of instruments through which the voice will eventually have to be clearly heard and understood. If you put the lead vocal on before adding strings, horns, synths, and the like, it will probably need a lot of brightening in the mix. Knowing this, record the voice brighter than you might like. This will also spare you boosting tape noise later on.

If you will be recording lead vocals for several tunes in sequence, I suggest you start with one in which the voice has the most competition in the arrangement. This tells you the furthest the eq will have to go. Providing the voice does not get too harsh in this context, you know that the right sound for other songs will be progressively mellower. The need for excessive vocal brightening should clue you that the instruments must later be mellowed during the mix.

In any case, always defer to the right vocal sound, unless the vocal part has no lyrics and is in fact instrumental in its function; the primary sales of the entire recording depend more on some other sound or element (for example, if the recording features an instrumentalist, and the vocals are an incidental filler or enhancement, in which case they should be mellower than the lead); or if a lead instrument will exchange phrases or sections with the voice in the recording. In this case equalize the voice and instrument so that they blend best and have the same relative weight and brightness within their respective pitch ranges.

A few words on vocal weight or dominance. A good recording should have all the impact of a live performance, and then some. Live, you witness the singer emoting and sometimes acting out the lyrics. Physical movements, gestures, and body language add a great deal of impact to the performance, and all of these are missing on tape. The tendency in the studio is to equalize the voice for intelligibility, forgetting that sheer power in the voice is just as emotionally convincing as clarity alone.

Vocal power is contained in the frequency range where the singer moves or "pushes" the most air—200 to 500 Hz for baritones and tenors, 400 to 800 Hz for altos and sopranos (what I call "chest tones"). If you are inclined to dip these ranges when recording so that you can boost tape level and intelligibility, be prepared to boost them again during mixdown. It is chest tone that gives a lead vocal physical command or dominance of the entire recording.

My own trick is to dip during record a 1-octave-wide band centered on a frequency about a musical fifth above the lowest pitch in the vocal part. This allows me to record the vocal several dB hotter and usually with less compression. Then, if the vocal needs more lung power during mixdown, I boost a broad band centered just below the lowest note in the vocal part. This seems to give back some of the physical presence or stature found in a good live performance. The listener can then sense the power of the singer's lungs and almost feel the air moving.

Recording with Reverb, Doubling, Delays, and Effects.   In general, I recommend that you cut lead vocals dry and add all ambience, reverb, and effects later unless the effect you want is predetermined, is a structural part of the song's principal effect, and there is no chance you will want less of it or a different quality to it during the mix; the effect is a known and expected part of the vocalist's normal sound in the same way certain stage devices are a part of the sound of various well-known guitarists; you know ahead that the device you need for the vocal effect will also be needed for a different effect on some other track during the mix; or the effect is needed only occasionally throughout the song, and it will be difficult to add it selectively during the mix.

Among the most popular effects that are often cut onto original vocal tracks are the Aphex Aural Exciter; doubling via ADT, flanger, DDL, or Harmonizer; slapback echo via DDL or tape delay; Vo-corder; normal reverb; and reversed reverb, also called *Preverb*. Of these, the only one that must be added prior to the mix is *Preverb*. This is made by physically reversing the direction of the tape so that the vocal track is heard backward. When you do this, the vocal will appear in a different module. For example, if the original vocal is recorded on track 2, it will now appear on track 23 and its corresponding module. Reverb is then added to the backward vocal and the composite signal bounced to an open track. When the tape is flipped to normal playback direction, the reverb will fade in prior to each note, anticipating it with a ghostly presence.

While there is always the danger that you will blend too much of the effect in with the dry signal, the natural tendency seems to be to use too little of the effect and wind up losing it in the mix. If preverb is an important effect, spend a few minutes recording different levels on several lines of the lyric, then flip the tape back to normal and pick the level that works best in context with the instruments. However, you may want to put such an ethereal effect only on a few words or lines of the lyric.

My general advice concerning effects and other special touches in your tapes is take risks and overdo things a bit. Today's listening audiences are on the fly and will miss all but the most blatant sound events in a tape. You cannot expect a listener to sit quietly between two speakers taking notes on delays and preverb, nor even on the lyrics themselves. If the words are lost in the mix or sung with little emotion, no listener will put in the effort to understand them. So whatever is special about your music, lay it on the line plain as day. Subtlety will get you nowhere with a mass audience.

Remember also to check effects levels by listening to them, in a rough blend with the rhythm tracks and anything else already on tape, in mono and at low volume on Auratone or other small monitors. When the effect is clearly noticeable without being obtrusive, you have chosen the right setting. Rarely have I regretted a recording decision made in this way, either during tracking or a mixdown. Some additional compression during mixdown will generally emphasize the effect if it starts to get lost. Of course, if it is too loud later on, you will know better during your next session.

Many of the same techniques discussed here will serve equally well on almost any wind, reed, or brass lead. Whatever the lead, it should have free rein to express itself fully in sound, dynamics, and emotion. The listening audience wants direction; it wants to have the main points of the record brought clearly to the fore without having to ferret through a maze of competing sounds. There are, of course, certain types of compositions where chaos and confusion are the point, for which other precepts will apply. In the vast majority of recordings, structure, order, and clarity of purpose are the ingredients for artistic success, sure communication, and audience satisfaction.

Level to Tape.   In general, I like to gain-ride vocals as they are recorded. This means learning the lyrics as the singer warms up, noting any particular notes, words, or phrases that are always too loud or soft, and boosting or dipping these during each take. This is a tricky and, since singers often try different phrasing on successive takes, not always dependable way of getting good tape levels. However, compact discs show excessive compression on leads, and gain riding is often less noticeable and objectionable than a uniform squashing of levels by compressor.

Because few lyrics have one word repeated many times in a row, momentary distortion on a vocal syllable can go by unnoticed by all but the most sensitive ear. For this reason you can cut vocals at levels hotter than might otherwise seem safe. With the longest, loudest sustained vowels set at $+2$ dB VU (or about $+10$ on peak-reading meters), a few sudden consonants or shouts may reach $+6$ VU (which is off scale) or $+14$ on peak meters. Unless you clearly hear distortion, or notice saturation compression, do not worry.

If you are recording without noise reduction, high levels will reduce effective tape noise in the mix. Just keep an ear out for excessive print-through, which increases noticeably with signals whose level is continuously in the red. If you are taping with noise reduction, levels should be a bit more conservative. Misalignment of record and playback noise reduction units is most noticeable on the lead vocal, and even more so where the level is way above 0 VU or the unit's threshold.

In an interview in *Recording Engineer/Producer,* George Massenburg discusses his approach in recording Linda Ronstadt's *What's New* album:

Very often engineers approach a project such as this with the idea of capturing "a sound" that is reminiscent of a particular era, and choose microphones accordingly. On the *What's New* project we found that the most important considerations for reproducing that genre of music were the arrangements and the vocal phrasing, as opposed to the engineering. We first referred to recordings from the '40s and '50s; as an example, listen to Frank Sinatra's *Only the Lonely* record. After listening, you're struck by the fact that you haven't really heard individual horn or string parts, because they blend very well. That's certainly a function of arrangements and vocal performances, rather than the recording.

John Neal ... was really a great help with the project. He's done hundreds of setups like this for television and films [at 20th Century-Fox, Warner Bros., etc.]. We used a basic orchestral miking approach to capitalize on the leakage from section to section. The overall pickup came from one good M-S mic [a modified AKG C24] that was very carefully placed. . . . Then we filled in with tight mics, including three on drums [one on the snare that wasn't used, and two overheads].

If you do this type of setup correctly, the actual balances are usually static. Like the Sinatra recording, the dynamics and movement take place via the arrangements (which were done so well by Nelson Riddle) and vocal dynamics. A lot of what happened in the sessions was really due to the quality of the arrangements and conducting.

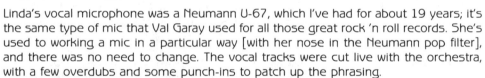

In engineering the vocals for Linda Ronstadt, Massenburg emphasizes that artistry, not technology, comes first:

Linda's vocal microphone was a Neumann U-67, which I've had for about 19 years; it's the same type of mic that Val Garay used for all those great rock 'n roll records. She's used to working a mic in a particular way [with her nose in the Neumann pop filter], and there was no need to change. The vocal tracks were cut live with the orchestra, with a few overdubs and some punch-ins to patch up the phrasing.

To get some isolation on Linda's vocal track we built a little booth out of seven-foot-high partitions. On the bottom were gobos [baffles 4' high, 4' wide, 9" thick] with Sonex [sound-absorbent open-celled foam] on one side and wood on the other, and then about three feet of plexiglas running above that on each panel. We positioned the booth right between the guitarist and the pianist [Don Grolnick] so she could see Nelson [the conductor]. She was pretty well isolated even though the booth was constructed only of gobos.

The room mic, which was positioned quite high, didn't pick up much leakage from her vocals. Only on one or two tunes when the orchestra wasn't playing at all, and when she was singing very loud, could you hear the leakage. Overall, it really wasn't a problem.

Linda generally stayed right up on the mic for a big, warm vocal sound . . . at most, she was two inches from the capsule. . . . I don't remember the exact eq settings for each performance, but it was relatively flat. Maybe just a little bit of high end. Certainly, there was nothing major. I guess the only special processing was the stimulating effect of chocolate-covered donuts on Linda's performance.

Massenburg also demonstrates the importance, for him, of "comping" vocals:

Some vocals tracks can be recorded basically in one pass, and then touched up by dropping [in] phrases, words, syllables, or whatever. But comping vocals [constructing the finished vocal from parts of several complete vocals recorded in parallel on different tracks] is becoming fairly common with a lot of singers, because it can actually improve a good vocal, and because it's convenient. You might have an extraordinary performance that is colored by one or two phrases having a mysteriously bad intonation. Replace those phrases and the performance blossoms. Phrasing is to a singer what interpretation is to Freudian psychologists.

The primary concern about combining vocal parts, though, is not to lose the continuity—the feel—of the song. . . . One way to improve the chances of getting consistent takes is to allow the artist to do as many complete vocal passes as possible at first, rather than singing one pass, listening to it, singing another, etc. If the artist can stay in the studio and keep the same, or similar, attitude through several performances—say three or four tracks—then you can work on all of them at once, and find the best sections to make one great performance. . . .

In a final phase the vocalist sings just a verse, or half a verse, or a chorus. The focus is to record a song that sounds like one complete thought.

GROUP AND BACKGROUND VOCALS

Background vocals generally serve one of three basic dramatic functions in a song:

1. When sung as word-for-word harmonies to the lead, they add weight, emphasis, or emotional color. If the harmonies are tight, two- or three-part lines written above the lead in pitch, they will lighten the lead, make it seem happier or headier. Parts written below the lead for the same song will generally make it heavier, more serious or urgent. On the other hand, if the harmonies are written in intervals of fourths or fifths with the lead, they can lend a stoic and contemplative feel.

2. Ooh-and-aah backgrounds often behave as purely instrumental parts, supporting the lead like a wind trio or quartet. Or they may punctuate specific lyrics with an emotional breeze, a momentary pluck at the heart strings.

3. Some backgrounds (with or without lyrics) are written as dramatic responses to one or more lines of the lead. These may restate or rephrase the lead singer's lyrics or play the role of a Greek chorus, exposing the lead singer's underlying or hidden feelings or motives. They may also portray the singer's conscience, the angel's or devil's advocate to the principal lyrics of the song.

The way backgrounds are recorded depends as much on their dramatic function with respect to the lyric and lead vocal as on the sound of the voices singing them. If they are an interior monologue or the lead's conscience, a warm breathy sound will probably work best. On the other hand, if they reinforce the overt meaning of the lead's lyrics, the backgrounds should be similar in tone to the lead, either mellow or bright in direct response to the lead's changing moods.

Because backgrounds are supplemental voices, they should never distract attention from the lead, and thus they normally require more processing during record to smooth out rough edges and mask the individual personalities of the voices singing them. This may mandate different types of miking and signal processing to highlight their function in each song of an album.

Let us presume, for example, that the backgrounds are intended to reinforce what the lead is saying. If they are to be recorded in stereo, they will work best if clustered around the lead, supporting it either X-Y or M-S in the mix. This mandates miking, which produces a natural left-to-right image. The lead and backgrounds will thus be a part of the same space. If double tracking is necessary for fullth, bounce the first background tracks with new live mics onto a second pair of tape tracks, switching the left-to-right perspective of the second group for uniform distribution of the individual vocalists in the composite stereo field.

If the lyrics are enthusiastic, aggressive, or hopeful, stereo background vocals will enlarge the lead singer's emotions. But if the lyrics express misery, loneliness, pain, or even timidity, consider recording the background vocals in mono. Such a treatment will render their emotional statement more recessive and may reinforce the lead singer's feeling of hopelessness. These are more production than engineering considerations, but illustrate precisely how the two aspects of recording affect technical decisions, and vice versa!

If the backgrounds are meant to comment on the lead or reveal its inner motives, they should be separate from the lead, occurring at distinct left or right image points and with distinctly different equalization and/or processing. This is best accomplished by recording the background vocals in mono, recording the same part again onto a second mono track, and placing each track left or right of the lead in the mix. Spatially, the backgrounds will now serve as a Greek chorus, commenting from offstage. This kind of thinking will carry you through mic selection, processing, choosing the type and amount of reverb and special effects, and so on.

Mic Selection, Pattern, Placement, and Dramatic Effect.   Take advantage of what you already know about mics. Dynamic and ribbon types, with smoothly tapered high-end response, will help blend a group of vocalists into a unified sound. Condensers, with more acute high-frequency response, will preserve awareness of the individual voices in the group. Similarly, X-Y pairs give a more unified sound with a smaller room size then a spaced pair. In the latter, when sound sources are crowded fairly closely around or in front of the mics, the difference in distance of the left- or rightmost sources from the two mics will exaggerate the spatial imaging and produce a broad stereo surround with less distinct imaging.

Processing.   The same kind of logic applies to processing. Gating is often necessary for dramatic and technical reasons. First, multiple-breath sounds will call attention to the backgrounds. In addition, groups of singers·clear their throats, shuffle about on the floor, turn pages, and even tend to whisper between vocal lines to count bars or rehearse phrasing and dynamics. All these sounds should be gated out, preferably during recording.

If it is important that the backgrounds be a constant, unobtrusive support or cushion for the lead, plenty of compression is in order. This will maintain an even level on the entire group, regardless of individual volume changes or group dynamics, and will prevent any single voice from sticking out. Again, use a fast attack and high ratio to catch every transient and maintain a plump vocal cushion. De-essing may be necessary depending on the individual singers.

How to make up for imbalances among the singers? If one vocalist is much more sibilant than the others, turn that person somewhat away from the mic axis.

Similarly, adjust volumes of the individual singers by moving them closer to or farther from a single omni- or bidirectional mic or a stereo pair, rather than setting up individual mics for each. And do not forget to note or actually mark their floor positions (with some duct tape or whatever) once the blend is right.

Remember, however, that compressors respond to level only and that with vocal groups the greatest level will be in the 200 to 400 Hz range for men, 400 to 800 Hz for women—the "chest tone" range. Aahs, oohs, and other long vowel sounds have higher level and will thus be highly compressed, while lyrics with long *e* and short *i* sounds may barely be touched. For this reason, the compressor will tend to reduce chest tone, so be prepared to add some back later with equalization. As with lead vocal, boosting at or just below the very bottom frequencies in the vocal part can add apparent weight or chest tone without increasing actual meter readings much.

Because many background vocal parts are sporadic, adding to already-crowded arrangements (especially in rock and synth pop), it may be difficult or impossible to ride their level as high in the mix as you might like without overloading. To ensure that the background lyrics are clear nonetheless, try boosting 10 kHz during record. The extra sibilance will not overload if you are compressing, but it will help lyrics cut through at lower volumes in the mixdown. In addition, it will allow you to treat the backgrounds as a part of the instrumental arrangement and construct a continuous bed or pad whose level does not leap every time a background vocal line occurs.

Special Effects. It is difficult to judge the right quantity of various special effects, delays, chorusing, or reverb to put on backgrounds until you hear them properly equalized and blended into the final mix. For this reason, add all effects during mixdown, except onetime or sporadic events that will be difficult to handle while mixing for overall feel. Lay in a delay or repeat of one word or phrase or heavy chorusing of a single phrase for ethereal effect while recording or in a bounce. This will save enormous amounts of time in mixing.

I also recommend that you do some gain riding of the backgrounds during record to lay each section onto your multitrack tape at the approximate relative volume that will be needed in the mix. This requires that you tell the engineer how these tracks will function and which choruses, words, or lines should be louder and softer. Again, this takes little time during recording but may save precious mixing time and allow you to concentrate on the structure of the mix rather than on decorations. Beyond this, there are few engineering tricks in recording backgrounds. The real trick is writing and performing them well.

Overdubbing. I suggest that you overdub the lead vocal after laying down basic tracks, before backgrounds and any decorative instruments that play fills, and so on. Although it is a bit tough to sing a lead over a relatively empty track, the finished tape will be stronger with backgrounds and fills tailored to fit a great lead than it might be if the lead is squeezed in around lots of decoration. Then, too, backgrounds and fills that are added later can be written or played to imply plenty of real-time interaction with the lead. This will help unify the entire performance musically and should rekindle some of the spontaneity that track-by-track overdubbing usually kills.

15

THE GRAND PIANO AND FENDER RHODES ELECTRIC PIANO

THE GRAND PIANO

Legend has it that the grand piano is the single most difficult instrument to record well. Legend may be right for several reasons. First, the instrument itself is physically large, and different portions of its sound emanate from each area. Second, its musical range of fundamentals stretches from 27 Hz at low A to 4,100 Hz at high C, with overtones right up to 20 kHz. Third, since notes are created when hammers strike strings, the piano is often considered a percussion or quasi-percussion instrument. With highly refined touch sensitivity in its keyboard and action, the dynamic range between a *pianissimo* melody and *sforzando* chords can be well over 50 dB, with very steep transients throughout the entire frequency range. All in all, the grand poses a severe challenge to every type of microphone and even the finest signal-processing equipment.

Sound Production, Amplification, and Propagation. Felt-covered hammers are propelled by the keys and strike steel strings, which then vibrate. A total of 212 strings, collectively stretched and tuned with a tension of up to 40,000 pounds, transmit their vibrations directly to a soundboard via a long, curved bridge. Bevelled and

208

sanded around the edges to under 1/8" thickness, the soundboard amplifies the string vibrations and couples them to the surrounding air. Soundboard area varies from about 12 sq. ft. in a baby grand up to 35 sq. ft. in the Bosendorfer Imperial concert grand, which has additional bass notes down to a low F that sounds at 21 Hz.

Here is where the fun begins. First, sound generated by any specific note takes a short time to spread throughout the soundboard and reach full acoustic amplification. The instrument does not, therefore, emit coherent wavefronts. (Perfect *acoustic coherence* occurs when each variation in air pressure caused by a sound wave emanates from a small or so-called point source in a neat, spherical pattern. Two audio signals are said to be coherent when their waveforms are consistently in phase with each other.) In fact, because wavefronts leave the piano in complex sequences and from various locations, internal phasing is an important characteristic part of the instrument's richly textured sound: witness the changing harmonics of a sustained mid-range note. Furthermore, because of the asymmetric shape and varying thickness of the soundboard, certain areas resonate in specific frequency ranges and are relatively dead in others. We have seen this phenomenon in the various plates and lobes of the acoustic bass.

Then there are the various mechanical noises that, while basically unmusical, are a part of the sound that most people identify as a piano. These include the percussive "clunk" of hammers hitting strings, the "pfft" of various felt parts of the action making contact, the metallic buzzing of strings as dampers stop their vibrations, the echoed whoosh and "thunk" made by the lifting and lowering of all the dampers by the pedals, and the mechanical operation of the pedals themselves, preferably without squeaks. These are all a part of a classical performance but of little use in rock recordings.

Finally, the instrument is not designed to be heard from directly above the soundboard but at some distance to the right-hand side of the performer. To accomplish this, a thick, reflective wooden lid, tilted up to an angle of about 40 degrees, bounces the sound from the board out to the audience. However, not all frequencies are bounced equally. The internal dimensions of the piano's case and lid form a complex acoustical amplification and projection system that defies even the most sophisticated computer analysis. This explains why the piano sounds available on so many synthesizers have thus far been unsatisfying to most pianists.

As with drums, no single piano sound is ideal for every recording. Classical piano is generally heard in a recital or concert hall, with the instrument some distance from the audience. For this type of recording, distant miking with a spaced pair will convey the large size of the sound source, preserve the broad dispersion pattern of sound bounced off the stage and lid, and capture the instrument's interaction with the hall's acoustics.

In rock recordings where piano will provide rhythmic support, a tighter and brighter sound is necessary. Sometimes you may want to hear every contact of hammer and strings, along with the metallic upper harmonics that are apparent inches from the soundboard but soften or mellow with distance. Furthermore, rock piano is often heavily compressed, both to control transients and to provide a steady cushion of rhythm on which vocals and other leads can float. The resulting sound has little to do with the way the original piano sounds, but it does what the music needs, and that is what counts.

Mic Selection and Placement. With so many sources of sound from one instrument, you should select mics on the basis of three criteria: the style of music being recorded, the sonic strengths and weaknesses of the specific instrument, and the parts of the sound you wish to emphasize and conceal.

The most natural piano sound results when mics are placed outside the case and fully raised lid, perpendicular to the strings, and at least three feet from the instrument. If leakage is no problem, this type of miking allows the wavefronts from the entire soundboard to blend. A listener at this position will note that the highest notes appear to originate from his left (nearest the keyboard). This is only natural, since energy from higher notes is concentrated in the small roughly triangular area of the soundboard beneath these strings. An X-Y or spaced pair should show this left/right imbalance. For classical or solo piano, nothing beats a spaced pair of omnis, say the B&K 4006 (condenser), the AKG 414 or Tube (both condensers). The resulting sound is smooth as silk.

I have never recorded rock or jazz piano without feeling the need to brighten the sound with eq. The brighter the mics you choose, the better. Neumann KM 87 or U 89 condensers or C-451 (with CK-5 capsule) work well in this X-Y context, set to cardioid and with no low roll-off. Shure SM 81s are popular for an open, uncolored sound. If you want a tighter sound with dramatic stereo imaging, move the mics in until they are over the right side of the case, midway between the soundboard and raised lid. Or switch to more directional dynamics such as the AKG 441 or Sennheiser 421U, again with no roll-off. These have natural boosts between 1 kHz and 5 kHz and will help the instrument cut through heavy orchestration.

If you prefer a less full sound but do not want the intimacy of close miking, try taping a pair of normal PZM mics (but not cardioid models) to the inside of the raised lid. They usually work best placed nearer the right side of the lid, at least one foot apart. Because the PZMs are at the surface of the lid, they hear no bounced sound from it but only the direct sound from the strings and board. The result is a purer tone, with little of the self-flanging generated by interaction of direct and lid-bounced sounds heard from audience position. In some ways, PZM sound seems half pickup, half mic, at least to my ear. PZMs are also known for producing the brightest piano sound around, one that is equally usable for rock rhythm or small group jazz recordings.

In most sessions, however, leakage is a problem, and interior miking becomes a necessity. Look for sweet spots: areas of the soundboard without serious local resonances or nodes. Have the pianist play chords and melody at medium volume. With one ear about eight inches above the soundboard, listen inside and along the curved surface of the case. Hopefully, you will locate at least one spot where the upper harmonics or midhighs of each note are clear and distinct and where no specific notes from the mid-keyboard (one octave below and above middle C) are unnaturally emphasized. There is no single spot that works well on all instruments.

If there is only one sweet spot, X-Y miking is the only alternative. A broad cardioid pattern will give a natural stereo, full bass response and pick up the largest possible area of the soundboard. Make sure that neither mic is aimed directly at the hammers and dampers. Mechanical noise is always annoying but even more so if only one of the paired mics is aimed toward the piano's action.

With two sweet spots at least a foot apart, you can try a spaced pair with both mics in omni. This will give a richer, more phase-coherent sound, though with more mechanical noise. (Coherence in discussions of stereo miking indicates that sound waves from various sources reach the diaphragms of both mics simultaneously or in phase.) Cardioid miking will solve the problem, but its tunnel view of two separate soundboard areas may produce an unnaturally broad stereo image with a hole in the middle. To fill a hole, with an X-Y or spaced pair, try switching only the mic aimed toward the higher notes to omni. This may offend your sense of sonic symmetry but will pull the instrument back together at the same time.

Three precautions, however. First, do not waste lots of time achieving more isolation than you need. In most types of recordings, a little leakage will not hurt much, so get what isolation you can quickly and then move on. Many times this simply means rolling off some lows from the piano mics, which has the additional benefit of preventing the piano bass notes from beating with or muddying the acoustic or electric bass sound. Second, do not go overboard with the stereo imaging of the piano. It is both artificial and ludicrous to hear bass notes from one speaker and treble notes from the other. Not even the pianist hears the instrument stretched out this way!

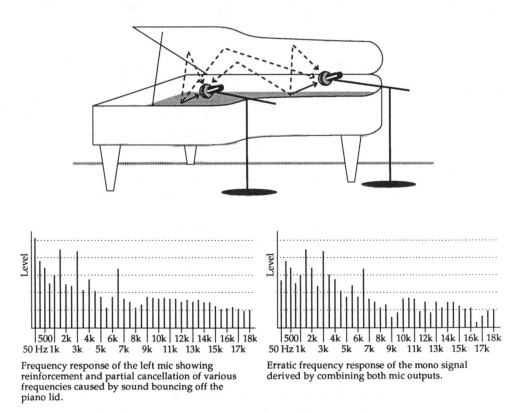

Frequency response of the left mic showing reinforcement and partial cancellation of various frequencies caused by sound bouncing off the piano lid.

Erratic frequency response of the mono signal derived by combining both mic outputs.

Figure 15.1. Side view of a pair of spaced mics over the strings of a piano, showing the direct (solid line) and bounced (dashed line) paths by which sound reaches each mic. Also the frequency response of a single mic and the combined signal from both.

Third and most important, whenever you mike a piano in stereo, switch your monitors to mono regularly in order to check for phasing problems. If there is a severe drop in level from stereo to mono, if the instrument's tone loses luster, or if you notice a peak or resonance that is not apparent in stereo, move one mic a couple of inches this way or that until the problem is minimized. Note or mark the final positions for next time, perhaps with a piece of tape on the lid (or, dare I say, a tiny marker on the soundboard itself). When you later cover the piano with sound blankets, the booms may swing left or right, destroying your coherence again. If I have time, the last thing I do when all the instruments are miked is to make sure the piano mics have not budged.

To obtain my all-time favorite rock piano sound, I set up a pair of AKG 414s, X-Y, mounted one over the other above the strings corresponding to A above middle C, just beyond the dampers. Both should be set to cardioid with their axes aimed almost horizontally, away from the keyboard—one toward the higher and one toward the lower area of the soundboard, but not necessarily a full 90 degrees apart. The resulting bass will be completely solid and coherent; midrange and treble will spread out with a crisp and beautiful sound, left to right. The directionality of the 414s should also reduce two undesirable sounds: buzzing of the strings where the dampers touch when notes are released and mechanical noise from the nearby action itself. Not too much ping, just pure bell-like tone.

Interior "Acoustification." Anytime you tight-mike a grand, and especially if you record with the lid on a short stick, you should deaden the lid directly above the mics (except PZMs, obviously). If, in recording position, the lid is 10″ above the soundboard, just 4″ from the mics, the difference in distance between the direct and bounced sound reaching the mics will be about 8″. Since this is about half the wavelength of 700 Hz, this frequency will be partially phased out, along with the higher frequencies for which 8″ is 1.5 and 2.5 wavelengths (namely 2 kHz, 3.2 kHz).

A separate series of frequencies (about 1.5 kHz and 2.6 kHz) for which this distance equals whole numbers of wavelengths will be reinforced. To minimize this acoustic comb-filter effect, tape a piece of a compressed fiberglass ceiling tile, or several layers of thick felt, to the inside of the lid, making sure it does not touch the mics when the lid is lowered into position.

If you prefer spaced sweet-spot mic locations and omni patterns, you can minimize mechanical noise by hanging a felt curtain from the inside of the lid. The curtain should be several layers thick and positioned just beyond the line of dampers. Cut the felt so that it just misses the strings when the lid is in recording position. This kind of treatment is similar to the felt cones suggested for tight miking of drums. Again, remember that mics are your recording ears. If they must be in an unnatural location, do all you can to shield them from leakage and proximity problems.

Isolating the Instrument. Because the soundboard is an acoustic resonator, it can pick up and vibrate sympathetically with sounds from anywhere in the studio. If you are recording piano with drums in the same room, you must isolate the piano from incoming drum sounds. You can begin by tight miking with the lid on a short support stick and draping sound blankets over and around the entire opening be-

A. Soundwaves are absorbed and/or deflected before arriving at the top of the soundboard, allowing the waves arriving at the bottom to move the soundboard.

Soundboard

B. Soundwaves arrive equally and in phase.

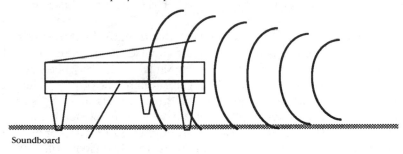

Soundboard

Figure 15.2. Two cross sections of a piano soundboard (seen from the player's perspective) reacting to incoming leakage. In A. the top of the piano is heavily baffled with sound blankets, allowing low frequency leakage from underneath to cause vigorous soundboard vibration. Without baffling (B.) the soundboard actually vibrates less, although there is more direct air leakage into the piano mic. Moral: For best isolation from ambient lows, shield the top and bottom of the piano equally, or not at all!

tween case and lid. However, the soundboard is open top and bottom. By blocking vibrations from one surface only, you may actually increase low-frequency leakage, since lows originally approaching both surfaces in phase (which might otherwise cancel out, failing to move the soundboard at all) are now free to move the soundboard from beneath. You really should surround the piano with dense, 3 or 4' high baffles that can prevent lows reaching the bottom of the soundboard.

Various companies manufacture piano bags—thick, absorbent tents that enclose everything to the rear of the music rack from the floor up, allowing room inside for mic stands and so on. In some studios the piano is permanently built into a recessed housing or isolation booth, with only the keyboard and music rack actually inside the studio. Both these methods work well, but they limit the seating arrangement of the band. A pianist who needs constant eye contact with other players may have a hard time taking or giving cues while facing a bulky tent or, even more inspiring, the studio wall.

Phasing Out Low-Frequency Leakage. What if the pianist prefers to be near the drummer? This comes up a lot in jazz sessions, and here too, the music rules. Set up the grand with the straight edge of the case toward the drums (so that the drummer is to the pianist's left). Locate an interior X-Y pair over an A-440, but also set up a third mic, a cardioid with full bass response, such as a U 87. Bring the cardioid into the console on a third module, set its level equal to the X-Y pair, and flip it out of phase. Then suspend it over the bass bridge, way up at the far end of the soundboard. Roll off the bottom end of the X-Y pair below 150 Hz and, via graphic eq, dip everything above 150 Hz from the bass mic. The bass mic should then make little contribution to midrange and high frequencies.

Now pan the bass mic to the stereo signal center, and moving it around inside the case, hunt for a spot where its signal seems to restore the bass taken out of the pair. Although the bass mic is out of phase, there is usually at least one spot near the bass bridge where the soundboard is moving almost 180 degrees opposite the rest at low frequencies. Remember that it takes time for various frequencies and ranges to travel through the board.

Some consoles have a built in *phase meter* that displays the degree of coherency of two signals. The scale on such meters generally reads from minus on the left to a center zero to plus on the right. If two incoming signals are fully coherent or in phase, the meter will read full positive and if they are totally out of phase, full negative. Comparing two totally different signals usually produces a zero reading, indicating that they basically do not interact phase-wise. For any pair of stereo mics (or for a stereo mixdown of any sort), the two signals should cause readings at or above zero most of the time, although an occasional minus is usually unavoidable.

The three-mic technique may not deliver bass quite as coherently as the pair, but we now have a unique situation. Low frequencies from the drums, traveling out in circular waves, will strike the pair and the bass mic simultaneously, since they are equally far from the drums. However, since they are out of phase, this low leakage will be pretty much phased out of the composite signal. If there is yet another source of lows in the studios (a bass amp, for instance), place it on the right side of the piano, and the same phase-out phenomenon will occur. Together with the baffling described above, you can get amazingly good isolation from a piano wedged in between bass and drums.

Signal Processing. Most successful piano recordings are a compromise between three factors: natural sound, the desired function the piano serves in the overall arrangement, and the sonic quality of the specific instrument at hand. Some pianos have relatively tame transients, a long sustain, and endless decelerating envelope in their release. Others can have a completely different sound envelope, even when comparing the same notes played at the same transient volume. Then again, changes in temperature and humidity can modify the behavior of a single instrument quite substantially from day to day. The instrument will sound fuller on damp days, when the soundboard is sluggish, and thinner on dry ones, when it can flex more quickly in response to higher harmonics.

As with drums, to determine the correct order for processing, determine the specific problems that processing is intended to solve, then identify those that are serious, generic flaws in the whole instrument. If your biggest problem is steep transients that threaten to overload on tape or force you to ride the piano level too low to fulfill its musical function, you need to compress first.

However, unlike drums, which are first and foremost percussive instruments, the piano is most often used for melodic, chordal, and rhythmic support. This mandates fast attack (under 2 ms), fairly high ratio (5:1 or greater), and a release time short enough to allow all piano notes and chords to be heard, even when there is a sudden change in level from one note to the next (well under 1 second). It is not necessary for every note to be above the compressor's threshold; this would sap all the dynamics out of the performance.

It is best to set the threshold only when you hear how the piano functions with other rhythm instruments. If it essentially carries the rhythm section, it may need more compression (a lower threshold) to provide continuous support. If, on the other hand, the piano exchanges phrases, lines, and fills with other instruments, raise the threshold so that the player can emphasize lead lines and participate in the desired musical and dynamic exchange.

Perhaps the most serious problem in the raw piano sound is one or more large response peaks caused by local resonances in collusion with tight miking, as we saw with drum miking. Also be aware that certain brands of pianos, notably Yamaha, are brighter than others and may have a peak in response somewhere around 2.5 kHz. In either event, sweep the entire midrange (300 to 3,000 Hz) with a narrow-band parametric equalizer to locate these peaks, determine their bandwidth, and finally reduce them in order to regain something like flat response. Then apply the desired compression.

The resulting sound will be balanced in dynamics and response but may still need overall brightness or more fullth for the particular song. A final eq can then be applied in the console. In most cases I overbrighten the piano during recording, shelf boosting everything above 5 kHz. Because there is not much in the piano's signal up there, this boosting will not overload the tape. If the instrument needs a midrange boost during mixdown, at least tape noise will not increase. If the highs are too hot then, roll them off and get rid of tape noise in the process. (You may have guessed by now that I am not a fan of noise reduction.)

Noise gating is seldom used on piano unless leakage of other instruments into the piano mics is horrendous and the piano part is intermittent throughout the song. In this case, the noise gate should be set for very fast attack to avoid clipping off the beginning of the piano notes. Set the threshold level well below the softest piano lines or chords in the arrangement. If the pianist uses a wide range of dynamics, it may be wise to compress or limit before noise gating in order not to need a low floor and engender clicks when the gate opens.

Hearing the leakage drop out between piano phrases can be distracting. You must set the floor and release time while listening to the entire rhythm arrangement. Reduce release time as far as possible without hearing the gate open and close and without chopping off the natural fade of piano notes and chords themselves. Likewise, lower the floor until you can barely hear the leakage going and coming through the entire arrangement; in most cases 10 to 15 dB down is plenty. By the time you've completed overdubs and added reverb and effects, you will no longer be aware of the gate's operation. Overall, be very sparing with piano gating. With luck you will not need it at all.

Level to Tape.   Coming up with the right recording level for the piano is a particularly touchy task. Because there is little signal above the 6-kHz level, analog tape noise will always be noticeable, even if you cut piano tracks very hot. Unfortunately, I cannot think of an instance where tape overload will actually help the piano sound, as it does with snare or kick drum tracks. You are trapped between noise and distortion.

In general, make sure the loudest parts of the piano chart do not exceed 0 dBVU or about +10 on peak meters. The purity of the piano sound makes distortion more noticeable at lower levels than it is on many other instruments. Then again, no matter how loud the pianist plays when you ask for a run-through, the instrument's volume will usually go up a few decibels when take one is slated.

Special Effects.   Anybody who has spent $30,000 for a grand piano will probably cringe at the thought of flanging its sound on tape. So would the critics and buying public, if you are dealing with classical repertoire. The piano is so much a part of the public's music psyche that even untrained ears flinch at hearing its sound manipulated unnaturally. Keep this in mind when you are adding effects to your recording.

Digital delays can be used without offending any ears, especially if the delay time relates to the tempo of the song. For uptempo songs—120 BPM (beats or quarter notes per minute) and up—a 16th-note delay time will generally add a bouncy, playful quality to the piano part. An 8th-note delay produces plain energy, and a quarter-note delay gives a halting or contemplative quality. If the lyric or feel of the tune needs this kind of help, do not be afraid to add it, even while laying basic tracks.

Short, arhythmic delay times can suggest playfulness, confusion, or clutter, while extremely long ones (longer than a quarter note) can create a feeling of whimsy, pensiveness, or even melancholy, depending on the music. Remember that the piano is often heard in a large hall with a natural delay time unrelated to the music. Thus, adding a hall-type delay will put listeners in a "concert state of mind," suggesting an intense listening experience. In this way, a delay can affect the listener's emotions and reaction to the music.

Whether to add reverb during recording depends on the pianist's pedaling habits. The internal sustain of a grand can mask large amounts of reverb, so there's no need to add reverb if the player applies continuous sustain. On the other hand, if the pianist rarely sustains, a touch of short decay reverb (under 1 second) recorded during tracking will help mask mechanical noises in the instrument and add a little apparent distance to the tightest interior miking. Remember that the piano case itself is in effect a small room intended to couple acoustic energy with the larger room around it. Short reverb will smooth out the overintimacy of close miking and add a warmth that is noticeable even if you add lots of longer reverb in the mixdown.

THE FENDER RHODES ELECTRIC PIANO

While synthesizers have eroded the popularity of the Fender Rhodes electric piano as an onstage instrument, the Rhodes has a unique combination of action and sound that many musicians prefer even to the finest synthesized or sampled equivalent. Unlike the grand, the Rhodes is generally considered a true percussion instrument whose keys drive felt-covered hammers that strike tuned metal bars. Vibration of these bars is picked up directly via magnetic pickups and sent for amplification or signal processing. There is no soundboard or acoustic *coupling* (transferring of sound) between the individual bars, and acoustic factors have no influence on the instrument's output signal.

This sound-production scheme has two problematic side effects for recording. First, the Rhodes produces very steep transients when full chords are struck. Instantaneous output levels of nearly a full volt can overload the input stage of everything from direct boxes and recording consoles to effects boxes and guitar amps. Second, from keys around C-5 (an octave above middle C) and upward, each note consists of an almost pure sine wave fundamental, with just a touch of upper harmonics. This tonal purity sounds wonderfully bell-like but is very difficult for recording tape to capture cleanly. The problem is further compounded by the fact that the output level of the Rhodes is highest in the octaves just above middle C.

To preserve the instrument's scant highs, and to combat transient distortion, it is critical that you use a low-capacitance cable and the finest direct (DI) box available. Simon Systems, Axe, and Countryman models should deliver an undistorted signal to the console. However, if you crank the mic trim up to get full VU level from the Rhodes, its transients will sometimes overload the console. One solution is to ride the mic trim down so that the very loudest chords just touch 0 dBVU, then route the signal to a parametric equalizer, where you can reduce the midrange hump and smooth out the overall response. The resulting sound can be boosted for taping by riding the channel fader above "0" or unity gain position.

Signal Processing.   Since Rhodes pianos have their hottest output level in the 1 1/2 octaves above middle C, to restore balance to the entire keyboard, try dipping the corresponding frequency range (centered on 400 or 500 Hz) by 4 to 6 dB. This (with a few dBs added at 5 to 6 kHz) brightens the instrument much more smoothly than boosting the direct signal heavily in the 3 kHz range. The latter gives the whole instrument a raspy, metallic sound reminiscent of a mellow clavinet. Of course, that sound might be perfect for certain blues, funk, or dance tracks.

It is immediately apparent that the Rhodes requires some limiting or compression—fast attack (under 2 ms) and a high ratio (over 8 : 1). I prefer limiting, since the Rhodes has plenty of natural sustain, and many players use the instrument's full dynamic range. In addition, limiting will help bring out specific dead or low-level notes, a foible even in the best-maintained Rhodes. With the transients brought under control, you can now boost the limiter's output before bringing the Rhodes back into the main module fader at the console. Finally—full level without distortion!

Some Rhodes have internal grounding problems or pick up RF interference, particularly in urban recording studios. The result is hum, noise, and audio garbage between notes. The solution (except for distinct AM or FM radio pickup) is gentle noise gating. Fast attack is necessary, but it will emphasize transients. Remember too that the lower you drop the floor, the quicker and farther the gate has to open when each new note is played. Too fast an attack and too low a floor will produce annoying clicks as the gate operates. As with the grand, set the release to allow for proper fades on sustained chords.

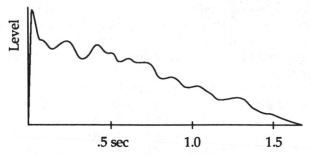

The envelope of a midrange chord played on
the Fender Rhodes, uncompressed.

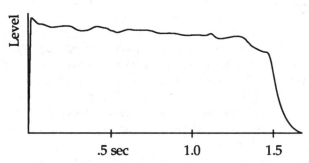

The same chord compressed at an 8:1 ratio as
described in the text.

Figure 15.3.   The envelopes of a Fender Rhodes piano midrange note uncompressed, then
compressed. The apparent level of the compressed chord is much higher because the output
gain is raised after the initial transient has been lowered.

Effects.   Since the Rhodes is solely an electric instrument, apply whatever effects achieve the emotional goals of the recording at hand. However, some effects
take to the instrument better than others. Because of its sustained purity of tone, a
DDL (digital delay) used for repeats will be hard to distinguish unless its level is very
high in the mix or unless the entire Rhodes part is played staccato.

In contrast, even a touch of slow, shallow flanging is immediately noticeable.
Pure Rhodes is so mellow that it often has to be boosted to an unnatural level in the
mix just to be heard. By varying the mixture of overtones in the Rhodes signal, flanging draws the listener's ear to the instrument at more modest mixdown levels. This
leaves the mix engineer lots of creative options. The internal tremolo on most Rhodes
works well but has only a single speed. And it undulates only the volume of each
note, doing little to bring separate harmonics to the fore.

Stereo chorusing gives compressed Rhodes a silky, evanescent quality, mysterious and with an illusion of space. This effect combined with a predelayed reverb
enables a Rhodes to replace many layers of synth pads, often with a warmth and
softness that would be hard to duplicate with a fine sampling synth. Yamaha's SPX 90

and Roland's DEP-5 series of multiprocessors offer a rich menu of layered effects, with full control of the amount of each and the order in which the effects are applied to the input signal.

One of my favorite effects is predelayed reverb (40 to 60 ms or more) with the return flanged. This leaves the actual notes played clean and separate, with a capacious, undulating space wrapped around them. One caution, however: all of this processing depends on phasing phenomena for its effect. First check your composite Rhodes signal in mono before laying it down on tape. Much advertising, film, and television music is still heard in mono—even records played on AM radio or television—and these media can lead to some of your best sales. If the studio console boasts a phase meter, check the processed Rhodes there too.

Unless the players must hear the Rhodes live in the studio, there is absolutely no advantage of running it into an instrument amplifier and miking that. Even if I amplified the instrument to enable the players to work without headphones, I would still record the Rhodes directly, using a good split feed box to drive the console and amp inputs without loading each other down. Taking the console feed of Rhodes sound from the line output of an instrument amp just adds noise and perhaps overload distortion to an otherwise pure signal. Of course, if you want the growly distortion of Rhodes played loud through a guitar amp, by all means set up a mic and go.

16

STRINGED INSTRUMENTS

ALMOST every nation and culture has a wide range of instruments strung with natural gut, plastic, or metal that are played by plucking or hitting the strings. From the Nubian oud, Bulgarian hammer-dulcimer, and Greek belzouki to the Japanese koto and biwa, the English lute, and, of course, the guitar, stringed instruments are the most popular family on earth, and with good reason. Except for the piano and harpsichord and their relatives, stringed instruments are lightweight; most are portable, easily tuned, need no assembly before every use, and produce enough volume to entertain a small audience but not so much as to mandate any distance between the player and listener. Conveniently, most are just loud enough to provide accompaniment to the unamplified voice and many hand-held winds.

BASIC PROBLEMS

It is worthwhile thinking carefully about the method by which this family of instruments creates, amplifies, and propagates sounds—more carefully than we did, for instance, with the piano—for one important reason. With most stringed instruments, the player can choose different strings, picks, pluckers, or hammers and make all kinds of adjustments that affect the quality of the sound the instrument produces. He or she can pluck or strike the strings anywhere along their length, even beyond the bridge or nut, for special effect. In the piano, most sound decisions are made by the manufacturer. Recording the piano is thus a matter of figuring out what has already been decided, but for most other stringed instruments, you must learn how your decisions can help or hurt you in the studio.

220

ACOUSTIC STRINGED INSTRUMENTS AND MAGNETIC PICKUPS

Sound Generation and Propagation. Of all groups of instruments, the plucked acoustic strings are inherently the easiest to comprehend. A stretched string passes over two fixed points located within its length. The nut, usually near the end of the string at which its tension and thus its pitch is adjusted, is a part of the rigid frame or body of the instrument and is not intended to vibrate. Near the other end, a bridge usually rests on the surface of a thin soundboard. The section of the string between nut and bridge is plucked or struck and creates the instrument's primary sound.

At its maximum deflection, the string forms a triangle with respect to its rest position. When it is released, the peak or apex of the triangle moves away like a wave from the point of pluckage and toward the bridge and nut simultaneously. This wave travels at exactly the speed of sound in the string itself, which in turn depends on the string's diameter, density, and flexibility and the tension with which it is stretched. These factors are analogous to those that determine the speed of sound in air, namely temperature, pressure, and relative humidity level. The fundamental frequency of the string's vibration depends on all these factors, plus the distance between nut and bridge.

The frequency content of the resulting note is determined by all of the above plus two additional factors: the sharpness of the angle formed at the pluck point (a function of the broadness of the plucker) and the location along the string's length where the pluck occurs. For the moment let us assume that the plucker is sharply pointed and that the pluck point is fairly near the bridge.

If the nut is indeed stationary (no energy is lost), the initial pluck-wave soon strikes the nut and bounces back and down toward the bridge. Every wave that reaches the bridge causes it to move and communicate energy to the soundboard, which in turn vibrates and distributes the energy over its entire surface. By coupling vibrations to the surrounding air, the soundboard functionally amplifies them. In general, the thicker, heavier, and stiffer the soundboard, the harder it is to move and the softer the resulting instrument sound. On the other hand, sound travels faster in a hard, dense, and stiff medium, which in turn enables such soundboards to propagate high frequencies quite efficiently.

As we know from our discussion of drums, acoustic bass, and the piano, the soundboard itself has various modes of vibration. Depending on its size, shape, and the material of which it is made, it can also contain smaller areas in which specific frequencies and ranges concentrate and resonate. Finally, the elasticity of the soundboard determines how quickly the original energy of the string's vibration is completely dissipated or how quickly each note fades out.

For two contrasting examples of propagation, let us briefly examine the banjo and harpsichord. The soundboard of the banjo is a stretched circular skin (made of vellum from animal skins or of plastic) very much like a drum head. The bridge, located near its center, excites only the lower modes of vibration, meaning that few high frequencies emanate from the head. In addition, because the head is extremely

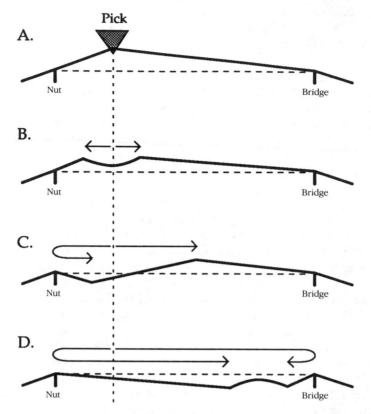

Figure 16.1. Side views of a string after plucking. A. At the moment of greatest stretch by a pick, B. Immediately after the string is released, C. After the initial "crest" (heading left) has bounced off the nut and is returning toward the bridge, and D. As the "crest" heading right bounces off the bridge.

flexible, it soaks up energy from the bridge, meaning that notes die out very rapidly—in less than 2 seconds. But for all the same reasons, and because the pluckers are usually wide metal finger picks that seriously deflect the strings, the banjo is quite loud for an instrument of its size.

The harpsichord also has metal strings, but that is about the only similarity. Its soundboard is a large, thin sheet of wood (usually poplar or spruce), much stiffer and heavier than the banjo's vellum. The pluckers are usually made of very thin quill or plastic, and consequently string deflection is small. However, thin pluckers mean a pointed, angular deflection that generates a lot of upper harmonics in each note. The stiff soundboard does not damp string vibration very quickly and amplifies high frequencies quite well. The result is a soft but very bright output, with long sustain—up to 6 seconds on lower notes.

A metal soundboard, in which sound travels fastest of all, should have the best response to high frequencies from the strings. The dobro guitar is the only widely known instrument that has a metal soundboard, and its tone is indeed bright, with steep high-frequency transients and dense upper harmonics. The only problem is that thin sheet metal has a tendency to "whistle" or ring in the 3 kHz range when excited, artificially sustaining the length of higher notes unless it is mechanically damped. A dobro player can apply damping as necessary during a performance; a harpsichordist using a metal-boarded instrument would have big problems. Pleyel brand harpsichords do in fact have metal soundboards and are extremely difficult to control for solo recording. They are quite loud and bright, however, and cut nicely through a large orchestra in live performances.

As you can see in figure 16.2, a thin plucker gives the string the shape of 1/2 a sawtooth wave. Anyone familiar with analog synthesis will correctly guess that the resulting note contains all the upper harmonics of the fundamental pitch. Assuming the plucker is sufficiently thin, the only other factor that can limit the highest frequency in these harmonics is the thickness of the string itself. A thin string bends more sharply, yielding higher overtones. Similarly, for lower notes requiring heavier strings (in weight per unit of length), a thin string wound with a metal wrapping will be more flexible and give higher overtones than a thick, solid string. Windings that have the smallest area of contact with the string will not interfere with its inherent flexibility. Thus, round-wound strings yield more and higher overtones than flat-wound (figure 16.3).

Given the type of instrument and strings, the variable that allows the player the greatest range of sounds is where on the strings the plucking occurs. If the player plucks precisely at the center of the distance between bridge and nut, the string is deflected symmetrically. The resulting sound will contain a high proportion of the fundamental (first-mode frequency). Moreover, every mode and frequency for which the center of the string is an antinode will be emphasized, and those for which the center is a node will be suppressed. The result is an output that contains all the odd-numbered harmonics and not much else, such as the full yet "shy" tone of a guitar

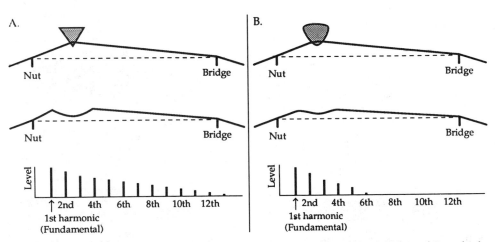

Figure 16.2.   String shapes caused when plucked by A. a thin pointed pick, and B. a thick felt pick. The sharper the plucking tool, the more sharply peaked the traveling wave crests, and consequently, the higher the proportion of upper harmonics generated.

plucked at midstring. If the string is tuned to 100 Hz, the played note will contain 100 Hz, 300 Hz, 500 Hz, 700 Hz, and so on. In a way, plucking at midstring introduces a kind of acoustic comb-filter.

Instead, if we pluck the string at 1/4 the distance from the bridge to the nut, the center of the string will be a node for the even harmonics (the first harmonic is the fundamental itself) while still acting as an antinode for odd-numbered ones. This results in a fuller series of harmonics, with one exception. Sound waves travel in both directions from the initial pluck point. Right-side-up waves coming back from the bridge might meet and cancel upside-down waves returning from the nut, and vice versa.

Such cancellation actually occurs for each mode that is a multiple of the fractional distance at which the pluck occurs. Thus, if you pluck the string at 1/4 its length, the 4th, 8th, 12th . . . modes (and harmonics) will be canceled. In the 100 Hz example, this cancels 400 Hz, 800 Hz, and 1,200 Hz, and so on. Plucking the same string at 1/6 its length—600 Hz, 1,200 Hz, and 1,800 Hz—would be missing. You need not worry about these losses but should understand that they give stringed instruments a part of their sonic interest.

The closer the pluck to the bridge, the higher the percentage of upper modes in its output, and thus the brighter its tone. Positions whose ratio of distances from pluck to bridge and nut is not a ratio of two small whole numbers will have the fullest harmonic series by including the most high overtones and partials. For every position at which one or more modes are conspicuously absent, the instrument acquires a different emotional quality: full and sincere, bright and cheerful, thin or nasal for a playful or cynical flavor.

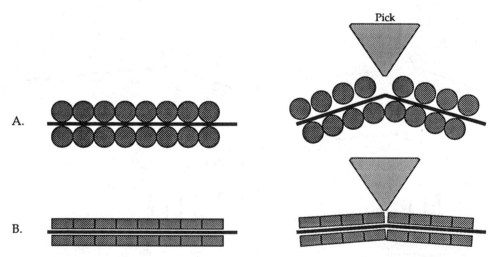

Figure 16.3.   Cross-sections of round-wound (A.) and flat-wound (B.) guitar strings, at rest (left) and at the instant of a pluck (right). The round-wound string can be bent at a sharper angle during plucking, and therefore emits more high frequencies.

Miking Considerations and the Danger of Magnetic Pickups. These days, acoustic instruments in almost any live performance are miked or amplified via magnetic pickups. Let us examine the difference in these two schemes. A microphone, even one fairly close to the body or soundboard of a stringed instrument, picks up sounds from all sources:

- the pluck itself, with string- or winding-scrape, and lots of high frequencies from the transient
- the length of the string, which can buzz against frets and fretboard, generating more highs (plus some unmusical vibrations beyond the bridge and nut)
- the soundboard(s)—front and back faces (as in the acoustic guitar)—the instrument's structural casing, or other sound-amplifying surfaces
- to a minor degree, the player himself, whose body, clothing, and seat may reinforce some frequencies and mute or absorb others

We can feature or subdue any of these sources by choosing the mic types and positions available to us.

A magnetic pickup senses only one source of sound: the relative movement of the section of strings immediately above its poles. The pickup itself may move up and down as the body or soundboard of the instrument vibrates, but by and large it hears only what is happening at one point along the strings. Suppose that point happens to be a node in the 4th mode of the strings. The pickup will never hear the 4th, 8th, 12th . . . modes at all. Conversely, if the pickup is under an antinode for certain modes, those modes will be unnaturally emphasized in its output. No amount of equalization can restore the instrument's complete, natural harmonic series.

Pickups can thus take some control of the instrument's emotional quality out of the player's hands. In any case, pickups never deliver the entire range of sounds that any stringed instrument is naturally capable of producing. The pickup inherently ignores much of what the instrument builder spent time on—a casing and soundboard that give every acoustic instrument an audio personality as unique as the materials of which it is made.

Mic Positioning. The pickup syndrome highlights the importance of listening to your instrument and finding the direction in which it projects the sound qualities you like and those you dislike for the song at hand. Let someone else play while you plug one ear and move the other around the instrument at close-mic distance (1'). If there is no other player handy, simulate this experience by having someone move an omni mic around the instrument while you listen to its output through headphones. Only in this way can you learn and take full advantage of your instrument's sonic vocabulary.

The dense, orchestral sound you get by miking the body of a harp's resonating chamber might be perfect for adding warmth to a ballad. For a harp solo, however, the right miking might be at midstring height, where you can pick up the player's finger contact with each string. Or perhaps you need a blend of mics at both locations.

What factors should you use to choose between stereo and mono miking? Simply, if the instrument is small enough so that it would be difficult to find two sweet spots more than 18 inches apart, stick with mono. You should record the mandolin, zither, ukulele, koto, balalaika, and autoharp in mono unless it is a solo recording and you have time to play with various coincident and spaced mic setups. If you have the tracks, record the hammer dulcimer, orchestral harp, harpsichord, and clavichord in stereo. You may argue that the autoharp's body is broad enough to get stereo separation between low and high strings. While this is true, remember that no audience hears the instrument that way, and spreading it out left to right in a mix will make the autoharp seem as large as the piano or drums. If you want that effect, fine. If not, do not waste the time. Sometimes a little touch of stereo reverb in the mix will give the impression that stereo miking was used, without the risk of phasing and imaging problems.

Selecting Mics. First of all, performers love to move around with hand-held instruments, and when they do, the direction in which the desired sound quality emanates will move too. Thus, unless you have leakage problems, I strongly suggest an omni mic. Then too, omni mics have little proximity boost of the bass frequencies that might reinforce unwanted body resonances in the instrument. Third, an omni mic will hear and blend sounds emanating from the entire soundboard, thereby reducing the effects of any local resonance from the part of the body nearest a cardioid mic.

My own first choices are the EV RE-55 for a dynamic mic or B&K 4006 and the AKG 414 for a condenser. If leakage is a factor, use the gentlest, least directional cardioid around; avoid super- and hypercardioid models. In addition to their audio tunnel vision, most highly directional mics produce high coloration of off-axis sounds, especially the leakage from other instruments. Thus, even if the on-axis instrument sounds better, the garbage in its signal may have a peaky, strained quality that degrades the sound on other tracks. Obviously, some baffling will help too, whether it is the felt coning technique suggested for drums or simply hanging a parka between the mic and other sound sources.

The dynamic/condenser question can be settled by two factors. If the instrument is to be a part of a rhythm section and you do not want a more intimate perspective on it than on other rhythm instruments, stick with a dynamic or ribbon mic and add top end above 8 kHz as necessary. This will give transparent highs rather than the striking and often distracting 4 to 6 kHz detail that comes with condenser mics. On the other hand, if the instrument is naturally dull (as often results with gut strings, vellum soundboards, and the like), reach for a condenser and be prepared to add top end anyway. One inexpensive mic that seems to like stringed instruments is Sony's ECM-23F, which gives a smooth and sparkling sound. Various Neumanns and AKGs also serve well.

Remember that in a live performance you can see the performer's fingers, picks, or hammers hitting the strings, plus body movements that give indications of timing and emotion. Just as you can understand muffled dialogue by lip reading, so visual information will make up for a lack of highs in a live musical performance. Conversely, extra highs from a condenser will help make up for missing visual information in a taped performance.

While low roll-off is almost always indicated except on the orchestral harp and harpsichord, which has fundamentals down to 31 Hz on some dual manual models, an internal pad is never necessary. The very loudest acoustic stringed instruments, excluding piano, produce little more than 110 dB within a few inches of their sound-board. This translates to an average SPL of 70 to 80 dB at a distance of 6′.

Inboard Processing.   To decide whether to add compression, you should pay more attention to the type of music and competition from other instruments than to the solo sound of the stringed instrument itself. All members of this family emit steep transients, meaning that average level is way below peaks. Therefore, to compete with rock drums or electric rhythm instruments, compression is a must—fast attack (under 2 ms) and medium ratio (5 : 1 or so) with the threshold set so that the required level of the instrument can be achieved without its transients overpowering the hi-hat, vocal sibilances, and other important high-end information in the completed track.

Beyond this, getting the sound you want is a matter of considering the inherent ADSR envelope of the specific instrument and how the part is played. To even out the volume of single-note parts played on an instrument with unpredictable, changing levels (banjo, for example), lower the threshold and go for a short release (under 0.5 second). In contrast, every note of a properly voiced harpsichord is virtually the same volume, no matter how hard the player attacks the keyboard. The only variable is the number of notes played simultaneously. Thus, a higher threshold and longer release will produce a smoother sound and subdue the clunk with which each note finishes as the released plectrum brushes by the string again on its way to rest position.

You should use noise gating only for effect. The release is an important part of the envelope of each stringed instrument and should not be eliminated. What holds the sound of these instruments together is how the body reacts to notes and chords as they die out, just as in the grand piano. Much of the warmth in strummed instruments (autoharp is a great example) comes from the way the body resonates with one note until the next is struck. Remove the space between notes or chords and you take away the instrument's weight, substance, and solidity, along with the feeling of physical contact between player and instrument. If leakage from other instruments is a prob-lem and the stringed instrument's part is intermittent, try gating with a threshold 6 to 8 dB lower than the softest passages and a floor of only 10 to 15 dB beneath that. In an emergency some help is better than none.

If you have located the sweet spot and chosen the right mic, beware of any apparent need to boost midrange and highs more than 6 dB. Equalizers can introduce severe phase shifts between the affected and nearby unaffected bands. This in turn gives a harsh, whiny quality that belies the basically open and gentle nature of most stringed instruments. Instead, introduce a broad dip in the mid lows. This will leave the important frequencies' phase coherent and achieve the desired shift of response. As with acoustic bass, drums, and other instruments, equalize before compression if you are eq'ing to dip body resonances and other narrow peaks, after compression if the sound coming from your mic(s) needs only a minor tailoring of response.

Level to Tape.   Distortion is a complex phenomenon because the ears do not work like test equipment. In some cases (notably drums and electric guitars), the human perception system may accept a certain amount of distortion as a desirable addition to a pure recorded signal. This is a function of experience and substitution. Most of the rock records we know and love have some type of significant distortion. In the same way that added high end on stringed instruments makes up for a listener's inability to see the performer, a controlled amount of distortion on some sounds makes up for our inability to play recordings of them at full, live volume. It reminds us of how music feels at 110 decibels. Electric guitar is certainly the perfect example.

On the other hand, acoustic instruments are never distorted nor terribly loud when heard unamplified. Thus, watch recording levels of stringed instruments carefully. Overloaded transients will create a teeth-gnashing harshness than can undo the most careful mic selection, placement, and processing. Check the level to tape with a peak-reading meter if possible, and keep the hottest peaks on full chords under + 8dB. Remember that if the player originally miked at 1′ moves 6″ closer to the mic during a take, the signal level increases by 6 dB. Overload on strummed rhythm parts will appear as a gargling lower-mid range or a muddy, underwater quality. If you notice this, check the compressor first. Many units overload only when their gain reduction is averaging more than 20 dB. If this is not the problem, simply reduce the input trim or level to tape until the overload vanishes.

Effects. I think that anything is fair in rock, pop, and the like, although for most types of acoustic-based music, I never record stringed instrument tracks with effects. Wait until the mix and see what is needed. One ironic pointer, however: having lobbied against using magnetic pickups as the primary recording source, I now suggest that if you want to add a delay, flanging, or almost any other effect, do it to a pickup's signal, rather than that from the instrument's main mic. Most pickups are lacking in frequencies above 10 kHz, the very range that, when delayed, chorused, or flanged and recombined with a direct signal, gives the most annoying phasing problems—spittiness, periodic swishing, and the like. In addition, most stringed instruments are soft and not easily baffled or isolated, and their main mic can and will pick up leakage from other instruments. Flanging or chorusing the mic's signal will also process the leakage, casting a fuzzy, artificial haze over other instruments in the ultimate mix. Instead, chorus the clean pickup output. You can then blend the effect back in with the mic, keeping the instrument distinct and separate, or record the effect onto another track for some special effect.

17

GUITARS

MORE musicians play the guitar—acoustic, electric, and its assorted cousins—than any other instrument on earth. While the ukulele (and its Latin American counterpart, the charango) and twelve-string represent the extremes of size and construction among acoustic guitars, they both produce sound in the same manner. Strings plucked or strummed by the guitarist transmit vibrations through a bridge and resonate a thin wooden body. These vibrations are further amplified by the internal volume of air, which is directly coupled to the surrounding air through one or more holes in the front surface of the body that faces the audience.

THE ACOUSTIC GUITAR

As with any acoustic instrument, there are at least two potentially problematical frequencies, namely those at which the wooden body (or armadillo hide used in an authentic charango) and the enclosed mass of air resonate. The larger the body, and thinner or more flexible the wood, the lower the frequency of the body resonance. A handmade Spanish gut- or nylon-stringed guitar, made extra thin because its strings are under less tension than steel strings, can resonate as low as 80 to 100 Hz, while the air inside resonates at perhaps 150 to 200 Hz. The lowest E on the instrument is about 80 Hz. The body resonance thus helps amplify the lowest notes, but the air resonance can cause a "proximity hump," muddying the lowest octave when close-miked.

Many guitarists who prefer to play seated contribute to response problems by surrounding and muting the instrument's vibrations with their own bodies and clothing. Shrouding the instrument reduces its high midrange output and produces a dull sound that is hard to brighten with equalization. In addition, chords and individual notes do not ring as long as when the guitar is played with little body-to-body contact. Compression will not restore its natural resonance. To maximize a guitar's high-frequency output, record with fresh strings, put on and tuned the night before the session. Unless it impedes proper playing, a thinner pick than the guitarist normally uses will also give the highs a lift. In the studio, volume is less important than clarity and presence.

Mic Placement.   Low frequencies emanate from the hole in a gusty burst. Miking directly in front of the hole can be disastrous unless you want a fat, puffy sound. Then again, miking farther up the neck can deliver an excessive amount of fret, string, and fingering noise. The correct miking position depends on the specific guitar, the player, and the effect desired. In general, the acoustic, which is quite soft, must be miked relatively closely to bring out its natural intimacy.

This mandates that you move one ear around in front of the body while the guitarist plays chords and lines. As with piano or acoustic bass, you will find at least one sweet spot where upper frequencies are bright and smooth. Even if resonances are also heavy there, that is the optimal mic position. The same is true whether you are recording a gut or steel 6-string, 12-string, lute, balalaika, mandolin, ukulele, koto, or kithara. Make sure the player understands the importance of the mic's positioning with respect to the instrument and does not change playing position or stance between or during takes. Moving even a couple of inches can totally change what a mic hears.

If the guitar is meant to add body to the rhythm arrangement, you want clear chords and not much fret noise. In this case, mike to one side of the bridge, whichever position is least in the way of the guitarist's movements (position A in figure 17.1). Miking on-center of the body (position B) accentuates the lowest octave and makes the instrument rather heavy. If you want a breezy sound, thin with an awareness of the instant each string is plucked, mike off center between the hole and neck (position C), again wherever the mic is least in the player's way.

Because the instrument is fairly small, with little room for individual frequencies to find local resonance spots, stereo miking can lead to phasing problems. However, you may find that one close and a second, more distant mike blended to a mono

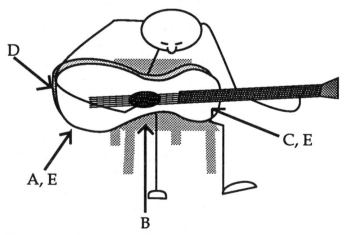

Figure 17.1.   View from in front of and above an acoustic guitar, showing various suggested mic positions for mono and stereo pairs as discussed in the text.

channel or track give a rich, almost flanged quality slightly akin to a 12-string. One mic in front and another behind the instrument (position D) warms up the bottom end. If you really want to record a single guitar in stereo (but not a classical guitar as in a live performance), find one mic position that would be the ideal single-mic location, then search for a second acceptable position, monitoring in mono to make sure that the composite signal is not worse than that from the first mic.

In my experience, two mics symmetrically located with respect to the center line or neck of the instrument give a balanced sound without phasing problems. Sometimes, as with acoustic bass, one side (either toward or away from the floor with respect to playing position) emits a clearer tone overall than the other side. In this case, position both stereo mics on the same side of the strings, one each in front of the bottom and top lobes of the guitar body (position E in figure 17.1). This approach also provides stereo separation between picking and fretting noises, along with a smooth interplay among the mid lows concentrated in and projected by each lobe. To insure solid lows while maintaining the spread between pick and fret sounds, an X-Y pair placed between positions B and C may be your best bet.

Mic Selection.   If you must close mike, the best sound will result from using an omni mic to pick up sound from the largest possible area of the guitar's body. Dynamic (such as EV RE55 or 635, etc.) and ribbon models (Beyer D160, etc.) produce a smooth sound; condensers (like our Neumann and AKG standbys) a crisper, sparkling high end. In any case, internal roll-off below 100 Hz generally takes the worst out of body resonances without thinning the muscial content too much.

However, if leakage is a problem, cardioid is the solution, particularly a model like the 421U, which will also boost mid highs and help the instrument cut through a large ensemble or dense arrangement. Placement is particularly critical with cardioids (especially when used in stereo pairs), since local resonances will be heavily featured at a distance of 6 to 8″ from the body. As with other stringed instruments, stay away from super- and hypercardioid mics if at all possible.

I have seen various lavaliers, such as the Neumann, Sony ECM-50 variations, and especially the Tram, give fine guitar sounds when mounted on the body itself, beneath and to one side of the bridge. However, such an extremely close perspective makes the instrument seem physically larger than life and negates some of its more delicate qualities. Make sure that lavaliers are not in direct contact with the wood. A thick cotton, felt, or cloth pad between the body and mic will greatly reduce the pickup of resonances and all mechanical noises generated during the performance. Be careful as well not to mount a lavalier right in the hole of the guitar, where the airflow generated by full chords and resonances can produce plosive blasts and a tubby sound.

Contact Mics and Pickups.   So far we have not differentiated between gut- and steel-stringed instruments. Obviously, only steel strings will produce any sound when a magnetic pickup is used. Such pickups effectively turn the acoustic into an electric guitar and will be discussed later. However, there are many good contact-type pickups usable on gut- or steel-stringed instruments. These units are designed to be mounted in or near the hole. In addition, their response is generally tailored to help subdue the excessive lows concentrated at this point. For the studio, use only low-impedance models that can be directly plugged into the mic input of the console.

Impedance matching via transformer is possible, but unless extremely heavy transformers are used, it often costs you a lot of the high-frequency response from the pickup. Then again, you may wish to broaden the pickup sound with a normal mic in a more conventional position, using the pickup to brighten the mic or the mic to warm or texturize the pickup's output. Regardless of how the pickup is used, be sure to check its phase relationship with the mic(s) at the console.

I prefer to mike the guitar normally, using the pickup only as the source for any effects—flanging, chorusing, or whatever—that must be added during record. The pickup does not hear leakage from other instruments, and as discussed earlier flanged leakage can "garbagize" any number of other tracks, especially the drums.

Processing. In comparison with electric guitar, piano, and most commonly used rhythm instruments, the acoustic guitar has little sustain, especially in its higher range. Picked notes have a severe transient, and they decay quickly. To make matters worse, high frequencies in each note decay faster than the rest of the spectrum. It is thus difficult to keep an acoustic lead or solo clear above a full rock or orchestral arrangement without heavy compression. Before trying this, however, reduce any egregious body resonances with one or two narrow bands of a parametric eq. Do not worry if the instrument seems a bit thin—it will strike the compressor more evenly this way, and you can restore the bottom with inboard eq after compression. Or better yet, record the track a bit thin but at relatively high level, and warm it up by boosting the lower midrange during the mix, reducing tape noise as usual in the process.

Many engineers summarily compress the acoustic no matter what its function in an arrangement—solo or rhythm. Fast attack (2 ms or less), medium ratio (in the 5 : 1 range), and short release (0.5 sec) will help mask the compressor's action. The threshold should be set with an eye toward what the instrument has to compete with in the finished mix. If the arrangement is fairly open, set the threshold so that the average strummed chord is just activating the compressor. If the arrangement will be more dense, the average solo guitar line may need 2 to 4 dB of compression, with loud chords topping 10 dB. Ideally, however—and especially if you are recording digitally—set the compressor threshold so that only full chords activate the unit, leaving the dynamics of any solos, fills, or single lines competely untouched.

If the idea (and/or the sound) of compression bothers you, remember that reverb will later help in two ways. First, it will mask audible compressor breathing or pumping you may hear in the dry guitar track. Second, it will sustain the rapidly decaying highs in each note, keeping attention on the acoustic even through some heavy midrange competition in the arrangement. Whatever you do, do not cut the acoustic track with reverb. After the other tracks are compiled, a reverb different from the one used on the other tracks can help highlight the acoustic in the mix without excessive level. By boosting mid-highs of the guitar in this reverb send, higher notes will be preferentially featured and sustained without heavy equalization of the direct guitar sound.

Effects. Like the piano, the acoustic guitar is an instrument that audiences are used to hearing pure and simple. That fact alone may deter you from cutting the track with flanging, chorusing, or other effects. However, as with the Rhodes piano, a touch of flanging can rivet attention on the acoustic. A neat trick is not to flange the direct signal but only the reverb send of the acoustic. Do this while laying tracks if you think the flanger will be unavailable for this detail during a mix, using a very short reverb time (well under 1 second) to allow room for your later selection of mixdown reverb. Or flange the signal from a pickup, as suggested earlier, leaving the mic signal itself clean and perhaps sending the flanged signal to a separate track for divergent panning in the mix. Either of these approaches should satisfy purists while adding sonic interest.

A DDL can help a 6-string imitate a 12-string. Set the delay time for 10 to 15 ms and use no more than about 20% of the delayed signal in the blend. A touch of very slow flanging on the delay will also add body to the finished sound. Since a 10-ms delay will partially phase out 55 Hz, 170 Hz, and 300 Hz (thinning out the blended sound), it is a good idea to shelf-dip the entire bottom end of the guitar signal before sending it to the DDL. This way you can get away with using a higher DDL percentage in the blend, if necessary. Better yet, apply the DDL in the mix and bring its return back into a separate module so you can take off a bit of its highs to preserve the guitar's own transients, and pan it differently than the direct guitar. Do not forget to check the composite in mono, though.

For a fuller rhythm acoustic sound without resorting to heavy compression, try one of the short reverse envelope reverbs available on the Lexicon 224 XL, Yamaha SPX 90 or Roland DEP-5 series processors. The effect may sound quite artificial when you solo the guitar track, but in context (and used modestly), it can sound as though a synth pad is doubling every line and chord played on the guitar. In some ways the guitar may actually seem to sing! If you want to use a lot of the flipped envelope, a touch of normal short-plate reverb will mask the fact that something strange is happening.

THE ELECTRIC GUITAR

The electric guitar appeared in the 1940s when magnetic pickups first became available. Initially the instrument was regarded as a loud but inferior substitute for acoustics in larger ensembles, bands, and orchestral performances in concert halls. Little music was written specifically for the electric guitar until about 1950, when Les Paul began recording hits, and until the beginnings of rock 'n' roll shortly thereafter. I bring this up only to remind you that the electric guitar is still in its historical infancy, and therefore open to every type of musical and electronic experimentation, signal processing, and trickery in the book. There is frankly no such thing as the ideal electronic guitar sound; there is only the right sound for each part in each song.

We should also remember that in many settings the electric guitar itself is only one part of a sound-producing chain that includes custom internal electronics, one or more preamplifiers, volume, fuzz-and-wah pedals, delay, flanging, chorusing, and other effects boxes, plus noise gates, compressors, and one or more amplifiers, each with their own electronic toys. Thus, to properly record the electric for any specific tape, you must think of the entire package as the instrument.

The guitarist must therefore make sure that every component of his or her system is in top condition, interconnected by properly grounded, low-capacitance cables, and that it performs at studio quality. You simply cannot expect an engineer to turn a Silvertone into a Les Paul Custom/Marshall combo with a few processing tricks. It is relatively easy to make a good recording of a fine-sounding instrument, impossible to make one of a junker.

Sound Production.   Electrics have solid and semihollow body designs. In solid bodies, body and neck are for all practical purposes mechanically inert in that they make no contribution to the musical output and have no mechanical resonances. Sound quality here depends solely on the type of strings used, the type and number of pickups, their mounting and relative positioning, and the type of electronics by which the signal from each pickup is ultimately delivered to the 1/4″ output jack(s).

Remember that electrics have the ultimate in close-miking problems. With pickups a few millimeters beneath the strings, we might expect all the local resonance and other problems of close-miking a grand piano with a shotgun (mic). It is not quite that bad, but the slightest problem in the string/pickup relationship can cause severe output imbalances. This makes fine adjustment of the entire movement absolutely mandatory prior to mastering sessions.

Semihollow bodies have relatively thick, stiff wooden faceplates, allowing at least some vibration of the pickups with respect to the strings. Although the sheer mass of the wood limits these vibrations to the lower midrange and bass, such vibration affords three distinct advantages. First, semihollow electrics have a warmer, fatter sound than most solid bodies. Second, the internal chamber does resonate, which in most models allows easier and smoother feedback and sustain effects than their solid-body counterparts.

Third and subtlest, the movement of the front face (and pickups) follows some unpredictable, composite waveform derived from the vibrations of all six strings. Thus, its phase relationship with the musical pitch of each string changes continuously as a chord rings, giving a very gentle self-flanging effect that is totally absent in solid bodies. When single notes are played, the body can mimic the vibration of each note directly. To my ear, this gives semihollow leads more weight and chords more sonic interest than those played on most solid bodies.

Strings, Pickups, and Internal Circuits.   Although it is not my intent to advise you on the selection of guitars or how to outfit the one you have, you should know the in-studio consequences of your decisions. While you are playing (live or in the studio), your ears are focused on the musical sounds you produce. In the same way a singer does not hear his or her own breaths, a guitarist probably will not notice the sound of finger slides on the fretboard, a string buzzing against the pickups, the fact that one string is louder than the others, or the hum, noise, and hiss from various effects boxes. While these types of sounds get lost in the ambience of rehearsal rooms and the audience noise of clubs and halls, you hear every nuance and flaw with dazzling clarity in the studio. To avoid wasting precious studio time adjusting your instrument or giving a drab performance because you are tip-toeing over the frets, you should be aware of the following:

1. Round-wound strings generally produce a brighter tone on tape, but they require greater clearance over the fret and pickups to avoid buzzing. This means that their output is generally a couple of dB less than that of flat-wound strings. Remember, too, that copper windings are nonmagnetic and will have even lower output, with proportionately more upper harmonics on the low E, A, and D strings.

2. Finger slides on the fretboard are much louder and potentially objectionable in the studio, especially with round-wound strings. Listeners expect these on acoustic guitar but not on electrics, especially in rock.

3. Extremely light strings may be easier to play, but their sound is inherently thinner or more shrill, and in a way that cannot be corrected with equalization. In addition, lightweight strings stretch a lot. If you play hard, the pitch of each note starts slightly above the note to which it is tuned and bends down as the vibration diminishes naturally. This may be fine on stage but can lend an unintended twang when heard in the studio.

4. Dirty or dead strings lose their high-frequency output and, worse yet, may be out of tune when fretted. This is because the extra weight of the dirt may not be evenly distributed or because the string may not have stretched evenly after long service, meaning its diameter varies over its length. Simply put, heavier sections of the string vibrate at a lower pitch than equal lengths of a thinner section.

5. If your pickups have adjustable pole pieces for each note, you can balance the output of all strings at home with a VU meter (on your cassette deck or mixer). When played evenly, the low E string should be about 3 to 4 dB hotter than the high E. Adjusting so that all the strings give the same VU reading will result in a thin, metallic tone in which the pitch of low notes played in chords is not easily recognized.

6. Any hum, grounding, or RF problem you can hear at home will render the instrument unusable for a master recording session. It is cheaper to have the instrument professionally repaired than waste studio time trying to work around the problem. You should, then, test your instrument thoroughly. Listening through a mixer or amp with the treble cranked all the way, search for problems through the entire range of the volume controls on each guitar pickup, both singly and combined; with and without your hands in contact with the strings; and when you stand near a fluorescent light or a tube guitar amp (if you have one handy). Then, if you use any effects boxes, add them to the signal chain one at a time and note how much noise, distortion, or other problems each of them generates.

7. Dead or dying batteries in guitar electronics or effects boxes can lower the output level of your signal, add considerable noise and hiss to the signal, generate distortion due to the underpowering of the electronics, and fail completely in the middle of your best take.

Effects. When the first fuzz-tone boxes appeared in 1965, we had no idea of what was to come. The first few generations of battery-powered, foot-switched devices made no attempt to deliver an output of studio quality. Circuits, and later chips, that could do this in a small package simply had not been invented. Many current effects boxes take advantage of custom chip designs that precisely manipulate the input signal with low-power consumption, noise, and distortion.

Furthermore, most of them are built by the same companies (Boss, Ibanez, Roland, Korg, Yamaha, Valley People, etc.) that make expensive rack-mounted studio devices for the same purposes. Attention is now on sonic quality. It is a fairly safe bet that the boxes you use on stage will work well in the studio, providing that the batteries are fresh in each and every device; they are all interconnected by properly shielded and low-capacitance cables; and the nominal operating level and input/output impedances of all are in the same range. Note that *mic* and *line level* are not precise terms, especially when used in conjunction with consumer products like effects boxes. The terms allegedly specify the input or output voltage corresponding to the device's so-called full operating level (beyond which there is normally another 10 dB of undistorted headroom still available). Different manufacturers use mic level to mean some specific value in the range from -65 to -40 dBV and line level from -15 to $+8$ dBV. Inputs and outputs on most consumer stereo equipment, for instance, use -10 dBV as their so-called line level.

Measured in volts, a 20-dB difference between two audio signals means the higher signal has 10 times the voltage of the lower one. Thus, one device whose line level output is at $+4$ dBV can severely overload another whose so-called line input is designed to receive -10 dBV. Because manufacturer's specs can be deceptive, even if all your effects boxes claim to operate at line level you should find the exact max settings that, with your guitar, still yield a clean, undistorted output. To do this, plug your guitar into the first effect, plug the output of that into your mixer or amp, and turn all guitar controls (volume and tone) all the way up. Turn the tone or treble controls up all the way on this amp or mixer without overloading it. Now, playing full chords at the loudest practical level, slowly increase the effect box's input level, threshold, or other gain control. Note and mark the setting at which audible distortion first creeps in. This is as high as you can safely drive that effect box with your guitar.

Coming down a bit from that (3 dB or so if you can meter it), now plug the output of the first device into the second and use the same method to find its maximum undistorted input setting. By repeating this process with each device in the chain, you will also find the combined settings that produce the least total amount of hiss and noise. If this noise level is too great for mastering, it may still be fine for a demo.

Remember too that the output signal of any (or all) of your effects boxes may be reversed in phase from the input, and this may only be true when the device is activated. If you ultimately want to bring the guitar into the console through two or more input modules (direct and amplified, for example), make sure that the composite signal remains phase-coherent by checking the combined signal of all tracks and effects in mono. A console phase meter will confirm this instantly.

In addition, you should ensure that the assorted foot switches and operating controls work relatively silently and are kept clean. To test for this, plug your guitar into the series of boxes, and turn the guitar's volume completely down and the mixer or amp gain up much higher than normal. Click each switch and turn each adjustment knob. Any that produce noise, clicks, or scratching need cleaning with audio solvent and/or a shot of compressed air to dislodge dust and gunk.

There should also be no grounding problems individually or collectively. Try every combination of all switches and test the entire range of all volume and effects controls, hunting for combinations or levels at which a humming, buzzing, or RF interference appears. Note any such ghosts and take the whole kit, guitar included, to a good electronics technician. The problem can be as small as one *cold solder joint* (meaning the solder did not melt completely when heated initially, leaving rosin or other material in the connection).

A unified *pedalboard* (with up to eight effects made by the same company, mounted on a single, prewired chassis for easy onstage foot operation) can be tremendously helpful for gigs. Before using such a system, even a studio-quality rackmount version, for recording, remember that every circuit or device in the signal path adds noise and distortion. If you need all the pedalboard effects within one song, there is probably no quieter way to hook them up than with the board itself. However, if you require only one or two effects, the recorded signal may be much cleaner if you remove these from the board and patch directly through them. Furthermore, just because a pedalboard is sold as one item does not mean the manufacturer has solved problems like phase reversal. Troubleshoot each component as carefully as you would if it were a separate device.

Guitar Amplifiers.   The basic job of any amplifier is to turn a very small voltage signal from a guitar into electric wattage, which in turn is transduced or converted into watts of acoustic energy by one or more loudspeakers. Like studio monitor amps and speakers, a good guitar or instrument amplifier does that job quietly, without distortion and without coloring the signal by adding a perceptible or characteristic sound of its own.

In theory, if all you want is unadorned amplification, the *wattage* and maximum undistorted output level of the amp should not matter. For studio use, a 20-watt amp can deliver as fine a sound as a 200-watt amp, especially if its input comes from a series of effects boxes that together produce exactly the sound you want.

In reality the 20-watt amp may have an advantage. Suppose you want 100 dB of actual guitar volume at the mic in the studio. Let us assume that the input gain and overall S/N of the 20- and 200-watt amps are identical when each is driven at full modulation. The 200-watter will deliver an actual volume that is 10 dB higher if necessary but with a continuous, 10-dB-higher noise floor. Thus, at any in-studio volume level or SPL, the 20-watt amp is actually 10 dB quieter. You may rarely need the extra 10 dB of guitar volume at the high end, but a higher noise floor always hurts.

Second, the larger the amp wattage, the more likely that its speaker cabinet has double woofers, separate tweeter(s), and perhaps even separate midrange drivers. There is frankly no way to close mike such a cabinet with one mic and get a balanced, coherently phased signal. Ideally, the instrument amp should project sound from a single point source such as one full-range speaker. By the way, it is quite expensive to build a speaker crossover network with low distortion and high-power handling capacity. Because of fierce price competition, most guitar amp manufacturers choose power over "cleanth" in their crossovers. This is another deterrent to multispeaker or multicabinet instrument amps for studio recording.

For studio use, find the cleanest, quietest, low-wattage, single speaker (or at most two-way) amplifier available, unless you want a guitar sound with mechanical distortion (such as overdriving of the speakers, acoustic sustain, or feedback of the guitar into the speakers; vibration of the cabinets; and acoustic coupling or reverberant effects of the studio itself); you need to use close and distant mics on the guitar amp for a big, ambient sound; or you have to play amplified guitar at the same time and in the same studio space as a loud drum kit. In the latter case the only way to reduce drum leakage into the guitar amp mic may be to generate the extra 10 dB of amplified guitar level and trim the mic gain in the input module by the same amount. At some point, though, you will finally get objectionable guitar leakage into the overhead drum mics.

In addition, you should consider a "dirtier" amplifier if your music (perhaps heavy metal) cannot be played correctly without the players feeling the same physical sensation around them to which they are accustomed onstage. Remember, sacrifice whatever is necessary in strict audio quality to get the right feel.

Most studios have one or more clean, small amps. Do not bother bringing your big stage amp if all you want is a pure sound. On the other hand, if your amp features signal processing, a tube output section, or speaker cabinets with a special sound, lug it to the session. Just make sure it is working up to specs and meets the low-noise requirements for making master tapes.

Vacuum tubes are preferred in output stages of instrument amps for three reasons. First, below their overload level, they provide a smoother, more musical tone. Their lower damping factor and relatively slow transient response more closely matches the capabilities of most speakers designed for high-volume service. Thus, tubes mask serious problems that many speakers have in reproducing high-level signals with steep transients and uncompressed highs.

Second, between the levels at which audible distortion begins and *clipping* happens (the condition in which any circuit or component is incapable of a higher output level, and therefore flattens or squashes output above this), tubes exhibit a sort of natural electronic compression. Unfortunately, since it is really the result of tube overdrive, the effect is often uneven or unpredictable. Nevertheless, this gives the characteristic soft-attack, highly sustained Clapton/Les Paul sound of the late 1960s, now duplicated and perfected (on a chip!) by Tom Scholz of the rock group Boston in various Rockman effects boxes.

Third, above the distortion threshold, tubes produce mostly second-harmonic distortion, while transistors generate third-harmonic distortion. The second harmonic of middle C is C2, one octave up. Its third harmonic is G2, a perfect fifth higher. Since perfect fifths are sharp compared to tempered fifths, transistor-generated distortion sounds rather grating, especially when added to every pitch in a chord or any complex musical signal.

Recording Direct Guitar. The raw signal from a guitar recorded via DI can have severe transients and should be treated carefully in the console. To prevent overload in the first stage of the module, the input trim should be adjusted so that when the channel fader is at 0 the instrument never exceeds 0 dBVU or about +10 dB on peak meters. If the player tends to smash chords now and then, raise the fader a few decibels and trim the level back the same amount, just to be safe. This will prevent overload in the first console preamp stage, a common phenomenon with instruments that put out sharp transients and dense clusters of overtones, as a guitar does with full chords.

Take the same precautions with level to tape. Transient and high-frequency content in direct guitar should warn you not to push tape levels beyond 0 dBVU or +10 peak. Regardless of how much care you take, the guitarist will probably get overenthusiastic in a couple of passages and hit +12 anyway! Beyond this, staccato rhythm guitar parts can engender lots of tape print-through, which is especially noticeable with signals so hot in the upper mid-range—all the more reason to moderate your record levels.

Because of their internal design, some guitar pickups ring or resonate in a narrow, upper midrange frequency band. Such a peak between 2 and 4 kHz creates a brittle, metallic quality that is further accentuated by flanging, chorusing, and other effects. To locate the source, see if the peak is there in the guitar's output or whether some combination of effects boxes is producing it. If possible, remove it with a narrow band of parametric eq at its source. If the eq cannot be patched in there, remove the peak right after the input preamp at the console, before adding any control-room processing.

No matter what sound you want, turn up the treble or tone all the way at the guitar, then adjust equalization in the console. Since even the finest guitar electronics are still noisier than studio equipment, it is best to send all the treble you have. This also helps to overcome high-frequency loss owing to capacitance in the cable(s). If you need to take highs off in the control room, you will get rid of noise from the instrument in the process. If the guitarist dislikes such a bright sound in his phones, record it bright and eq the signal separately for the cue mix. This will elicit the best possible performance.

If you decide to gate the guitar, do it last, after any other effects you are adding during record. Use a fast attack, a threshold just above the noise you wish to lose, and, as with piano, use a modest floor (perhaps 15 to 25 dB)—just enough to clean up the track without leaving dead air between notes and chords.

If the dry guitar sounds scratchy, too tight, or clinical in comparison with other instruments, record it with a touch of short-plate (or digital-plate) reverb in the 0.5 second range. This will give some of the feeling of recording through an amp in a real room and will help the guitar blend in with the rest of the band when it is time for mixdown. Remember that few record buyers ever hear an electric guitar direct. It can seem brittle and metallic to the untrained ear without some ambience, chorusing or other built-in accommodation.

Miking Guitar Amps.   Close-miked guitar amps rarely sound as good as the guitarist expects. The major reason is that the mic misses the acoustic interplay between the amp and the room, just as it does in close-miked drums. Moreover, the guitarist hears this interplay in stereo in the room, while the mic's signal is delivered to the console in mono. Then too, the amp's problems—perhaps a rattling speaker cone or the narrowly beamed ringing from the metal dust domes common in full-range speakers—are smoothed out by interaction with the room but heard full force by the close mic.

To hide these defects and reduce leakage it is best to use a cardioid dynamic mic capable of good performance when subjected to high SPL levels (up to 140 dB in front of a stack of Marshall speakers). The Shure SM 57 and 58 are the most popular choice, with the EV RE-15 and Sennheiser 421U close seconds. Because of the high directionality of all three, you may do better to move them back two or three feet from the amp, especially if the cabinet has separate bass, midrange, and treble drivers. Give these individual bands some room to blend into a composite sound. The alternatives—separate mics on each driver or a bidirectional mic adjacent to the amp with its axes pointed vaguely toward the drivers—are generally much inferior.

On amp position in the studio, if you have no leakage problems, bring the amp out a few feet from the wall. Even with close miking, this will help flatten out its mid-low frequency response and give a better sense of space. Also, try to decouple the amp from a wooden floor, perhaps by hefting it onto a chair with a sound blanket folded beneath. If it is too huge to elevate, slide the sound blanket(s) underneath and mic the uppermost of its speakers. On the other hand, if you have to enclose the amp with baffles near a wall, aim mic and amp toward each other, with mic and speaker axes both parallel to the wall, to minimize the effect of resonances caused by proximity to corners and surfaces.

Multiple Miking.   If you are overdubbing guitar, and leakage is no problem, turn up the guitar amp and set up both close and distant mics, with the latter at least 10 to 15′ away. This will enlarge the sound and put back some of the room interaction, even if both are blended onto a single track. Omni mics give the fullest distant sound—anything from an RE 55 to a condenser or even a PZM mounted on a stool.

To further accentuate the ambience, try a ribbon or bidirectional mic as the distant pickup, setting its axis at right angles to the amp itself. This mic will only hear the room's response to the amp, with little direct sound. Now you may notice the time delay between the close and distant sound. If this effect helps, fine, but if you feel that multiple attacks of each note or chord confuse the timing of the part, you might introduce a digital delay into the close mic's signal and bring it back into time alignment with the distant signal.

If, for example, the distance between the two mics is 16′, the sound will take 16/1,100, or about 0.015 seconds, to reach the distant mic. Thus, a delay of 15 milliseconds should do the trick. In essence, you are moving the close mic back by 16′ while keeping the sonic intimacy of its proximity to the amp. This trick does, however, delay the entire guitar part a bit and can subtly affect its feel with respect to other rhythm tracks. On the other hand, if a guitarist tends to push the tempo of the track, this trick may lay him or her back in the groove. The drums will now assume a more commanding lead within the rhythm section.

If you have studio time and an extra track to kill, set up a spaced pair of distant mics. Split these left and right into a pair of tracks, with the close mic up the middle, and blend to taste. For extra space, patch one of the distant mics through another 20 ms of delay before blending and recording. This gives a wall-of-guitar effect with enormous depth and physical power. For even more variations, apply some of the thinking we used in deciding what dramatic effect the background vocals serve in a song and how to use audio trickery to create that effect.

Recording Direct and Amplified Guitar.   If you have extra tracks and do not want to spend lots of time getting the best combination of direct and amplified guitar sounds while laying basic tracks, assign the direct and amplified sounds to separate tracks. You can then choose among them in the mix, panning and processing each differently and even featuring one or the other in different parts of the song.

Make sure that both tracks go down in phase, and set the level on the amplified track (with all effects) about 2 dB lower than the direct. The direct guitar has sharper transients in general, but the amplified track will have peaks at certain notes that are not present in the direct signal. These stem from acoustic resonances inherent in the amp, speaker, and room acoustics of the particular amp/mic setup. A note that is relatively dead on the direct guitar may produce a 6-dB peak when amplified. This is why you need extra headroom on the amplified track.

Processing for Direct and Amplified Signals.   I would no more advise you on the right guitar sound than jump into a cage filled with lions. However, I have repeatedly seen guitarists wish they had applied less processing during record because the song needs different processing when mixdown comes around. The assumption that the kind and amount of effects that work on stage should be recorded verbatim is often a grave error, since tape picks up details and nuances that are lost in crowd and room noises at live performances. While recording basics, less is often more.

The most common mistake is overcompression. Compressor/limiter boxes for stage use, especially combined with a noise gate, do help you maximize your projection and achieve a real physical impact live. But home listeners just do not play rock at 120 dB, so you simply cannot make your point on tape by vaporizing their living rooms. Instead, you need dynamics and a tone that does not compete with synths and the other midrange instruments for clarity and dominance.

You should compress during record only as much as necessary to achieve the desired sustain, and not a dB more. That means setting a threshold high enough to allow much of the part to go uncompressed; medium attack (usually under 8 ms but long enough to allow every string pluck to cut through); and a ratio low enough (under 5 : 1) to ensure that fills and lead lines punch through the rhythm section and need little boosting during the mix. Train yourself to substitute dynamics for sheer volume by monitoring as much as possible on small speakers, even Auratones.

To avoid legislating my own taste in guitar sounds, I have discussed only destructive equalization. However, few guitar amps put out much usable signal above 6 kHz. It helps to shelf-boost the top end during record, even if only to shelf-dip it during the mixdown and get rid of some tape noise. Although it is the 1 to 3 kHz range that gives amplified guitar its bite, top end adds acuity and an open quality that allows you to ride the guitar lower in the mix without sacrificing its command. This is especially true if you also boost the low midrange in the 200 to 300 Hz range—a technique we used on vocals. As suggested earlier, a sonically gentler, less grating way to achieve both boosts is to dip the midrange broadly, centered perhaps on 0.8 to 1 kHz. On the other hand, if a song is about frustration, rebellion or anger, boost away for added bite.

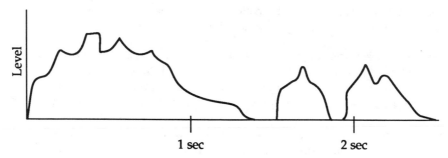

A. A guitar chord and two notes recorded through a Direct Box.

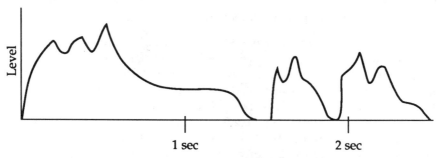

B. At medium volume through a miked guitar amplifier.

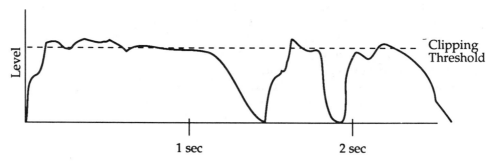

C. At high volume through a tube amplifier.

Figure 17.2.   Envelopes of an electric guitar. The same chord and notes recorded via a D.I. box (A.), a miked amplifier (B.) and an overdriven amplifier (C.). Due to the mechanical characteristics of the guitar amp speaker and its interaction with the air and mic diaphragm, the undistorted amp signal (B.) has sharper transients and a more physical impact than the original signal (A.). The overdriven amp in C. is incapable of putting out another decibel, i.e., it is clipping. In this condition it essentially limits the signal in the same way it might be affected by a compressor with a high ratio.

Delays, chorusing, flanging, and the like are all wonderful effects in the right place, but they dilute the guitar's raw attack on notes and chords. If the song itself calls for an atmospheric rhythm section or a very three-dimensional lead sound, lay the effects on thick and heavy. However, for high rhythmic impact, be very sparing with digital effects during record. Wait until you have the entire tune on multitrack, then see if you need guitar effects in the mix. You can add more later, but not less.

For the most dramatic stereo and spatial effects, record two separate but identical guitar performances on two separate tracks. The rhythmic tension between two takes is much more interesting than a single performance with stereo processing added in a mix. Yes, this does require the extra studio time to play two equally perfect performances, but that may be less than the mix time spent later, adjusting a phalanx of effects boxes to make one guitar track sound like two. Why not go for the real thing? Two separate tracks will also give you more flexibility with panning during mixdown, and you can use separate effects or reverb on each.

18

WOODWINDS AND REEDS

$\mathbf{I}$N actuality, woodwinds, reed instruments, orchestral brass, the pipe organ, and penny whistle all produce sounds by the same principle. An outside source of steady airflow causes the air inside a tube to vibrate with the help of a vibration starter such as a single or double reed, a knife edge in the air path, or the player's own lips. Although we will examine each group separately, the following discussion applies to them all.

BASIC PROBLEMS

For purposes of recording, we need to look at five factors about each group of "blown" instruments:

- the air source
- the source of vibration
- the dimensions of the tube and its construction
- the mechanism by which various pitches are produced
- the acoustic environment in which listeners are accustomed to hearing and remembering a specific instrument.

The first four factors help determine the objective quality of sound produced. Then, depending on the type of music being recorded, the last, subjective factor comes into play. For this reason, a pipe organ would sound as strange without reverb as a penny whistle might in a cathedral.

THE ORGAN PIPE AND FLUTE

The organ pipe, the simplest of wind instruments, demonstrates how these five factors affect the recording of all its relatives. In cross-section, most flue (not flute) pipes consist of a thin metal tube with an opening at both ends. (Some flue pipes are actually square in section and made of wood, but they function the same way.) Air flows in through one end of the tube and is focused so that it passes by a knife-edged surface. When a stream of air passes by a sharp edge, it flows alternately over one side of the edge, then the other. The speed of its flip-flopping depends on the speed and width of the airstream, its placement with respect to the edge, the sharpness of the edge, and its angle with respect to the airstream.

Even without the attached pipe, a sound or *edgetone* will be produced by this flip-flopping. This unmusical whistling sound consists of an unrelated bunch of upper-midrange and high frequencies, plus a general steam tone. However, with the pipe in place, each time the stream flops over the edge and toward its interior an internal puff or wave of increased air pressure is created, which then travels (at the speed of sound in air) to the other end of the pipe. As the excess pressure meets open air, pressure in that end of the pipe dips below normal, creating a low-pressure wave that travels back toward the air source. When it reaches the knife edge, this low-pressure wave draws the airflow inside again, and the entire cycle starts over. In this way, the length of the pipe controls the rate at which the airstream flops back and forth across the knife edge.

As you might suspect, the time it takes for the high- and low-pressure waves to travel up the pipe and back equals one full cycle of the pipe's fundamental frequency. The length of the pipe from knife edge to open end equals one half the wavelength of that note. Thus, a 4' long pipe produces a tone with wavelength of 8', or about 130 Hz (1,100' per second / 8'), an octave below middle C.

The C flute, with about 2' between the mouth hole and furthest tone hole (at which point the enclosed air column meets open air), resonates at 260 Hz (middle C) when all its tone holes are covered. If the flautist opens a hole at half the length of the instrument, the internal waves meet open air after traveling only one foot, and a 520 Hz tone is generated. A simple and logical mechanism!

Remember, however, that it is not the pipe but the volume of air inside it that actually resonates owing to its own dimensions. What encloses that air may affect the tone, but it has no effect on the fundamental pitch produced.

If a pipe is stopped or closed at its far end, the initial high-pressure wave bounces back off the stopper and returns toward the knife edge. Only then, when the pipe exhales, can a low-pressure wave enter and travel up and back. In fact, the interior air pressure is higher (or lower) than normal for the entire time it takes each wave to travel up the pipe and back. Because the positive and negative waves each travel twice the length of the pipe, the note produced will have twice the wavelength of an open pipe of the same length and will thus be one octave lower.

On the other hand, if we increase the air pressure in our original open pipe, we can overblow it, causing it to sound at the second harmonic (twice its normal frequency, or one octave higher). It hardly matters if the pipe is open or closed; either

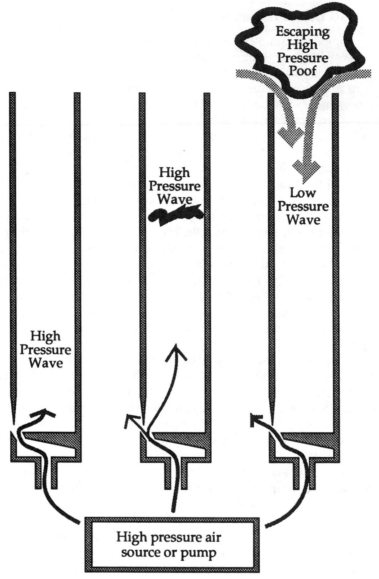

Figure 18.1.   Cross-sections of a four-foot organ flue pipe. A high-pressure wave forms at the pipe's lip, travels up the pipe, and exits. A corresponding low-pressure wave then enters and travels down toward the lip, completing one cycle of the fundamental note. The flow of air from the pump is then drawn in again, creating the next high-pressure wave, etc.

way, a second high-pressure wave enters the pipe when the first is only halfway down the pipe. Still stronger overblowing will generate the third harmonic, and so on. The multiple pressure waves engendered by overblowing pass through each other without any interaction.

Even when a pipe is not overblown, its output will contain some of the second and higher harmonics. Their volume in the pipe's sound is greater with respect to the fundamental if the air pressure increases, the knife edge splits the airstream exactly in half rather than intercepting it at an angle or off to one side, the pipe is made narrower in proportion to its length, or the walls of the pipe are made thinner, allowing the pipe walls themselves to vibrate at their own resonant frequencies and harmonics.

In the flute, for example, the first two factors allow the player to adjust the brightness of the instrument's tone while varying air pressure and the position of his or her lip with respect to the knife edge on the mouthpiece. The third factor dictates that lower notes have the highest proportion of overtones. Because the diameter of the metal tube remains constant, the ratio of diameter to speaking length increases with higher notes. The pipe gets proportionately fatter, and fatter pipes (like thicker guitar strings) have fewer and softer overtones. Because the walls of the flute are relatively thick, they hardly vibrate at all and thus add few overtones. This is why the flute's sound is so pure.

Some woodwinds, such as the recorder, have tapered interior bores. This suppresses lower-numbered harmonics and produces a smoother spread of highs in the edgetone. The result is a broader, silkier high-end output. We will examine this phenomenon in detail with the conical, tapered metal bodies of saxes and brass, where vibrations emanating from the sides of the body itself create a substantial part of the instruments' characteristic timbres.

With all this in mind, let us investigate how to record the families of instruments whose sound are produced by vibrating tubes or columns of air.

THE WOODWINDS

We already know a great deal about flutes. Their fundamentals and related overtones emanate from either end of the open tube, although the far end of that tube moves as the flautist opens and closes various tone holes along the instrument's body. Edge- and wind tones emanate almost entirely from the mouthpiece (which is also the stationary end of the air column), with another small beam of highs following pressure waves down the tube and out the nearest open hole. Very little sound radiates from the metal body itself.

Mic Selection and Placement.   Because the flute's output consists mainly of a fundamental and edgetones (with few musical harmonics), it is important that a mic pick up any overtones that are present. Otherwise, its purity (like that of a Rhodes piano) can easily be buried by brighter instruments. Moreover, flute notes have a relatively slow attack, which further masks their *onset* (a synonym for attack when talking about the instrument's envelope) and makes it difficult to keep a flute solo clear without excessive level. For this reason, the edgetones themselves (from 3 kHz on up) are quite important for clarity.

The best solution is a good cardioid condenser mic with crisp response to 20 kHz. As with the human voice, high frequencies emanate upward from the mouth hole at an angle that varies with the flautist's lip posture. In general, upper-midrange frequencies (3 to 6 KHz) are pushed out rather horizontally, while real highs (above 6 kHz) rise almost straight up. For this reason, and because the 5 to 6 kHz range has a harsh, metallic quality that most flautists dislike, place a close mic perhaps a foot in front of and above the mouthpiece.

Moving a mic toward the center of the flute's body will thin the tone. Why? The high-pressure wave of each fundamental exits the far end just as the low-pressure wave enters the mouthpiece. The air at one end of the flute is thus rarefied as the other end is compressed, and then they switch. At a central mic position, high- and low-pressure waves partially cancel, reducing lows in the mic's signal. For a thin flute sound, mic the center of the body; otherwise stick with the ends.

Oddly, the fullest tone is available at the far end of the tube or above and to the left of the mouth hole, beyond the short end of the tube and out of the stream of highs. Remember that the farthest tone holes and mouthpiece are where the lowest notes escape. Some internally mounted pickups are tucked inside the far end of the tube in order to catch the greatest volume of the flute notes below 500 Hz. Although the instrument may need brightening when amplified, the extra low response helps keep the flute signal free of low-mid leakage from other onstage instruments and can thus help prevent PA or amplifier feedback.

Other pickups consist of so-called peanut microphones that clip on to the top edge of the mouthpiece, right in the path of dense highs. Both types deliver a surprisingly even output, one that is more earthy than airy. A flute sound without some audio space around it is somehow disconcerting. If you must record with a pickup because of leakage in the studio, blend in at least some of an external mic. This will restore some lightness to the sound, without which the flute may sound like a good synthesized imitation of itself!

Dynamic Problems.   Although the flute does not have an especially great dynamic range (perhaps 30 dB, loudest when extremely high notes are overblown), compression may be necessary for three reasons. First, when low notes are played, the ratio of speaking length of the internal column of air to its diameter (called the pipe's *scaling*) is highest. As we know from organ pipes, the skinnier the pipe, the softer its sound. Thus the lowest octave of the flute is softest, while higher notes are louder because the speaking column is proportionately fatter. With organ pipes, volume can be made uniform from low to high notes by keeping the scaling fairly constant for each pipe in a rank (the group of pipes designed to produce a certain sound over a range of several octaves).

Second, when the flautist stops a note, for example, at half the instrument's length, the unused portion of the body with its many open holes now comprises a series of short open pipes that can resonate or sympathetically reinforce harmonics of various played notes. As shown in fig. 18.2, the short sections of the flute between these open holes have no harmonic relationship to each other. Chance reinforcements of notes above about 1.5 kHz can thus occur in a rather unpredictable manner. This phenomenon is much more pronounced in thin-walled reeds like the saxophone, where the instrument's body can resonate with and amplify these spuriously created harmonics. The result may be an inexplicable harshness on certain notes.

Third and most important, because the wavelengths of notes in the bottom two octaves of a flute are in the 1-to-4' range, the physical positions of the flute and mic in a studio can easily work with the studio's own room acoustics to reinforce some notes and kill others. For example, assume the flute is played by someone standing

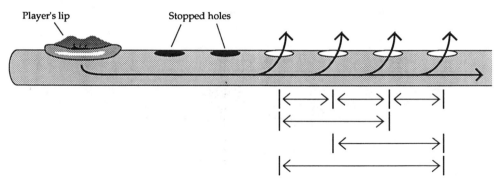

Figure 18.2. **The tubular sections of a flute beyond the holes currently stopped can reinforce upper harmonics.**

in a room 10′ high. If the mouthpiece is about 5′ above the floor, the distance sound travels from mouthpiece to the ceiling or the floor and back is 5 + 5 = 10 feet. This equals 2.5 wavelengths of 275 Hz, the lowest D of the C flute. The result is that in this situation the bottom half-octave of the instrument is partially canceled right at the mouthpiece. If the mic is mounted 5′ high, the low C to G range will be weakened in its output. At the same time, because 10′ = 5 times the wavelength of the C one octave up, at 520 Hz, this range will be reinforced at the mouthpiece and in the mic. Overall, we have an acoustic comb-filter with peaks and dips all the way up the frequency spectrum. There is no way to totally eliminate the comb, but we can adjust it to prevent the acoustics from affecting the bottom octave by moving the flautist and mic up (or down) just 6″.

Now the distance from mouthpiece to ceiling to mic is 9′, from mouthpiece to floor to mic 11′. The difference is 2′, which means that the sound bouncing off the floor at 260 Hz is a half-wavelength out of phase with that bouncing off the ceiling. The result here is that the mic hears the flute's lowest notes without any change of amplitude due to phasing probs. Of course there will still be some cancellation at frequencies where 2′ = 1.5, 2.5, 3.5 ... wavelengths, that is, 825 Hz, 1.37 kHz, 1.83 kHz, and so on. If we want to boost the lower notes acoustically, move the flautist and mic up another foot (or have the flautist play seated, mouthpiece about 3′ above the floor). Now the difference between floor- and ceiling-bounce paths is 4′, about a full wavelength of the lowest note.

These problems are somewhat unpredictable and, in small studios, unavoidable. Furthermore, they only affect flute and other acoustic instruments in which the absence of many harmonics brings every interaction between the fundamental and room acoustics to the fore. However, the anomaly does reveal why the flute usually needs compression when recorded in relatively small rooms. The mic's response can seem totally erratic, with peaks and valleys of 6 dB on selected notes throughout the flute's range. Fortunately, such problems vanish in concert halls and taller studios, with instruments that are close-miked relatively near the floor (seated acoustic musicians or speaker cabinets for electric instruments) or with any instrument miked at a great distance.

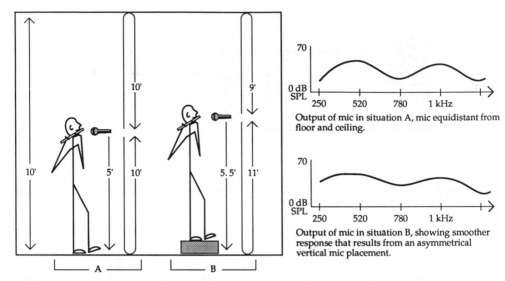

Output of mic in situation A, mic equidistant from floor and ceiling.

Output of mic in situation B, showing smoother response that results from an asymmetrical vertical mic placement.

Figure 18.3. Soundwaves bouncing off the floor and ceiling into the flautist's mic can cause an uneven apparent frequency response in the mic through cancellation and reinforcement.

To strengthen weak transients, use a long compressor attack (10 to 20 ms), but to ensure that lower and deader notes are not entirely lost, use a short release (under 0.5 second). The threshold and ratio will depend on how much competition the flute has in the musical arrangement. Low threshold and high ratio will hold it at a relatively constant level in spite of the flautist's dynamics and the room acoustics. The opposite will allow the flautist plenty of dynamic range but may let weaker notes submerge in the midrange bulge of other rhythm instruments.

Final equalization is a matter of taste and necessity. The more importance the flute has in the arrangement, or the more competition it has from the rhythm bed, the more brightening it will need. Boosting the 1-to-2 kHz range lends a sultry, wooden feel; the 3-kHz range gives a reedy, almost oriental flavor. Way up in the 10 kHz range you will find a mysterious intimacy that can beckon the listener's ear (like background vocals singing oohs and aahs) through the densest arrrangement. The flute, after all, is one of the few instruments that emits high frequencies continuously rather than in a transient burst. Use these highs to good effect.

Effects During Record. The flute's relatively slow attack allows a greater freedom with added effects. As with the Rhodes piano, which also has a high proportion of sine waves in sustained notes, effects on flute can bring the instrument to the listener's attention at a much lower level in the final mix. My favorite is slow chorusing or a gentle flange. Because the flute's lowest note is 260 Hz, delay times under 10 ms can be used without fear of serious phasing or comb-filtering problems.

If you want to make one flute feel like two by using more than about 25% effect in the blend, the phasing problem will become apparent at frequencies where the nominal delay time equals 1.5, 2.5, 3.5 ... the period of one full cycle (for a 5-ms delay these are 340 Hz, 560 Hz, 700 Hz ...). Phase awareness can be reduced by bringing the chorus in on a separate module from the flute itself and using a parametric eq to dip the midrange band in which the most apparent phasing occurs.

However, what really gives electronic doubling away is the way the high frequencies in the doubled signal exactly mimic those in the original. The result is a hollow, tooth-gnashing spittiness. To defeat this, sweep the highs of the flanged or chorused signal with a parametric, find the half-octave or so in which the edgetone is most pronounced, and dip this while auditioning the combined direct and processed flute signals. If this works, and if you have an extra track, record each separately so you can pan them differently in the mix.

Reverb sounds great on the flute but will further weaken the already soft attack and blend one note into the next. Thus, do not cut flute tracks with reverb. Later, if reverb submerges the flute in the mix, try two tactics: a long predelay (60 ms minimum) and separate equalization of the flute send to reverb, dipping the 400 to 600 Hz range. These touches will keep the instrument clean and distinct from the reverb and add depth to the entire mix.

THE REEDS

The single-reed wind instruments are next on our ladder of complexity. Functionally, this group includes everything from the clarinet to the saxophone, two instruments rarely mentioned in the same breath. Although they are made of completely different materials, have diverse interior designs, and use their bodies in totally different ways with respect to defining a sound quality and projecting it, we will learn by comparing this duo. First, though, let us consider their simpler cousin, the single-reed organ pipe.

In the strictest sense, a musical reed is any tapered piece of material that can vibrate when the thicker end is held fixed and the other is pointed into an oncoming stream of air. Because of their rigidity, the metal reeds used in organ pipes will vibrate at only one frequency, which is determined by their size, shape, and the specific metal or alloy of which they are made. As in the sax and clarinet, the reed is solidly mounted alongside a cavity called the *shallot* (also the name for the clarinet mouthpiece) and shaped so that, when the oncoming air flexes it, the reed closes the shallot and momentarily stops the airflow.

At this point, the reed snaps back to its normal shape, opening the shallot, and the cycle begins again. Slapping against the shallot many times a second, the whole apparatus creates a buzzing sound whose rate or fundamental frequency is the natural resonance of the reed itself. The puffs of air that make up this buzz pass through the shallot and into a metal pipe whose thin, tapered body rings almost like a bell, amplifying the rich series of harmonics present in the sound.

The more flexible the reed, the higher the air pressure, and the thinner the walls of the pipe, the louder it speaks and the greater the proportion of high frequencies in its output. When the length of the enclosed column of air is half the wavelength of the reed's fundamental (as in the open flue pipe discussed earlier), it resonates and helps keep the reed vibrating. It can even help start the reed vibrating with lower external air pressure. If the pipe is tuned differently than the reed (longer or shorter than half the wavelength), it can partially or fully stop the reed's vibration.

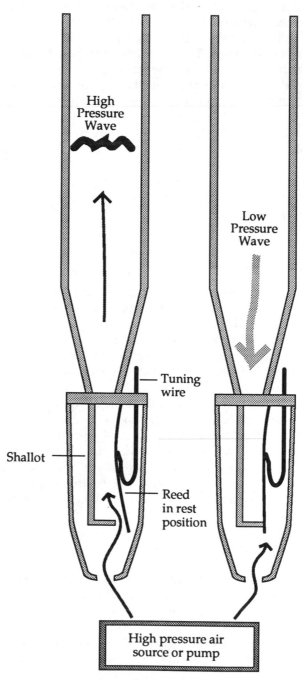

High
Pressure
Wave

Low
Pressure
Wave

Tuning
wire

Shallot

Reed
in rest
position

High pressure air
source or pump

Figure 18.4.   Cross sections of a reed organ pipe showing how air pressure momentarily flattens the reed, closing the shallot and shutting off the air flow. The natural spring of the reed then reopens the shallot, allowing the cyclic process to repeat again.

In contrast, the clarinet, sax, and other single-reed winds have a series of tone holes like the flute, allowing the player to vary the length of the pipe. Also, the reeds used in these instruments are not metal but actual organic cane, which can vibrate through a wide range of frequencies depending on the applied air pressure. Most important, the cane reed will vibrate at any frequency suggested by the current pipe length, namely, the note being played by the performer. Further softened by the performer's own saliva, cane reeds can be made to slide smoothly from one frequency to another and, with careful overblowing, sound at octaves and other intervals of the played note. In doing so, the reed itself flexes not in one smooth, first-mode arc but in the rippled shapes of its second, third, and higher modes.

Sound Propagation.   Like reed organ pipes, all of the single-reed winds have a flaired bell at the end of the pipe. This serves two purposes. The very highest overtones of the buzzing reed, extending up past 20 kHz, beam straight down the pipe and out the end. The bell, like a dispersion horn coupled to a high-frequency loudspeaker, spreads these highs over a broader angle. Except for horizontally mounted organ pipes called *trompetes en chammade,* most reed pipes are aimed upward at church ceilings and need all the help they can get to broadcast highs to the congregation. Second, because the bell is essentially a rapidly expanding section of the body, it gives harmonics in the 2-to-4 kHz range an extra boost as they leave the pipe.

The result is that the brightest, clearest tone from any single reed is available directly in front of its bell. But a mic located here misses a lot of the instrument's warmth and character, since much of the fundamental exits at the first open tone hole (the one for the note being played), and the body itself is designed to vibrate at midrange frequencies. These waves leave the instrument in a cylindrical pattern that melds with its bell output only at some distance. While we recognize the sound of a clarinet miked at its bell, the sound most listeners imagine at the mention of the word *clarinet* is the smooth tone of Benny Goodman (miked to the side or at several feet) or of an orchestral clarinet miked anywhere from 15 to 30'.

Double Reeds.   English horn, bassoon, and oboe are the only double-reed instruments used much in Western music. In all of them the second reed replaces the shallot, the sound being produced as two small, identically sized reeds held inside the player's mouth buzz against each other. Their vibrations are carried through a very thin neck (less than 1/4" in diameter) to the wooden body, which has a series of tone holes. As you might expect, the skinny neck severely limits the amount of airflow, and thus the ultimate volume.

Without the benefit of a solid shallot, everything about the sound of the instrument depends on the player's wind pressure and control. Thus, all double reeds have somewhat unpredictable behavior both in terms of volume and tone. In all other ways their sound is generated and projected exactly as the single reeds. However, because the reeds themselves are much smaller, constantly wet from saliva, and do not slap against a hard surface, the double reeds have less upper partials and a gentler, rounder tone than any of the single reeds.

Close-Miking Single and Double Reeds.   Like the flute, the clarinet has a cylindrical bore. Because the vibrating air column is proportionately narrowest for low notes, these have the richest series of harmonics. The wooden body resonates in the

300 Hz range, which amplifies the lowest octave and gives a fat, warm tone even to much higher notes. This functions like a singer's chest tone, which boosts subharmonics of notes actually sung and thereby conveys an added impression of audio weight. In addition, certain mid-high frequencies are boosted or reinforced as they bounce back and forth laterally and diagonally within the tube. The clarinet's uniform bore of about 3/4″ thus reinforces frequencies whose wavelengths are 3″ and less (about 3.5 kHz on up). It also emits a uniform series of very high frequencies in the reed buzz no matter what note is played. Harmonics between the highest note (about 1,200 Hz) and 3 kHz are sharply attenuated by the body, giving that familiar shy tone.

In contrast, the bore of a sax diverges at an angle of about 3 to 4 degrees (depending on maker and range, bass to sopranino). In the tenor, this means the tube varies from less than 1 to about 4″ in diameter, not including the bell. The bell, made of relatively thin brass, collects and broadcasts upper frequencies generated at the various cross-sections of the body. With maximum wavelengths of 4 times the bore, or from 3 to 14″, these frequencies span from perhaps 800 to 3,500 Hz. There is no big hole in the midrange, as with the clarinet. Beyond this, we again have a relatively full series of upper partials that speak regardless of the note being played.

A mic placed in front of the sax bell will miss a lot of the instrument's fundamentals, which exit through tone holes, and the cylindrical "body waves" that fatten its midrange harmonics. If you are overdubbing or can live with a little leakage, I advise miking reeds (single or double) at 2 to 3′ but not right on axis. Try placing the mic 20 to 30 degrees above (or to the side of) the line coming directly out of the instrument's bell. This way you will pick up a smooth combination of bell and body waves without too much spittiness from the mouthpiece.

At these distances a cardioid condenser will maximize detail in the high end. For the mellow reeds (oboe, English horn, clarinet, bassoon, and the like), try a Neumann U 87 or KM 89 for a bright solo sound and an AKG 414 or equivalent for a mellower section sound or if the arrangement allows a gentler solo to cut through. For a sax, with its dense series of overtones and loud reed buzz, try a dynamic or ribbon first. The RCA 77DX (the familiar, capsule-shaped radio mic of the 1940s) gives the very smoothest sound of all, though it needs heavy boosting in the extreme highs. The EV RE-20 and RE-16, Shure SM 57, and others provide crisper sounds.

If section mics leave the low end a bit weak, you may need to sneak a couple of close mics in on bassoon, bass clarinet, or the like. To deemphasize the close perspective, mic from either side of the instrument, not right in front of the bell. The Shure SM 81, EV RE-20, and, surprisingly, Neumann's cardioid lavalier have very smooth off-axis sounds and should cause no trouble when blended in with the main stereo pair. For alto or bass flute, the Neumann lavalier suspended left or right above the mouth hole provides a smooth, warm sound with just enough transparency to cut through louder and higher winds. In any case, just a touch of these close mics should bring the section back into harmonic perspective without confusing the stereo image. Be sure, however, that the close mics are panned to coincide with the left-to-right position of the same instrument as heard through the distant stereo mics.

If leakage is your primary consideration, drop back to a cardioid dynamic or ribbon mic: the Sennheiser 421, 441, or Beyer 160 to brighten the mellower reeds or give a bright solo; the EV, AKG, and Shure dynamics for blend and fullth if you want a smooth section sound or if you must mike a sax solo right at the bell. In my opinion, except on flute, internal pickups and contact mikes are strictly for stage use. No matter how you process the signal from a pickup, it is very tight and usually has too many narrow response peaks (and holes) to give any sense of the instrument in a real environment. Together, these give most pickups a hollow, nasal, or sickly sound. In addition, most pickups simply do not have the real high-end response to convey the airy quality of winds and reeds, even if you boost heavily above 8 kHz.

Buzz Tone and Mechanical Noise Considerations. Although it is tempting to accentuate the direct sound of single or double reeds by miking nearer the player's mouth than the bell, consider for a moment that all reed players are behind the reed, shielded from its harshest high frequencies by the mouthpiece and their own face. Then too, some of the fundamentals exit the body at the mouthpiece. Thus, a reed or sax player hears his or her instrument with a mellowness akin to the sound in the tenth row. Oboists, bassoonists, and clarinetists dislike hearing a lot of the 2-to-5-kHz range in recordings of their instruments. Do not fall prey to the tendency to preferentially mike or boost this range during recording. Instead, look higher and boost the 10-to-12-kHz range. Let every breath be heard, but not the spittiness and phlegm that reed players go to such lengths to eliminate!

The mechanical sounds of fingering keys, key pads, valves, and other parts on winds, reeds, and the like are magically lost in the ambient or background sound of most concert halls. However, use of close mics during record will catch every finger movement and felt pad. What to do? First make sure none of the pads or parts has an especially loud slap or click. If so, refelt the offenders before the session. Second, listen to the instrument in the studio to determine the direction in which most of the mechanical noise is projected. If these sounds are loudest above the instrument, mike from either side. Third, if the noise is really bothersome, use a more directional mike—super- or hypercardioid as necessary.

Lastly, do not hesitate to erect a *gobo,* or shield. Find your best mic position for the instrument's sound. Then, using two mic stands as supports, stretch a scarf consisting of several layers of thick felt or other absorber between these stands. Position the entire contraption between the mic and the source of mechanical noise, leaving sound from the end of the instrument's body (bell or mouthpiece) a direct shot at the mic. This is the same kind of thinking a painter with a good sense of lighting puts into a portrait, selectively lighting or masking various parts of the subject's face to highlight the best features and subdue others.

Compressing During Record. Because of player variables, internal design, and the ever-changing performance of wet reeds, single and double reeds have rather uneven outputs over their entire range. Pinched upper notes on the oboe may sound at under 60 dB SPL (the level of moderate humming), while a lower note at the primary resonance of the body may peak near 100 dB. As with all reeds, it takes very little to keep a note going once it is instigated, resulting in a relatively high dynamic range.

Thus, except in classical recording, compression is virtually a must. What kind and how much depends on the specific instrument and player. Stiffer reeds, as on the sax, take a lot of wind to start up and therefore produce a strong transient attack. (In addition, the sax can put out over 130 dB SPL right at the bell.) At the other extreme, the English horn has little attack, no matter how hard the player blows. Thus, use faster attack (under 6 to 10 ms) and a higher ratio (5 : 1 or more) on single reeds than on double reeds, and set the threshold and release to produce the desired amount of dynamics in the recording with respect to the speed of the part itself. A fast release will allow the unit to be more responsive if notes played in rapid succession also sound at different volumes.

For solos on the sax, which generally has the widest dynamic range of all reeds, do not hesitate to pull the attack down to 2 ms and put almost every note above threshold if the arrangement is dense. When listening to the sax alone, a ratio over 6 : 1 can sound artificial, bottling up the reed in a way that calls attention to the processing rather than to the instrument itself. Remember, however, that the compression will be much less apparent when heard along with the reverb and the rest of the instruments.

Again, the faster the part, the faster the release needed to ensure that sudden soft notes are not lost. For more languid parts, or if you want the wind and reed parts to provide a smooth bed, opt for a release closer to 2 seconds. This will help suppress the player's breaths at the same time.

Unless the player is prone to making outrageous amounts of noise between desired lines, do not noise gate while recording. Noise gating can cut off the attack, especially on soft notes, and totally eliminate breath sounds. Remember that, as with a vocal, a wind or reed track with no breaths at all sounds very unnatural, even if the breaths are likely to be drowned out in the final mix. It's an emotional consideration, but one worth noting.

I hate to admit it, but you may find it necessary to gently noise gate distant-mixed wood-bodied winds and reeds depending on the ambient noise level in the studio itself. These instruments are all relatively soft in the *p* volume range, and many inexpensive studios have less-than-ideal noise floors, with air conditioning and exterior noise at substantial levels. If this is the case, be sure to set the threshold of the gate just above ambient noise level, with an attack and release slow enough not to cause any jarring on/off leaps in level. And do not reduce the floor or range any more than is necessary to diminish—not eliminate—the ambience between charted lines; 10 or 12 decibels is often quite enough.

Effects During Record.   Except for the saxophone, reeds seem to be a sacrosanct genre in the recording studio. Their airy high end does not take well to digital delays, and flanging or chorusing gives an electric edge that can defeat the purpose of using these instruments in the first place. As with the flute, you can approximate doubling with a slow flange or chorus, provided that you bring the effect in through a separate module and remove the high end of the effect return before it has a chance to combine harshly with the direct signal.

Again, as with flute, you may wish to record the mellower reeds with a predelayed reverb. This gives a broad quality with a sense of space, calls attention to the reed parts at a lower volume in the mix, and imparts a degree of acoustic freedom that can distract the ear from even the most severe compression, which you may have introduced to preserve clarity among the reed parts themselves. If you opt for using a predelayed reverb, do not overdo it. Leave enough room to add more of the primary

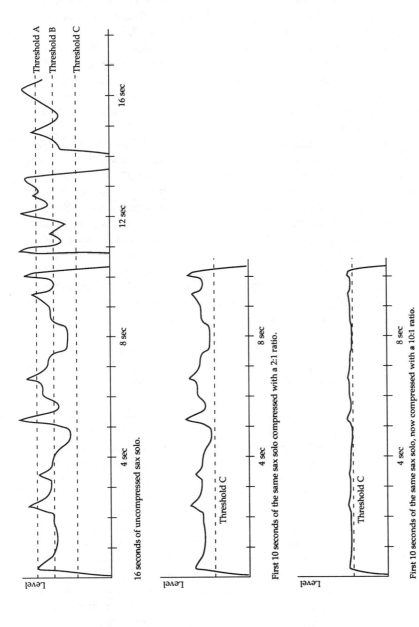

16 seconds of uncompressed sax solo.

First 10 seconds of the same sax solo compressed with a 2:1 ratio.

First 10 seconds of the same sax solo, now compressed with a 10:1 ratio.

Figure 18.5. The envelope of a 16-second sax solo. Saxophone is unique among reeds in its ability to emit transients almost as sharp as those from drums. To tame these spikes we might set a compressor threshold at A. If the softest notes get lost in the arrangement, a threshold set at B would still preserve much of the player's dynamics. In a dense arrangement it might be necessary to lower the threshold to C, where every note would be compressed. This would sound artificial when solo'd, but might work fine in the context of the entire band. Using threshold C, notice that a 2 : 1 compression ratio reduces the height of each peak to 1/2 its original value, while a 10 : 1 ratio reduces the height peak to 1/10 its original height, essentially taking out all the dynamics.

reverb you select in the mixdown. Putting the reeds entirely in their own space can be distracting and emphasize the fact that they were overdubbed (even if they were not!).

Stereo Distant Miking for Solo Winds and Reeds and Sections. We've discussed close miking and its normal follow-up processing in such detail not because it gives the best wind and reed sounds but because most multitrack projects are close miked from bottom to top, regardless of the kind of instruments used or how they are heard live. Frankly, except for reinforcing lower wind parts or a wind or reed solo, I prefer distant miking of all sections for a number of reasons. First, arrangers who write for sections generally intend the instruments to be sensed more as an ensemble than as separate lines. You can only get this kind of melding (and very simply at that!) with distant miking.

Second, the unevenness of various ranges in the flute, oboe, bassoon, and other reeds allows a playful interplay among the individual parts of a wind chart. Miking and processing all winds or reeds separately flattens their individual foibles and takes the dynamic interplay out of the whole section. Third, distant mics mask mechanical noise, reed buzz, edgetone sibilance or spittiness, and the players' own breathing at rests. Fourth and most important, most listeners think of winds in their orchestral setting, a gentle, textured, and alluring bed of harmonies, lines, and decorations. Why spend lots of time trying to mimic this feel with close miking and processing when a pair of mics and two compressors can do it better in five minutes flat?

Remember, however, that flutes (and all thick metal- or wooden-bodied winds) and the traditional (wooden-bodied) reeds all speak in the same volume range and cannot be recorded on the same mics as saxes and their louder, thin-walled, metal cousins. In any case, unless the producer has a specific left-to-right arrangement planned, allow the players to seat themselves for necessary eye contact and cueing (a broad arc or semicircle is usually fine), and set up the mics at the focal point of this curve, perhaps 8 to 10' away, at least 6' above the floor but not less than 2' from the ceiling. A sound blanket folded in several layers under both stands will get rid of more ambient lows, even if the mics are already shock-mounted.

There are a number of dramatic and spatial considerations when selecting mics. Coincident miking gives the most natural left-to-right image on a section, with the fewest phasing problems when heard in mono. However, as with background vocals, the winds may serve a number of different dramatic roles depending on the song itself. If they should coddle the lead vocal or solo instrument, reinforcing its emotion or giving it support, coincident miking is the right choice. Your engineer will know which variety of X-Y works best in his own studio.

On the other hand, you may want an exaggerated stereo spread if a song is about loneliness or unrequited emotions, it is an interior monologue, or if it has a dense arrangement that may obscure the solo or lead without lots of room in the mix. In these cases, go with a pair of mics at least 2' apart. Omnis give an open, airy feel but will also pick up ambient noise and any acoustical imbalance in the studio itself. Cardioids give more left-to-right separation of individual instruments and leave more of a hole in the middle for the lead or solo part. You can always pan cardioid-miked section tracks in toward the center during the mix, but you cannot pan omni tracks further out.

I have so far avoided naming specific mics for three reasons. First, all winds and reed instruments sound unique. Second, all studios have different acoustics, even in various sections of the same room. Third, who knows what the producer's taste may dictate! Generally, I prefer an X-Y pair, definitely condensers—AKG 414s or their Tube for an intimate, breathy sound; Neumann KM89s for a bright, upfront tone. Sanken, Sony, and Telefunken condensers are also great but not available in too many studios. Let your engineer choose if you decide to go with an *M-S* (Middle-Side, using a cardioid mic aimed at the center of the section and a bidirectional mic with its axis perpendicular to this) or *Blumlein* configuration (two bidirectional mics aimed 45 degrees left and right of the section's axis).

Recommendations for a spaced pair depend on what you want. EV RE-55s give a thinner version of what you get with the 414s (used in omni); Beyer M-300 and Sennheiser cardioids have a bit more aggressive quality (hotter upper-mids, less real highs) than their condenser counterparts. To find the right mic for the studio and specific instruments, set up three different types and listen to the oboe and flute playing together. Choose the mic that subdues the oboe's pinched nasality and the flute's metallic upper midrange. Just make sure that when these two instruments play a couple of scales in unison, you can clearly tell the difference in their sounds. The wrong mic will render them indistinguishable about one octave above middle C, where their overtone structures are most similar.

For saxes and any other reeds that produce a bright tone with a full series of harmonics, I would generally stick with ribbons or dynamic mics, say the RE-20 or RE-15, and avoid those that have a peak in the upper midrange. The mellower condensers, U 47 and SM 81, can bring out a solo nicely against a fuller arrangement. The same choices hold for bagpipes and a whole range of medieval and Renaissance instruments sometimes used for effect in rock or pop genres. You can add some top end above 8 kHz for a sheer, gossamer quality, while these mics naturally tame the oft-grating buzz range between 4 and 6 kHz.

Compression.   Compression is particularly noticeable when applied to stereo mics on a full wind or reed section. However, because of the unpredictable response at certain notes, it is often necessary, if only to prevent overload. Use a pair of matched compressors electronically "tied" together for stereo operation. When either compressor begins operating, the other reduces gain similarly, even if its input is still below threshold. Applying an identical amount of compression to both channels ensures that individual instruments maintain their chosen left-to-right imaging positions regardless of an individual or group burst in level. Otherwise, if the left compressor, but not the right, reduced gain suddenly, the whole section would slide right for a second, then back.

Unless you are certain that winds and reeds will be lost in the mix, set the threshold so that a solo forte line causes a gain reduction of just a couple of dBs. This will allow the separate parts to intertwine naturally at lower volumes and smooth out the blend in louder passages, where one wind or reed is most likely to hit a momentary peak.

Mixed Miking.   In orchestral performance, it is expected that the lower notes of bassoon and oboe may be indistinct—just a part of the wind and reed texture. In studio recordings, this may be unacceptable. If you decide to beef up the sound with a few close mics, keep in mind that sound arrives at these mics sooner than at the distant mics, confusing the transients or onsets of the close-miked instruments. To disguise this flaw, roll off the top end from these mics, and make sure you blend them into the stereo image at the same left-to-right positions those instruments occupy in the image of the distant pair.

To restore actual time alignment, you might introduce digital delays on the close mics, moving them back however many milliseconds it takes to synchronize their signals with that from the stereo pair (a process suggested with close and distant miking of guitar amps). Sometimes, however, the apparent doubling generated by two mics picking up each wind or reed instrument at slightly different times can create a fuller overall section sound. In this way, certain sloppy recording techniques can actually improve the results. Let your ear be the judge.

For additional ideas applying to woodwind and reed sections, turn to Chapter 20, Strings. Several of the tips for creating a phantom auditorium and filling out small sections via multiple miking and modest processing of strings can be equally well applied to winds and reeds.

19

THE BRASS FAMILY

FROM the double B-flat tuba to the piccolo trumpet, brass instruments produce fundamentals ranging from 40 Hz to 4 kHz. Because they are constructed of relatively thin metal that vibrates in response to the internal air column, all brass instruments broadcast dense series of overtones and partials stretching past 20 kHz. And since metal bodies and flared bells are much more efficient than wood at amplifying internal vibrations and coupling them to the outside air, some brass instruments can produce upwards of 130 dB at the bell. These factors, combined with steep transients produced by the higher brass with certain blowing techniques, makes the entire family a recording challenge par excellence.

BASIC PROBLEMS

Sound Production and Propagation. All brass instruments are essentially cylindrical or tapered conical tubes. The method by which fundamentals are produced is exactly the same as for winds and reeds. Thus, I will discuss here only the differences between brass instruments and the instruments I have already discussed.

We might more accurately call brass instruments lip reeds, because the player's lips serve the same function as tapered reed in the oboe, bassoon, or any double reed. Air pressure inside the player's mouth pushes against his or her lips, which are pressed against a metal mouthpiece. At a certain threshold pressure, the lips will separate, allowing a puff of air through, then slap shut again in exactly the same way as a pair of wet cane reeds. The length of the instrument's tube of air "suggests" to the player's lips the frequency at which to vibrate, exactly as the length of an organ pipe determines air behavior at the knife edge.

However, whereas the tone holes in wind reeds are closed by fingers or key-operated pads, the length of the tube in brass instruments is changed by selecting longer or shorter available tube paths via a series of valves (as in the tuba, French horn, and trumpet) or by mechanically extending the tube via a movable sliding section (as in the trombone). The first method offers a choice among several predetermined lengths, while the latter offers a continuously variable range of tube lengths.

All brass instruments, including the sax and all blown reeds whose bodies are made of thin metal, have bodies that vibrate very much like a bell. Consider our earlier discussion of vibrating membranes, specifically drums. When a drum head is struck off center, vibrations travel both across and around the head, causing up and down movement of the head analogous to the surface of a circular pool when a stone is dropped in. The speed of sound in the drum head together with its size, thickness, inherent stiffness, and the tension applied by the rim determine how fast the waves will travel. Where the head is struck determines which modes are excited, and these in turn predict the frequencies at which the head will resonate and project sound into the air.

A cymbal, which has no rim to apply tension, maintains shape through its own rigidity and is deformed in exactly the same way when struck. Because the speed of sound in metals is very high (as much as 20,000' per second) and because the cymbal is ground to different thicknesses over its area, it emits frequencies right up to and past 20 kHz. If the cymbal were stretched out vertically by its mounting hole, we would have a short cone not too different from a bell. Struck anywhere on the edge, vibrations will travel around and over the body of the cone, exciting various modes and characteristic resonances. An outside source of sound at any of these frequencies will also cause the bell to ring sympathetically. If you sing into a cymbal, it sings back.

Now stretch the bell out until we have a very long, highly tapered metal cone. The walls of the cone are quite thin and its diameter fairly small, greatly reducing its tendency to vibrate in the lower modes. Its original outer edges now form the wider end of the tube and simply cannot flex as much as they used to. However, this tube now contains a column of air that can be excited by some outside stimulus like a reed. By adding a mechanism for varying the length of the tube, we have invented a thin-walled metal wind instrument.

This instrument will produce fundamental frequencies determined by the range of lengths to which the tube can be adjusted. Its series of overtones, however, will be largely dependent on the frequencies at which various parts of the body resonate by virtue of upper modes and local resonances—similar to that of a cymbal.

As with other winds and reeds, fundamentals radiate primarily through the end of the bell. But while various amplified harmonics follow suit and exit with fundamentals, a large proportion of midrange frequencies exit directly through the side walls along various parts of the tube. The very highest overtones and partials, plus the actual buzz of the player's lip reed, exit the bell in a narrow beam. Because this frequency range can be so harsh, some Renaissance and Baroque composers of brass music instructed players to aim their horns at the walls of the church or hall rather than the audience. Using architecture to spread the highs around also expands the audience's sense of space.

TECHNIQUES FOR MIKING BRASS

Close-Miking Alternatives.   There are two alternatives available for close-miking brass instruments. If the bell projects the sound away from the player, he or she hears and feels the fundamental and lower harmonics directly but gets frequencies

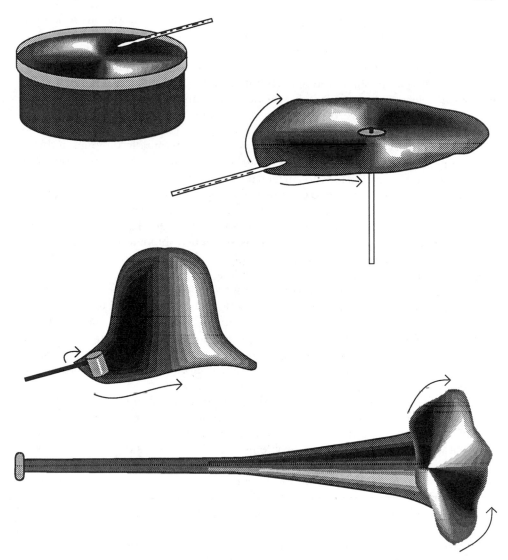

Figure 19.1.   Four instruments vibrating in their second "pie-shaped" modes. Exaggerated views of a drum head, a cymbal, a large bell, and the bell of a brass instrument. The ability of all these surfaces to flex in various modes produces their unique overtone structures. Sound waves move around their surfaces in both directions, passing through each other repeatedly.

above about 3 kHz only if they are reflected back to him or her from the walls or stage. Thus, most brass players like a fuller sound than is available (without lots of processing) right at the bell. Many engineers assume the contrary and go for all the high frequency bite they can muster. For the fullest sound, position a mic two or three feet beyond the bell, with the mic about 20 to 30 degrees off the axis of the bell, aimed toward the instrument's body,

With any mic, this positioning helps collect frequencies from various sources in the instrument and melds them into a full, round tone. If you must close mike single horns or pairs in a section, this technique gives a blend not unlike what you might get from single-pair stereo miking of the entire section. You can also use the instrument and musician to shield the mic from mechanical noises by choosing your off-axis position left or right of the bell, whichever is farthest from pistons and valves.

From the perspective of the audience, a trumpet with bell aimed directly at listeners and blown evenly over its lowest two octaves exhibits several peaks in its averaged frequency response. (Its lowest note is E below middle C, about 160 Hz.) The first peak is about 1.5 to 2 kHz (well into the harmonics of its lowest fundamentals), another closer to 3 kHz, with smaller peaks extending up to 6 kHz. Way up top, around 10 to 12 kHz, there is one narrow peak of lip tone that is produced regardless of the note played. Almost every brass instrument has a characteristic lip-tone cluster between 6 and 12 kHz. Even though stage and walls help amplify fundamentals and lower harmonics, what the audience hears is still much thinner and more piercing than anything the player hears onstage (except with the French horn, which projects sound to the player's rear, away from the audience).

In recording, this direct sound is best captured just a few inches from the bell, with the mic off center just a bit to avoid the worst spittiness in the 5 to 6 kHz range. This produces the familiar pencil-thin horn sound of R&B and dance hits, where the horns provide sharp punctuation marks for the lead vocals or overall rhythm arrangement. To my ear this is not a satisfying sound for lead horn lines or legato section parts, although some gentle processing can make it more useful in these roles, as we will see later.

Miking brass directly at or inside the bell is not recommended. Although I hear this technique on plenty of rock and pop-jazz records, to my ear it produces a dry and buzzy sound, small and closed, like a kazoo. Whatever the cause, instruments miked this way seem to have sinus problems. If an artist is used to in-the-bell miking from live gigs, I might set up a dummy bell mic for his or her playing comfort but record the instrument through a more distant mic for fuller sound. The dummy mic can also prevent the artist from moving off mic during takes.

To determine the kind of mics to use, in general follow the principles described for the sax. The closer to the instrument you decide to mike, the less you need a condenser. Use brighter dynamic mics or ribbon models (Sennheiser, AKG, and Shure) for the lower horns—tuba, sousaphone, French horn, trombone, and even flugelhorn; use the smoother dynamics (EV and the like) for the trumpet on up. Any of these choices can be brightened above 8 kHz to restore a silky, airy top end. At the same time they will all subdue that grating 5 kHz bite that can fry eardrums and push horn parts to the fore even when they are meant to serve a subtler musical purpose.

The only exception to these credos might be if you are close miking a number of brass instruments, only one of which will solo. In this case, pick a solo mic one step brighter than you might if the same instrument were just a section member. Better to have the added edge from this mic, taming it as necessary with eq, than to boost midhighs from a dull mic, a process that with brass can only lead to a whiny, nasal quality. In any case, be prepared to use the mic's internal pad. To avoid the proximity boost of cardioid mics on low horns, you should consider a low roll-off filter in the mic or board.

Section Miking.   As with winds and background vocals, the important criteria for selecting and positioning a pair of mics for a whole brass section is the section's dramatic function in the piece being recorded. In particular, if the brass should wrap around the lead giving it tight support, any of the coincident miking schemes (X-Y, for example) is the ticket. Its phase-coherent bottom end provides a solid, centered low end (especially important with trombones) and a clear stereo image of each player's position. For a broader stage with an exaggerated sense of physical depth, use a spaced pair of omnis. The wider the spacing, the bigger the resulting hole in the middle, a tool you can use specifically to reserve plenty of space for a mellow lead vocal or instrument to cut through heavy brass charts.

You should also determine how much you want to hear the separate parts or players. For a big, gushy horn pad with little separation among parts, the RCA 77DX is unbeatable. It will need lots of brightening in the 8-kHz range, but the basic sound is extremely full, and warm as toast. Newer model dynamics and condensers produce a less colored sound and should not need quite so much added high end. The B&K 4006 or EV RE-55 are fine in spaced pairs, the RE-20 and broader-field cardioids for X-Y use. All of them give a more intimate, private sound than any condenser.

For an open, blazing sound, all of the large-diaphragm condensers are great. The Neumann U 47 and AKG MC740 give big, round lows and a very silky, almost elusive high end. AKG 414s and the C 451 are neutral and should not fry too many ears even with a full complement of flaming trumpets. For aggressive leads or an edge-of-your-seat section sound, Neumann 87s and 89s are the ticket. Using any condensers as a stereo pair, you may need to add a close mic to beef up the low horns. In this case the Neumann KM84 or KMfi cardioid lavalier should do the trick.

French horn presents a special problem, since its bell faces downward to the rear of the player. In addition, it is the mellowest member of the entire brass family. As a result, it is nearly impossible to hear the horn clearly in a large brass section. In a symphonic setting, French-horn notes fold under and expand upward behind the orchestra, using the entire stage backdrop as a soundboard. In a studio this effect is lost; the only solution is to place a separate tight mike behind the player. Again, the Neumann KM84 and lavaliers work well if the section mics are condensers. Otherwise, try a Sennheiser 421 or any other bright dynamic. The warmest sound, again, is available off center of the bell and perhaps one or two feet away. If high frequency leakage from other instruments invades the horn mic, a gobo or felt cone should cure the problem and allow you to brighten the horn as needed.

Engineer Al Schmitt discusses how he recorded the brass section for *Rosanna:*

I started with a stereo mic about 10 or 12 feet back—that's the mic I opened first to get my big room sound. Then I added the mics on the individual sections, gradually getting my presence. There was one U 47 on the 2 trumpets, maybe 5 feet in front, and one U 47 about 3 or 4 feet in front of the one trombone. I used 3 U 87s on the 3 saxes, open all the way around so I could get some leakage back and forth. The individual sax miking gives me the definition.

[Although most engineers close-mike saxes with a cardioid], I try to back the mics off a little bit. If there are two or three saxes, the alto can leak into the tenor, and vice versa. The ambience seems to open up the sound more.

Next time you're overdubbing a guitar or something, try putting up a mic in the cardioid position. Then flip it to omnidirectional, and the difference is *amazing*—the sound just opens up. The cardioid pattern has the back blocked off. Opening up the back of the mike seems to let the sound follow right *through* the mic.

Sometimes the weirdest things work for me. I learned a long time ago that the first place I go is to the exact opposite of what I normally think would work, and that's the answer!

Processing.   Brass instruments have no single body resonances or other peaks in output that need destructive equalization. However, as with sax, most solo and section horns—especially when close miked—require compression. They also require fast attack (2 ms or less), medium ration (6 : 1 or so), and enough room in the players' dynamics below threshold to allow expression while preventing overload on high staccato notes or forte lines. As usual, if compressed brass sounds artificial when soloed dry, the addition of a little reverb will make the effect disappear, especially when other instruments are masking its action. Because brass instruments are so loud, you should not need to noise gate the track(s) during record. Ambient studio noise, foot shuffling, and the like will generally be inaudible between lines.

To obtain the pencil-thin horn sound described earlier, you really need heavy limiting. Use a low threshold, high ratio, fast attack, and release, and do not cringe if the compressor registers 15 dB or more of gain reduction on the loudest spikes. This keeps the brass at a constant, controllable level and prevents them from dominating a lead of any type, regardless of how enthusiastic the horn players get during the take. The price for this control, however, is hearing every breath, page turn, and foot shuffle between horn lines. Use noise gating to lower the floor by at least the same number of decibels by which the compressor is reducing signal peaks.

Doubling, Chorusing, and Effects.   The dense series of overtones and partials that characterizes brass makes it difficult to disguise attempts to enlarge a section through electronic doubling. A small amount of chorusing can fatten a section yet be inaudible in the final mix. More than about 20% of the effect in the blend will turn real horns into synthetic-sounding imitations. The same is even truer of simple DDL and flanging effects. The reason is grating collisions between the jagged high-frequency waveforms of the original and replicated signals. If you must use these devices when laying tracks, take the top end off their return before reblending with the direct horns. Otherwise, leave all this type of processing for the mix.

Noise Reduction and Level to Tape.   If you have compressed the horns, you can get away without noise reduction and print tape levels fairly hot, say + 1 dB VU or up to + 10 on peak-reading meters. With or without compression, levels any higher than this usually cause severe print-through. However, for big band, jazz, or any music in which the full range of brass dynamics must be preserved, it is hard to get away without using noise reduction. The range of volume from a mild French horn line to 14-piece staccato brass stingers can be over 50 dB. This leaves you two choices: learn the part and gain ride, or use noise reduction. I apply modest gain riding even if using N/R, simply because it reduces the amount of riding necessary during the mix. In this case, hold your VU readings down a touch. It is hard to anticipate the exact level of upcoming lines, so it is better to settle for a little noise than lots of distortion and print-through.

20

THE STRINGS

EXCEPT in the roles of country fiddle and solo instrument for a few jazz ensembles, the violin, viola, and cello are rarely recorded one at a time. After all, who ever played rhythm viola for a rock band? Our main studio challenge with this family of instruments is therefore recording groups of strings, from the familiar quartet on up. And here, our listening audience has lots of preconceptions. Everybody "knows" what a good string sound is, even though a very small percentage of the public has heard unamplified strings in the last decade.

BASIC PROBLEMS

With a few minor differences, all strings produce their sound in the same manner as the acoustic bass. In general, the higher the range of the individual instrument, the more its high frequencies (upper partials and rosin tone) are beamed out perpendicular to the top face. It seems odd that orchestral violins and violi shoot their clearest tone up into the rafters of the stage house, but it is true. One reason hard-topped stages are acoustically better for orchestral performances is that live strings have both a left-to right and a stage-to-ceiling stereo image. Their highs literally spray down on the audience after bouncing off the ceiling.

There is a way of implying the vertical dimension in a two-channel recording, but this quality is not necessary or appropriate for every recording. Other problems include the fact that many engineers have fixed notions of what makes for good strings, regardless of their musical context. The frequent but lamentable lack of communication between client and engineer about the dramatic function strings should serve in a particular recording is even more lamentable when you consider the cost of hiring a 20-musician section and writing arrangements and charts for it.

More than most instruments, strings elicit an immediate emotional response in listeners. Thus, the way in which they are recorded can reveal how the artist or producer wants the audience to react to the song's story or lyric. A case in point is the string quartet in the Beatles' classic "Yesterday." Why such a tight, dead, unreverbed

string sound? Simply because the lyric is stoic, not Wagnerian. It is an interior monologue in which the character looks at his problems face to face, not at a distance. His
reserved emotion, reflected by dry strings (though very poignantly written and
played), underscores his loneliness. This in turn draws the listener into the man's
problems, eliciting a more direct outpouring of emotion than if we could keep the
protagonist at a distance with a fuller, reverbed string quartet.

The same is true of "Eleanor Rigby." Dry strings here point out the tragedy of
a life lived by the book. Poor Eleanor never gave herself the latitude to be human,
and the rigorous string sound (and writing) makes this theme perfectly clear. For
contrast, consider "The Long and Winding Road" or "Something"—same band, same
producer, but here we have a full reverberant string sound because here the lyric
stands back and comments on life as a whole. There's no personal drama, just philosophy at a distance. "Something," on the other hand, is a rose-colored view of the character's lover, soft-edged and idealized. Dry strings in either of these would bring us
too close to reality, instead of supporting the singer's romantic view of his subject
matter.

Miking for Dramatic Effect.   Here we might ask some of the same questions
posed about background vocals and other sections. Are the strings intended as a sympathetic support for the emotion conveyed by the singer, or do they reveal what is
going on behind a stoic exterior? Perhaps they are an outside commentary on the
singer's situation. For the moment let us assume that the task is to record a full string
section—a dozen players or more—in stereo with a single pair of distant mics. What
are the options?

Coincident X-Y miking using a pair of broad cardioids will produce a warm,
cradling string sound through its phase-coherent bass and lower midrange. The
stereo image will be fat and seamless, with no hole in the middle. This is great for
thickly written string parts that will be featured in the final mix. The wall of midrange
built by such strings will mandate riding the singer relatively high in the mix but will
also provide a solid bed beneath the vocal.

A spaced pair of omnis or cardioids (at least 4' apart) will divide the string
section laterally. The phasing between channels will heighten the drama but provide
less low-end stability than the X-Y setup. And there will be a definite hole in the
middle for the lead vocal or instrument, whose volume will not need to be pushed.
The broader the mic separation, the bigger the hole. This technique is good for sporadic or intermittent string parts, particularly where they are meant to comment on
the singer's tale from an outside perspective.

To make the strings reveal the singer's private thoughts or emotions, switch to
tighter miking of each player or subgroup (separate mics on violins and violi) and
construct a stereo image in the console. Dividing the members of the section in this
way sounds artificial. It is a constructivist, manipulated view of their sound and can
be made to imply a whole range of interior emotions depending on how the individual strings are panned. Panning basses and cellos hard left or right can give a real
sense of imbalance and insecurity. Splitting the entire section with broad panning can
make the singer seem trapped; the strings will have almost the same presence as the
vocal and sonically surround it.

Suppose the string parts are meant to change their function or perspective dur-

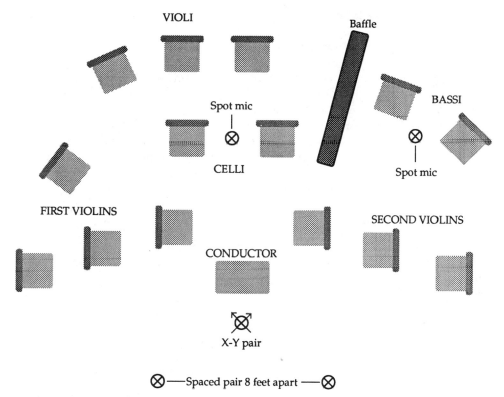

Figure 20.1. Suggested seating plan for fourteen string players, showing positions for X-Y mic and a spaced pair on the entire section, plus close mics on bass and celli.

ing the song. Set up two types of miking and fade or shift balance between them in various sections. Or you might record the two setups on separate pairs of stereo tracks and later blend and rebalance them during the mix.

In general, condenser mics are best for distant pairs, dynamics for individual tight miking. Individual players will be heard only if the mics have enough upper detail to separate the rosin and bowing sound from each instrument. At a distance, Neumann U 87s or U 89s do this admirably, though their overall tone may be a bit aggressive if the strings are part of a musical bed. For a warmer sound that retains the detail, try 414s, AKG Tube condensers, or the Neumann U47. For spaced pairs, the B&K 4006 omnis give much the same clarity as the condensers above. So do EV RE-55s, although they may need a bit of top-end boost.

In all distant cases, the mics should be suspended several feet above the section and at least 6 to 8′ in front of it. Remember that highs from cellos and basses project forward, and it's more important for clarity among the parts to capture these than the very top end of the violins and violi.

Tight mics on violin and viola can produce a gritty quality unless you use smooth dynamics or ribbons such as the EV RE-20, Beyer D160, or even—for ultimate nostalgia and romance—the RCA 77DX. Avoid placing the mic closer than about two feet so that the instrument's local resonances and other imbalances have some space to meld together. Also, mike closer to the top or bottom lobe of the body, rather than directly above its center. Undesirable wood and body resonances are strongest there, while low notes will sound fuller and more even if a mic is aimed up toward the bridge from above the tailpiece. Remember too that even seated string players like to move their upper torsos. Give the mics enough room to allow for this without hearing shifts in volume, response or imaging.

Rather than miking each string player separately, you may find it best to double up, mounting a wide cardioid over pairs of players or a bidirectional mic between each pair. This certainly saves setup time and reduces inter-mic phasing. However, you may need to angle the bidirectional axis a bit away from the player to the left of the mic (as seen from audience perspective). Bowing and rosin sounds from his instrument have a clear shot at the mic, while those from the player to the right of the mic may be absorbed by his own clothing.

Combo Miking and the Three-Dimensional Soundstage.   One mic seems to accomplish an audio impossibility: it creates the illusion of a three-dimensional space through simple stereo reproduction. The Calrec Soundfield Mic (with a cost approaching $6,000) has three pairs of internal diaphragms: one pair senses left-to-right stereo, one picks up sounds coming from above and below, and a third senses sounds approaching the mic from the front and back. The mic's custom preamplifier/mixer allows the engineer to blend the outputs of these pairs to achieve the best effect for the type of music and the room in which it is being recorded. Alas, very few studios have Calrecs. Conversely, since the Calrec highlights a studio's acoustics, it should not be used in small or dead rooms.

However, with a little thought and a bit of studio time, we can use ordinary studio equipment to simulate the three-dimensional effect of a Calrec in a fine hall. The primary differences between sounds approaching the ear from each of these six directions are when the sounds arrive, the ratio of the levels of direct and bounced or reverberant sound from each direction, transient quality, and frequency content.

For instance, in an average auditorium, a sound originating from a position onstage in front and to the left of a listener seated in the fourth row arrives first from that direction with a high proportion of direct sound and with undiminished transients and frequency content. The same sound bounces back to the listener from the right rear of the hall (diagonally opposite the source) perhaps 120 milliseconds later with no direct sound and a high proportion of early reflection reverb, with greatly reduced transients, and usually with a peak between 300 Hz and 1 kHz, containing little above 4 kHz. The exact response of reflected sounds also depends on the wall surfaces and any draperies or coverings used. Sound reaching the listener from the auditorium's ceiling arrives even sooner, with less and shorter reverb (given that the height of most rooms is smaller than their lateral dimensions), higher transience, and fuller, flatter response.

To approximate all these variables, set up close and distant mics on your string section. A distant cardioid pair re-creates the ensemble sound that a listener might hear straight from the stage. Next we can use the closer pair to simulate the up/down and front/rear signals. At their input modules, eliminate the direct signal from the monitors and use two pairs of aux sends to input the pair to two different digital reverb systems. On the first select a room program with under 1.5 seconds reverb time and introduce a 50-ms predelay, then bring its output back into another pair of modules, panning these returns somewhat left and right of center. Boost one channel a bit at 400 Hz, the other at 600 Hz for a little left/right imbalance. Believe it or not, this audio charade can add apparent height to the string section, simulating the relatively short up/down reflections generated in an auditorium.

Also, send the close mics into the second reverb unit and dial in a hall program reverb time of between 2.5 and 3 seconds. Select a predelay of 100 to 120 ms and bring the outputs back into yet another pair of modules, in full stereo but reversed. Boost one channel at 200 Hz and 1 kHz and the other at 300 Hz and 1.5 kHz to suggest a horizontal imbalance in hall acoustics, and take the top end off both. These parameters should simulate the front/back reflections of a hall. By blending the distant mics and two pairs of reverb returns, an auditorium should now begin to surround you. For the final touch, use the aux sends on each pair of reverb return modules to send some of the up/down reverb into the front/back unit and vice versa. A touch of each exchange should do the trick.

This procedure requires a lot of modules and processing to create an illusion, but it also proves an important point about psychoacoustics (the study of how various sounds effect the human mind and emotions). If you give the ear the right kind of sounds at about the right times with respect to a direct sound, the brain imagines they are being generated by the kind of space in which you would normally hear this music, a phantom auditorium. Vary the parameters and blend until you have the overall sound you want. The effect is quite striking. One problem: you will probably have to do all this during record, simply because not too many studios will have four spare console modules and four channels of reverb that can be dedicated to strings during a mixdown.

String Pickups.   Several brands of contact mics can be mounted near the bridge of various strings. The best among them are wonderful for live gigs, where normal mics would surely feed back. However, unless you must record strings in the same pass and in the same room as full rhythm and horn sections, do not use pickups for string recording. Except for the interior-monologue string sound already mentioned, pickups are just too close to the sound source to give any perspective. In addition, they cannot deliver the full bottom end that results when waves emanating from the instrument's body converge at a mic some feet distant.

The only instance in which I might use the pickup signal, but then only to beef up freestanding mics, is on the bass or cello, as discussed in the chapter on acoustic bass. As with the lower winds, bass and cello tend to get lost in a mix containing lots of rhythm parts. The added focus of a small amount of pickup signal will enable these instruments to cut through a lot of midrange fullth, mainly because the upper frequencies and rosin sound will be accentuated. This may sound abnormal when the strings are soloed, but it does restore better balance when they are laid into a dense arrangement. To coordinate the pickup sound back into the whole section time-wise, delay its output by 10 to 20 ms before blending it with live mics.

Compression.   I hate to admit it, but compression is almost a must unless your string section and conductor are experienced studio players who realize that for tape, pianissimo and double forte are only 10 or 12 dB apart. A single violin has a gentle attack; ten violins hitting each note at slightly different times have hardly any attack at all. Use a 10-to-20-ms attack, low ratio (4:1 or so), low threshold so that most of the part is above threshold, and a very long release time (2 to 3 seconds). In my experience, string players tend to make more mechanical noises (feet shuffling and general instrument clatter) right after a phrase rather than before the next one. With luck, the long release time will help suppress this unwanted noise without gating.

Reverb, Effects, Doubling, and Chorusing. Generally the problem with strings is that you do not have enough of them. These days there are all kinds of devices that profess to enlarge a section, but real strings can sound like a synthesizer if these gadgets are overused, especially during record. Here are a few general pointers:

1. If you mike strings in full stereo and add chorusing or other doubling, keep the doubled sound closer to the center of the stereo image by hiding it in the section rather than allowing the listener to separate it from the real sounds.
2. Equalize the return from the chorus or doubler for two effects. First, take the very top end down (shelf-dip above 6 kHz) so that the ear will not hear grittiness caused by interference of the delayed highs with the direct ones. Second, find any frequency bands in the direct signal that are weak and boost them a bit in the doubled signal. This way the doubling will fill in holes without competing with bands that are strong in the direct string sound.
3. Even if you want to record the direct strings dry, add a little very short reverb to the doubled sound while it goes down to tape. A 0.5- to 1-second plate reverb will make the section seem larger and take the rough, electronic edges off the doubled signal. For even greater warmth and a real sense of depth, try light flanging on the return from the reverb.
4. If you have to record strings simultaneously with other instruments and encounter leakage in the stereo pair, use tight mics or string pickups as the source for any chorusing or other electronic doubling. Chorused or flanged leakage will stick out like a sore thumb in the mix, giving away your attempts to enlarge the string section. The cleaner signal from string pickups or close mics may not basically sound as good but will have little leakage and give a better illusion of more players. Add a bit of reverb to the doubled signal to smooth out its rough edges.

With the right combination of these tricks, you should be able to turn 8 strings into 20. However, be very careful when trying to stretch a quartet up to a dozen or more pieces. The best bet here is simply to double-track the players and apply the electronic doubling in a bounce pass. Of course, that takes a total of six tracks (four of which can be wiped clean afterward). The best advice is to plan ahead—more players cost more but will take less studio time (and dollars) than double-tracking and bouncing.

Equalization of the Completed Section Sound. Remember that a string section playing in a live auditorium has a full, smooth sound, not a shrill screech. Halls tend to boost low mids, while studio bass traps eat them up. An auditorium's reverb will stretch highs and rosin tone into a thin, silky presence; a dead recording studio, which preserves and separates every rosin-scrape with little chance of smooth blending via artificial reverb, is just not the same. Lacking an enormous studio, if you want a natural sound, eq in the missing hall effects. Scan the highs with a parametric to find and dip the rosin-scratch range—usually just a quarter-octave band in the 6 to 7 kHz area. Then boost above this for more silk.

Again, since equalizers afford a gentler sound when dipping than when boosting, increase the midbass by dipping the range just above it, perhaps one octave wide around 500 Hz. This will also give an effective boost to everything above 1 kHz. If you want a superbright sound (e.g., for a dance or funk record), it is better to dip the low mids 6 dB and boost the upper midrange by 3 dB than to leave the bottom flat and boost upper mids by 9 dB. Too much boost in any range generates phasing problems within the equalizer, giving rise to a harsh, metallic string sound—a leftover from late 1970s disco. All in all, treat strings gently, like a lead vocal. Anything too far from reality will undo the significant investment it takes to put good string section on your tape in the first place.

21

THE TUNED PERCUSSIONS

O F all the instruments discussed so far, only the Fender Rhodes piano bears any direct relationship to the vibraphone, marimba, xylophone, orchestra bells, chimes, steel drums, and the other tuned percussions. Yet even its connection is rather slim. The Rhodes produces sound when its tuned metal bars are struck, but it is strictly an amplified instrument. All the other tuned percussions are acoustic. While today's pickups for tuned percussions are not up to the demands of serious recording, they have vastly improved the sound quality obtainable from this family on stage. Thus I am mystified that these instruments have not played a larger role in popular recordings or on the rock stage because the tuned percussions as a family offer a wide range of sounds and emotions.

BASIC PROBLEMS

Sound Production.   Except for chimes and steel drums, most tuned percussions have wooden or metal bars sized and shaped to produce chromatic notes spanning a 2- to 5-octave range. Because rectangular bars are quite stiff and (like stiff soundboards) prone to emitting a high proportion of upper harmonics when struck, most wooden tuned percussion bars are shaved thinner in the center of their underside. This promotes more vigorous vibration at the fundamental, the depth and arc of the shaving determining the proportions of lower harmonics produced when each bar is struck. In addition, shaving increases overall volume and helps sustain notes that would otherwise die out almost instantly.

Oddly, the bars of tuned percussions behave much like organ pipes closed at both ends. The energy imparted by a mallet sets the bars resonating much like the action of wind at the pipe's knife edge. Sound waves travel back and forth inside the bar at the speed of sound in the specific wood or metal of which that bar is made.

274

Strictly speaking, these waves bounce off each end with no direct outlet to the environment. Since the bar is actually a closed system with no fixed attachment at its end (such as the bridge and nut of a stretched string), its resonance varies inversely as the square of its length. This simply means that when one bar is twice as long as another (all other factors remaining the same), its pitch is 1/4 the original frequency, or 2 octaves lower. The pitch of organ pipes, you will remember, descends one octave for every doubling of length.

The way that the proportion of various harmonics produced varies with the striking position is almost opposite from the way this relationship works in plucked-string instruments. Striking the bar at its center will produce little vibration at the fundamental but lots at upper harmonics. To get the fullest tone, bars are struck near either end, causing deflection of their entire length in a single arc.

A soft mallet, which flattens against the bar when they meet, acts like a broad pick, suppressing upper harmonics. It literally damps vibrations whose wavelengths (inside the bar) are as short or shorter than the length of bar/mallet contact. Hard mallets have a point contact with the bar, bend the bar at a sharper angle on contact, and like a thin pick, produce a sharp transient containing two groups of high frequencies: one made up of musical harmonics of the bar's fundamental resonance and the other a simultaneous burst of inharmonic highs that I call "impact noise," the contents of which is virtually identical, regardless of which bar is struck.

To further boost the level of fundamentals and increase the instrument's overall volume level, vibes and marimba have resonating tubes mounted beneath each bar. The air column in these tubes provides a kind of mechanical feedback to the bars themselves, helping prolong each note just as a reed instrument's air column keeps the reed vibrating. The xylophone, orchestra bells, and other unamplified tuned percussions depend on their intense series of upper harmonics to provide enough volume to compete with an orchestra or marching band. Fundamentals in the metal-barred instruments are elusive if not downright inaudible. For this reason, they are rarely scored without other instruments either doubling their parts or otherwise defining an underlying tonality above which their harmonics add a distinctive texture.

TECHNIQUES FOR MIKING TUNED PERCUSSIONS

For recording, the important physical parameters of tuned percussions are their large size and broad frequency output. If one plays any sort of lead part, stereo miking and tracking is the obvious solution, even if the entire session is being recorded direct to 2 track. Because tuned percussions have no unified soundboard, the fundamentals and overtones of each note originate from completely separate positions. This mandates some careful thinking about stereo imaging and phasing problems, especially since lower notes and most fundamentals are already a bit weak. In addition, we must deal with the added problems of a very large dynamic range and potential leakage from other instruments played simultaneously in the studio.

Clearly, to maintain the highest possible phase coherence and the cleanest L/R image for the fundamentals of a vibraphone and marimba, we should use coincident miking, with the mikes far enough from the bars so that the relative distance to each bar is fairly uniform. For vibes, which are almost five feet wide, a mic positioned 2' above the center bar is over 3' from the highest and lowest notes. If all notes sound at equal volume, there is already a 3-dB difference between the end and center bars' level to the mic. Moving the mics farther than about 4' away may make the instrument sound distant in comparison to other close-miked sources.

The upper harmonics from each bar travel mostly upward, while the impact sound travels out more laterally. In addition, as with organ pipes, those fundamentals reinforced by resonating tubes are strongest above the mouths of the tubes. Thus, the fullest and clearest sound is above the bars and the murkiest and most percussive at their own level, out front in the direction of the audience.

All in all, the instrument itself gives us few choices, except when it comes to mics. Here, I would suggest the brightest condensers in the house—for two reasons. First, although vibes and marimba (the two most popular tuned percussions for recording) can emit extremely steep transients when played with hard mallets, most players prefer to work with softer mallets that allow them to inflect wide dynamic changes within the grace notes or passing tones of melodic lines. The greater our ability to distinguish each transient, the better, even if it is later necessary to apply compression to the stereo signal.

Neumann U 89s in X-Y configuration with crossed wide-cardioid patterns are by far my first choice. Although 414s may produce a slightly more transparent sound during instrument solos, experience dictates that the toughest problem is getting the tuned percussion to cut through a rhythm section in the mix. Any extra brightness available during record definitely helps. If leakage from other instruments is a problem, try a pair of tighter cardioid dynamics a little closer to the instrument, and shelf-boost the top end during record. Remember, however, that a super- or hypercardioid pattern may deliver impact sound only from those notes on axis for each mic, with a big hole in the middle.

The spaced pair of wide cardioids is also popular, but it has an inherent flaw. If the mics are 2' above the bars and 2' apart, the lowest bars are about 3' from the treble mic. The difference, 1', equals about half a wavelength at 500 Hz. Thus, the entire range around 500 Hz will be partially phased out in the lowest notes, especially when the recording is heard in mono or the mics are panned in from full left and right. With the lower bars weaker in level already, losing some of their harmonics can sap fullth from the entire sound. Even when a spaced pair is used for its open sound quality, it seems unnatural to hear the notes of vibes span the entire L/R sound-stage. Be careful to create a realistic stereo image during the mix, no matter how broad the stereo you may have obtained while recording.

Concerning mic input level to the board, ask the player to strike chords that are as loud as possible and set the mic trim so that with faders set at 0, VU level in the modules rarely exceeds 0 (with corresponding peak levels at +10). The reason for this is that although the instrument is not loud enough to require padding at the mics, its transients and sustained tones can overload the mic preamps in some boards. Better to keep input level down and boost gain (after processing) at the module faders, just before the signal goes to tape. In addition, the player's so-called loudest is likely to increase during takes with the entire band.

The steel drum presents a completely different set of recording challenges from other members of the tuned-percussion family. It has individually tuned plates mounted on a single resonating surface or soundplate, very weak transients, no highs above about 4 kHz, and a relatively unpredictable output level from one note to the next, even in the hands of a good player. For these reasons, and because of its small size compared with other tuned percussions, it is a good idea to try a pair of Sennheiser 421s in X-Y configuration first. Mount the mics above the far edge of the drum's soundboard to get the best upper harmonic clarity, as well as to allow the player a fair shot at each note.

Vibes Pickups. None of the contact and magnetic pickups that I have seen are suitable for recording solo or featured vibes. The reasons are manifest. There is little room to fit a pickup anywhere except directly beneath the bars of the vibes, where transient levels can reach 150 dB, threatening in-console overload even with a pad. Since there is little room to adjust the pickup position, you may wind up placing them directly under nodal or antinodal points for certain harmonics of each bar, where they will deliver a frequency response riddled with notches and peaks. In addition, a magnetic pickup misses all the warmth added by the resonating tubes. Unless the vibes play a small role in the music, do not let a little leakage deter you from using normal mics. Frankly, except for large-hall situations in which the vibes must be heard above a big band or orchestra with lots of horns, I would just as soon use mics even on stage.

Chimes and Bells. The transients for chimes and bells are so steep, especially when the metal bars and tubes are played with hard mallets, that dynamic mics are a must. Then again, the upper harmonics of these instruments are so dense that a bright dynamic will make most listeners' hair stand on end. Stick with a good omni, say the RE-55, or a smooth cardioid like the RE-20 if leakage is a problem. Boosting a little above 10 kHz will open up the harmonics without throwing sonic darts at your ears.

Although orchestral chimes are large enough to use X-Y stereo miking with the mikes criss-crossed horizontally and aiming broadside at the vertical chime tubes, the resulting effect is dizzying. If the player's part is mostly staccato, or if the player damps notes liberally, go for stereo. Otherwise, record chimes and bells mono, since the metal bars of these instruments throw out their upper harmonics in a rotating pattern. A pair of mics hearing various harmonics at slightly different times can produce a rolling, seasick sensation that draws listeners' attention rapidly from side to side.

Equalization and Compression. The vibes are by far the most difficult tuned percussion to record, because each bar and tube produces a nearly pure, ringing sine wave at its fundamental. (A true sine wave contains no harmonics, only a single fundamental frequency.) Played in rapid succession or groups, these sine tones pile up in lower midrange clusters that seem to highlight every weakness in the recording chain—from harmonic and IM distortion in mics, console, amps, and speakers to dropout and *modulation noise* (spurious noise created in proportion to the signal level) in the tape itself. Therefore, use a parametric eq to introduce a broad midrange dip (centered between 300 and 500 Hz) to forestall the buildup of sine clusters. This will also help rebalance the keyboard if X-Y mics are closer to central bars (above middle C) than end ones.

Compression itself is quite noticeable on vibes unless very critically adjusted.

To hear the onset of each note, impact noise should pass through untouched, while smooth, slowly released gain reduction is applied to the prolonged note that follows. This can be achieved by a little sleight of hand—slow attack (5 to 10 ms), high ratio (over 6 : 1), very slow release (2 seconds or more), and a shelf boost, after compression, of the top end. Transients will pass through the compressor unscathed, while the sustained level of each note or chord is tightly controlled. The postcompresion eq will mimic an expander on the highs, adding percussive quality if you push the impact range (4 to 5 kHz) or a silky presence if your boost is above 6 kHz. For tuned percussions with shorter sustain (e.g., marimba and xylophone, compressor attack and release times should be reduced proportionately perhaps to 2 ms and 0.5 second, respectively.

Incidentally, stereo compression is a continuing point of debate on vibes. In theory, if we use coincident miking, the compressors should be tied together so that whenever one operates, the other does the same. This keeps the instrument's stereo image from straying left or right when only one compressor acts. My own choice, however, is not to tie the compressors. Many vibes players exaggerate their dynamics quite intentionally, with the result that lower notes get lost in the blend. In this event, I would rather have a loud high note compressed while its lower, weaker companion comes through the other mic unsquashed.

Level to Tape. Even with compression in place, go easy on the level of vibes you put on tape. The loudest transients can tip +3 dB VU without problems, but sustained sine clusters over 0 dB VU produce excessive modulation noise, which shows up as a garbled throatiness that sounds like tape dropout. If the vibes will be the lead, take a couple of short segments at various levels and see how far the specific recorder and tape can be pushed before this problem sets in. On marimba, xylophone, and tuned percussions with sharper transients and shorter sustain, transient level is the limiting factor. Even then, do not count on the compression to save you—record and play back a sample to test the limits of the system at hand.

Be particularly careful with tape level on orchestra bells and chimes. Their upper harmonics are so dense and ringing that they cause apparent overload even at relatively modest recording levels. Sometimes peaks of +3dB are the highest the tape can handle smoothly. Besides, in most cases these instruments are used in the background, so mixdown playback level and its associated tape noise will be low. When mixed up front, the bell harmonics themselves can mask lots of tape noise.

Reverb to Tape. In general, the shorter the sustain on a tuned percussion, the more I would consider cutting its track with a little short reverb built in. Some reverb will reinforce the ear's awareness of the fundamental of each note played, particularly if the top end of the reverb is rolled off when it is returned to the console and blended with the mic signal. In addition, tuned percussions are often employed as decorative touches within larger arrangements. Because of their transient nature and low mix volume, they often seem to elude the action of the main reverb used in a mixdown, no matter how high their individual reverb send level during that mix.

Effects. To my ear, most effects added to tuned percussions make them sound more like synthetic than acoustic instruments. Vibraphones obviously have a built-in tremolo effect that, as is the case with the Rhodes, can help call attention to the instrument at lower volumes in a mix. However, the sound envelopes of the faster-decaying instruments are too short to make much use of flanging and chorusing unless huge amounts of the effects are applied. In this case the transient is smeared out over a period of time, rendering the instrument even more difficult to feature in the mix. Instead, try a straight digital delay to increase awareness, setting a delay time to relate to the tempo of the specific song or to an unrelated interval just to call attention through a crowded chart. If possible, return the delay on a separate module and shelf dip frequencies above 4kHz to prevent hearing two distinct transients on each note. This technique will seem to sustain notes on xylophone or marimba without cluttering their parts rhythmically.

22

PERCUSSIONS

FOR some reason, percussions are the cause of more remixes than any other family of instruments. I cannot count the number of times I have brought a mix home thinking it was perfect, only to find the percussions way too loud, lost in the mix, or sticking out by virtue of an overbright eq applied to their tracks during mixdown. There are a number of possible reasons for such problems and, luckily, several ways to prevent them with a little forethought.

BASIC PROBLEMS

First, consider the difference between how percussions function onstage and on tape. Unless a percussionist onstage has separate close mics on each item in his kit, one or two all-purpose mics will pick up a lot of leakage, degrading the impact of other instrumental sounds. For this reason, sound-reinforcement engineers tend to run percussions low in a house mix. In spite of this, the audience may feel the percussion level is fine, if only because the percussionist himself is a magnet of visual attention, moving around rapidly among a large variety of easily seen toys. What the audience sees can make up for a lack of actual sound level.

On tape, rack and hand percussions are invisible sources consisting mainly of highly transient sounds in the midhighs and above. Furthermore, they have two inherent level problems. First, individual percussions project sounds at wildly different levels, from 70 dB or so for a shaker played in a light samba rhythm to 140 dB or more for a double-rank tambourine or cowbell. Second, the level of individual percussion notes or hits in a continuous part can vary by over 20 dB without the player or (sometimes) the engineer noticing. This is part of the inherent nature of the instruments. Finally, percussions play a wide range of dramatic functions in different songs, here reinforcing or even replacing the weight and tonality of drums, there evoking an atmospheric ambience in combination with deep reverb or other effects.

280

TECHNIQUES FOR MIKING PERCUSSIONS

To tackle these problems we need to borrow from the thinking applied to the recording of many instruments. For hard-edged functions such as conga, timbale, or bongo parts that carry a song's rhythm, use "tom-tom logic." Locate and emphasize the frequencies that embody the instantaneous attack and the tonal weight of each percussion or those that convey the emotional intent of the instrument in the specific song's context. For example, if two congas are tuned to 130 and 190 Hz, their sound rings longest at these frequencies. To ensure they are heard through a dense arrangement, boost these resonances a little for added sustain.

Also, find a narrow band that focuses attention on the hand/skin contact. This slap contains frequencies from 4 kHz on up. Boosting in the 5 kHz range will give the congas an aggressive edge that is great for rock, while a boost way up at 10 kHz may give the slap a transparent quality more appropriate for a ballad. Later, a little extra reverb on congas and their relatives (real plate is best) will also add sustain, but the variation in reverb levels on loud hits can call attention to any uneven playing. Ultimately, the only way to really smooth out and control levels is with compression. Very fast attack (1 ms or under), medium ratio (say 5 : 1), and a short release (under .5 second) should do the trick. To make sure the effect is constant, lower the threshold until even the softest hits cause a touch of compression.

If several percussions will be played in sequence and recorded on one track or a stereo pair, try to record them at relative tape levels that allow each to be heard properly in the song without constant level changes during mixdown. A tambourine recorded with peaks at 0 dBVU sounds a lot louder than congas with identical peaks. To get the same apparent level on these when monitoring the entire rhythm section, it may be necessary to set the congas peaks at +8 and lower the tambourine peaks to −6. By the book, you will hear a bit more tape noise during tambourine parts. However, without an automated mixdown, you are better off spending your mix time working on the leads and structural aspects of the entire tape rather than adjusting myriad percussion levels.

If you are recording percussions in stereo, proper imaging can help replace some of the visual excitement of seeing the player live, as long as you do not overdo it. Many engineers automatically tight mike each conga and send their signals to two separate tracks. If these are panned hard left and right during the mix, the conga player seems as broad-sounding as the whole group—a very artificial effect. Instead, here are two good reasons to use an X-Y pair. First, a pair mounted as shown in figure 22.1 receives coherent lows from each drum, distributing its low-frequency energy among both tape tracks and delivering a full sound. Separate tight mics or a spaced pair will generate a variety of phasing problems on both drums.

Second, the audio separation of each drum by the X-Ys will be more gentle than that obtained either by tight mics or a raised spaced pair. If this still sounds artificial during the mix, you can pan the tracks toward the center (or place the stereo percussion image anywhere on the stage) without fear of the lows suffering via phasing.

For rack and hand percussions such as wind chimes, assorted wood blocks, bells, shaker, and tambourines, a spaced pair gives a greater sense of the room in

Figure 22.1. Two mic pairs for a percussionist: an X-Y pair for congas, with a highly directional spaced pair above for hand percussions. Left and right stereo pan positions for each mic as shown.

which each sound occurs and can allow the player to have fun with the stereo sound-stage while performing. One way is to move the shaker slowly from left to right, implying a movement across the stage. Another idea is to phrase the shaker, clave, or tambourine part so that downbeats occur toward the left and upbeats more on the right, and so on. Spatial effects like this can focus attention on percussions while maintaining a much lower volume in the mix than might be necessary if you tape only one mono percussion track.

Of course, in order to avoid hearing conga leakage through the raised mic pair and vice versa, the engineer must learn the arrangement and mute any mics that are not used as each take progresses. It also helps during takes if the engineer has a clear view of the player, who can give visual cues to indicate where he or she is headed next. Communication is the key, whether that be via printed charts or cue sheets, sightlines, or even a vocalist or roadie who knows the arrangements and cues the engineer in the control room.

If you decide to compress percussion tracks, the situation is a bit more complex. First, depending on how many percussions the player uses, it will be necessary to blend up to eight mics, selecting panning positions for each and sending the entire group through two identical compressors on the way to tape. This again underscores the importance of monitoring through the tape deck itself. Then, to ensure that various percussions are compressed as evenly as possible, the percussionist may have to adjust his normal rack setup so that each pair of mics receives about the same level from the instruments it covers. Although it is customary to tie the compressors to-

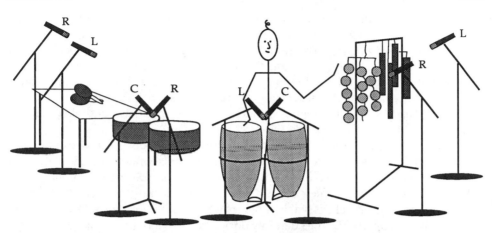

Figure 22.2. Four mic pairs for an elaborate percussion set-up: Two X-Y pairs on congas and timbales, with two highly directional spaced pairs for the percussion rack and assorted hand percussions, respectively. If the mics are mixed and distributed to two tape tracks as indicated (L, C, R,), the congas will be leftish, the timbales rightish, with the rack and hand percussions spread across the stereo field.

gether for proper stereo use, I find that leaving them untied helps keep individual percussion hits out front. After all, who is ever going to hear the percussion tracks soloed again?

Miking and Processing. Concerning mic selection, bear in mind that many rack and hand percussions create their sound by the combined action of between dozens and thousands of events—individual tambours clinking, beads shaking, and chimes ringing. If you want to emphasize the separateness of each event, choose condenser mics. For a smoother sound with more emphasis on texture, go with dynamics. Because of the similarity between congas, bongos, and timbales and their tom-tom cousins, I prefer 421Us, 441s, or their equivalents. Again, one mic is naturally bright; the others offer a treble boost switch. If you opt for an edgier condenser sound, be prepared to use internal pads. A loud conga player can generate over 130 dB at the mic position.

For rack and hand percussions, I generally reach for a pair of broad cardioid condensers, especially if I can get the mics back a couple of feet. No pads are necessary at this distance. But if percussions are played in the same room with the rhythm section, reach for the tightest super- or hypercardioids available, say RE-15s, using the internal low roll-off. These will probably need a high-end boost at the console but should provide good isolation, especially if aided by properly located baffles and even the felt cones, gobos, or "baffle-ettes" suggested for toms and hat. Of course, the percussionist must realize that these mics are directional and play all of his part directly on the mic's axis.

Be careful of audible overload at the input stage of the console. High-frequency peaks much over +3 dB may not look disastrous on meters but can push certain processing gear, not to mention recording tape, beyond its limits, leading to a crunching distortion that cannot be fixed in the mix. For that reason, check percussion levels with peak-reading meters, if available, and trim your console mic inputs enough so that the main faders for percussions are always at 0 dB (unity gain) or better. Then set tape levels so that the percussion that must be loudest in the final mix peaks highest, and so forth on down the line. It is best to record a short piece and play it back to test for distortion if you have any doubt. And just for kicks, see if these peaks are showing up as crosstalk in adjacent tracks. Tambourine that is audible on a bass guitar track will be no help during the mix.

Even if leakage is a mild problem while recording, I do not advise gating the percussion mics unless a single mic or pair of mics picks up much more leakage than the others. In this case, gate only the culprits, flooring the leakage down only to the leakage level in the other mics. Because the gate attack must be virtually instantaneous, any gate-opening clicks will be quite obvious once they appear. This problem is less likely to crop up if you gate mildly during record and again during mixdown, rather than applying one emergency gate job in either phase. Either way, it is not necessary to eliminate leakage totally between percussion notes. Set the threshold relatively low to ensure that all notes come through, and release long enough so that the gate operation is not too bothersome between adjacent notes in any percussion part.

Special Effects. It often helps to add some short reverb to percussion tracks during record, since this extends individual notes or hits, making them audible at lower mixdown volumes. In addition, by virtue of the transient nature of percussions, to get the same degree of "wetness" on percussion as on other instruments, it is usually necessary to send higher levels of them to reverbs during the mix. The result is that the percussion send level may overload the reverb inputs and/or generate noticeable springlike flutter echoes that interfere with the reverb on other instruments. Some prewetness added during record can obviate the need for high send levels or for a separate reverb unit to create reverb-soaked percussions. Regardless of where the reverb is added, keep your ears open for distortion, spring or digital fluttering, and other audio defects that often accompany steep transient inputs.

Unless you have a specific effect sound in mind for one percussion that will be blended in with many others on a mono or stereo pair of tracks, save flanging, chorusing, harmonizing, and the like for mixdown. As with many instruments, it is very difficult to predict the necessary kind and amount of an effect until you can hear the percussions in context with a finished instrumental and vocal blend. Too much of one effect will draw attention from the lead and create a parody of what was originally intended.

Concerning levels during mixdown, I find it helpful to decide which instruments the percussion tracks are most intended to support, decorate, or blend with. When your mix is built enough to include all these other elements, then it is time to add percussions and equalize them for proper impact. This can prevent you from going overboard on their level or equalization, a tendency that seems to set in when percussions are added last to the mix.

23

RECORDING "LIVE" ENSEMBLES, BANDS, AND ORCHESTRAS

S O far we have concentrated on the techniques of recording on multitrack, close-miking most or all of the instruments and vocalists. However, if you want to record an ensemble, band, or orchestra whose blend and sound onstage are fine, and whose performances derive excitement and energy from a high degree of communication between the conductor and various players, you should not submit to the audio dissection procedures described above. Do not presume that the requirements for good recording are at odds with whatever helps you perform. Perhaps it would be difficult or impossible to deliver the kind of controlled sound on each instrument that we have described above. But for your type of music, this sound may not be necessary, or even appropriate, especially for a group whose audience is used to hearing a unified live sound.

What you want in a recording studio, therefore, is the closest possible approximation to the best hall in which you ever performed, with plenty of square footage and studio height for good conductor sightlines and elbow room, risers or whatever staging you are used to having before a live audience, and an open, supportive acoustical environment in which every member of the band hears what he or she needs directly, without headphones, knowing the entire ensemble sounds wonderful to the mic in the proverbial tenth row.

Opt for a big studio with 2-track digital rather than 24 or 32 tracks, a live room rather than a dead one, and an engineer who has done live sound for large groups rather than lots of synth pop. Moreover, insist on working with few if any baffles between players or sections; place music stands wherever you need them. In short, choose a studio and engineer that meet your musical and human needs and will bend their equipment and techniques to give you the most natural sound available. Do not be bamboozled into working in an environment or under technical conditions that sap your enthusiasm and ability to put out a great performance. Then be willing to make a few compromises in the name of sound.

Recording a large ensemble is kind of like taking a fine black-and-white picture of a large landscape. The landscape may be lit by a single broad stroke of sunlight, yet, the visual contrast between objects facing the sun and those under a tree is very large. In life we may be able to distinguish shadow details, because each object has a unique color. In black and white, however, only the amount or level of light from each source registers on film. A medium green and red will be rendered as the same middle gray tone on the negative. Our colorful, three-dimensional reality is thus reduced to two dimensions on black-and-white film.

The photographer's job is to capture the essential unity of the entire view and do everything he can in the darkroom to reestablish the original separation and clarity among various objects. He can "dodge" the print, lightening one area of the picture by underexposure and darkening another by overexposure; he can select higher or lower contrast printing paper; or introduce intentional out-of-focus effects here but not there. All these efforts lead the viewer's eyes to the important parts of the original scene and reestablish among them something approaching their original emotional or pictorial weights and relationships.

Similarly, a big band has many instruments spanning a large physical area, with frequency outputs over the entire range of human hearing. Many of them, however, compete for clarity in the upper midrange. Some of these, by virtue of their unusual dynamics, attack, or overtone structure, easily capture a listener's ear. Others that might steal attention live because their players' movements are visible cannot be seen on tape, and thus get lost in the audio crowd. Thus, two three-dimensional experiences (sight and sound of the original performance) are reduced to one two-dimensional left/right stereo image on tape.

Clearly then, no simple two-mic recording can entirely reproduce the live experience. An engineer's first job is to find a single location from which to capture the essential scope and balance of the original (like selecting the right camera angle), then to select mics with the best sound and pickup pattern (analogous to lens focal length). Next the engineer needs to identify instruments overwhelmed by their competition, lost in the shadows of masking, or whose solos are not properly featured and highlight them with a touch of close miking and processing. Like the photographer, the engineer may have to control the overall contrast or dynamic range by subduing highlights or peaks with compression, rebalance various exposure or frequency ranges within the entire picture with equalization, and take hard edges off sounds intended to blend better with some reverb.

PRIMARY MIKING

The big factors in primary miking are studio size and low-frequency content in the music. At certain points in relatively small rooms, low-frequency nodes and anti-nodes produce uneven or unpredictable response. When recording a large ensemble in a small studio, do not use a spaced pair as primary mics. For an a cappella women's choir, whose lowest notes might be in the 200 Hz range, no problem. However, using spaced mics to record a big band with string bass or low brass would give them an insubstantial foundation. Unless a studio has 15-foot ceilings (height is usually the smallest dimension), or unless its floor area is large enough to really let you spread out, use coincident mics as primaries.

Within this category, the next question is how good the room itself sounds. If it is large but fairly dead or if it really does not sound very good, there is no sense in miking for ambience. Concentrate on the source itself by using an X-Y pair of cardioids, aimed between 35 and 60 degrees left or right of the center of the musical source (depending on how broad the cardioid pattern and how much room there is in front of the entire group).

How far you should set the mics from the group depends on how wide the entire group is. In general, the mics should not be much closer to the group than half a group-width. If the ensemble is 15' wide, suspend the mics 6 to 8' from the center of its first row and wrap the players into a mild arc. If the group is also relatively deep, say 12', move the mics a couple of feet farther back to make sure front-row players are not overemphasized in the blend.

If the studio ceiling height is 12 feet or greater, mount the mics a distance beneath the ceiling equivalent to the average height of players' instruments above the floor. For a standing choral group, hang the mics 5 1/2' below the ceiling; for seated winds, 3' or so (unless ambient room noise prevents distant miking). As explained in the woodwinds chapter, this relationship ensures that the distances by which the sound first reflects off the floor and ceiling to the mics is equal, minimizing the worst vertical phasing problems. However, if the ceiling is low, do not suspend mics closer than two feet from it, regardless of the bounce distances.

On the other hand, if the studio has a pleasant live quality, try an M-S (Middle-Side) mic setup. This setup requires one cardioid mic aimed at the group and a coincident bidirectional mic aimed perpendicular to the cardioid, with the dead axis of the bidirectional aimed at the center of the group. To record this pair properly, you will need an M-S matrix, a circuit explained earlier. The result will be a very natural, stereo with a feeling of space and plenty of ambience. The same source-to-mic distance relationships apply. If your engineer suggests a more exotic 2-mic configuration, set this up along with a simple X-Y configuration, using identical pairs of mics. Record a short take with each and choose the one that fits your music best. After all, it is only a 4-mic setup, not 14.

To choose between condensers or dynamics, first determine how tight a blend you want. Turn back to the miking discussions in the chapters on background vocals, woodwinds, and brass to review the alternatives. In general, though, the larger the group, the faster I reach for condensers. The mellower the music or deader the room,

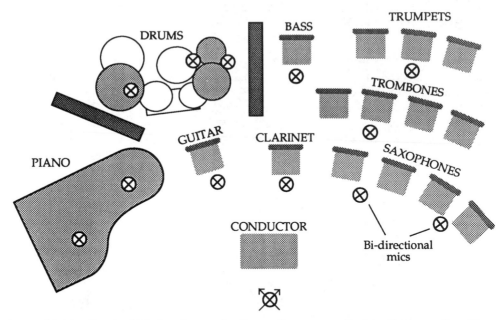

Figure 23.1A. Standard big band setup for live performance, miked for live recording. The main X-Y pair is behind the conductor, bi-directional fill mics are used on the saxes; cardioid spot mics are placed for clarinet, lead trumpet and trombone, piano, guitar, bass, with a spaced pair over the drums and spot mic on the snare. The only concession to the recording has been the placement of two 4' baffles near the drums to control leakage.

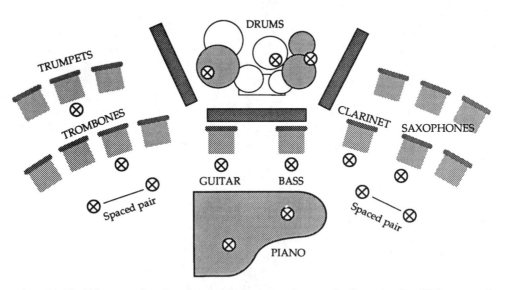

Figure 23.1B. The same band as they might be set up in a studio for recording. Using spaced pairs for brass, reeds, drums, and piano, with spot mics for brass soloists, clarinet, guitar, bass and snare.

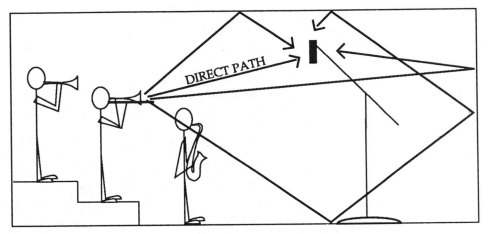

Figure 23.2. If the mic is placed at the same height as most of the players, there will be many symmetrical paths, causing uneven frequency response due to phasing problems and often leading to several distinct echoes that can be distracting. If the players are at several heights and none of them at mic levels (as shown), the increased number of path lengths will smooth out phasing problems and smear out the audible echoes better.

the brighter the condenser, and vice versa. On the other hand, for a small group that wants a very tight blend—no rough edges or solos—it is dynamics all the way.

REINFORCEMENT WITH CLOSE MICS

In a choir, soloists can step forward to approach a mic, but in most ensembles the players are firmly planted behind music stands. Because of this, be prepared to tight-mic solo instruments unless their solos can be heard clearly above the entire group. Obviously, check the individual chapters for miking techniques on each type of sound source. For starters, do not bother with heavy baffling, isolation, and signal processing. It is not worth the time and effort to fine-tune the close-mic signal if it will be used only to supplement the distant sound. Moreover, a close-miked instrument with full processing will stick out like a sore thumb from the natural blend provided by a stereo pair. Sonic consistency is more important than introducing a high-tech element here and there.

If the group is used to hearing bass through an amp, do not be talked into taking it direct. Performers need the musical foundation in order to emote properly, so go with the amp. However, to get a tighter sound and limit leakage, turn it down a bit lower than the group is used to, and thin out the sound a touch at the amp. Now close-mike the amp and equalize the lows back in at the console. If the group can live with less-than-normal bass level in the studio, the added bass tightness will unify and solidify the entire sound on tape. You could also take it direct and blend the amp and direct signals at the same time with no one the wiser.

Other instruments that may need close mics are piano, low winds and reeds,

French horn, and sometimes trombone. If these instruments are paired, use a bidirectional mic between each pair, rather than twice as many individual cardioid mics. Obviously, a lead vocalist will need separate miking too. To avoid band leakage into the vocal mic, use a super- or hypercardioid mic on the vocal, and have the vocalist(s) face the rest of the group, perhaps from directly across the studio, unless that ruins visual communication or makes the singer ill at ease. Only as a last resort would I put the vocalist in a separate room or booth. Certainly, the isolation would be better that way, but feel and performer comfort come first.

The only instrument you may have to isolate is the percussion. Did you ever notice how a tambourine, wood block, or triangle can overwhelm the level of a full symphony orchestra in a concert? The same will happen in the studio, especially with smaller ensembles. Short of placing the percussionist in a booth, have him play everything behind a chest-high baffle, making sure not to cut off his view of the conductor. If percussions still stand out, a booth it is. Sometimes just having the player inside the booth with the door open works better than setting up a separate booth mic. If the booth is behind or beside the rest of the group, you can use its door as the volume control, exactly as is indicated in some orchestral pieces by twentieth-century composers!

CONTROL ROOM DECISION MAKING

We have gone to great lengths to bring a natural stereo sound into the console, relying on a single pair of mics, a little reblocking of the group's onstage setup, minimal isolation, and a touch of close miking to burn in details just as a photographer does while making a print. If you are suspicious of a setup relying so little on signal processing, bring to the studio an LP or CD copy of a fine recording in your genre of music. A-B a section of this against a trial take of your own setup, and use your judgment to decide on equalization, compression, and artificial reverb. Nine times out of ten, this comparison will put to rest any fears of underengineering your tape.

This minimalistic approach is designed to get a large group organized and recording in the least possible setup time. The more people present, the easier it is to lose control and focus in the session. Anything that can be done to speed things up will result in higher player enthusiasm and more good takes, and it will save you a good chunk of time and money in the process. Setup time will be much less than for a fully tight-miked treatment. And if you record direct to 2-track, no overdubbing and mixing will be needed (or possible!).

On the average session, I estimate that this approach will cost between 30 and 40% of the more elaborate multitrack alternative, both in studio time and tape. If you are really hell-bent to spend some of the difference, go to the best studio around and record direct to 2-track. With jazz, gospel, vocal, classical, and other nonrock formats, and especially with the success of CDs, more and more labels are buying independently produced masters recorded direct to 2-track. For spontaneity, natural dynamics, and overall warmth, it just cannot be beat. What is more, critics and the public seem to agree!

24

SAMPLING LIVE SOUNDS

IN a few short years the technology of digital sampling has opened up a whole realm of musical creativity. Combined with the powerful sound-manipulation capabilities of current synthesizers, sampling has improved "traditional" sounds used in established genres such as rock and pop and invited the creation of new sounds that now color everything from jazz and classical to folk and ethnic genres. As with any new technology, however, sampling hardware has stolen the media spotlight from what, in my opinion, makes the process inspiring to musicians and appealing to music lovers at large—the collection and use of great samples.

PROCEDURES

A *sample* is basically a recording—usually a digital one—of any naturally occurring (in the loosest sense) sound or group of sounds of short duration. Because the recording is stored as data, there are many computer-based procedures by which the raw sample can be instantly accessed and varied through synthesizer keyboards and other controllers. Yet the underlying concept and procedures of digital sampling are analogous to those by which composers of *musique concrète* working in the 1950s (Varèse, Stockhausen, Dockstadter, et al.) manipulated samples recorded on short pieces of tape. A short list of these procedures includes:

1. *Instant playback* of the sample is triggered by a synthesizer key, sequencer, drum machine, pad, or other Go message. The speed at which data can be handled allows us to say Go as often as necessary, cycling instantly back to the beginning of the sample.

2. *Variable-speed playback* of the sample allows the control voltages of various synth keys to specify the playback speed of the data every time a new Go is

issued. If the original sample is assigned to a middle C on the keyboard, then the C above this (C2) will play the sample back at double speed, and it will sound one octave higher. Like a tape played at double speed, it will last only half as long, from attack through release.

3. *Portamento, breath, or pedal control* and other *manual variable speed devices* allow the player to change the envelope or bend the pitch of each playback for expressive control in exactly the same way that he or she can manipulate preset synth patches.

4. *Editing or trimming* can be done by examination of the sample's waveform on a CRT (oscilloscope) or other readout. Sections can then be edited out (hopefully without hearing the splices), either to shorten the envelope of the sound or to combine it with part or all of other samples.

5. *Looping* can be done by examination of the sample's waveform again, this time to join two points in its envelope so that the enclosed section repeats endlessly at a designated interval. Or we may find a section of its waveform that, if looped, gives the illusion that the sound's sustain continues as long as the triggering Go signal is held. The latter may be achieved by connecting attack/decay and release samples to the front and rear ends of a repeating sustain loop.

6. *Reversing the sound* can be accomplished by simply playing the sequence of digital data backward, perhaps in combination with other procedures above.

7. *Mixing or blending samples* occurs when using analog and/or digital equipment to combine two or more individual samples into a new one. With the right equipment, the operator can continuously vary the level of each component—its dynamic range (via compression and gating), equalization, and all normal recording parameters—and even add reverb or ambiences to mask the combining process or change the composite sample's quality. Most current top-end sampling systems provide visual software that allows most of these operations to be conducted entirely in the digital domain.

How you intend to manipulate samples should govern how you record them in the first place. Some of the operations just mentioned can highlight flaws in the way the original sample is recorded. And because many samples have to be made on location and thus in less than ideal recording environments, it is important to think about various techniques for getting what you want in the field, applying whatever processing is necessary to optimize the best and hide the worst in each sample and thinking creatively about how real life can provide raw material for your musical imagination.

As with any recorded sound, the raw material you take for a sample contains three elements:

1. The direct sound of the instrument, voice, or effect you want, as it might sound in an anechoic (acoustically dead) chamber. If the sample is electronically derived, as from a synth patch, the direct sound is the patch.

2. The acoustic response of the place in which you are taking the sample—its resonances, reverb, and rattling in response to the direct sound. For elec-

tronic sources, this may include any internal imbalances in response or intentionally added modifications to the basic patch.

3. Ambient sound of the space itself, including noise from heating systems, nearby traffic, hums and buzzes from fluorescent lights, and the like. Electronically, we are talking about noise in all its ugly forms.

Our ears are both selective and optimistic. When you hear proposed samples live, you tend to focus on the first element, and ignore those portions of the latter two elements that you do not want. This is an extension of the so-called cocktail party effect, which enables listeners to focus on one voice in a crowd. A mic or DI is far less selective: if you do not ensure that it picks up only the desired portions of the entire sound, the sample will be unusable when you get back to the studio.

SAMPLING SUGGESTIONS AND PRECAUTIONS

Problem 1. When a sample is sped up (played at a higher pitch), all three components are raised. Even if the direct sound works when raised or lowered on octave (the sample does not fail via helium or Mickey Mouse syndrome), the room resonances and the ambient noise may sound very artificial at the new pitch. In general, the more you raise or lower the sample's pitch, the more you will notice these as separate components. This will also give away the fact that you are using a single sample over a broad keyboard range, thereby cheapening the effect.

A solution is to make sure you get as much direct sound as possible. Tight mike, noise gate, and destructively process the sample until all undesirable parts are gone. You can always add a little reverb or other clean, artificial ambience in a second generation, but you cannot take natural reverb and ambiences away. If the natural sound is available over a wide range, take at least three raw samples, one each near the bottom and top of its range, and another in the range you anticipate using most frequently. This gives you a record of how the sound's natural overtones (timbre) and envelope vary through its range.

If you later decide to use a higher or lower pitch, make a blend of two samples that work best in the range you finally decide to use, again adding reverb and ambience during this process. Or if your sampler/synth combo allows split keyboard use, assign each of the three (or more) samples to different key ranges, so that a single performance over a wide pitch range sounds relatively natural.

Problem 2. For editing purposes, it is crucial that the envelope of your raw sample be complete and that ambient noise be low in comparison to the peak signal. Just as undesirable parts of a sound become more obvious with pitch changes, they also stand out when they stop instantly, as when you release a keystroke when playing the sample. (Gated reverb, for example, sounds very artificial when heard in solo.) The exact difference in level (S/N ratio) necessary to avoid this problem depends on the kind of sound.

Again, one solution for any type of musical sound sample is for the sustain of its envelope to be at least 40 dB above ambient or system noise. An organ pipe or any nontransient continuous sound is quite usable when you have miked it such that the room sound is 40 dB below its "speaking" or sustained level. A sampled harpsi-chord, with steep transients, may be unusable with less than 60 dB between its peaks and the room ambience. Obviously, the more going on in the arrangement of a song, the less you will notice background noise in a sampled sound. But the next time you use the same sample might be in a very open, quiet piece, where its ambience is quite obtrusive. This holds true for musical and nonmusical samples.

Problem 3.   For looping of continuous sounds, record a long enough sample that any fluctuations in the level or tone of the raw sample are not heard as timed repeats in the looped version. Except for organ pipes, almost every acoustic instru-ment has some change of level and/or tone in the sustain portion of its envelope. Suppose you wish to loop one note on a vibraphone, prolonging the sustain indefi-nitely. Even if you hold the level of a fading note perfectly steady for several seconds by gain riding, the higher overtones decay faster than the fundamental. When looped, the looped sample will get brighter at the beginning of each repeat.

I suggest you blend a forward and backward example of the same sound, so that the reverse envelope, with its reversed shift in frequency content, counteracts the normal changes, producing a constant level and tone over an extended period of time. You can loop this section of the sound and connect it to the vibe transient saved above. It may take some trial and error to determine the right timing for the forward/backward overlap, but this should provide a long enough section of constant volume and tone to make a usable seamless loop. If there is still a noticeable click or disconti-nuity at the splice point, try adding a little reverb to the forward and backward sounds while resampling the composite.

In addition to its advantages for sequencing parts and improving the quality of sounds, sound sampling can help you save studio time. A sample that needs to be fully processed every time you use it is a time waster. You may think, "Ah, I've got a digitally recorded kick drum sample," but if it needs to be destructively eq'd, gated, compressed, and final eq'd every time you use it, the fact that it is digital will not matter a fig or save a buck.

For this reason, spend a little studio time at the end of your demo and mastering sessions to generate properly miked and fully processed samples for later use. When taking samples on location, at least use the right type of mic, position it correctly, and take the sample at the highest possible level, with as much high end as you can find. Then, keeping the original sample for future modifications, make a processed copy in the studio, storing that directly back to digital again. Now you have something to call up instantly, knowing it needs little work. In essence, once you have invested in sampling hardware, invest some time and money in your own unique software.

If you do a lot of live sampling, let me suggest that you put together a kit consist-ing of two inexpensive and bright-sounding cardioid mics: a dynamic and a con-denser. With their low roll-off and crisp response curves, the Sennheiser MD421U or 441 and Sony ECM 23 are fine choices. You should also have one good DI—the Axe, Countryman, or equivalent—along with a set of balanced low-impedance XLR and low-capacitance 1/4" and/or RCA cables to prevent high-frequency loss when deriving samples from electronic sources. Of course, if you want to generate stereo samples, you will need two of everything. Total price is about $800 per channel, tops. Not cheap, but much more economical than investing in the synths and sampling devices that store and manipulate the data.

Be careful before investing in a portable digital recording system of one kind or another, perhaps a DAT machine. Consumer devices are not cheap, and most of them become obsolete almost as fast as they hit the marketplace. At least for now, it makes no sense to recommend specific models of samples, synthesizers, or control and triggering devices. To date there have been no enduring standards in the marketplace.

Part IV

MOLDING, SHAPING, AND PACKAGING THE SONG BEFORE AND AFTER RECORDING

25

THE MIXDOWN

T HE seeds of a good mix are sown while planning and recording every instrument and sound on a multitrack tape. Mixdown is simply the last step in the ongoing production process. Some topics discussed in earlier chapters may be left for decisions during the mix: the dramatic role of various instruments, the emotional effect of different approaches to reverb or stereo imaging. In other chapters, notably those on bass, piano, and lead vocal, considerable space was devoted to specific mixing techniques. Looking ahead this way enabled you to view recording as a unified thought process rather than a series of unrelated artistic and technical operations, each pursued according to its own standards of excellence.

As you read on, refer back to the earlier material to bring the new material into focus, and reflect on how your studio chops have evolved in the intervening pages. Then, as new topics and techniques come up, look ahead to the survey of great sounds in Appendix A. Nearly every subject discussed in this volume is demonstrated brilliantly on one or more of those classic recordings. If the producer's job is to find what the artist has in common with the audience, all good producers must approach their jobs in essentially the same way. After all, audiences are people, and—notwithstanding rumors to the contrary—so are musicians and producers!

THE ROUGH MIX

Mixing is easily my favorite part of every session. If recording can be likened to shopping for a dinner, then mixing is certainly cooking the meal. The processes really are very similar. A good cook has the entire dinner planned out (arranging, programming, rehearsing for a session); finds all the right ingredients; cleans, chops, and prepares them for cooking (laying all tracks—basics, overdubs, sweetening); and then begins to cook. Similarly, you cannot concoct a good mix without the right building blocks, though I must admit that last-minute surgery can be fun—filling in where the tune needs a line, effect, or "event."

On the other hand, the mix will tell you how well you made all your musical and engineering decisions on the tracks. In a lot of ways, you never really know if the overall tempo is right for the song, if the individual sounds on which you lavished so much time and energy work well together, or if the musical material and quality of the performance is clear, strong, and unified enough to convey a central thought or emotion until you hear all the parts together during mixdown.

Mixing also reminds me of assembling a jigsaw puzzle. Blank multitrack tape is the surface on which a musical painting is realized. Supplying the mixdown engineer with the musical contents of dozens of separate tracks is similar to handling that painting in pieces of all sizes and shapes. Somewhere in the tune he may find pieces missing, moments where the music itself needs reinforcement or help. These he fills in with reverb, delays, effects, editing—every trick in the book or a few made up for the occasion. The finished tape, however, must be a complete picture. Today's listeners are used to a high level of artistry in sound engineering; they expect every source to be clearly recorded and set in an audio space that immediately establishes the song's mood.

The Purpose of the Tape.   Who are you making this tape for? Is it for booking agents to help secure live gigs or an A&R person at a major label to encourage a signing? For yourself to work on an arrangement in preparation for a master tape? Or is this the master—the pass/fail product that will entice radio programmers, dance floor dj's and, of course, the buying public? In any case, whether your budget is in the quick demo or master range, your goal is the same: to create a strong impression on a first listening and the desire to hear the finished tape repeatedly. The key words here are *first listening*.

Most people hearing a new recording for the first time retain very little of it even if they like it. They may recall the tempo, feel, central emotion, perhaps a part of the chorus or lyric, a fill, or a rhythmic phrase or two. But few listeners are professional musicians who instinctively analyze everything they hear. Few play their stereos at studio volumes or have studio-quality systems in their living rooms, and most living room acoustics are not conducive to careful listening. So the question in planning a mix is, What elements of this tape/song *must* come across on a *first* listening?

This kind of thinking leads one to an architectural approach to mixing, one that stresses foundation, structure, and decoration. If it offends some readers to impose a formula on the mixing process, bear with me. When learning to play an instrument, you have to build a toolkit for your trade—scales, chords, and exercises. Next you gain confidence by learning techniques that help express your style and musical goals, and so on. Similarly, good craftsmanship in mixing is an achievement that will ensure your tapes get the best possible first-listening reaction. Artistry in decorating a cake has little use if the cake itself falls over. The greatest reward in the studio is knowing that you did what you set out to do and that it works!

As Daniel Lazerus remarked in a recent interview,

I really see mixes like paintings framed between the two speakers. What I try to do is get a left-to-right panorama of that painting, but also create a three-dimensional feeling—as though you could almost walk into the mix and grasp a specific sound. It's a matter of using a lot of properly controlled echo and delay: those are the elements that allow a lot of dimensionality, like a guitar that's here, with its echo over here [begins pointing in various directions]. A vocal that has its echo over here, plus a delay that's sitting over here . . . things like that make the mix "breathe."

[When starting a mix], I build all the foreground elements first. The kinds of things that have spins and spirals are built on after the foreground parts, which shouldn't be washed out or lost—bass guitar, in particular, is something that can readily be lost as the mix builds. . . .

I generally use a snare drum to check all my effects, because it's a regular, strong beat. I like to use three EMT plates—left, right, and center—and I make sure that they are balanced, decaying in the same time, and sound similar.

I start going for my drums dry—eq'ing them in solo mode; same with the bass, guitar, and keyboards. Then I'll put up a mix with drums and bass, and start to add echo. . . .

Even the drums might have certain effects, but I add those before I continue. As far as setting delays and echo decays, to me that all depends on the drum sound. I'll solo whatever is the smallest increment of time on the track—usually it's the hi-hat rhythm—and use that in setting delays. I'll listen to the return of the delay on the lead vocal and make sure that it's just disappearing perfectly with the hi-hat. . . . On many of my mixes there are as many as seven or eight very different delays.

Ordering Mix Time (and Budget) Priorities.   In most rock, pop, R&B, country and western, and related records, four or five elements constitute the foundation and structure, that part of the record that sticks on a first listening:

Lead Voice

Main rhythm instrument(s) or "bed" sound

------- Drums ---- Bass -------

This simple graphic layout demonstrates several important relationships. First, the sonic weight of drums and bass really is the foundation of the record. Each should have equal power in its own role and a roughly equal ability to attract the listener's attention at certain moments.

Second, the lead vocal or instrument should ride above the foundation. Not a single note should be obscured by the foundation when the overall blend of these three is right. If there is any argument about what ambience or reverb is right for the record, choose the one that best reinforces the lyric or emotion in the lead. Finally, there is usually one or perhaps one pair of rhythm instruments that establishes the feel of the tune and that, along with the lead, determines the structure of the tape. Certainly every player's part is important, but in most tunes we must admit that there is one instrument without which the whole feel just crumbles.

When mixing a budget demo, spend most of your time getting sounds on the tape and blending these few elements. If these do not work, the tape probably will not get a second listening. On a really tight budget, or if the levels of foundation and structure need continuous attention during the mix, go so far as to rough-blend everything else—all the decorations—to one pair of buses. Compress this whole sub-mix, and bring it back into the console on a single pair of faders just to make sure none of it grabs attention from foreground elements.

Rough mixing is both a challenge and, in its own way, an art, a little like writing haikus or penning a quick portrait of a friend. Almost any 24-track tape that is decently recorded should be rough mixable in 90 minutes or less, especially when the engineer knows the contents of each track. The pressure of having to capture the essence of the song keeps you focused on one goal and prevents you from spending an excessive amount of time on any detail or sound. Then, too, the rough mix, taken home and played for innocent bystanders, can tell you exactly what is needed in the final mix. Moreover, a good rough mix serves as a psychological safety net. So many times I have spent four to six hours perfecting the sounds in a final mix only to find that the rough mix had better overall energy or feel.

This experience can be very frustrating, but it tells the mixer that the necessary elements are there, as long as there is consistent focus on the right goals. When a final mix gets too polished, or if you just go overboard with processing, clear the entire console and start again. The final mix is no good if it is not better than the rough. But since every final mix starts as a rough, let us think about overall parameters and the right order in which to deal with them.

Drums and the Audio Stage.   You should first determine how crowded the finished "stage" will be and where you should place the major players and singers. This requires a decision on which perspective the listener should experience—the players' or the audience's. We touched on this in chapter 12, which focuses on drums. Drummers hear the hi-hat on their left; the kick, snare, and rack toms fairly well centered; the floor tom(s) to the right; the crash cymbal on the left; and the ride on the right. All these sounds are spread out around the drummer in very broad stereo.

To a live audience, on the other hand, the entire kit occupies a small L/R space. Within this space, hi-hat is toward the right and floor toms a little left. Before processing anything, bring all your drums tracks up and select the right position and breadth for the kit. The overhead tracks contain some of all the drums and should indicate accurate left-to-right positions for every drum and cymbal. Once you have positioned the overheads, pan the individual drum tracks to the same position each occupies in the overhead image. If you decide to position the entire drum set left or right of center, make sure the kick and snare are centered on the overheads with no individual drum track outside the stereo overhead image.

To make full use of both stereo channels to maximize drum punch, it is conventional in rock to spread the drums out symmetrically around a centered kick and snare. That does not mean you have to separate rack and floor toms hard left and right. This dissects the kit, making it as wide as your entire stage, bigger than life. On the other hand, for a jazz ensemble, why not put the entire drum kit a little right or left of center, occupying a third of the apparent stage? That is the way listeners are used to hearing jazz live. You might as well give them a familiar setting on tape.

Defining the Weight and Space of the Mix.   In most of today's "chart-bound" records, drums are the loudest instrument. Their sound establishes the overall weight of the song, and their interaction with reverb and ambiences indicates the type of acoustic and emotional space in which the artist wishes to place the listener. Often, if the weight and space of the song are familiar, the listener will mentally place the song in correct musical genre without knowing the lyrics or hearing any leads. This reference point invites closer listening.

Up-tempo pop records, for example, traditionally have a light drum sound. The

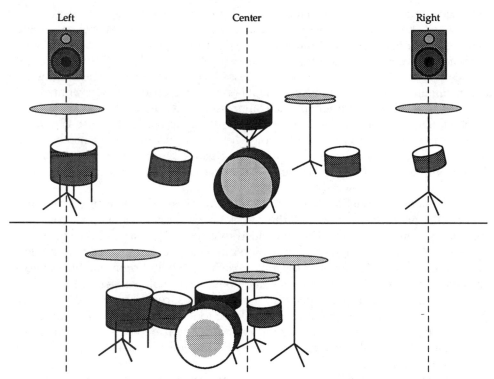

Figure 25.1.   The left/right stereo soundstage, with a drumkit (top) spread out as is common in rock recordings, and (bottom) condensed and placed left of center, for a realistic representation of a live performance on stage.

primary sound goal of the record is to project well from small speakers at low volume in mono. Although AM radio and network television are now converting to stereo, the continued prevalence of mono television receivers and next-room listening means that mono is still an important mixing consideration. For this reason, and because small speakers in reverberant rooms tend to smear details in a recording, tracks for pop records are highly noise-gated and mixed brighter in the upper midrange than are records intended for critical home listening or FM broadcast. Any sense of real space is unimportant; it's "radio space" that counts.

Heavy metal, at the other end of the rock spectrum, depends on high drama, Wagnerian dynamics, and effects. Average metal listeners crank their home or car systems up high and can therefore hear musical details more clearly than pop listeners. As a result, heavy metal uses thicker sounds and textures and less noise gating (which in turn preserves the kit or ensemble feel among the drums or several guitar and vocal parts) than pop. This approach allows us to place the music in a large, reverberant space that is heroic in proportions and reminiscent of the major halls and arenas that are the true home of metal.

Beyond musical space, there is also what I call "record space" to consider. Listeners may not realize it, but years of hearing music on radio, television, vinyl records, and analog cassettes have subtly taught them that recorded music is compressed music. Most all the recorded music they hear is subjected to fast-attack, slow-release compression or hard limiting. Compression keeps record grooves to a safe maximum width and prevents radio and television transmitters from clipping. In addition, it enables the overall level that is broadcast, pressed, or "cassett-ified" to be maximized, thereby minimizing any awareness of the inherent noise problems in each medium.

The fact is that most listeners like compression and miss it when it is not there. For the trained audiophile, compression makes listening harder because it reduces musical dynamics, but to the average home listener, it makes hearing much easier. One of the original complaints about the high dynamic range of CDs was due to the lack of compression. On some classical discs, one is continually turning soft passages up and loud passages down.

For a demo or rough, either compress the entire mix or patch stereo compressors into the monitor buses, even if the 2-track tape itself is made without compression. Heavy compression can later be added to a second-generation dub made for cassette duplication, and lighter compression can be added when acetates and/or lacquer masters are cut. For greatest flexibility, patch the left and right mix buses into a matched pair of the best compressors in the house, tie the units together for tandem operation, and set the attack to between 3 ms and 5 ms, release to about 2 seconds, and ratio to 6:1 or higher. Input level should be tone-set so that a 0 dBVU tone just nicks threshold. Since the actual amount of compression depends on the mix bus levels, adjust them so that average levels in your music cause perhaps 3 dB of gain reduction by the meter.

If you want the compression to go to tape, patch the compressor into the 2-track mixdown recorder and set the compressor output levels so that the recorder gets the same level it would without the compressor patched in at all. If not, bring the outputs of the compressors back into the console at another line input in the control room monitor section. You can now set the compressor outputs so that the listening level remains fairly constant when you switch from the uncompressed mix buses to the compressed signal. Remember that the higher the mix level in the console, the more gain reduction will be applied by the compressors. Thus, for levels continuously above 0 VU, you may have to increase the compressor output levels to get a fair A-B level comparison.

Adding Effects to Drums.   There are as many "right" drum sounds as there are songs or recording artists. For rock/pop/R&B, however, I equalize and balance the kick, snare, and hi-hat (including the overhead tracks) so that—before adding heavy effects—they seem equally audible in their respective ranges (bass, midrange, and treble) on studio monitors and Auratone minicubes. Pay no attention to their relative meter levels; concentrate only on how easily the kick, snare, and hat catch the ear. Spend just a few minutes roughing in the backbone of the drum set. Do not labor over each sound. To determine the starting level to tape, set kick and snare no higher than 0 dBVU or +10 peak, depending on your metering. Note these benchmark levels and do not let everything creep up as the mix proceeds.

Now is the time to add some reverb or ambience. With so many choices of digital reverb programs, you can spend or waste a lot of time adjusting fine parameters. But for now, select the general amount and type of reverb that sets the proper emotional space for the entire mix. For a rock ballad, perhaps a bright hall is appropriate, 3 to 4 seconds reverb time with a predelay that equals a 16th note in the song's tempo. As suggested earlier, set reverb level by listening to the Auratones in mono. Apply the reverb to the snare track first, then put enough on overhead and hi-hat tracks to smooth out rough edges. Kick drum? For metal, add at least a touch of reverb; for other genres, let it go for now. If just enough reverb on Auratones seems like too much in stereo on large studio monitors, leave it for a while to get used to it, then reduce the level if it still annoys.

If adding the toms tracks dilutes the punch or edge on the snare and kick, reach for noise gates and reduce the noise floor just enough to restore the loss. It is not necessary to eliminate snare or kick leakage on these tracks completely. As during record, 20 dB of extra separation via gate is usually plenty. And because tom-toms have more natural sustain, it often takes a bit of extra reverb on them to make them play nicely with the reverb. Moreover, the reverb from off-center toms will pull the ear across the stereo image.

Next add in the bass. In general, bass level and eq should be such that on small speakers it carries at least the same audio weight as the kick drum and such that kicks can be heard clearly through simultaneous bass notes. For rock the bass is generally centered left to right. However, if you move the drums off center in one direction to imply a stage location, balance them with the bass on the opposite side. If the bass is heard alone in the tune, even briefly, a touch of reverb will put the bass player in the same room with everyone else. Or if you prefer a dry bass for the body of the song, reverb can be added only in "solo" sections—if you remember it later.

The Equal-Loudness Curves. In Part I we saw that the human ear has different frequency response at various listening levels. To reinforce the importance of monitoring at reasonable levels, consider these three curves (part of a series known as *Fletcher-Munson* or *Equal-Loudness Curves*):

Each curve in figure 25.2 shows the volume level at which different frequencies sound equal in volume to 1 kHz heard at a known level. To match the level of 1 kHz heard at 70 dB (bottom solid curve), a 40 Hz tone has to be played at 90 dB (20 dB louder than 1 kHz), a 7 kHz tone at 77 dB. At that listening volume, therefore, the low notes of a bass guitar registering 0 dB on the VU or peak meter will sound about as loud as a flute registering at −20 dB.

Now look up to the 110 dB curve, which corresponds to the onstage level of an average rock band in a small club. The 40-Hz tone now has to be played only 10 dB louder to sound equal to the 1 kHz tone at 110 dB. Our ears thus have a flatter response at high volumes than low volumes. This means that if you set relative mix levels when monitoring at 110 dB, bass and kick drum will seem relatively weak when the tape is played at lower levels. A 70 dB listening level is rather modest when you consider that the average AT&T desk phone (bell set to low) produces 75 dB at 3 feet and a canister vacuum cleaner produces at least 90 dB when you stand next to it. And yet 80 dB is well above the average home listening level for most music.

The solution involves compromising on levels and equalization. In general, I set the level of low-frequency instruments while listening in the 80 dB range, then adjust their equalization so that at 100 dB they are not overly ponderous. This may involve dipping the deep bass a little, boosting the midrange a bit (500 Hz to 2 kHz),

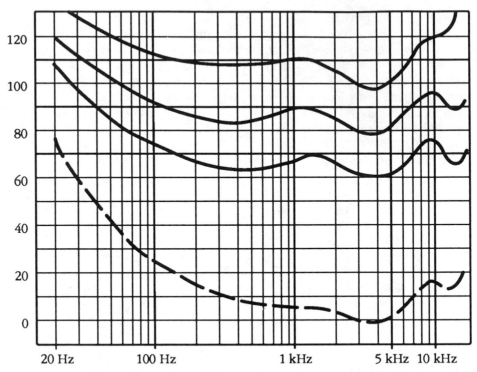

Figure 25.2. Three of the Fletcher-Munson Equal Loudness Curves, referenced to a 1 kHz tone at 70 dB, 90 dB and 110 dB SPL (sound pressure level). The dashed line represents the threshold of hearing, i.e., the level necessary at each frequency for the average listener to hear it at all, even in a totally silent room (anechoic chamber).

or both. If the overall level of the instrument is affected by the boosting, reset this at the lower volume again. To a lesser extent the same is true of real highs (such as percussion and vocal sibilants). Set their mix level while monitoring modestly, then adjust eq at a higher volume to make sure they are not spitty or harsh.

   Lead Vocal or Instrument. What qualities make for a commanding lead sound? Weight, clarity, and crispness (sounds like an ad for wine). All too often vocals are eq'd for clarity and crispness only. Boosting the mid and high frequencies will increase intelligibility (as you can see in the equal-loudness curves, the ear is most sensitive to frequencies around 3 kHz anyway). However, when the resulting vocal sound is properly mixed with the bass and drums, it will not "push air" or have enough fullth to grab attention from foundation sounds. Thus it is very important to give the vocal proper weight.

   Make sure you do not lose now what you did to capture weight or chest tone when laying tracks. Keeping that weight may involve boosting midbass a touch or dipping a broad midrange band to feature weight and intelligibility. A vocal track that has plenty of weight when soloed may sound quite thin when mixed with a snare track to which you have added lots of low-mids. If the best obtainable vocal sound still does not compete with the snare for attention, dip some midrange in the snare rather than altering or thinning out the vocal sound.

On the other end of the spectrum, crispness makes the difference between easy intelligibility and tough listening. It is the complement to weight, the very highest highs in the lead part and just beyond. The airiness of a flute, sibilances of a voice, highest partials of a trumpet or sax: each lead has a unique, high frequency range. This range should be hot enough to stand out clearly above any other sounds at these frequencies. For example, vocal sibilances (8 kHz and up) should be right up there in level with the hi-hat or ride cymbal. The air of the flute solo should cut through the combined rosin tone of a full string orchestra. That is one reason I recommend boosting this range when you cut tracks. Another reason is that boosting it during the mix adds tape noise.

Use additional compression on the lead only if, when its loudest notes or words are in proper balance with the foundation, some of its softest sections are masked or lost. Even then, I prefer riding vocal or lead gain during the mix to compressing. Now add reverb to the lead, setting reverb level via small mono speakers. Even good reverb can muddy up the clarity range a bit, and if it does, eq the reverb returns to reduce the conflict. Or if you really like the lead and reverb sounds but still lose low-level syllables or notes, increase the compression on the lead a touch.

In any case, once you have pretty final drums/bass/lead sounds and balance—a blend that sounds equally good on small and large speakers at medium and high volume—mark your fader levels and eqs. A major goal from now on is not to make major changes in these settings. Work everything else in around this core, processing each added track so that it serves its functions without detracting from the drums/bass/lead unit. It is these core sounds by which most listeners will judge the overall quality of the recording. A less-than-ideal piano, synth, or guitar sound is less of a problem than you might think, since the home listener will never hear these instruments soloed. Your compromises will be well hidden by the mix itself.

Adding the Key Rhythm Track(s). Everything we have done so far is basically mono. In rock, the kick, snare, bass, and lead instrument are usually centered, with only the overhead mics and reverb returns in stereo. Rhythm instruments give you a chance to really define the width of the soundstage. Presuming that one guitar and piano define the rhythm and density of the arrangement, start by splitting these broadly around the lead. If the piano was recorded stereo, you need not spread it full left and right. A left-to-center spread will give the piano 50% of the entire field and a more definite image. Then place the guitar opposite to this, center-right, for example.

For a starting eq on rhythm tracks, solo the guitar and lead vocal and push the guitar level up until it starts to distract your attention. With a parametric equalizer boosting a 1/2-octave band, sweep through the midrange from 300 Hz to 3 kHz and locate the range that conflicts most with the lead or obscures lyrics. Now dip this band as much and as broadly as is necessary to refocus your attention solidly on the lead. Then boost the eq'd guitar level to make sure it will not interfere, even when you push it higher than it will ever be needed in the mix. You may not be in love with the resulting soloed guitar sound, but the song needs this sound for unity. Finally, adjust low- and high-frequency guitar eq for the proper weight and bite.

Repeat the same process with the piano. Listening in mono at a low volume, set the overall levels of the guitar and piano against the drums/bass/lead, and add enough reverb to put them in the same space. If the guitar and piano (or whatever your key rhythm tracks are) do not provide enough support, compression may be necessary. For now, just note the problem until more rhythm tracks are added.

Now check the compressed mix against the straight version. If the addition of lead and rhythms is causing too much compression, simply lower the master fader, which feeds the compressor inputs. However, if the master is down more than 6 dBs and the stereo levels are still too hot, reduce each module fader by 6 dBs and bring the master back up. Otherwise, you may overload the console's output stage and engender electronic distortion.

Compression should add punch and unify the entire blend without crowding the lead vocal or instrument. If the compression clearly helps, use it; if its effect is minimal, inaudible or detrimental, eliminate it. Whichever you choose, tape a verse/chorus section of the tune at this stage. If the mix gets too crowded or confused later, the taped section can help restore proper order and musical perspective.

This entire procedure should take no more than an hour. In most cases, the whole song will work well and make its point in this skeletal version. If not, no amount of added tracks, decoration, and fancy processing will save it. To complete a quick and effective rough mix, return to an earlier suggestion: take the remaining rhythm tracks (such as synth pads and additional guitars, plus winds, strings, and brass) out of mixdown status by removing them from the mix buses. Submix these to two channels or output buses, spreading them out for a balanced stereo stage and applying a quick single-band eq to any tracks with a problem frequency range. Then run this submix through stereo compressors to clip off high transients, and bring their outputs back into the mix through two new faders. Add reverb to this submix here, rather than at the original faders from each tape track.

You should now be able to run a rough mix with three fingers: one on the lead vocal fader and two on the submix faders. Ride the submix up between lyrics or at any point where a dramatic crescendo is needed; ride it down wherever the lead needs space. Together, these tracks can be used like a painter's brush, to dab a little color in between foreground objects, to splash in a momentary highlight, or to punctuate an important lyric or musical event. You will not be featuring every riff and fill that you may need in a final mix. The important thing now is to capture the overall build, energy, and feel of the song in a single pass. This will force you to make the song work via the music, rather than the engineering. When you later tackle a final mix, the rough will remind you that a great feel is both achievable and more important than any individual sound or effect on which you may fritter away lots of mixing time and money. Humberto Gatica, in an interview in *Recording Engineer/Producer,* revealed some things about his mixing technique that support this advice.

When I mix, I literally create a picture in my mind; I see things like placement and depth. . . . I begin to create my balance, and determine how the rhythm parts should blend. I begin to put this instrument against another, to create maybe one solid rhythm part. But then if you want to separate them aurally in the mix, you can. It's a marriage of the individual parts into one flowing piece.

If you take the last ten albums I've done, there is a consistent overall concept. But there are also very different types of approach to match the specific musical concept. If it's a rock album, I have a lot of ways to get into a "punch" concept. And if it is an R&B project, the choice of eq will be different. I record vocals in ways that match the type of music by choosing mics that suit the particular characteristics of whatever style we're working with. For example, I don't want to have a beautiful concept album with some strange, heavy digital effect on the vocals.

Even though I have a strong background in the technical aspects of recording, I am not a technical engineer or producer. I like to do things by instinct. I pull [effects] out only for specific reasons. Using outboard gear wisely, and only when it's effective for the record, is one of the secrets of a good mix.

I hear the lead vocal being right in the center of the mix, and up front, but it must have a depth to it. What helps me most with that aspect is the EMT 250 Digital Reverb. I can dial in a very short reverb time so that it sounds like a perfect resonance in a normal room—a natural room sound. On top of that I use a short echo. Actually, there is plenty of echo, but it disappears very fast. I want just enough echo for some depth— a third dimension—but not so much that it will run into the background vocals that are making the line behind it.

Background vocals are two distinct signals. I can achieve the effect of a full wall of sound by running them through a stereo Eventide H949 Harmonizer. The vocal track on the left is set a little flat a 99.6% pitch shift, and the signal on the right has a slight delay of 20 or 21 ms. This creates the illusion that they are connected by a solid line, yet you can hear them as two separate tracks. It makes the vocals very "thick". . . .

If I want to separate them [lead and backgrounds] to make two distinct parts, I increase the delay to 25 ms on the left, and 45 ms on the right vocals in the back. In essence, it's like telling the singers to step back a few paces, and sing their parts from there. There's a slight ambient kind of sound on the track that detaches the two vocal parts. . . . I like distance and clarity together. Less lows and more highs seems to achieve that.

Acoustic piano works well up front—dry with no effects—and positioned as though it were being viewed from the audience. I mike the piano towards the center with two mics about one foot apart, and about one foot above the strings. The bass mic is angled about 30 degrees, while the treble mic is facing straight down. This technique gives me the capability of spreading the piano out across the entire front of the stereo spectrum. I'll pan only the acoustic piano and strings to the 7:00 and 5:00 positions [full left and right]; any tighter and the acoustic piano will start to sound mono.

Rhythm guitar fills the space between about 9:00 and 3:00. A lead guitar, sax or synths fits well just to the left or right of center—never in the middle. That's only a personal preference. I like to keep the lead instrument at least a short distance from the bass and central drums.

I've worked with a number of producers who look at the board and tell me the settings don't look right. I try to remind them that where the knobs are doesn't mean a thing. If the music sounds right and feels right, it is right.

PROBLEM-SOLVING TECHNIQUES

Before continuing I must note that you cannot mix according to a formula. What I have presented so far is just one possible approach. Many engineers and producers have entirely different procedures and techniques; some attack each mix differently, with no routine or starting points. There is no right way to mix; whatever gets the results you want is right. However, you can learn a lot by considering at least one ground-up approach. Next we will investigate some proven techniques for saving time, ensuring mix quality, and cooking up a few of the more popular sounds used in past and present chart toppers.

Mixing is a lot like filmmaking. Good directors do not ask audiences to react to each shot; they command, using every artistic and technical tool at their disposal to force an intense physical and mental reaction to the scene. This sounds manipulative, and it is. Consider a scene in a thriller: husband and wife are having dinner at home with no apparent tension and pleasant conversation ... but the director wants the audience to realize the scene will end in tragedy. How to make the audience sweat? Subdued warm lighting suffuses the dinner table, but the knife on the meat platter in the foreground catches a glint of bluish streetlight from the adjacent window. As the camera pans and tilts with the wife bringing things to the table, the foreground knife is always there—a third character that commands the audience's attention and establishes a threatening mood. As dinner conversation heats up to accusations of unfaithfulness, the knife begins to dominate the screen. When the wife reaches for it suddenly, all hearts skip a beat as ... she carves another slice of lamb. False alarm! The audience wipes its brow.

The moral for mixing is: Be manipulative, aggressive, decisive, unsubtle, even hoaky if necessary, but make sure there is a good dramatic or emotional reason for every effect you use. Make sure each effect gets the listener reaction you want. Ride gain on the vocals to make sure every word is clear; push fills and musical hooks right up front. Do whatever it takes to keep a verbal, musical, rhythmic, or purely dramatic element (like a sudden stop) in the foreground continuously. Most important, listeners—booking agents, A&R people, club owners, or radio programmers—give you only one chance to make your point on tape. A strong reaction, even a negative one, is better than a shrug.

In dramatic terms, try to mix so that you get a balance of two listener reactions: *aah!* and *oh! Aah* indicates satisfaction; once the opening sounds of your tape identify its genre, go for an aah until that genre is completely established. The basic structure of most pop tunes (intro, verse, chorus, verse, chorus, bridge or solo, chorus, and repeat) and the standard blues chord progression are both aah devices. So are the wall of sound in heavy metal and the gated snare in current synth and hard rock.

Oh indicates surprise (pleasant, we hope!). Oh devices include editing out half the second verse of a pop tune to get to the chorus quicker, adding extra beats to prolong a turnaround between sections of a tune, inserting a key change between choruses, and adding sound effects to paint the situation or emotions described in the lyric. These are all legitimate methods of preventing listener boredom or complacency or misunderstanding of what the song is about, dramatically or emotionally.

Of course, if you have not built ohs into your taped arrangement, there are two solutions: edit down the song until the aahs alone carry it, or create dramatic events during the mix by muting and unmuting drums, soloing fills, hooks, or adding perhaps just the tambourine for two beats and a repeat to an important note or word. There is nothing sacred about an onstage arrangement if it does not work on tape.

Each medium has its own strengths and weaknesses, and many's the master tape that was saved by the razor blade.

In my experience, few studio engineers are formally trained in composition and arranging or in psychoacoustics. As different as these subjects may appear, they share many of the same goals. The arranger learns the capabilities of each instrument and a wide variety of methods for using instruments to achieve different moods, emotions, or impacts on a client's audience. The psychoacoustician learns how various sounds, studio techniques, acoustical environments, and their interactions affect the mood or psychological state of listeners. Insomuch as music is a subset of all sounds, both jobs really have the same goal: control of a listener's attention, pulse, heartbeat, desires, and emotions.

The engineer who thinks the job stops at making "good" recordings of individual sounds and ensembles denies that every twist of an equalizer has an emotional impact on the listener. And yet most clients confine their mixing requests to piecemeal technical operations: "Can we brighten the kick drum, fatten the guitar sound?" If asked to help convey a specific emotion or mood, the engineer might have dozens of ideas to make the listener tap his toes, or bring a tear to the eye. A good engineer can sharpen your arranging skills and bring to bear his or her grasp of studio pshchoacoustics—if you ask. Otherwise, you are only getting half of what you are paying for!

It is impossible to list every correlation between studio processing and listener emotions. In addition, there are many procedures and effects that can have opposite results in different musical contexts. We can, however, demonstrate the kind of thinking by which pure engineering techniques can solve the most common recording problems. Again, as in cooking, once you develop the nose and toolkit for reliable results, the rest is a matter of experience.

Problem 1.   Let us assume that you have done a good job writing, arranging, and performing your music in the studio, but the tape still lacks the right energy. First, determine where it lacks energy. Is it consistently sluggish, from the intro straight through, or does it just need a lift in the choruses? You really have to dissect things this way, because there is only one way to fit the jigsaw puzzle together, namely with all the pieces in hand.

Low energy is often a result of the inherent difference between multitrack recording and live performance or even rehearsal. When playing live you hear everything at once; in the studio you focus first on rhythm instruments, then overdubs (often one at a time), and then vocals. Live, you instinctively feel the right timing for fills and know how loud to play them and when to add a tambourine hit. The constructivist, building-block approach of multitrack works against unity of performance and puts each overdubber in the spotlight. On top of this, each sound is usually processed for its own quality, not how it blends with the full ensemble. There is no unifying audio treatment to suggest the performance could have been a real, live take.

A possible solution is to add compression on the whole mix (but not the kind applied to prevent overload). Done properly, this submits the entire group to one unified processing and implies an all-at-once feel. Furthermore, by proper setting of attack and release times, you may be able to lift the energy level or change the rhythmic emphasis to a number of ends.

Suppose you have a midtempo rock or dance tune that needs heavier backbeat feel to get people out on the floor. Boosting the snare track will not shift the entire band's feel. The real problem is how to modify the envelope of the whole arrangement from 1–3 rhythmic emphasis to a heavier 2–4 feel. Even better would be to create a slight anticipation of each 2 and 4 for added drive. Let us play a bit with the completed rough mix.

The kick (on 1 and 3) has a slower attack than the snare, so that fast-attack compression will be more noticeable on the snare than on kick. We really want the opposite, so use a slow attack (10 ms or higher). Furthermore, to compress kick more than snare, feed the compressor's keying input with an equalized version of the mix, boosting where the kick is loudest, at perhaps 70 Hz. Now we are compressing beats 1–3 more than 2–4. To get the bouncy anticipation of 2–4, we want the compressor to release almost fully after each 1 and 3, allowing 2 and 4 through at full level. Set the release to about 0.8 second and you have it.

The music will seem to surf on the compress/release cycle, bouncing off 1 and 3 and taking a big breath going into 2 and 4. In addition, the very pumping of the compressor will lend a physical quality to the mix that just was not there before. Such simple techniques will not resurrect a dead performance or pull a sloppy one together, but they can certainly give some edge to an overly careful performance on tape.

What if you already considered and rejected this make-it-sound-like-a-record compression? Remember that recording is illusion, and compromise! You owe it to your music to make it as appealing as possible. No one will care about sound quality if the tape does not grab ears and emotions or make people dance.

Problem 2.   Let's assume that your recorded performance has good energy overall but does not build and subside from verse to chorus and back—it just sits there for 3 minutes. This time we have to look for something internal to the mix that can be emphasized or used to lift the choruses. Obviously, we could mute one or more instruments during the verses and bring them in during choruses. But if after trying this, the verses seem empty, what should you do short of adding some new tracks?

A possible solution is to double or quadruple the time-feel of one or more tracks or instruments during choruses. If this suggestion seems to come from left field, consider how what I call time-feel is an energy-defining parameter.

Suppose our midtempo rocker is paced at 120 beats (quarter notes) per minute and that the drummer plays 8th-note hi-hat through the whole tune. Eighth-note time-feel thus predominates. Even if the rhythm chords and bass part are busier in choruses, the hi-hat puts a lid on the energy level of the whole tune. With this lid on, the song may seem to slow down when added instruments crowd in during the choruses. Musical weight, therefore, does not increase apparent tempo; it reduces tempo.

The human brain takes tempo cues more from purely rhythmic sounds, even subtle ones, than musical ones. Thus, the first thing to try is a digital delay on the hi-hat, creating extra hits between each 8th note played. This delay will not only seem to accelerate the tune; it can actually change its basic feel depending on the delay time selected. At 120 BPM each quarter note equals 1/120 of a minute, that is, half a second or 500 milliseconds. Consequently, an 8th note equals 250 milliseconds. Straight 16ths will result from a 125-ms delay time applied to the hat. Even a touch of this will lift the apparent tempo and energy without changing the basic rock feel.

Suppose, however, that the lyric is about a tension and release situation—for example, the verses pose a lover's dilemma and the choruses reveal his hoped-for solution. Certainly the choruses demand a more lilting feel, not just more speed. Instead of straight 16ths, go for a triplet 8th feel with a delay of around 170 ms (2/3 of 250 ms). Since the middle 8th of each triplet is omitted, the whole chorus takes on a carefree bounce that is more akin to skipping than running.

You have a whole range of feels available with a twist of the delay time control. Up around 200 ms (with a song tempo at 120 BPM) results in a lightheaded, giddy feel that may help reinforce a lyric here and there. Below 125 ms the delay will begin to add a nervous quality. At 63 ms (a 32nd note at this tempo) each hi-hat tap will be sonically underlined, giving a confident, emphatic feel that is great in small doses. And by bringing the delay back into the mix via a second module, you can vary the balance of the delay versus direct sound in different parts of the song.

Going a step further, delays can paint or imply dramatic motifs not contained in the lyric or arrangement. For example, time is a driving force in many tense human situations, and as every movie director knows, the sound of a clock makes an audience nervous. We can create the audio image of a clock by panning the 8th note hi-hat and its 16th note delay to right-center and left-center of the mix, respectively. The result is a stereo left-right tick-tock feel that can make listeners subliminally nervous. In addition, each repeat is at a precise, metronomic 125-ms interval, far more clocklike than any drummer could play a continuous 16th note part in real time.

In a slow ballad, another dramatic imaging technique involves generating the feeling that the singer is alone in a vast emotional abyss. How can you do this without just piling on reverb? Paint a sonic canyon with one or more rhythmic elements or musical phrases ricocheting left and right off its distant, granite walls. Use two aux send channels to deliver signals to a stereo tape delay (or two DDLs capable of perhaps 500 ms of delay with full frequency response). Bring these delays back in to the console on a pair of modules and split them hard left/right in the mix. Now feed the snare (always good for a ricochet) into the first delay and send the return of that (via the corresponding aux send on its own module) into the second delay. To keep this going, feed the second delay back into the first via its aux send, as diagrammed in figure 25.3.

If the snare plays rim shots on 2 and 4 of each measure, each shot will originate in the center, then repeat left-right-left-right as though bouncing off ever-receding mountains. The volume of each repeat and how long the series continues can be adjusted by the relative aux send and return fader levels of each delay channel. The effect can be used continuously or just where the lyric is meant to send a chill up the listener's spine. Or you might send one or two important words of the lyric through the same setup. Every module of the board has the same aux sends, so you have instant canyon or loneliness at the twist of a rotary pot.

The delay interval you choose can reinforce many different emotions. For a lyric that expresses confusion or isolation, choose a nonrhythmic delay time. The seeming randomness of the repeats will confirm the lack of order in the singer's environment. If it is one of those look-at-me-now lyrics, a straight quarter-note delay time will give

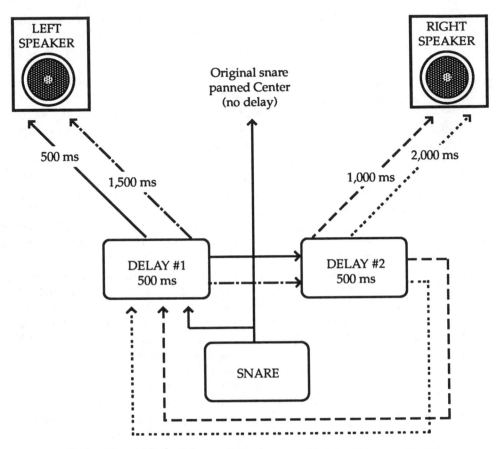

Figure 25.3.   Block diagram of the stereo multi-delay "canyon effect."

the impression of a mirror image on each delayed sound. Of course, in a happier song, the random delay time might imply a playful state of mind, the rhythmic delay a tendency toward conformance.

Suppose we decide our rock tune needs 16th-note feel for the choruses and 32nds for a few 2-measure turnarounds, but we want quarter-note hat for the first verse, perhaps to give a more labored feel or suggest dogged determination. The 32nds can be created with a 65-ms delay and regeneration for added repeats between each real hit, but how to eliminate every other hat hit to come up with quarter notes? Run the hi-hat through a noise gate with the floor or range set very low (− 50 dB), attack set to 100 ms, and the release time set to 300 ms. The 100-ms attack will let one tap through, then shut down for 300 ms, lowering the next tap by 50 dB. This way, every other hit is attenuated by 50 dB. If you really wanted to get baroque, you might add triplet 8ths by putting a 335-ms delay on the output of the gate. By this time you should consider bouncing all these changes to a clean track so you do not have to worry about the hat during the actual mix.

By the way, whatever works on the hi-hat can be used continuously on a tambourine, shaker, snare, a percussive rhythm guitar track, or even a lead vocal (as artists have been proving since Buddy Holly's day), and intermittently on everything from kick drum to sound effects from a Three Stooges film. It is just a matter of how much lift the tune needs in each section and whether it needs the added dramatic weight of musical delays and repeats in addition to purely rhythmic ones.

Problem 3. Suppose our tune has a track of sustained synth chords that supports the vocals well and acts as a pad but does not have much dynamics. It might be nice if there were a second track of the same sound with syncopated, staccato accent chords at the same pitch or an octave higher (similar to "second touch" in certain synthesizers). This would definitely give one or another section a distinctive bounce. No need to record this; we can create it fictitiously.

Find some sound in the tape that happens regularly at or just before the point in each measure where you want these accents. For simplicity, suppose you want the new chords on the second eighth note of each measure, and the kick drum happens right on each upbeat. Perfect—we can use the kick drum to key open a noise gate and let the sound we want through. First, patch a multiple of the synth chords into a noise gate and set its attack very fast and floor or range very low. Now make a multiple of the kick track and send it into a delay line. If the song tempo is 120 BPM, 250 ms still equals one 8th note. Delay the duplicate kick 250 ms and send it into the key input of the synth gate, adjusting its threshold so that the gate opens at each kick hit.

Now we have synth chord accents beginning at the right spot. The hold and/or fade controls of the gate can be used to set the length of each accent and its release. Moreover, the resulting accents can be placed anywhere left to right in the mix or given separate reverb treatment. And if we want the accents up an octave, simply run the original synth multiple through a harmonizer before processing.

Perhaps this effect is too regular, and what you would really like is to add these accents as fills here and there between certain lyrics and in varying rhythms. Simple enough, but it will take a spare track. Set up a mic and have someone tap or beat the rhythm you want, recording the taps onto the spare track. Now use this track instead of the duplicate kick to drive the keying input of the gate on the synth multiple. The rhythm can be as complex as necessary as long as you do not exceed the ability of the gate to open and shut in response to each tap. This process will only take a couple of minutes and is much quicker than recording a new synth track to do the same thing, perhaps less accurately.

Of course we are not really triggering events here, just allowing something that is happening silently (the synth) to be heard on human cues delivered via the gate. What can be done today with the entire range of synth-triggering devices and MIDI control is in another league and beyond the scope of this book. Yet an artist who does not base his or her sound on MIDI'd synths may not have, or know how to use, synths for the few studio tricks needed. Instead, learn to think creatively and be resourceful with traditional studio gear. And if you need a certain effect but do not know how to get it, ask your engineer.

Gating on reverb and ambiences can create a whole range of emotionally charged spaces. The most familiar of these effects is gated reverb on the snare, created by assigning the snare a separate reverb unit, setting a fairly long reverb time, and

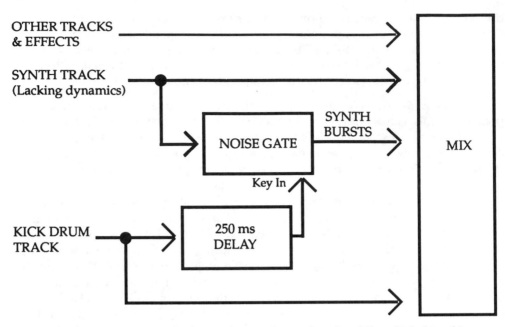

Figure 25.4.   Block diagram for keying bursts of a synth pad to follow kick drum hits, as described above.

bringing the returns back into the mix through a noise gate. Turn the return up high enough so that it seems to sustain the impact of the drum, then set the noise gate to close completely (− 70 dB floor or range) about 200 ms after each snare hit. The effect can be made even more explosive by eq'ing the reverb to match closely the sound of the drum itself. Used dry on a slower tune, this gives a very mysterious, threatening feel to the snare. Or adding normal reverb on the gated reverb and a lower gating time, you can just use the gated snare for a thunderous sound on straight hard rock.

Of course there are variations on these effects. One is to bring the gated reverb back into the mix in mono for some parts of the song and use stereo for others, or even pan the gating back and forth behind the snare. The eye and brain will follow something as prominent as the gated reverb, chasing it from left to right. Use whatever effect supports the song's lyrics or underlying emotion.

Try predelaying the snare reverb. The reverb will seem to ricochet and then cut off instantly with the gate. By adjusting the predelay time to an interval equal to a 32nd or 16th note in the song, you can speed up the apparent tempo of the song. Setting the predelay to a triplet 16th interval, you will add a bouncy, almost reggae feel to the snare itself. It is amazing how one trick can alter the feel of the entire tune. (Draw a mini flow chart or patching diagram for each of these examples. Doing so will help you understand them, and give you ideas for other potentially useful setups.)

Suppose now that you need a liquid ambience for a certain song to illustrate insecurity portrayed in the lyric, to get a weepy feeling, or just for a weird audio space. Try flanging or chorusing the reverb send(s). The result gives the impression that the room is swirling or pulsating around the music. If you want the effect only on specific sounds, use a separate reverb for these, flanging its input(s) and sending only selected notes or words. For an even stranger space, flange or chorus the reverb returns (an effect suggested earlier to thicken strings). Used slowly and lightly, this effect will charge the mix with eeriness; the space around the music will seem to breathe as if alive.

Remember that there are basically two reasons to use such studio-manufactured tricks: either they fit the lyric, emotion or style of your song, or you need something to cover up a musical or performance weakness. The song might work without such tricks, though effects themselves can help drive a point home. However, even when an effect is used cosmetically, it should still relate to the song's lyrical or emotional message. Without such a connection, the effect will weaken the underlying performance. In the end, you cannot rely on effects to save a bad tape. With so many basically good tapes on managers' and record company desks, you would be wise to spend your money on more and better takes of your tunes, then apply effects sparingly.

26

PRODUCING RECORDS AND TAPES

P*RODUCED BY* may be the most sought-after and least understood credit in the English language, at least to people in music. Having produced hit records is a sign of power and glory, as well as communion both with musical artists and their public, not to mention a lucrative way of making a living. And yet there is no uniform, inclusive definition for the artistic contribution of a producer. Even in the business or organizational sense, a producer may have total control or be completely outside the planning and budgeting phase of the record, depending on who hires him and how and when he becomes involved with the specific project. For purposes of sanity, let us examine a typical major-label scenario in which the A&R person, having signed a new artist, hires someone to produce the album.

THE TRADITIONAL RELATIONSHIP BETWEEN PRODUCER, LABEL, AND ARTIST

In most cases, the selected producer brings three primary ingredients to this project. First, he has already made critically and/or commercially successful music for the market in which the label hopes to launch the artist—the dance market, metal, or country. Within this market, he is known either as a purist or pop producer. Every label hopes a new artist's record will cross over to the pop charts, but the basic goal is to get the artist clearly established in one market or genre. This will bring name recognition and a following on which to build future hits aimed more and more toward the Top 100.

318

Second, the label looks to the producer to help the artist hone his or her reper-
toire down to a group of songs that demonstrate a central recurring theme, feel, or
style with just enough material apart from this to give an indication of future musical
directions. No matter which songs the label picks as singles, radio DJs and their listening audience often react more strongly to an album cut that is slightly off center of
the group's primary sound or genre. The producer's role here is to help the artist put
out feelers to test a number of markets that are right next door.

Lastly, the label wants a producer who can fill in any gaps or inexperience that
it perceives in the artist. If the artist has not done much recording, the producer
should be able to organize, schedule, and book the sessions, work with the artist to
develop arrangements or modify existing ones, and keep the artist focused on making
music in an unfamiliar studio environment, rather than worrying about the technical
aspects of the project. On the other hand, if the artist is overprepared studio-wise or
has artistic tunnel vision, the producer must be able to dislodge the artist's preconceptions and realign them with the label's expectations for the finished product.

An artist whose goals are already close to what the label has in mind does not
need much active production, just someone to keep the energy level up and the
whole project on budget. Some producers, however, want a say in every note played
or sung. While labels do try to hire producers who can work with artists in a relationship of mutual respect, the bottom line is that the producer is the label's legal agent
for the sessions whose word is final on all creative matters. Producer and artist are
employees commissioned to create a product on which the label will be happy to
spend even more money in the release and promotion phases.

Certainly, there are cases where the label hires a producer for name value. Radio
DJs are more likely to give a known producer's work a spin; critics are more likely
to review it. Or the project may demand a producer known for strong business control of his projects—for dealing with unions, publishers, arrangers, and other creative
"suppliers" in a time- and cost-efficient manner. Whatever the selected producer' cre-
dentials and abilities, a major label will pay him between $12,000 and $20,000 to turn
in a finished, headed-for-the-charts album. A big name will get more, or a project
entailing special mixes for dance markets, videos, and the like.

This same fee level applies to any major label product that may have the ability
to cross over into the pop album charts. However, fees paid to the producer of an
authentic country, a dance-only, blues, or main-line jazz artist will be scaled down in
proportion to the lesser potential market for the finished album. From $5,000 to
$10,000 is normal here, depending on the artist's stature and the complexity of the
whole process. Of course, even the larger "indie" (independent) labels cannot pay
such fees. Here, producers' fees for a new rock artist might be in the $3,000 to $6,000
range, lower for dance and other nonpop product.

The key to all these deals is points and options. No producer worth his salt will
put hundreds of hours into a project unless future royalties are likely to make up the
difference between the upfront fee and the real value of production time and effort.
As you know, producer royalty rates on major label projects vary between 5 and 7%
of the adjusted wholesale receipts, with royalty payments beginning before or, at latest, at the artist's breakeven point in units sold. Any legitimate producer you contact
will quote in this range. And he may ask to be named producer on one or more future

albums unless the releasing label chooses someone else. For a complete discussion of such business topics, refer to the companion volume, *Sound Advice: The Musician's Guide to the Record Industry.*

Do You Need a Producer for Self-Financed Masters?   The simple and definitive answer to this question is yes! A producer is just as essential on a self-financed master tape as on one a record label has commissioned. The reason is that, above all, a producer's job is to bring out and reinforce what the artist's music and personality have in common with the audience. Some artists immediately assume this means selling out—searching for the lowest common denominator between their music and public taste. ("Let's see, the average rock hit has a tempo of 128, a kick drum sound boosted at 2 kHz, Aphex Aural Exciter on the lead vocal, so . . .") With a good producer, this is certainly not the case.

Music is a very basic form of emotional expression and communication. Whether dance or Gregorian chant, music invites listeners to participate in a physical, intellectual, or a ritual act that reinforces something important, and perhaps central, to their enjoyment of or frustration with life itself and of the society in which they live. Every musical artist tries to share some common human experience. The classical musician demonstrates that he and the audience are made of the same emotional stuff that ruled the lives of the great composers. The same is true of the blues guitarist, the rock drummer, synthesizer programmer, or lead vocalist. Each uses his or her medium and toolkit to share and celebrate (or lament) a part of what it is to be human. However, once an artist gives his emotions vent by writing a new song, he or she may become more interested in the musical or technical details of how it sounds. Here the producer's job is to ensure that every chord and delay line still express the emotion that first inspired the song.

OBSTACLES IN THE RELATIONSHIP BETWEEN ARTIST AND AUDIENCE

In some cases, emotions actually prevent artists from looking clearly and objectively at their own work. More specifically, emotions divert attention from the crucial balance between the whole and the parts. You are no doubt familiar with the temptation not to like your own performances unless they are technically perfect. Yet would the average listener call the tiny imperfections that bother you mistakes? Probably not, except in classical music, where a listener might actually follow along with the printed score. The rock or pop listener recognizes out-and-out clams but would have no idea that you played a note, line, or passage in a way you did not intend or plan.

Moreover, many artists feel that the notes alone, if properly played, will deliver the same emotion to a listener that the artist feels while writing or playing them. However, audiences do not listen to music like musicians, searching for the important lines, analyzing rhythms, lyrics or sounds. I venture to say that most audiences hear music rather than listen to it. Then too, there's so much free music around that listeners are saturated and spoiled, responding only to those records whose personality or complete image grabs their ear and commands, "Feel this way!" Only after submitting to the gut power of the record will the listener look for lyrics, lines, or sounds that support his or her instinctive reactions with a rational basis.

These days, our society places high value on tactile musical experiences: those that surround and physically move us (such as the high-decibel level of rock concerts or discos) or those that tickle the neurons of our inner ears (like digital sound itself). The same is true of sounds that soothe body and nerves (e.g., new age and other textural music, which a friend recently described as "the hot tub I can't afford") and those that bring us to the edge of our seats to admire or participate in an intricate, three-dimensional reality. Here we can cite the best of current jazz and conceptual rock pieces by artists from the Police to Paul Simon and the fabulous synth renderings of Bach by Wendy Carlos.

In a world that offers performing artists an infinite variety of tools—from digital guitar effects and hundreds of different sax mouthpieces to breath-controlled MIDI keyboard racks—it is easy for artists to become fixated on making ideal sounds with their instruments or voice. No music seems possible without achieving this first. Since few can afford the ultimate in current technology, many musicians give up on reaching an audience. However, as with the performance mistakes, the audience does not know what sound you have in mind. If the sound you choose conveys the basic emotion you feel, mass audiences are quite content to accept and buy that sound, state of the art or not!

Another factor that keeps musicians and their audience separated is too much hanging out with other musicians. Rather than focusing energy on what can be done, musicians often reinforce each other's justifications for failure. "I could really wail with that new processor!" says one. "Man, it's all over the new record by so-and-so . . ." responds the next. Better yet, in response to an A&R person asking what kind of music is on a demo being submitted, I have heard many artists reply: "It's only 8 tracks, but you'll get the idea, I hope." As if the only important thing about the demo is the technical limitations endured while recording it.

THE PRODUCER'S ROLE

Clearly, a producer has to minimize the effect of all these distractions on the finished product. First, the producer must force the artist, if necessary, to identify what the music is intended to communicate; what aspects of the material and performance achieve this; and what aspects need help. Do not forget that A&R people are people first. No artist is signed until the label feels that he or she can speak heart to heart with humanity.

Second, the producer ensures that every detail of the recording—notes, performance, and sound—makes the same emotional statement and that there is no moment on tape when the audience loses sight of, or interest in, this statement. Some artists work best with producers who verbalize or interpret every detail of their performance. For example, the producer might say, "This guitar sound is too sleazy," or, "The way you sing that phrase does not capture the tragedy in the lyric!" Other artists prefer not to pin literal meanings on such details and respond better to producers who present suggestions without the verbiage. Here again, the producer must adopt whatever mode of communication elicits the artist's best efforts.

Then, the producer may have to convince the artist of the need to overstate his case. Just as many chefs tend to underspice a dish because they know exactly what went into it, an artist may think his guitar sound, the amount of delay or reverb on this or that track, and the extent of bent notes or overall schmalz level of his performance is blatantly obvious or embarrassingly melodramatic when in fact the audience is barely aware of each of these factors.

Remember: you are an entertainer first. Your audience and label expect you—in fact pay you—to take risks, to stand up there, onstage or in the studio, and expose your deepest feelings without reserve. In turn, you encourage the audience to do the same—perhaps quietly at home, where no one can see them dancing around like maniacs; perhaps in the anonymity of a crowd, where everyone expects unbridled enthusiasm from the nameless person in the next seat. Few people call something art until it is bigger than life. Why buy a record if it is just more of what life feels like every day?

A good producer also keeps you thinking objectively, showing in a nonjudgmental way what everything about your recording means, or fails to mean, to the audience. In addition, he or she is like the host at a good party who plans ahead to put each guest in the mood to enjoy a common experience and makes sure nothing that happens during the party derails that experience. Some guests know ahead what kind of party is planned and come dressed, physically and mentally, for it. Others may have had a bad day and need a lot of help to find the right mood. Still others may simply be too timid or modest to let loose and enjoy the party.

As host, the producer must know what is being recorded in each session and plan so that each player is at the right energy level and in the right state of mind for the specific song. If an argument with a spouse or a towed van keeps one of the players from the right mood, the producer must talk those problems away. For sessions where a down mood is needed, he has to create it, even if everybody in the group just won the lottery. Or if the lyric demands more anger than the singer can muster, the producer may have to provoke an argument to put him or her on edge! Whatever emotion the song calls for, it is the producer's obligation to make sure the whole group is there, together, as though their combined performances were the work of one human being whose heart is on his sleeve.

Here is what Phil Ramone says about the purpose of a producer:

My working knowledge of the studio and my techniques are of little value unless I can stimulate the artist and combine our two talents to bring out the music. As a producer, I must be a highly receptive and objective viewer and I must be knowledgeable of the artist's potential.

The word "producer" is really misleading terminology. It is more a job of directing—the flow, the song, the talent—into an area that can bring about the best musical sounds and a certain amount of comfort in the studio. The musicians *have to* feel comfortable in order to play.

Only the producer, artists and a few others know how, where and what went on during the recording. And that's the way I like it. It's the privacy that I think is so important to the artist, because it [the session itself] is the most tender and creative time in his life. Care should be taken not to take the artist into an embarrassing situation. After all, there would be no producer if there was no artist.

HOW TO SEARCH FOR AND FIND A PRODUCER

The first hurdle is admitting that you honestly need a producer, and that is a matter of deciding to let another person join your creative effort on an equal footing with an opinion you will value as highly, or even higher, than your own. The issue is not whom you can trust, but more fundamentally, whether you can trust at all.

If your ability to trust allows you to work with a producer, then a love of your own material will help you select the right one. Your own ability to say what your music is about will bounce back at you larger than life from the right producer. The producer not only understands what you are saying but will enlarge your own view of your material or performing abilities. A producer is not a yes man to your musical whim but someone who can relate your abilities to those of other artists in the same market—past and present—and make you aware of strengths and weaknesses that you just cannot deny.

Furthermore, the producer may bring out things you have in common with completely different artists or types of music. This kind of collaborator can divert your attention from the lesser objective of self-expression to the ultimate target of shaking up the average listener's mind! Short of this kind of input from a prospective producer, I would only consider him or her if you honestly do not know how to get from here to a master tape and are willing to entrust your artistic life to an expert. This in itself is a sign of strength, not weakness, in your artistic vision.

Consider for a moment that even the wealthiest person hires an architect to build a dream house. Clients may have a good idea for the basic layout or look, but only an architect can design a house that stands up; relay exact specifications and techniques to the contractor who, after all, has to bang the nails and solder the pipes; and give the clients a good idea of what the finished house will actually cost. The architect asks the client a million questions about life-style, tastes, budget, habits, and foibles, plans for family, at-home work, and recreation. In the end, however, the architect must simply be trusted and allowed to design the client's future home.

A well-designed house can surprise the clients with how much the architect knows about them. Similarly, the finely produced master tape will show the artist depths or details of an emotion that were hidden before the producer's help arrived. The tape can be a map, suggesting future creative routes for the artist. It should also encourage the artist to reach for goals he or she may never have considered possible.

[For Quincy Jones, the relationship between artist and producer is] a very personal relationship that lets the love come through. Being on the other side of the glass is a very funny position—you're the traffic director of another person's soul. If it's blind faith, there's no end to how high you can reach musically....

There are two schools of producing. The first necessitates that you totally reinforce the artist's musical aspirations. The other school is akin to being a film director who would like the right to pick the material. As to what production style I adopt, your observations and perceptions [of the artist] have to be very keen. You have to be able to crawl into that artist and feel every side of their personality to see how many degrees they have to it, and what their limitations are.

[Then] you have to dig down really to where you think the holes are in that artist's past career. I'll say to myself "I've never heard him sing this kind of song, or express that kind of emotion." Once you obtain an abstract concept or direction, it's good to talk about it with the artist to see what his feelings are, and if you're on the right track. In essence, I help an artist discover more of himself.

[Quincy Jones also reveals how he works with musicians to get good sound to tape:] I like to work out in the room with each player, running the chart down and guiding the feel of the tune. We will usually run it down once, then I'll get behind the glass to hear the balance and what's coming through the monitor speakers. Once I get the foundation of the tune on tape, and know it's solid and right, it is easy for me to lay in other elements to the song. It's the song itself that's the MOST important element we're dealing with.

Bruce [Swedien] is very careful with the bass and vocals, and we try to put the signal through as little electronics as possible. In some cases we bypass the console altogether and go direct into the tape machine. Any processing, in effect, is some form of signal degradation, but you are making up for it by adding some other quality you feel is necessary—we always think of these considerations.

Lots of times we'll avoid using voltage-controlled amplifiers because there will be less signal coloration. Also, if possible we avoid using equalization. Our rule is to be careful and pay close attention to signal quality.

THE PRODUCER'S COMPENSATION

Paying producers is tough for artists working on low-budget masters. However, if you find a producer you can trust and who thinks a collaboration may lead to a label deal and ultimate financial success, don't hesitate to propose a spec deal. If you can secure a commitment from a recording studio to front all or part of the time needed or give you a great deal on a block booking, so much the better. This puts you more in the owner's seat.

In my opinion, you will only get the best from a producer if you pay him, at least partially, while you are recording. After all, if he does not have legal ownership of the tapes, the producer's effort will only bring a return if you follow through and get the tapes sold and released. It is thus necessary to draw up a separate agreement that specifies the following:

1. The total dollar amount of the producer's fee or payment(s)
2. What part of this total you will pay before and during production and on completion of the tapes
3. On what date or under what circumstances you will pay the balance of the total
4. When and how often any subsequent earnings will be paid.

When a label acquires the masters, and when the balance of the producer's fee can in fact be paid, it is best to have the label pay his future royalties directly. That takes the burden of accounting and payment off your shoulders.

What if the current tapes cannot be sold but serve only as demos that enable you to be signed to a label? Does this producer have any rights in that case? Do you owe him part or all of the balance of his deferment upon such a signing? Yes, but a reduced amount, perhaps the balance of half the total fee he might have received if the tapes he produced were bought and released. However, if both you and the label want the same producer to continue producing when the label signs you, the simplest thing is to wipe out your whole starting deal with the producer at that point, forget the remaining deferment, and let all his future payments come from the label's recording budget, as if you had been signed first.

Last but not least, should this producer receive any part of the publishing rights and/or royalties in the tunes to which he "adds value" by virtue of his production? In my opinion, the answer is yes if he agrees to deferred payment of most of his total fee. What percent of the publishing? Never more than 50%, and perhaps a maximum of 25% unless he brings studio time or backing to the project. Under no circumstances should he have administration of the copyrights, unless it is only through his resources that the recordings are made at all.

Concerning actual producer's fees, you should never pay anywhere near what a major label might for a producer's services. Where $15,000 would be a healthy producer's fee for a rock album produced on label funds, I would propose an up-front payment of no more than a quarter to a third of this amount, with the balance of the agreed-upon total deferred until first monies from a master purchase. If you spend a total of 200 hours in rehearsal, recording, and mixdown, a $4,000 fee averages out to $20 per hour. No legitimate name will work for less than this without getting a piece of publishing, then only if he really believes you have a potential hit or wants to try his hand at a new type of music.

Hiring a producer out of your own pocket may mean that you do not produce a whole album but only three or four songs. Recording three songs at a modest professional facility with the aid of a seasoned producer is a better way to spend limited funds than cranking out a whole album at a semipro studio without good production. Not every artist/producer collaboration works, but remember that like preparing to gig, recording with a producer takes practice. Would you rather pay a modest amount for the experience now or bet that your first producer collaboration—when you are signed to a label and your career is on the line—will be a sure winner?

FINDING HELP FOR PRODUCING YOUR DEMOS

You may not be able to find an experienced producer to take on the project of producing your demos for little or no pay. A producer with no financial link to the project cannot accept the same level of bottom-line responsibility and obligation as a hired pro. More than ever, the question revolves around whom you can trust. Remember that three of the fundamental resources a producer brings to each project are objectivity, a sincere enjoyment of your music, and a broad knowledge of other artists in your stylistic ballpark.

These criteria might lead you to ask a music critic who gave you good reviews, the professional booking agent who helps you get gigs, or even an enthusiastic and knowledgeable disc jockey or record store sales person to "produce" your demo. Think about it: these people know the material and sounds of many established artists, and they already like your music. A brief discussion should give you a feel of whether he or she wants to play producer and whether you share the same basic values about your potential products. If not, try someone else. What have you got to lose by asking?

If you arrange one of these situations, the producer need only attend two or three rehearsals, help select the songs to be recorded and slice their arrangements into shape, and bring his or her objectivity to the sessions to keep you from diverging from the genre in which you mean to compete. If a critic or disc jockey accepts the role, make sure that he or she understands the limited level of responsibility that will be expected. Consider all of this person's suggestions and criticisms seriously, but do not take them as the law. After all, in this case it is your demo, your budget, and your artistic neck on the line, not the producer's.

Whoever accepts this role will learn a lot about the studio recording experience, and this may be his or her only payment. Beyond this, the critic-producer may later write up the experience and give you some unexpected press. A booker-producer might get more excited about promoting your live gigs. A disc jockey or record store employee might later be your best sales person if you release the product locally and may bring it to the attention of promo people from major labels who come in weekly to place new product in the store or club.

Why not simply ask the engineer at the studio you have booked to produce your tape too? First, because he or she probably does not know your material and will not have time to spend in rehearsal with you. More important, however, the engineer's "creed" is not to comment on the artistic validity of what clients are playing. Opinionated engineers generally chase future studio business away. Even when asked for musical judgments, most engineers are reluctant to be as open or blunt as you should expect a real producer to be. Besides, your engineer has plenty to think about just getting good sounds on tape.

27

THE PRODUCER'S "TOOLKIT"

T HERE are an infinite number of possible approaches to producing records, each derived in part from the specific producer's personality, career experience, and study of the work of others. Although no single approach guarantees a greater percentage of great tapes or hits, it may be helpful to look at one method of operation I use when producing rock or pop tapes, especially those with emphasis on the vocals. The method is a conceptual toolkit, a group of questions and analyses applied to the raw material—such as the song and artist—that together can suggest appropriate decisions for the arrangement, tempo, performances, engineering and mix techniques, and sounds. By getting "inside the song," what needs to be accomplished quickly becomes clear and unambiguous.

Looking at production so logically may seem abhorrent or anticreative to some of you, and I fully understand this reaction. To some extent, imposing any system can take the magic out of the creative act. Yet I do not recommend that you adopt my method of operation as your own unless it feels natural for you and works. Instead, examine it under the microscope, then identify raw materials inside yourself from which to develop your own toolkit. Once that kit exists, you can consciously work on improving each production skill, knowing that whatever the project, your toolkit can help you achieve professional results each time. Good reliable craftsmanship is the first step toward artistry. "Art" itself is an honorary title that only the audience can bestow upon your work.

Most songs tell a story, even if only a sketchy one. These days many such stories are expanded and pictorialized in music videos. My own background includes years of film and video production, from television spots to documentaries and sales films, plus recording and mixing soundtracks for dramatic shorts, features, and series. Perhaps because of this, I love producing songs whose lyrics evoke strong visual images. When such a tune appears, I automatically start writing the video screenplay mentally. In a nutshell, this is my method: to paint a detailed mental picture of the dramatic character singing the song, the setting in which this event or situation takes place, and the conclusion or final act of the drama. The first phase of this search can be reduced to just six basic questions about the story:

1. Who is the person or dramatic character singing?
2. To whom is he or she singing?
3. What is the basic human situation about which he or she is really singing?
4. Where might this reasonably be taking place?
5. What does the singer want to accomplish or to have happen as a result of the song?
6. Does the desired result come to pass?

Let me illustrate with a song I produced a while back for a hard rock group called the Edge, formerly artists for Casablanca Records. The lyrics tell the story well enough to show this technique even without hearing the tune.

SOCIAL ARMY*
© 1982 Boston Skyline Music (ASCAP)

1st Verse	We are the generation who will run the world, everything . . . the galaxies! We have got the power to make it work! Oh yes, we are the youth. We have the energy.
Chorus	Rally Round. We've got the cause worth fighting for . . . Rally Round. We've got to stand up and fight, fight, fight!
2nd Verse	Woodstock heroes of the past searched out security: joined the club, made the sale, got their warrantee. You can hear them rumble in the streets underground A swell . . . commuters . . . a show and tell. Chorus.
Bridge	Revolution on the horizon. We are the Social Army. Revolution, it is rising. We are the Social Army. Common enlist with me, enlist with me. Common enlist with me. Solo. . . Chorus.
3rd Verse	We are not as disorganized as you think, That's right; look around, and you will see. We have got the numbers to overpower them all. We are the youth. We have the energy.

> Chorus.
>
> Bridge.

Coda   We are the Social Army, We are the Social Army,
(Spoken)   We are . . .

*Used by permission of Hubie Davis and Kenneth Evans, Esq.

This lyric answers all six of my production questions in graphic detail, with lots of imagery to spare.

1. The singer is obviously young and discontent with society. We do not know his specific complaints, but that allows listeners to fill in their own best gripes. Beyond this, we can tell the character is not a Ph.D. by his clipped phrasing and simple vocabulary. He seems to come from a blue-collar background and has little money; we can almost see his jeans and sneakers. In keeping with the song's many references to the future, I imagine him more as a Han Solo than a Luke Skywalker. However, I also get the feeling that the singer fashions himself in the image of a George Washington or Paul Revere. Though his future may be in the stars, his heart is steeped in revolutionary emotions of the past.

2. He is singing to a crowd of other youths directly, not parenthetically. They are right there, hearing his best sales pitch.

3. At first, the song's subject seems to be discontent itself, but the bridge really gives it away: this song is about the need for social revolution and for an army, led by the singer, to make it happen.

4. This event is definitely happening in a big city, daytime, outdoors, with the singer up on a soapbox or some building's steps. He and his army-to-be could not afford to rent a convention center, public address system, or for that matter anything, so he is shouting directly to them.

5. He wants people to enlist in his army. Make no mistake: this guy wants to lead a grass-roots revolution.

6. The last verse is open to interpretation, but I believe the singer gets his army together. Battle lines are now drawn for the revolution to come.

My second step is simple: identify the bottom-line emotional goals for the production. On a first hearing of the finished record, what one or two feelings must it evoke in every listener? The singer of "Social Army" never really identifies the "cause worth fighting for." His bottom-line goal (and therefore mine) is to stir excitement (literally to increase male pulse rates) with thoughts of future military glory. The U.S. Army has exactly the same goals in its current television ad campaign, "Be all that you can be." If we were working on a ballad, the goals might be to evoke tears, a lover's yearning, or simply to make the listener pity the singer, depending on the lyric. Whatever the goals, once identified, everything the producer does must further them. And having such goals makes production a more organized and sure-footed endeavor.

Next comes free association based on the six answers and goals specified above.

What kinds of lines, harmonies, tempo, instruments, vocal parts, percussions, recording and mix techniques, reverb, ambience, and overall sound will ensure that the story and goals come across loud and clear? In many projects, certain of these parameters are preset. For example, the Edge is a hard rock group, and the record must clearly state this from the beginning with lots of electric guitar and driving drums. Radio programmers will then be able to recognize the genre instantly and focus on the contents. Too many sound effects or distractions in the first minute might cast it as a novelty record or some confusing hybrid.

Allright, free associate! Appropriate sounds? Field drums, guns, cannons, marching, trumpets playing reveille, drill sergeants, anything military and warlike, particularly sounds referring to traditional field warfare. Musically, distorted guitar chords, metallic rhythm plucks, backup vocals reinforcing cries of "rally round" in each chorus, followers repeating the singer's words in second and third verses, enlistees shouting "fight, fight, fight!" List anything that might reinforce the military images of the lyric. Some of these ideas will be used, others discarded, but for the moment, just get them all out on paper.

Dramatically, "Social Army" will only work if listeners feel the need for revolution. Thus, the intro must convey a state of chaos or impending danger, an ominous situation that will be solved by the creation of the proposed army. Well, how was danger announced to the public in 1776? By chaotic ringing of the church bells. We can mimic that with a distorted guitar chord—six strings playing a big, open ninth chord—with heavy reverb and a delayed repeat. For a rock tempo without order, I would use a heavy quarter-note snare beat, unaccented or phrased and tuned low to sound like a field drum. Start with the bell phrased in 3–4, then insert the drum beat, and chaos! The singer's raspy voice can then come in over these two elements to impose order, followed by a full rhythm section on the phrase "run the world . . ."

No gimmicks, no sound effects. Just let the natural rock drive of the group carry the first two verses and choruses. Then comes the fun. We can add arpeggiated synth trumpets in the bridge for extra military feel. These lines will also call up other rock war anthems, like "Baba O'Reilly" by the Who. Do not be afraid to quote from successful records that shared the same underlying subject. Listeners will remember these sounds subliminally and put themselves in the right mood to hear your message.

The army itself can then come together during a synth solo following "Enlist with me . . ." Start with slightly ragged marching, then make it tighter and more determined, panning the troops left to right like a real army on bivouac. One or two members of the group can inject a few military commands and whistles, whipping the recruits into shape. This lyric is ripe for creativity, but once the situation is clearly stated, let the listeners fill in the details.

After the army sings its chorus anthem again, we can use the "fight, fight, fight" part for a dramatic stop to refocus attention on the lead singer. Drop back to the original quarter-note snare and bell chords, but modulate up a half step because now the singer has his army, and the excitement is rising. In the final chorus, groups of soldiers can shout "come-on" answers to his "rally round," with bigger three-part harmonies to suggest the army's continuing growth. The marching continues, and the whole record climaxes with the final "Enlist with me," inviting listeners to consider their next move.

We decided that the ending should tease the listener with the unanswered question "should I?" Thus, in our production we broke down to just the lead singer with a plucking rhythm guitar. As he echoes "We are the Social Army...," more and more voices join in from both sides, the marching picks up again, and under the leadership of the drill sergeants the whole army moves off into the distance via increasing reverb and a fade. The listeners are challenged to get on the boat before it leaves.

This production plan includes many of the elements a video director might use to dramatize the lyric. In that way, we can actually make the video much simpler to conceive and produce. In this day of $80,000 and up dramatic video budgets, any major label would appreciate the help. Moreover, this production should quickly focus the first-time listener on the singer's story, drawing the listener further into the plot as it progresses. Beyond this, the record needs the standard ingredients: hooks (repeated musical or rhythmic phrases that stick with the listener) and an energetic performance that communicates the excitement of enlisting.

Now the big question. Do successful producers always think so analytically? Certainly not. Yet there are lots of hits that when analyzed reveal such a constructivist approach. Are these accidents? No again. While I enjoy planning this kind of production in detail, then incorporating spontaneous ideas as they come, other producers might make many of the same decisions instinctively. If the song itself is strong and complete, providing clear answers to all 6 questions above, it would probably create similar images in most producers' minds. Thus, whether a producer verbalizes everything or follows his or her nose from demo to master, the emotional results can be very similar. Each producer, however, will have favorite sounds or studio techniques that distinguish his work from his contemporaries.

When the song does not answer all 6 questions, a producer can provide his or her own answers, suggesting a possible location by choosing reverb, sound effects, and other ambient elements. To suggest a dramatic outcome, the producer might opt for a hard ending to portray strong conviction or a long fade drifting into reverb if the drama is unresolved. The central process is to develop a complete and consistent mental picture of the play or drama, then to stage this on tape using components of the chart, performance, miking, equalization, type of reverb, whatever. Every decision in the production must be guided by this picture. What sounds nice is less important than what works within the picture.

Moreover, the producer makes these decisions and fills in answers in the way he or she believes will best connect artist and audience. The audience for "Social Army" is made up of young people in their late teens and early twenties who are reliving the late 1960s and rebelling against the pressure society imposes on us all to conform. With this in mind, my 6 questions can be rephrased:

1. What kind of dramatic character will the audience be most likely to sympathize with as this song's singer? Does the artist himself fit that description? If not, what can shape his performance or image more in that direction?

2. What is the audience's self-image? Does the lyric fit that perfectly, or should we tailor it to fit? Notice that "Social Army" puts the singer and his audience in the same club (i.e., "we") and credits this club with nothing less than

controlling the future. Very flattering. What audience would not respond to such powerful compliment!

3. Is the underlying emotion of the song demonstrated by situations or lyrics that are meaningful to the artist's audience today? If not, we need to make more changes to ensure that as many listeners as possible get the point and react instinctively to the record's impact. "Social Army" creates that bond via reference to the Woodstock generation that "sold out," namely yuppies.

4. If you were filming the video, what location would best communicate the artist's message to the audience or most surely put the audience in the right mood to hear his message? Young audiences respond to motifs that suggest freedom. An outdoor podium in "Social Army" implies the listener is free to take in the singer's pitch or to leave. Listeners usually have to buy tickets to indoor events, and paying for something is a psychological sign of submission.

5. Is the singer's goal something that most of his audience will identify with? If not, few will care whether he achieves it or not. Perhaps it needs to be restated, broadened, or related to events or motifs the audience would recognize. Enlistment in a "Social Army" offers listeners the promise of excitement and a better future, plus a leader who really sounds in command of things, whatever they actually be.

6. Are such goals ever achieved in similar real-life situations today? Or is the story's last act futile, hopelessly romantic, outright impossible, or in any way demeaning to the audience? If so, listeners will not want to associate themselves with the record for fear of being rejected by their more sensible peers.

The Edge brought "Social Army" to me in an advanced state of development. The bell and drum intro and musical arrangement had been built in rehearsal, undoubtedly without heavy analysis. It remained for me to recognize the song's structure, reshape it a bit, and suggest where to add fills, sound effects, dramatic *hits* (in the film-scoring sense, musical moments that synch with or punctuate specific images or on-screen events), and decorations. All I really did was to broaden the group's concept into a complete entertainment event, a little movie on tape.

It is exciting to work with an artist who can take his raw material to this stage. Ideas fly like sparks in the studio, and—hit or no—the process of making masters is charged with energy and enthusiasm. I would not trade these moments for the world. In real life, "Social Army" was never finished. The label went into financial and functional hibernation due to ongoing post-disco legal problems and the untimely death of its founder. Very unfortunate for the Edge, but one often cannot control outside factors. Just make the best music you can within the budget, and keep your fingers crossed.

A good rough mix of the finished tracks for "Social Army" appears on the second CD of the *Sound Advice* compact disc package. Give a listen for elements I overlooked here.

THE "GREAT SOUNDS": AN INDUSTRY SURVEY

If I asked you to name a few of the great recorded sounds of the multitrack era, you might rattle off a list of singles and albums with stellar drums, bass, piano, and the like. But this is a loaded question because each listener's answers come from totally different pools of experience, background, and taste. A pianist may consider herself an authority on recorded piano sounds. Regarding drums, however, answers might reflect not the quality of drum sounds alone but how they worked in the context of a whole production. Moreover, many respondents would answer through the rose-colored glasses of memory. Nevertheless, a large sampling of opinions does carry weight, especially when members of many professions or backgrounds repeatedly single out the same recordings for this or that sound.

Over a six-month period we conducted a phone and mail survey of some 165 people in the following music-related professions: about 30 recording engineers and producers, mostly working in Boston and New York, but including a dozen from Los Angeles, Nashville, and Miami; 35 professional musicians; 20 record company staffers, from A&R people to regional promo managers; 15 music and studio engineering teachers; 25 full-time music students; a sprinkling of critics who write for trade journals from *Billboard* to *Downbeat* to *CD Review,* formerly entitled *Digital Audio*; and even a few dance-floor and on-air disc jockeys.

We asked each to cite the best recorded (not played) example in the 1960s, 1970s and 1980s of 17 different instruments, sections, or vocal sounds—drums, acoustic bass, electric bass, and so on—basically, all the sounds covered by chapters of this book. Their answers were not restricted to any particular genre of music, and represent a fair profile of the entire United States record industry. About 45% of the "great sounds" are from rock and pop records, 25% from R&B/dance, and the remainder divided among jazz, classical, folk, and other musical genres.

Furthermore, we asked surveyees not to respond in any category unless their opinion was very strong for one artist, single, or album. Of the 57 possible responses from each person surveyed, we got an average of about 20. Oddly, even among engineers and producers, about 75% of all the choices were from the 1960s and 1970s. At face value this means there have been fewer great sounds in the 1980s than in either preceding decade. Finally, respondents were asked their principal occupation and what instrument(s) they play, if any.

Comparing the collected responses from engineers and producers with those of musicians and other respondents, it was surprising to find the list of greats cited by each fairly similar. In fact, in spite of several attempts to find "loaded perspectives" in the survey, only the critics seemed to be aware of a few obscure gems that slipped by everyone else, notably several jazz and classical releases. Moreover, few of the records cited received engineering Grammies or other technical accolades at the time of their release. This may be a comment on the tendency to confuse the excitement of a recent hit with its actual recording quality when Grammy time comes round each year.

And the Winners Are . . .   Space does not permit us to print the complete survey, nor would it be particularly useful. The table shows the singles, albums, and artists repeatedly picked for one or more of their excellent sounds. Some respondents chose particular records for overall excellence, rather than for any one sound. To save space, the winners are listed alphabetically by artist, the specific song or LP, and year of release, with sound category noted thereafter. A *G* next to the year of release signifies a Grammy as best engineered recording or best producer of that year. *E* and *P* identify the engineer and/or producer, respectively.

Artist	LP/Song	Sound(s)	Engineer	Year
Beach Boys	*Pet Sounds*	Group vocals	no credit	1966
	"Good Vibrations"	Electric bass		
Beatles	*Sgt. Pepper's Lonely Hearts Club Band*		Geoff Emerick (E)	1967
	"When I'm 64"	Solo wind		
	"Sgt. Pepper"	Drums		
	"With A Little Help . . ."	Electric bass		
	"She's Leaving Home"	overall		
	Abbey Road		Geoff Emerick (E)	1969
	"Come Together"	Electric bass		

Artist	LP/Song	Sound(s)	Engineer	Year
	"Hey Jude"	Piano		
	"Oh Darling"	Solo voice		
	"Because"	Group vocals		
	"Eleanor Rigby"	String section	Geoff Emerick (E)	1966
	"Yesterday"	String section	Geoff Emerick (E)	1965
Blood, Sweat & Tears	"Spinning Wheel"	Brass section	Roy Halee (E)	1966
Boston	*Boston*	Electric guitar	Scholz/ Dewey (E)	1976
	The Third Stage	Electric guitar	Scholz (E)	1986
Boston Symphony	*Rite of Spring* (Ozawa) (Philips LP 416 246)	Orchestra	unavailable	1971
Gary Burton	*Crystal Silence*	Mallet percussion	Jan Erik Kongshaug (E)	1973
Wendy Carlos	*Switched-on Bach*	Keyboards	Carlos (P,E)	1968
The Cars	*Heartbreak City*	Electric guitar Group vocals	Green (E)	1984
Chicago	*Chicago 17*	Drums	Humberto Gatica (E)	1983 G
	"Hard Habit To Break"	Group vocals	Humberto Gatica (E)	
Phil Collins	*No Jacket Required*	Drums	Hugh Padgham (P,E)	1985
John Coltrane	*Giant Steps*	Solo reed	Tom Dowd, Phil Iehle (E)	1959
Dire Straits	*Brothers in Arms*	Drums	Neil Dorfsman (E)	1985
Thomas Dolby	*Golden Age of Wireless*	Keyboards	Lacksman/ Shipley (E)	1984
Donald Fagan	*The Nightfly*	Group vocals	Scheiner/ Lazerus (E)	1982 G
	IGY	Drums, keyboards	/Nichols (E)	

Artist	LP/Song	Sound(s)	Engineer	Year
Fleetwood Mac	*Rumors*	Group vocals	Ken Caillet (E)	1977
Peter Gabriel	*SO/ Sledgehammer*	Solo voice	Daniel Lanois (P)	1986
		Drums, keyboards		
Getz & Gilberto	"Girl From Ipanema"	Acoustic bass	Phil Ramone (E)	1964
Jimi Hendrix	*Axis, Bold as Love*	Electric guitar	Eddie Kramer (E)	1969
	"Little Wing"	Drums		
Michael Jackson	*Thriller*	Keyboards	Bruce Swedien (E)	1983 G
Billy Joel	*The Stranger*	Grand piano	Jim Boyer (E)	1977
Kenny Loggins	*Keep the Fire*	Solo voice	Tom Dowd (P)	1979
Chuck Mangione	*Feel So Good*	Solo brass	Mick Guzauski (E)	1977
Manhattan Transfer	*Vocalese*	Group vocals	Elliot Scheiner (E)	1985
Wynton Marsalis	*Hot House Flowers*	Solo brass	Tim Geelan (E)	1986
Pink Floyd	*Dark Side of the Moon*	Drums	Alan Parsons (E)	1973
	The Wall	Drums, piano, electric guitar, group vocals	Guthrie (E)	1979 G
The Police	*Synchronicity*	Mallet percussions	Hugh Padgham (P,E)	1983
Linda Ronstadt	*What's New*	Orchestra	George Massenburg (E)	1982
David Sanborn	*Straight to the Heart*	Solo reed	Elliot Schiener (E)	1984
Paul Simon	*Graceland*	Acoustic guitar	Roy Halee (E)	1986
Simon & Garfunkel	"Bridge Over Troubled Water"	Acoustic guitar	Roy Halee	1969 G

Artist	LP/Song	Sound(s)	Engineer	Year
Steely Dan	Aja	Drums/elec. bass Group vocals	Roger Nichols (E)	1977
	Gaucho	Drums	Scheiner/ Nichols (E)	1980 G
Supertramp	"Breakfast In America"	overall	Henderson (E)	1978 G
James Taylor	J. T.	Acoustic guitar, solo voice	Val Garay (E)	1977
Mel Torme	A New Album	Strings, winds, and reeds, solo voice	Norman Schwartz (P) Keith Grant (E)	1979
Toto	Toto IV/ "Rosanna"	Brass/ keyboards	Schmitt/Knox (E)	1981 G
Andreas Vollenweider	White Winds	Harp, percussion	Eric Merz (E)	1985
Weather Report	8:30	Electric bass	Roy Thompson (E)	1980
Steve Winwood	Back in the High Life	Reed section	Tom Lord Alge (E)	1986 G
Stevie Wonder	Innervisions	Solo voice, keyboards	Dan Barbiero (E)	1972 G
Yes	90125	overall	Gary Langan (E)	1983

If you do not agree that all of these represent the finest recordings of all time—not to worry, I do not agree either. Nevertheless, there is no debating that they are all well recorded and produced, and for that reason alone they stand as benchmarks. Furthermore, the engineers whose work is represented above have each done dozens of other albums, among which we would doubtless find some of our own all-time greats.

PAINTING WITH SOUNDS: RECORDING AND PRODUCING *FULL CIRCLE* FOR CBS RECORDS*
CBS LP # 40966

Since the early 1970s the engineering and production of jazz artists has taken a number of distinct directions. Some artists like Wynton Marsalis maintain the traditional dominance of music over technology. My hat goes off to Tim Geelan (Wynton's engineer of late), who builds a strong stage for musical genius but takes no place on it. Lacking the slightest hint of audio guile, the music simply "happens" in what seems to be a small club with wonderful acoustics; it is real, three-dimensional, intimate. "J-Mood" and "Standard Time" are the culmination of an engineering modus that Rudi van Gelder fostered on so many great albums of the 50s and 60s: the art of artlessness.

*This article by the author originally appeared in the May, 1988 issue of *Mix Magazine*.

A second faction, including Steps Ahead, Ritenour, Klugh, Spyrogyra, and much of the GRP roster, has adopted rock engineering and production techniques to capture the hard edge of drums, brass, and almost every instrument and vocal. Tight miking, individual compression, noise gating, and signal processing are used on virtually every sound source. Impact is the prevailing audio statement, and the players meet in an electronic, studio-defined space. While this approach suits the music at hand, it separates the listener and players. They are clearly on opposite sides of a studio control-room window. One is continuously aware of an unseen hand controlling each element, maintaining a balance and sound image not determined by the players themselves.

The third and most recently founded school of jazz production and engineering is the impressionists, including DiMeola, Metheny, and a growing number of artists who use live instruments plus synthesizers and the studio itself as a palette with which to render musical paintings. With the exception of early painterly work by Miles, this approach derives not from the jazz itself but from other musical and nonmusical idioms. In any case, Full Circle's music clearly demanded an impressionist or visual treatment.

During preproduction I discovered that composer Karl Lundeberg's instincts are those of a painter or filmmaker as much as a composer. He is very concerned with portraying places and environments via his music. We also share an overriding love of acoustic instruments and determined to use synths primarily to define new types of acoustic sounds. Synths and studio provided endless orchestral voices that could be used like unusual voicings and combined sections in 20th century classical works. We furthermore decided that, despite using lots of synths, all performances must be live rather than sequenced. This would emphasize the organic qualities of the music and keep tempo control where it belongs—with the rhythm section.

Five of the seven tunes on the album are named for actual places or are openly suggestive of a specific locale or cultural ambience. Harmony lines, rhythmic textures, counterpoints, and many of the studio effects used invite listeners to close their eyes momentarily and mentally to join the group in one port of call or another. Many jazz artists evoke geographical settings via their writing or performance style; for this project we pulled more than a few tricks from the same bag as Holst, Stravinsky, Rodgers, Ives, and more recently, Steve Reich. Liquid textures, for example—from cosmic shrouds and Pacific waves to mirages—play prominent parts in works like "The Planets," "Victory at Sea" and "Desert Music." The power such pieces have to put listeners in space, at sea, or behind Don Juan's eyes derives from more than the notes of their scores.

Each of these works engulfs the listener in a broad stereo soundstage, not unlike that created by 6-channel 70mm surround sound in major motion pictures. Many parts are scored for oversize orchestral and vocal sections, the composer employing the natural undulation among many players for its hypnotic effect on the audience's mind. Similarly, where Full Circle's "Con Leche" opens and ends in the misty depths of a rain forest, we needed an acoustic-sounding organ pad more ethereal than any single stereo synthesizer or sampler could deliver.

To get the right texture, Karl and Jamshied Sharifi (an affiliated artist at M.I.T. who also teaches at Berklee and consults to Kurzweil) programmed a bank of eight Yamaha DX-7 modules (a TX-8 rack), plus Kurzweil loaded with combined wood flute and flue organ pipe samples, all controlled via MIDI from one keyboard. Each of the 10 sources is slightly detuned and separately chorused at a different rate for added fluidity, variously equalized to emphasize a syrupy lower midrange and steamy top end, and finally panned to one of 10 different left/right stereo positions. The resulting blend was then recorded to 2 pairs of tracks on 24-track tape, keeping the stereo Kurzweil and TX rack separate.

Seeing an opportunity for even more texture during the mix at his Rainbow Studios in Oslo, Jan Erik Kongshaug (with dozens of ECM albums and the mix of the Grammy-nominated *Lyle Mays* LP to his credit) sent each track into two or three separate reverbs, chorusing one or more of their sends or returns. The result is a background of damp and eerie musical fog that one can almost smell. Within this setting, "cinematic events" such as intermittent percussions, ersatz animal sounds, and bird calls complete the musical picture.

Such synth and chorus layering generates 20 or more sounds from each note of a keyboard performance, subtly mimicking the sonic "size" of an orchestra, even when played pianissimo. Beyond this, we included specific audio hints about the size of the space in which the music happens. For example, in a real rain forest one might be able to see only a couple of hundred feet in any direction but would be aware of a larger dimension by the way sounds reverberate among unseen hills or ruins. If the synth pad above defines the size of the immediate surroundings, a different treatment of event reverbs can evoke the mysterious beyond. For this we used a separate Lexicon unit set to 3 or 4 seconds reverb time, with left and right channels predelayed different amounts, about 0.8 and 1.1 seconds, respectively. (The exact numbers are unimportant.) Since sound travels at 1,100' per second, these delays indicate reflecting surfaces about 350 and 500' away. To broaden the audio horizon, sounds originating on the left, for example, were sent to the right reverb input, thus echoing first from the right. A portion of the right reverb return was then sent to the left reverb input, producing a second, more diffuse bounce from the left, and so on.

A terse flute run or bird call thus repeats several times from left and right, each reflection timed differently and receding into the forest. The same effect applied to twin acoustic bass pedaltones evokes a tremulous low-end rumble that rolls in from distant hills. To suggest forest sounds happening all around the listener, we recorded rain, percussion, and bird sounds rather oddly. Two spaced pairs of RE-15s faced opposite directions, each pair picking up separate people making sounds. One pair of mics was in proper phase, but we reversed phase within the other pair. The result is a natural spread of effects between left and right speakers with intermittent effects that, by phase reversal, seem to originate behind and above the listener. Disturbingly real when heard in stereo headphones, these effects disappear when the mix is played in mono.

Such cheap cinematic tricks are not specifically planned ahead. Like lines of a solo, they just suggest themselves as each piece develops, and you try them out sans verbiage. They are also suggested by passages in orchestral works from Stravinsky's *The Rite of Spring* and Grofé's *Grand Canyon Suite* to Philip Glass's *Akhnaten,* where rapid repeats of certain phrases bouncing around the orchestra indicate the size or grandeur of the dramatic location. In still other modern pieces, composers indicate that certain instruments are to be played off stage, in the wings, or even up in the balconies or rafters.

It may seem that no instrument on the album escaped unprocessed. In reality, we did little of the protective processing used on most multitrack sessions. Drums, for instance, are tight miked à la rock, with one noise gate on the kick, but otherwise recorded and mixed entirely without gating or compression. The snare is limited to the loudest sections of two songs to fatten its sound and prevent tape overload. Acoustic bass, grand piano, flute, and even percussion tracks are stereo-miked but uncompressed and ungated. Because all compression changes a performer's attack and dynamics, I try to avoid it at all costs, especially in jazz and classical projects.

Instead, uneven fret- or keyboard response can often be smoothed by parametric equalization. Beyond this, engineer Robin Coxe-Yeldham and I used manual gain riding to boost low-level passages of several tracks, even while recording basics. This requires learning the musical charts pretty thoroughly, but it is worth the effort to know that you are stretching every possible ounce of quality out of the analog multitrack medium. In "Croton Drive" and "Con Leche," for example, the overhead drum mics are boosted almost 12 dB for the long intro and coda, where drummer Russ Gold barely touches the cymbals and snare with brushes. On synths tracks, however, we rode gain to add dynamics and emphasize attacks on certain lines (moves for which there would never be time during the mix) and to rock certain lines left and right in the stereo pair, adding lateral movements to the part that would later play nicely with the reverbs.

The *Full Circle* album represents an unusual approach to jazz production and engineering. Delivering a natural sound in the CD medium demands that one preserve full musical dynamics. At the same time CDs allow the slightest nuance of texturizing to shine through clearly. Our main concern was to create new "acoustic" textures through the subtle blend of real instruments, synths, and vocals. Some effects sounded just plain horrendous and were junked immediately, but the key was to try anything that might enhance the visual or sensual aspects of each song.

SUGGESTED READINGS

The following books are the best I have found in their respective fields for nontechnical readers. There are more theoretical books on recording than Eargle's, but these are intended for future audio engineers and equipment designers. Lengthy math and physics training would be required for full comprehension. I am not saying that the books I have selected are lightweight—decidedly not. However, they are written in a style, and at a level of detail, that will enlighten rather than frighten. I hope there will soon be many more titles that reveal the intricacies of business, law, and technology to readers whose thoughts and backgrounds are overflowing with music and creativity, not necessarily with graduate degrees.

Building a Recording Studio, by Jeff Cooper
  (1984, Synergy Group, Calabasas, CA) Paperback.

If you are planning a basement studio, demo studio, or even a multimillion-dollar facility, buy this book. Jeff Cooper explains some rather esoteric principles of acoustics and sound behavior with practically no math, yet in a fully rigorous and informative manner. You can construct a tight little room with this book as a guide. Or, if you are going for multitrack digital, you will save a lot of money by learning what to discuss with designers and contractors and how to define the line (in quality and budget) between your real needs and niceties. The book should also prove helpful to musicians who spend a lot of time in studios, both by explaining how various rooms behave and by hinting at how to avoid the worst acoustical problems.

The Complete Guide to MIDI Software, by Howard Massey et al.
    (1987, Amsco, NY) Paperback.

An up-to-date catalog of MIDI-based programs available for every type of personal computer, with full technical data on the types of synths and other devices with which each software package works well or poorly. Since many commercially available programs cost hundreds of dollars, buy this book for a frank look at the strengths and weaknesses of any software you are considering for purchase. Better to spend a few dollars up front before discovering that your new software will not interface with a certain type of sync pulse, time code, sampling rate, or whatever!

Dictionary of Music Production and Engineering Terminology, by Wayne Wadhams
    (1988, Schirmer Books, NY) Hardcover.

The only dictionary covering fifteen different topics and industries, from business, publishing, and union terms to those of record, jingle and film/TV production, as well as the most current digital, synth, and computer terms. The definitions are easy to read, mostly nontechnical, and intended to improve communication among music producers, their clients, and the engineers who will help create music for any medium. Over 125 detailed illustrations of every track format (audio, video, and motion picture), cue sheets, flow charts, every major type of equipment, and the like make this book as useful for working engineers as for students.

Digital Delay Handbook, by Craig Anderton
    (1985, Amsco, NY) Paperback.

Not a theoretical tome, but a catalog or "recipe book" of sounds and effects that can be produced by various types of delays, flangers, harmonizers, vocorders, and the rest of the "digital kitchen." As with any such book, brands and models have changed since its writing, but the underlying recommendations on how to imitate Leslie speaker systems, fatten synthetic string sections, and create a host of nonexistent spaces and effects remain as useful as ever. The book is also a big help in adding production value to even the simplest of home recordings.

Guitar Gadgets, by Craig Anderton
    (1983, Amsco, NY) Paperback.

Craig Anderton, currently editor of *Electronic Musician* magazine, is indeed the authority on the seemingly endless crowd of devices, effects, and whole pedalboards made for on- and offstage use. Although the book discusses many models (and more than a few brands) no longer in production, the basic concepts have not changed. This is solid, useful advice on how to get the most out of your time and dollar investment in portable outboard signal processors.

Handbook of Recording Engineering, by John Eargle
  (1986, Van Nostrand, NY) Hardcover.

At the moment, this is the most complete and up-to-date textbook on the theory and practice of studio engineering. While little time is spent on recommended creative uses for various processes and equipment, the underlying concepts are clear and concisely stated, especially for the serious student who has not encountered similar material elsewhere. Many other books, more loosely styled and organized, serve better as review texts for experienced engineers and studiophiles. Bring along a scientific calculator and good grades in several college-level math/physics courses to take full advantage of everything this book offers.

Making Music, edited by George Martin
  (1985, Morrow, NY) Paperback.

The finest book of interviews I have ever encountered. George Martin, best known as the Beatles' producer, interviewed and solicited short essays from about seventy professionals in every musical nook and cranny—from songwriting and performing to engineering, production, and the various music industries themselves. His questions are penetrating, and most contributors get right to the heart of their field, avoiding the all-too-usual "and-then-I-starred-and-triumphed-in" syndrome. This book also gives a wonderful sense of the history and traditions behind each major area of study, factors that are lost in the endless "how-to" books that become obsolete as soon as the equipment they feature is outmoded.

MIDI for Musicians, by Craig Anderton
  (1986, Amsco, NY) Paperback.

Another winner for Craig Anderton, mainly because of its nontechnical, informative style. This is the book for anyone just buying his or her first MIDI instrument, or beginning to play in a group where such instruments are featured. MIDI is a very powerful tool, but, like any system with so many possibilities, it can be conceptually intimidating to the novice. The book does not presume that the reader owns or has daily access to sophisticated synths or drum machines. Even if you do have such equipment and learned how to use it largely from manuals and hands-on experience, this book can structure your knowledge and open up whole new areas of creative thinking about MIDI.

Modern Recording Techniques (2nd ed.), by Robert Runstein and David Huber
  (1986, Howard Sams, Indianapolis, IN) Paperback.

When this fine book first appeared, Bob Runstein was an active engineer working with many non–math-trained artists. The book was organized according to topics of technical interest to engineers but written in a way that was understandable to lay readers. David Huber's update is in the same spirit, but he adds new chapters on digital recording and synchronization. In addition, he has completely rewritten the chapters on tape recorders and consoles, automation, noise reduction and signal processing, and the current manufacture of CDs, LPs, and cassettes. The math is still light and the explanations clear and concise, although there is little creative advice to help readers get specific results in their demos and master tapes.

Music Through MIDI, by Michael Boom
   (1987, Microsoft Press, Redmond, WA) Paperback.

A good complement to the Anderton book two entries above. Michael Bloom covers some of the same basic information but spends much more time on how to use MIDI creatively in the process of making music. The conceptual connections between traditional compositional and performing techniques and systems, and those available with MIDI, are particularly fascinating. This kind of knowledge may help bridge the creativity gap for musicians who feel that their entire past experience and musical knowledge are quickly being rendered obsolete by the development of MIDI and each new wave of computer-based technology.

Principles of Digital Audio, by Ken Pohlmann
   (1985, Howard Sams, Indianapolis, IN) Hardcover.

The one and only thorough and accurate textbook on the theory and practice of digital audio recording. You may be familiar with Ken Pohlmann's reader-friendly equipment reviews and articles in *Digital Audio* and other magazines, but this book is carefully written for the math- and physics-trained engineer or equipment designer. Do not expect light reading but rather a careful and well-grounded theoretical treatise. Although the material is complex, the style is free-flowing and never strays beyond the reach of logic. My respect and gratitude to the author for a uniquely accessible treatment of tough stuff.

INDEX

Italics indicate pages where terms are defined.

A

Absorption of sound, 50
Acoustic amplifier, *176–77,* 208–10,
  221–23, 229
Acoustic chamber reverb, *53*
Acoustics
  concert hall, simulation of, 270–71
  studio and control room, 46–50,
    248–49
Active electronic circuit, *12,* 76
Address, SMPTE, *88*
Administration of copyrights, 325
ADSR (sound envelope), 67, 136–39,
  148 (fig. 12.4)
Air resonances, 141, 179, 245,
  261–63
AKG spring reverb systems, 53
Alternating current, *13*
Analog recorder or recording, *56,*
  119–21
Anechoic chamber, 136
Antinode, *140,* 178, 221–22
Aphex Aural Exciter, *80*
Arco, *176*
A&R Department at labels, 96–97, 99
ARMS console automation, 85–86
Attack (envelope), *65,* 148 (fig. 12.4)
Attack curve, compression, *68–70*
Attack time, *67,* 151 (fig. 12.5), 162
  (fig. 12.9)
Aural exciter, *80*
Auto-locator, 44
Automation, console, 7, *83–84,* 85–
  87
  ARMS system, 85–87

master module, *28*
moving faders, 85
Aux (auxiliary) send and return, *31*

B

Background vocals, dramatic func-
  tions of, 205–7
Baffles, 48 (fig. 4.3), *49–50,* 105–6
  felt "mini baffles," 157, 255, 283
  problems with uneven baffling,
    211–13
Ballistics, meter, *25*
Bandwidth, *76,* 77–79 (figs. 7.1–7.3)
Batteries, effect on electronic perfor-
  mance, 235
Beatles, 4, 6
Beats per minute, 312–13
Beck, Jeff, 6
Bells, miking of, 277–78
Bidirectional polar pattern, *13,* 19
  (fig. 2.4)
Big band recording, 285–90
Binary numbers, 58–59
Bits (computer data), *58*
Blumlein stereo miking, *259*
Body resonances
  in acoustic bass, 179–80
  in acoustic guitar, 232
  in brass, 266
  in drums, 141–42
  in organ pipes, 247
  in stringed instruments, 227
Bore (woodwinds and reeds), 247,
  253

349

L

M